AF843600

THE NEW RIVER

The Property is now offered for Sale in Lots to suit all classes of capitalists, and consists of Valuable

FREEHOLD ESTATES,

COMPRISING

Two Fifth Parts and a Fractional Part of a Share

IN

THE KING'S MOIETY,

AND

One Eighth Part of a Share

IN

THE ADVENTURERS' MOIETY,

OF THE

Grand and Unique Trading Corporation.

HISTORICALLY KNOWN AS

THE NEW RIVER

With a Revenue last year amounting to the enormous sum of nearly **£400,000,** being an increase of **£15,000** on the previous year, conferring the *Parliamentary Franchise* on its holders, and returning an *annually increasing Income*, derived from *Land and Water*, which has *doubled within the last ten years* (during which period two large bonuses have been declared), and is without limit as to future accretions.

ALSO

FIFTY £100 NEW SHARES (fully paid)

IN

THE NEW RIVER,

Participating equally with the Original Shares in all the advantages of the Company.

Auction particulars, 23 October 1878

THE NEW RIVER

A Legal History

BERNARD RUDDEN

CLARENDON PRESS · OXFORD
1985

Oxford University Press, Walton Street, Oxford OX2 6DP
London New York Toronto
Delhi Bombay Calcutta Madras Karachi
Kuala Lumpur Singapore Hong Kong Tokyo
Nairobi Dar es Salaam Cape Town
Melbourne Auckland
and associated companies in
Beirut Berlin Ibadan Mexico City Nicosia

Oxford is a trade mark of Oxford University Press

Published in the United States
by Oxford University Press, New York

© *Bernard Rudden 1985*

All rights reserved. No part of this publication may be reproduced, stored in a retrieval system, or transmitted, in any form or by any means, electronic, mechanical, photocopying, recording, or otherwise, without the prior permission of Oxford University Press

British Library Cataloguing in Publication Data
Rudden, Bernard
The New River.
1. New River Company—History
I. Title
338.7'6281'09421 HD1697.G74L6
ISBN 0-19-825497-0

Library of Congress Cataloging in Publication Data
Rudden, Bernard
The New River: a legal history
Bibliography: p.
Includes index
1. New River Company—History
2. Water—Law and legislation—England—London—History
3. London (England)—Water-supply—History
I. Title
KD8962.W3R83 1984 343.421'421'0924 84-20674
ISBN 0-19-825497-0

Set at the University Press, Oxford
Printed in Great Britain by
Butler & Tanner Ltd, Frome and London

Our mercenary stream
No grandeur boasting, here obscurely glides
O'er grassy lawns or under willow shades:
As, thro' the human form, arterial tubes
Branch'd every way, minute and more minute,
The circulating sanguine fluid extend;
So, pipes innumerable, to peopled streets
Transmit the purchas'd wave.

John Scott, *Amwell: a Descriptive Poem* (1776), lines 123–30

Contents

Illustrations

The illustrations are reproduced by courtesy of the following: Bodleian Library (Nos. 2, 5, 11, 15, 16); British Museum (Nos. 4, 7); *The Engineer* (No. 1); Greater London Record Office (Nos. 6, 8, 17, 18); Guildhall Library (Nos. 3, 10); Trustees of the National Portrait Gallery (Plates I and II); Thames Water Authority, North London Division (frontispiece, Nos. 9, 12, 13, 14).

Explanations and Acknowledgements

THE sources spell many of the key names in several different ways. 'Myddelton' is the form always used by the founder of the project himself, but his associates and descendants differ. The Backhouse family name was usually spelt thus, but sometimes appears in other versions; the name of their Clerkenwell land is given as Commandery Mantles, although there are innumerable variants in the sources. Chapter 9 is devoted to the Crown Clog, although until this century the name often appears as Clogg. The natural river is almost invariably spelt Lee by Parliament, and Lea by everyone else; the latter has been preferred save in direct quotation. Finally, the phrase 'the New River Head' is used—as it always was—to mean, not the source of the water, but the place at Islington where the aqueduct ended.

The precise locations of manuscripts are given, save in the case of those held by the Company itself. These were consulted at its office at 30 Myddelton Square, Islington; but that office was recently closed and the documents moved. At the time of writing it is likely that most of them may eventually be deposited with the Greater London Record Office.

The dates given are those in the sources, but the year is taken to begin on 1 January. Statute references follow the style adopted by the *Chronological Table of the Statutes* (HMSO) and are given in the book's Table, being repeated in the footnotes or text only where there might otherwise be risk of confusion. Footnote references are grouped, with the cue being given at the end of a paragraph. Quotations and transcriptions of original manuscripts preserve their spelling and punctuation, but the tilde and macron are omitted.

My warmest thanks must be given to the Company secretary, Mr R. A. J. Bennett, a worthy successor to William Lewyn, appointed to that post by James I. Mr Bennett not only permitted me the freedom of the archives but provided a handsome room overlooking Myddelton Square, where they might be studied in elegant comfort. Much of the source material is now held by the Thames Water Authority, whose Administrative Manager, Mr A. C. Longstaff, and staff have afforded me many hours of cheerful courtesy. In particular Mr W. J. Whitehead placed at my disposal his unrivalled knowledge of the hundreds of thousands of their terriers and other documents which are so daunting to the stranger.

The archivists and librarians of many institutions have also been of great assistance, particularly Mrs J. Kenealy, of the Greater London Record Office, and the staff of the Guildhall Library, Kent County Archives, The British Library Manuscript Department, and the Public Record Office. To the Bodleian Library, where this work was written, and to its helpful and patient staff, I owe more than I can tell. Particular permissions to reproduce illustrations and documents are acknowledged in the appropriate places.

Being merely a lawyer, I have had to draw upon the learning of many academic and professional colleagues and must sincerely thank the following: Dr J. H. Baker, of St Catherine's College, Cambridge; Mr J. Barton, of Merton College, Oxford; my old pupil, Mr D. Brodie, for his advice on accountancy principles; Mr I. Gray, secretary of the Amwell Society of Islington; Dr C. A. Haigh, of Christ Church, Oxford; Dr D. J. Ibbetson, of Magdalen College, Oxford; Mr J. Kaye, of The Queen's College, Oxford; Mrs M. Prestwich, of St Hilda's College, Oxford; Dr G. M. Saul, of Brunel University; Mr F. A. Sharman, of Wolverhampton Polytechnic; Professor A. W. B. Simpson, of the University of Kent; and Mr N. G. Watson, of Charterhouse Japhet Investment Management Ltd. Two Oxford friends have read a draft of the whole work and given unstintingly the benefit of their keen eye and shrewd sense: Mr J. S. Anderson, of Hertford College, and Mr J. Hackney, of Wadham College. Needless to say, I alone am responsible for all mistakes.

The New River Company Ltd. kindly provided the funds to include illustrations which both lighten and give point to an often austere text. I am, and the reader will be, deeply grateful for this generosity.

B. R.

Brasenose College, Oxford
Christmas 1983

Abbreviations (*non-legal*)

APC	Acts of the Privy Council
BL	British Library
CJ	Journal of the House of Commons
CSPD	Calendar of State Papers (Domestic)
CTB	Calendar of Treasury Books
DNB	*Dictionary of National Biography*
EHD	English Historical Documents
GCM	New River Company General Court Minute Book
GL	Guildhall Library
GLRO	Greater London Record Office
GM	*Gentleman's Magazine*
HC	House of Commons
HL	House of Lords
HMC	Historical Manuscripts Commission
LJ	Journal of the House of Lords
M	New River Company Minute Book
MDR	Middlesex Deeds Register
M/GC	New River Minute Book, General Court Meeting
MWB	Metropolitan Water Board
NR	New River Company
NRCD	New River Copy Deeds
NRRP	New River Register of Proprietors
PC	Privy Council
PP	Parliamentary Papers
PRO	Public Record Office
Q	Question
RC	Royal Commission
SC	Select Committee
SS	Selden Society
SPD	State Papers (Domestic)
TW	Thames Water Authority

CHAPTER 1

Introduction

THE NEW RIVER deserves a book. The aqueduct of that name rises at Chadwell Spring, just south of Ware, is soon joined by a cut from the River Lea, and brings drinking water south to London over a distance—as the crow flies—of some twenty miles. Work started in the spring of 1609, the official opening took place four years later, and the river is running to this day, looking in places much as it must have done almost four hundred years ago.

The man whose enterprise achieved this feat was Hugh Myddelton. He and his associates were incorporated in 1619, and his Company—though, like the river, somewhat altered—is still in existence. Until 1904 it ran a public utility and then, when the whole of London's water supply passed into the hands of the Metropolitan Water Board, was transformed into a modern property company to manage its considerable landholdings. Taken over by London Merchant Securities PLC in 1974, it still exists as a separate entity within that group. From the purely legal point of view the history of the whole undertaking reveals features that are both unique and eccentric but which none the less cast some light on the development of the law of business corporations and on changing perceptions of property.

Leaving aside ecclesiastical bodies, the early corporations fulfilled purposes of public benefit—including governance—and were imbued with notions of both comradeship and monopoly. The city or borough provided for local, and the craft guild for economic, development. But although these legal institutions helped the merchant to withstand feudal control—so a London burgess had no lord save the King—the members' common interest was independent of the corporation: they lived in the same street or by the same trade, or both. While the great Livery Companies represented the trading capital invested in the particular activity in London, membership of them merely reinforced, but did not create, the common interest. The members traded, not with a joint stock but for their own account, limited membership of their company to sons and apprentices (so that the concern was still a family business), and carried out the regulation of monopoly power in collaboration or competition with the borough. The benefit conferred on them was the liberty to trade under the shelter of corporate organization—it was a protected 'freedom' rather than a 'share'.

The early foreign trading companies were likewise seen as organs of public utility in which people with a common interest come together. Incorporation was necessary because the government of, say, India could not efficiently be carried on by sporadic associations of merchants combining for occasional voyages. Their enterprise was charged with public functions and so needed permanence, while the stimulus to the private investor was provided by the grant of a monopoly. But incorporation facilitates economic change: the single-voyage venture is replaced by long-term planning; double-entry bookkeeping provides an account of a running balance and, when needed, an instant appraisal of the overall position; and the traders go to the public to raise the necessary funds. The thousand people who, in 1617, subscribed the £1½m. needed to finance the East India Company's voyage were very disparate: earls, countesses, knights, widows, clerics, merchants, and tradesmen. The only thing they had in common was the newfangled 'joint stock'; the only place they met was in the Company's books.[1]

Yet investment in many of these bodies conferred—at least in formal terms—the privileges and duties of members of a guild, so that, for instance, the East India shareholders are called 'brothers' and its first Charter of 1600 (like those of the Levant Company in the same year and of the French Merchants in 1611) envisages that only sons and apprentices of the original members will be 'admitted to become free of the said Company'. This recalls the admission to borough and guild and suggests that the entrants' investment is perceived first and foremost as a claim upon the *corporation*, an attitude expressed in the East India's early practice of dividing its capital at the

[1] The background is admirably set out in the works of Scott, Carr, and Cooke. For the East India's second joint stock raised in 1616–17 see Scott ii 104; Cooke 57–8.

end of each voyage. What took longer to emerge was the idea of such an investment as primarily a marketable asset to be realized by selling to a stranger the claim on the company, while leaving undisturbed its balance sheet. To make this generally practicable, a stock market has to exist, and this did not develop until the late seventeenth century under the pressure of Government borrowing.[2]

The New River does not fit the older pattern of craft guilds, nor the equally ancient partnership of the law merchant, nor the structure of a trading company. Like a partnership, its investors were few—and, as we shall see, membership of the Company, in the sense of having a voice in its management, was until this century limited to twenty-nine. Unlike a partnership, Hugh Myddelton's friends invested money, not skills or enterprise, and their shares and the rights attached to them were freely transferable from the very beginning of the venture, several years before incorporation. Unlike the trading companies, the entire amount invested in the enterprise by these twenty-nine 'Adventurers' (and the King) was immediately and irrevocably expended in capital construction. This had several consequences. Firstly, the money advanced by one was at once irretrievably commingled with the rest. Secondly, while the enterprise was a going concern, the investor could never expect his *capital* back—all he could hope for was a return on it from a share in the profits produced by sale of the water. This leads to the third feature, namely that the investment cannot be seen as a claim on the undertaking recoverable on demand or after even prolonged notice: thus, the only way in which an Adventurer could disinvest was by share transfer. Finally, the money advanced was immediately sunk into the earth itself—what more natural than that it should be seen as a stake in land, and the investment it represented be classified as real property?

Thus, for almost three centuries, a New River holding is unique and, by the nineteenth century, is described by its owner and the Company as 'an undivided share'. This is the phrase used by lawyers to denote the interest of a tenant in common

[2] For the East India Company see Scott ii 89–206. His account of the New River is scattered throughout vol. i and in vol. iii 18–31. The Levant and French Merchants' Charters are printed in Carr, *Charters* 30 and 62.

in land; but, although the word is used in the New River documents as if it meant the same, in reality it refers to a share in the business; or—to anticipate the story—in half the equity of the business. Thus, the New River illustrates vividly an intermediate stage in the notion of a company share. In 1612, at the time of its first traceable 'share issue', the interest of a tenant in common of land itself had been long understood; that of the investor in a modern company was not to be fully comprehended until this century—if then. The New River shares fall neatly between these two concepts.

The shares of the old trading and of all modern companies are fixed as to nominal value, but not (within limits) as to number. New River shares, by contrast, resemble those of a tenant in common or (in the law merchant) of a partner, in that they are fixed by number but not value. For reasons that will be related, the maximum number became seventy-two, but over the years the market value of each rose from some £77 in 1626 to over £125,000 in 1898. Like the interest of a tenant in common, but unlike that of a partner, however, New River shares together (where appropriate) with membership of the Company were always freely assignable.

The New River was a project with none of the risks of business partnership or foreign trade, and one whose profitability was as sure as that of land, for it was an investment by a few into what is a necessity for everyone. Just as we all must have somewhere to live and to work, so we all need water to stay alive. Consequently, the financial turmoils of the late seventeenth and early eighteenth centuries left the Company unscathed, the Bubble Act of 1720 passed it by, and limited liability remained a matter of complete indifference to its shareholders.

Expressed in modern terms, the constitution of the Company itself is also very strange—Scott calls it 'unique'. Before incorporation, James I had met half the expenditure in return for half the profits, so that the 'equity' was held half by the King and half by twenty-nine citizens holding thirty-six shares. In granting the Charter, James could not—or at least did not attempt to—incorporate himself: consequently (and until 1904), the Company consists of twenty-nine people and the 'liability' side of the balance sheet is divided into two moieties:

that of the Adventurers which is itself subdivided into thirty-six, and that belonging originally to the King. Twelve years after incorporation, the latter was transferred, not to the Company but to Hugh Myddelton, and was later itself divided into thirty-six. The holders of the King's shares, however, remained forever outside the Company or, in modern terms, without votes. But, as their 'undivided shares' were real property, they were consoled by the acquisition of not one but two parliamentary votes for the counties of Hertford and Middlesex, through which the river flows.[3]

The consideration for Hugh Myddelton's purchase of the royal half of the equity was his 1631 covenant to pay £500 a year for ever to the Sovereign. Although it was framed as only a personal obligation on him and his heirs, payment was later made by the Company and in 1911 the House of Lords (erroneously) held it to be a liability of the undertaking. It was not redeemed until 1956.

A final striking feature of the Charter was that by it the King—so far as he could—attempted to grant the assets side of the balance sheet, together with the balance on the profit-and-loss account, to be held of him in socage tenure. And the whole history of the treatment of the river bed reveals another unique characteristic of the New River and one which was to haunt the development of modern company law. By the initial Act of Parliament of 1605, ownership of the bed remained in the neighbouring landowners; they were subjected merely to a compulsory servitude *aquae ductus*—a kind of public-law easement. Later, the Company bought bits of the bed here and there, together with other land. Remembering, however, that the investors held 'undivided shares', the lawyers decided that it was they and not the Company who owned the land itself.

For reasons that will be explained in Chapter 10, the Industrial Revolution, the later growth of joint stock companies, and the development of a modern company law prompted the application of ancient techniques of property law to newer forms of wealth. The older generation of doctrinal writings (represented at its best by Hargrave's and Butler's editions of Coke on Littelton) dies out and is replaced by newer texts which can make little of the New River. They do not even

[3] Scott, iii 22, says of the Charter 'this document is unique'.

remark its oddities, but simply state that its shares are realty and pass on to clearer things. The typical place for the Company is in a footnote: it is there that it appears briefly as 'an exception' to the author's system in all twenty-four editions of Joshua Williams on Real Property; it is there that it appears—if at all—in the new generation of works on company law.[4]

The major difficulty in presenting a legal history of the New River has been the coexistence of different kinds of problem. At one level, the tale is tangled but not intellectually difficult. At another level, however, many of the sources are concerned with extremely technical legal issues: the application to a share of the learning on words of limitation, on disseisin, and on the calculus of estates; the development of the Rule against perpetuities to deal with 'entails' in seventeenth-century trusts of long leases; the relationship between a shareholder and the fixed assets of a company; and so on. If discussion of such topics were prefaced with an elementary explanation of the relevant law, this work would have had to be twice as long. Consequently, the text does at times change gear, moving with some rapidity from the domestic details of a family story to the high arcana of the great conveyancers. One solution might have been that adopted by Miss Stella Gibbons, whose purple passages in *Cold Comfort Farm* are indicated by helpful asterisks. Modesty prevailed, however, and it has been left to each reader to pass over the sections which are not to his or her taste.

[4] Williams, *Real Property* lst edn. 8 fn. (h), 24th edn. 29 fn. (o). Similar treatments will be found (in chronological order) in Cruise, *Digest* i 58; Roper i 342; Flintoff i 23–4; Crabb i 61 (s. 83); Tudor 42; Raleigh 8; Strahan 275; Lindley, *Companies* (1902) i 630 fn. (o). Challis ascribed the New River's oddity to statute (1st edn. 33, 2nd edn. 38). His editor, Charles Sweet, was persuaded to argue from the Charter (3rd edn. 57–8). It was left to an American to note some of the difficulties: Samuel Williston (1888) 2 *Harv L Rev* 150–1.

CHAPTER 2

Beginnings 1600–1619

2.1 The Project

THE City of London was once well watered. The Thames formed its southern boundary, the Walbrook wound from North to South, the Fleet ran on its western side, and, further to the East, the River Lea flowed into the Thames at Leamouth, which later ages were to call Limehouse. The terrain included water-bearing gravels underlain by clay so that, as the Elizabethan antiquary John Stow puts it, 'they had in every street and lane of the City divers Wells and fresh Springs'. The growth of population and building, however, had its inevitable effect, until the citizens 'were forced to seek sweet Waters abroad'. Consequently, from the thirteenth century adjacent landowners of Tyburn and Paddington (with royal prompting) granted powers to the City to run conduits and pipes from their springs 'for the profit of the City and good of the whole realm thither repairing: to wit, for the Poor to drink and the Rich to dress their Meat'.[1]

The first roving commission to bring in water was given by statute in 1543. The Act observed that the City 'hath been before this time well furnished and abundantly served till that now of late . . . the accustomed course of the waters comming from the old sprynges and auncient heads are sore decayed diminished and abated', but that the Mayor had not only discovered sources in the suburbs 'but hath divised the conveyaunce thereof by cundytes vautes and pipes to the said citie'. It then enacted that it was lawful for the City to enter private land (save houses and the like) and 'there to dygge pittes trenches & diches and to erect heades lay pipes & make vaultes . . . for the conveyaunce of the said water'. It must be emphasized—for reasons which will loom large later—that the City was given no powers compulsorily to acquire land. The Act empowered the acquisition of a right to run water—a

[1] Stow, ed. Strype i 23, 24; Barton, chap. I; Clifford ii chap. VIII; MWB, Water Supply of London (1961) 1–4.

servitude *aquae ductus* or kind of public-law easement—on payment of compensation to be assessed, where necessary, by a body appointed by the Lord Chancellor. This feature is made vividly clear by the provision which stipulates that if the springs on Hampstead Heath are tapped then the City must pay to the Bishop of Westminster and his successors a rent (backed by distress) of a yearly pound of pepper 'in and for the acknowlegeinge hym and them for the lordes and very owners of the saide heath'.[2]

Despite the breadth of the powers granted, the attempt made in 1589 to exercise them by drawing water from Hampstead Heath was unsuccessful—'much money being therein spent the effect failed so that the Brook [i.e. the Fleet] by means of continual Encroachments upon the Banks, getting over the water, and casting of Soilage into the Stream is now become worse cloyed and choaken than ever it was before'. Nine years before this, however, a more effective means had been found to improve the water supply by harnessing the drop in the Thames caused by London Bridge. Peter Morris took a 500-year lease of the northernmost arch (and later of others) and installed 'a most artificial Forcier'—a tide wheel which pumped water to the South and East of the City. The business continued in his family until the eighteenth century and formed the London Bridge Water Works, taken over by the New River Company in 1822. In 1858 much the same fate befell the later children of the 1543 statute, the Hampstead Aqueducts.[3]

The need for a fresh source of household water became urgent in the early seventeenth century. By then, London and its suburbs held a quarter of a million people—one-twentieth of the population of England and Wales—of whom some 30,000 died of the 'plague' in 1603. That one cause of the disease was the 'fowle and unsavory ditches' was expressly recognized in the Letters Patent of the following year granted to Edmund Colthurst. Since Elizabeth's reign he had been agitating for permission to run water from springs in Hertfordshire. The City had approved, and commissions of *ad quod damnum* had issued

[2] London Water Act 1543; cf. Gloucester Water Act 1541.

[3] Stow, ed. Strype i 23, 25. The City Rebuilding Act of 1666 provided for the reconstruction of the works to supply water 'as it for almost this hundred years hath done' (s. 41); London Bridge Waterworks Removal Act 1822; NRCD F/674, 685, 690, 692. See Chapter 6.5.2.

into the counties concerned; the consequent inquisitions had reported in favour provided that the aqueduct was limited to six feet in breadth and that the owners of the land through which it was to run were 'satisfied and contented for their particular losses'. Accordingly, in 1604 the King granted Colthurst 'full power licence and authoritie' to bring the water from the springs—as yet unnamed—within seven years. In return for a payment of £20 per annum the Letters Patent gave 'to him his heires and assigns for ever all the whole and entire benefitt pfitt and comoditie which may come arise or growe by conveying or disposing or in any way imploying the said water'.[4]

According to a slightly later account among the Tanner manuscripts in the Bodleian Library, the grant was made to Colthurst 'in recompense of his longe service in Ireland', and he invested a great deal in procuring the patent and in preliminary work. Certainly, he remained actively involved and—as will be seen in section 2.3—became the first tenant for life of four shares in the unincorporate New River undertaking. The City, however, decided to place the venture on a sounder legal basis and in 1605 began the process of obtaining an Act of Parliament. By this time the most suitable sources of the water supply were being identified, for we read in the records of Middlesex Sessions that on 22 December 1606 two London butchers were sentenced to hang for robbing Robert Boothe of his clothes and 'a parchment map called "the Mappe of the new Cutt to bringe the water from Amwell to Tibbolls" worth fifteen pounds'. Colthurst protested against the Bill to Robert Cecil—later the Earl of Salisbury, Lord Treasurer, and much involved with the project—and was invited to be heard at the Committee stage before a body which included several who were to become the first Adventurers (or shareholders, in modern terms), one of whom was Hugh Myddelton. At the third reading Sir Henry Montagu (Recorder of London and an early investor) promised that the City would recompense Colthurst, and the Bill was carried by 60 to 49. In the Lords, Colthurst's deserts were stressed but the Bill passed rapidly.[5]

[4] Kenyon 14–15; Letters Patent of 18/4/1604 at TW, Strongroom B30, box 79; CSPD 1603–10, 93; NRCD B/184.

[5] Bodl. Tanner MS 98 fo. 113; HMC Cecil MS xvi 55; *Middx County Records* ii 245; CJ i 262, 310, 311; LJ ii 442.

The Act as it finally received the Royal Assent is printed in Appendix A.1. It identifies the source of the water as being only springs at or near Chadwell and Amwell (and not the river Lea) and gives powers to the City in terms which—for reasons which will appear—are here emphasized:

[I]t shall be lawful for the [City] . . . to begin and continue the laying out of such convenient limits of ground for the making of the trench for the said river at the breadth of ten foot . . . and . . . to have and take for the purpose aforesaid *the use and liberty* of such and so much ground . . . for the conveying of the said water . . . *leaving the inheritance of the new cut in the owners thereof.*

Thus, the only compulsory power is to acquire a watercourse, the statute sensibly—in case of failure of the scheme—leaving the fee simple in the bed with the landowners. As will be explained in Chapter 5.3, at least one tribunal (the Court of Requests in 1637) may have taken this to mean not merely that landowners could not be forced, but that they were not permitted, to convey the land itself.

The statute also provided for compensation to be adjudicated, where necessary, by Commissioners. Section 7, however, is in these terms:

That until or before a full agreement with the lords, owners and occupiers of the premisses be had, or that such order and means be devised and agreed upon by the commissioners . . . it shall not be lawful for the [City] to put the said digging, trenching or new cutting of the said new river from the said springs in execution.

Given that the proposed watercourse was almost forty miles long, the statute appears to enact that nothing can be done until everything can be done.[6]

The engineering problems were then studied; William Inglebert advised that the water be brought in an enclosed channel, and in 1606 the City obtained a short Act for that purpose. John Aubrey—who enjoyed being indignant at virtue slighted—gives Inglebert credit for the whole scheme and paints a sad picture of him in later years 'in a poore Rug-gowne like an Almes-man, sitting by an apple-woman at the

[6] According to the recitals in the New River Company's Act of 1852 its statutory history begins in 1570. In fact that statute is concerned with navigation on the River Lea (13 Eliz. I, c. 18).

Parliament-stayres'. The City did not act precipitately to exercise its powers, and its hesitation has been greatly misconstrued. Thus, the sententious Anthony Munday, in 1618, says:

I spare here to speak of the Length of Time that such an Intent was in talking on; like much good Matter well motioned, though long minded, long debated but never concluded.

Eighteenth-century historians went further, with Pennant alleging—quite falsely—that the City opposed the grant of its statutory powers, and all of this was to provide ammunition for the nineteenth-century opponents of public ownership of London's water, culminating in the Parliamentary witticism that the City merely 'rested on its oars'. In fact, apart from the difficulties of section 7 of the statute (above), the main problem seems to have been financial. The City had the powers but, perhaps remembering the Hampstead failure of sixteen years before, was understandably reluctant to venture public funds in an untried and potentially endless commitment to capital expenditure. By 1609, however, there had emerged the man to money the business: Hugh Myddelton, whose name still adorns the streets and schools of Islington.[7]

2.2 The Prime Mover

The sixth son of a Denbighshire landowner, Myddelton was born about 1560, followed his elder brother Thomas to London, and was apprenticed to a goldsmith, becoming a liveryman of the Company in 1592, Warden in 1604, and Prime Warden in 1610 and 1624. He prospered in his trade, supplying gilt bowls to Gerard Malynes (whom we shall meet in Chapter 10.7), pearls to Queen Elizabeth, and 'a pendant of one diamond' bestowed by James I upon his wife. He sat as Member for Denbigh in all the Parliaments of James I, and being entitled to practise any trade, as a member of one of the great companies, he seems to have diversified diligently into mining, engineering, textiles, and buccaneering. Indeed, tradition credits him with promoting the custom of smoking tobacco by

[7] Aubrey, ed. Clark ii 1; Stow, ed. Strype i 25; Pennant 197; Hans. (3rd Ser.) ccclxxxv 1207.

doing so in public with his friend Sir Walter Ralegh. He married first a widow almost twenty years older than himself, who died childless, and then his brother Thomas's step-daughter, twenty years his junior. She bore him fifteen children.[8]

The first entry in Hugh Myddelton's own accounts of the New River is dated 20 February 1608 (i.e. 1609) and covers a disbursement for legal fees. The second records the payment of 2*s.* 6*d.* via Colthurst 'to give the officer for warninge the Comitty to meate in that business'; the Common Council did indeed meet and, in March, resolved to accept his offer to carry out the work at his own cost, and to appoint him their deputy in the exercise of the statutory powers. In April they gave him letters of attorney followed by a formal agreement drafted by Sir Henry Montagu; they then wrote to the Privy Council requesting that instructions be sent to the Justices of the Peace in Hertfordshire and Middlesex to assist Hugh Myddelton and his men 'all in their power'. Various extensions of time were later given and, on 28 March 1611, a formal agreement was executed which superseded the earlier arrangements and remained effective until 25 July 1904.[9]

It is printed in Appendix B and merits reflection. In the first place, it jars upon modern assumptions as to constitutional propriety. The City, we may think today, is a creature of public law and the two statutes conferred upon it public powers which, in principle, may not even be delegated, let alone given away. But of course the exercise of such powers by private citizens was central to feudalism and not unknown to the seventeenth century: had not 1604 seen yet another lease of the Great Farm of the Customs to a group of notables who promptly (though not without comment) sublet to a syndicate? In the usual transfers, however, the public power at least got something in return, some certain and covenanted yield; Myddelton got the powers (and the profits) with no such burden. He covenants to do his best to bring the water to the City at his own expense within seven years, to compensate the land-owners, to comply with

[8] *Pell Records* 19; Malcolm i 217; Pink 47 ff.; CSPD 1603–10, 187; Gough 6; CJ i 899, 917, 1021.

[9] PRO LR 2/27; City indentures of 27/2/1611 and 28/3/1611 at TW, Strongroom B30, box 79; *Remembrancia* 555; NRCD B/179, 181, 183, 186.

any Commission of Sewers, and to bear the risk of failure—'the sole and onely hazards and adventure'.

In return the City Fathers do two things. Firstly they appoint

Hughe Midleton his heires and assignes ioyntlie and severallie their true and lawfull Attornyes Deputyes and Agents in their names But to the onely benefitt and behoofe of the said Hughe Midleton his heires and Assignes to doe execute and pforme whatsoever by the said Actes of pliament [the City] are authorised to doe or may lawfullie doe.

Secondly, in consideration of his undertaking to try to run the river, they 'graunte convey assigne and confirme unto the said Hughe Midleton his heires and assignes the whole entire and sole profitt benefitt comodity and advantage whatsoever' of both the bringing and the selling of the water. Thus, the transaction straddles agency and grant, being a delegation of the powers together with, in return for their exercise, a gift of all the profits. The other striking feature of the indenture, and one which will give rise to three centuries of unique, if costly, privilege, is that it is couched in the language of real property. The correct conveyancing techniques are used and the appropriate words of limitation; but the property involved is not land in the sense of a corporeal hereditament, or power to acquire a freehold. The substratum of the whole enterprise is a watercourse.[10]

It will be recalled that section 7 of the founding statute appears to provide that the consent of all landowners must be obtained before any work is put in hand. That Myddelton ignored this and began at once is clear from his accounts. First of all, he had to know whom to approach and seems to have guaranteed his informants anonymity: on a page of his disbursements studded with the names of his labourers (at 6*d.* a day) appears the discreet entry for 3 March 1609/10 of 7*s.* 3*d.* 'to certen men to give knowledg of the owners of groundes to London'. James I approved a Commission to settle cases of dispute and, where necessary, they fixed the appropriate amount.[11]

Myddelton also took receipts from landowners, and a selec-

[10] Heckscher i 245; Lewyn's accounts (1609–30) at NR; PRO LR 2/34.
[11] PRO LR 2/27 (2/8/1609); M vol. A/13 ff.

tion is printed in Appendix C. He was soon using a standard-form document, as is evident both from the texts and from the fact that, in some of the manuscripts, not enough space has been left for particular details. The typical receipt acknowledges payment from the City by the hand of Hugh Myddelton of compensation for damage caused by cutting the river. Occasionally, of course, there are variations. Thus, the Vicar of Amwell allowed passage through his lands at no charge 'for the uttere love I beare to the said Cittie' (Appendix C.1). At the other extreme, some owners haggled, as is shown by the weary note endorsed on one by Hugh himself (C.6). Sometimes the receipt refers to the 'passage of the new Ryver by Acte of pliament' (C.2) or covers compensation merely for a temporary disturbance to grazing rights (C.3). The document in Appendix C.5 is that relating to the New River Head, which was to be the subject of a century of dispute and litigation. In all the receipts it is abundantly clear that the arrangement was merely for a wayleave and not for a grant of any greater interest in the land. He dealt with over 300 landowners and others, paying them a total of £341. 2*s.* 0*d.*[12]

In early 1610 work stopped and remained at a standstill for almost two years; virtually the only disbursements shown in the accounts are for the mole-catcher's wages and overtime. The reason is recounted in a manuscript preserved in the Bodleian Library entitled 'The state of the cause concerning the Water work'. Clearly the work of a Myddelton supporter, it begins the process of exaggerating both the capital and the labour involved which was to persist until this century. It avers that Colthurst had laid out £1,000, though he himself put the figure first at £300 and then £700, and describes a labour force of 1,700, although the accounts show that it was nearer 250, some of whom were part-time. After recounting the collaboration of Colthurst and Myddelton it says that the latter 'hath brought the said streame tenn miles or thereabout of the way' and has 'compounded with everie man through whose land the same shall passe except Mr Purvey and 2 more who will not be compounded withall'. The latter are said to have 'begunne all theis mischeafes out of mallice and splene' and to have preferred a Bill to repeal the statutory foundation 'upon pretences and

[12] GL MS 4883/9; accounts abstracted in Chapter 3.5.

suggestions which cannot be proved'. Certainly William Purvey was in royal favour, being Auditor of the Duchy of Lancaster, and was able to muster a number of landowners in support of the Bill to repeal 'the acts for the river from Ware' which reached the Commons in May 1610. The City, of course, opposed the move and sent a deputation to lobby Sir Julius Caesar—then Chancellor of the Exchequer—and other notables. Many of the objections were trivial—that the cut was dangerous or that tithes would be lost—but two were prescient: the damage to the River Lea and the fact that the City had 'by an acte of Comon Councell irrevocable granted their whole interest in fee simple to Mr Middleton and his heires who doth the same for his private benefitt'. The reply is a cogent demonstration of Pareto-superiority (someone gains, no one loses): 'yf the cittie finde good and the Countrie noe hurt, though Mr Middleton gaineth by it, he deserveth it well.' After its second reading the Bill was referred to a Committee, ten of whose members were to inspect the river. Whether they ever did so is unknown; but, in the following February, Parliament was dissolved not to meet seriously again for a decade.[13]

2.3 The Royal Investment

Immediately on the dissolution of Parliament, Myddelton obtained from the City a further five-year term in which to finish the work. Opposition had not ceased, however, and objections were being made both to the City's actions in transferring their powers and to the result—'that which was intended for a public good shall be converted to a private gain'. Myddelton's next move, therefore, was prompted by political and financial prudence and was a common precaution of entrepreneurs of the day—to involve the King. The obvious contact beween the promoter of smoking and the author of the 'Counterblaste to Tobbaccoe' was Salisbury; the river ran through his land at Hoddesdon, he had been paid for the right of passage, and he

[13] Bodl. Tanner MS 98 fos. 47–9, 113; copies of the first two are at PRO SPD Jas. I 78 No. 106; Sharpe ii 22; CJ i 429, 442, 445, 450. The idea that the original work cost £500,000 is repeated as late as 1980: Braun 2. The true accounts are abstracted in Chapter 3.5.

negotiated further with Myddelton during the summer of 1611. Eventually a deal was struck and embodied, first in an agreement with Salisbury and finally in a formal indenture under the Great Seal dated 2 May 1612.[14]

The document is printed in Appendix D. It expresses royal support for the City's transfer of its powers to Hugh Myddelton, gives him a free right of passage through the Royal Park at Theobalds, promises assent to any further necessary legislation, and envisages the investment of other 'adventurers'. It also prohibits, on pain of high displeasure, any interference with the work and permits Hugh Myddelton 'at his proper cost and charg to derive a quill out of the mayne pipe . . . to serve the poore people gratis about St Johns Streate and Aldergate Streate which are not able nor fitt to paie for their water'. The two most important provisions are that the King will meet half the expenditure incurred and that, in return, he will receive 'for ever the one halfe of the benefitt profitt and comoditie of the said water and of the conveying of the same . . . so as the interest shall and maie still be setled and kept in the subiecte and not in His Maiestie his heires or successors'. The reason for this last clause seems to be to avoid any misgivings felt about the Crown as partner.[15]

In any event, to secure both the King's commitments and the corresponding share of the profits, the deed contains elaborate provisions for the keeping of accounts. It is this royal interest which has ensured the preservation of so many of the early documents. The Public Record Office holds a set of books covering the years 1609–30. They are kept on the single-entry principle: the first nine record disbursements, beginning in Myddelton's hand and continuing in the hands of his clerks Edward Hughes and William Lewyn. The royal involvement is shown by the countersignatures on the records of expenditure of Sir Julius Caesar, then Miles Whiteacre, and finally Edward Ball. Another nine books record the income, beginning in March 1614, listing all the customers under the appropriate parish; at certain intervals of about a year is found a list of

[14] HMC 3rd Rep. Appx. 45, 58; CSPD 1611–18, 128; *Pell Records* 156, 172, 190; indenture of 2/5/1612 under the Great Seal at TW, Strongroom B30, box 79.

[15] Blackstone ii 409; Charles II was apparently acceptable as a partner in the Africa Co: Carr, *Charters* 176.

arrears due. There is also a bundle of drafts and fair copies of 'balance sheets' and other documents, and William Lewyn's final list of arrears and oath that they are 'desparate'. The sums paid piecemeal out of the Treasury totalled £9,262. 9*s*. 6*d*., which, according to an account in Myddelton's own hand dated 24 February 1625/6, was half the amount disbursed; in fact it was 6½*d*. short of that figure but thereafter the total expenditure is given as £18,524. 19*s*. 0*d*. At the Company's head office is still to be found a detailed summary of Hugh's account with the King over the period 1609–30 (including a charge and discharge of uncollected rents) prepared by William Lewyn and audited by James Weston, Baron of the Exchequer.

As will be recounted in later chapters, there were several attempts by nineteenth-century Commissions and Courts to ascertain the capital expended by the Company, on which its revenue was by then reaching half a million pounds. The Company answered that it did not know, and referred (quite truthfully) to a fire at its head office in 1769. A century before that date, in reply to similar queries put by the Privy Council, it was pleading the Great Fire of 1666. The existence of Lewyn's accounts, on four parchment membranes wrapped in red leather, was apparently overlooked by all concerned. A set of the Treasurer's accounts for 1670–84 (with half-yearly balances) survives in 185 folio pages in the British Library and will be discussed in Chapter 3.4. Meanwhile, to meet his own commitments Hugh Myddelton needed outside capital.[16]

2.4 The Adventurers

One reason for getting royal finance was, no doubt, to ensure support against the land-owning opposition to the project. In order to raise further capital, Hugh Myddelton did what the

[16] Lewyn's accounts (1609–30) at NR; PRO LR 2/27–33 (expenditure), 35–43 (income), 34 (miscellaneous copies of deeds, draft abstracts of Lewyn's accounts, Hugh Myddelton's account of 24/2/1626); 44 (list of bad debts and Lewyn's oath that they are desperate) (of the expenditure ledgers, the pages of the volume at LR 2/32 are uncast and unverified, though the book is audited like the others); BL Harl. MS 3604. CSPD 1611–18, 364, misprints the total of the royal investment—see CSPD 1631–3, 160, and *Pell Records* 156, 172, 190; *Hertford Records* 18. William Lewyn is the hero of the deservedly forgotten novel, *The New River* (1885), by 'Edward Fitzgibbon'; the characters also figure in a children's book, *Water for London* (1956), by A. Ashton.

modern entrepreneur will do: he issued shares. The fact that the enterprise was as yet unincorporate seems to have proved no hindrance—the Bubble Act was a hundred years and more ahead. The earliest traceable example is printed in Appendix E. It was made just six days after the formal royal investment described above, between Hugh and Sir Henry Neville of Billingsbear, Berkshire. The latter's earlier investment of £200 is recited, and he covenants to pay what would nowadays be known as 'calls' up to a maximum of one-sixteenth of the amount by which one-half of the expenditure (the King bearing the other half) exceeded £3,200. It is clear from the document that another fifteen had already invested and received shares, and it may be that this last sum represents the total capital by then paid up; certainly by 1619 there are twenty-nine 'Adventurers'. In return for his past and future investment, Neville is to receive one-eighteenth of one-half of the profits. This figure is arrived at as follows: the deed provides that neither Hugh nor his heirs

> shall grant out of the profitt of the premisses or charge the same with more than sixe and thirtie partes, the totall and entire to be accounted and devided into sixe and thirtie parts and the parts in this present grant and others formerlie made being accompted.

In the operative words of the instrument, Hugh grants

> unto the said Sir Henry Nevill his heires and assignes for ever two full and intire sixe and thirtieth partes of the said water works river and new cutt and of the profitt benefitt gaigne comoditie and advantage which (such moietie or halfe of the profitts and comodities thereof due and to be due to the Kinges Matie aforesaid according to the true meaning hereof excepted and allowed) at anie tyme hereafter shalbe made or raised by or out of the said river and of all rents somes of monie and other profitts . . .

A final clause repeats that the whole transaction, both as to calls and dividends, relates only to the Adventurers' moiety.

Neville was thus to bear one-sixteenth of half the cost (over a certain amount) and to receive only one-eighteenth of the profits. The reason for this disparity is explained in the indenture. In consideration of the 'greate labour and endeavour by him bestowed about the said worke', Edmund Colthurst is to have four of the thirty-six shares 'for terme of his naturall

FIG. 1. Boring machine for wooden water mains, 1615

life'. On his death two of the shares are to go to Hugh and his heirs for his 'great industry travell and paynes taking'; the other two are to go to Colthurst's estate (in fee simple) if he survives the completion of the work and, if not, are to be shared rateably among the shareholders. It looks, therefore, as if, during Colthurst's life, only thirty-two of the shares are to be subject to calls; but together they must make up the whole moiety of expenditure and so, as Nevill holds two, he must pay one-sixteenth thereof. Since the shares remained in his family for many years (the story is told in Chapter 4.3), it is impossible to say exactly what calls they had to bear. If, however, we calculate at the moment the King stopped paying—by which time income was marginally exceeding expenditure—and take the initial total cost to be £18,525, each Nevill share would have had to bear some £189 in calls, giving a price per share—or 'par value'—of £289. As will be shown later, however (Chapters 6.5 and 7.3.2), capital investment was financed out of net income until the nineteenth century, a process which may be compared with further calls or new share issues.[17]

[17] Indenture of 8/5/1612 at TW, Strongroom B30, box 79. The estimate of £289 is of the same order as that of Scott (iii 21 ff.), who gives a fraction over £257; he seems not to have known of Colthurst's life estate. In 1626 the share was valued at £76. 16*s*. 9½*d*.: PRO LR 2/41. Hugh Myddelton also raised an unsecured loan of £3,000 from the City: Sharpe ii 25; Berry 41; Gough 65.

2.5 Making the New River

The River Lea drains a valley in the great chalk ridge which intersects Hertfordshire. At the foot of the chalk hills near Ware, and about 100 feet above sea level, there were two plentiful springs: the upper named the Chadwell and, below Ware, the Amwell. These (with assistance from the Lea as described in Chapter 3.3) formed the source of Myddelton's water. It is not the purpose of this book to describe in detail the engineering of the river, but the story—and its interruptions by political and financial difficulties—can be traced in minute detail from the books of expenditure.

The entry for 5 May 1609 records a payment of £20. 3*s*. 0*d*. 'to Mr Wright for his 3 sevall surveis to Amwell and back againe to Islington'. The surveyor was the mathematician Edward Wright, Fellow of Gonville and Caius College, Cambridge, and author of works on logarithms and navigation. In addition, Edmund Colthurst is receiving 14*s*. a week 'for his entertaynement' until August 1616, when presumably he died. The plan was simply to dig a cut about five feet deep and ten wide following the contour line southward, looping to the west to cross the valleys of the tributaries of the Lea, with a fall of about five inches in a mile. Where necessary, banks were to be built up and bridges constructed to carry the roads over the river. Levels had to be estimated by plummet, for the spirit-level was unknown. For the last half of 1609 between fifty and a hundred labourers were employed, assisted by 'the Ingen', whose maintenance occasioned a number of disbursements. Aubrey tells us that this was the invention of 'a Country Fellow [who] said that he would save them 2,000 pounds, that is he would turn up the Earth with a Plough; and had strong Ploughs and Harness made purposely, which was drawn by 17 Horses, and sav'd a vast deal of Expence'. Presumably the device failed, for it is not mentioned in the books after 1609.[18]

For the reasons decribed in the previous sections, work virtually ceased during 1610. After the royal investment and failure of the opposition in Parliament, however, it resumed briskly under the technical direction of Edward Pond, mathematician

[18] PRO LR 2/27 (first book) 14 and 28/10 and 11/11/1609; Aubrey, ed. Dick 198.

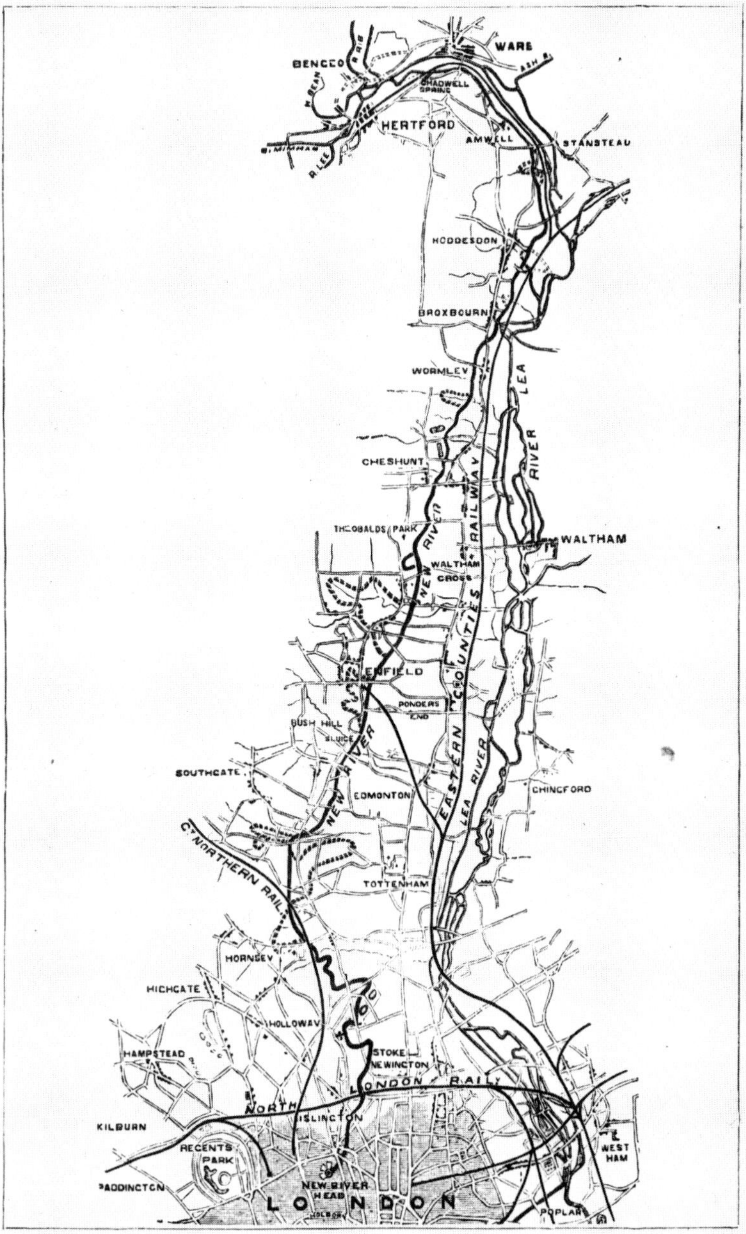

FIG. 2. Map of the New River (1904). The dotted loops to the West show the original course. The river now ends at Stoke Newington, save for an ornamental stretch at New River Walk, N1.

and publisher of almanacs; his signature appears as a witness to the compensation receipt of 13 December 1612 printed in Appendix C.3. Baskets were bought 'toe carrie earthe' and hods for 'where the wheele Barrowes cannot goe' and the cut continued southwards through or near Wormley, Cheshunt, Theobalds, Enfield, Winchmore Hill, Hornsey, Stoke Newington, and Ball's Pond until by the spring of 1613 Islington was in view. At Bush Hill, near Edmonton, the river was taken across the Salmon Brook in a long wooden frame, which excited much admiration. Meanwhile, at the head of the river a 'Cistern House' was being built and the pond prepared.[19]

2.6 The River Running

The official opening on Michaelmas Day 1613 was celebrated in the presence of the Lord Mayor, the Lord Mayor-elect (Hugh Myddleton's elder brother Thomas), Aldermen, and a huge crowd; the festivities included marches, music, and very bad verse. Edmund Howes has left us a description which, while not without charm, seems to owe more to Euphues than observation:

> Chadwell, the remotest of the two Springes yet ever heretofore emptied her wasted waters into the river of Lea untill now being taught a new course, she poureth her rich spoyles into the bosome of her sister, and so hand in hand runneth along with her to London. The other spring which heretofore sporting herself upon a playne bed of gravell was wont wantonly to wash the pebbles with her christall waters and so (as careless of her own worth) to bury her pearls in the lappe of Lea; But now being taught to esteeme better of her self hath been pleased to view her selfe in a fair poole and there sportfully to wrastle with her sister.[20]

The scene of these frolics can still be discerned in the car-park behind the Thames Water building on Rosebery Avenue.

Bringing the water to London was itself no mean feat of

[19] Pond appears regularly from PRO LR 2/27 (second book) December 1611. An entry for 30/11/1611 (PRO LR 2/27, second book) shows that John Blagrave was also involved in the survey; described by à Wood (ii 96) as 'the flower of mathematicians', he died soon after. Disbursements on river and Cistern House are recorded frequently in both books at PRO LR 2/28; (1784) 54 *GM* 43.

[20] Howes 1015 (abridged).

engineering; but the distribution of it through pipes of elm sunk in the streets involved heavy expenditure and the citizenry seemed in no hurry to take—and pay for—the new water. The normal charges (for instance, what John Milton's father paid) were 5*s*. for connection and 6*s*. 8*d*. a quarter: exactly what was paid almost 300 years before by those citizens lucky enough to have private channels from the Tyburn conduit. In addition, the transaction costs were heavy. To the seventeenth-century lawyer, the important feature of the arrangement with the customers must have been that it was intended to endure. The law of contract was equipped to deal mainly with the instantaneous transaction—sale is the obvious example. For legal regimes involving the element of time, the law of real property supplied the machinery. We shall see that the Charter empowers the Company to 'demise' the water and lays down limits—twenty-one years or three lives—appropriate to other fields of investment. The document printed in Appendix G shows that the arrangement was cast in the form of a lease. The connection fee is a 'fine' and the quarterly payments a 'rent'; covenants are inserted restricting the user to private consumption of the water; the interdependence of obligations is shown by the clause which permits the rent to be withheld if the supply fails; and the standard forfeiture clause provides the sanction for unjustified default. One feature which remained constant to this century was that, in general, payment does not vary with consumption.[21]

Despite the heavy outgoings, there were only 384 'tenants' by Ladyday 1615, and the income was under £1,000. In addition, the New River was experiencing a difficulty which was to continue for centuries, that of vandalism. In June of that year the Privy Council sent an open warrant with a vivid description of the problem:

Whereas Hugh Midleton hath brought a river of water unto Islington and from thence convayed the same by pipes into divers partes of the citty of London, to the great benefit and comodity of the inhabitantes of the said citty; forasmuch as complaint is made unto us of many abuses and misdemeanors daylie committed and donn in and upon the said river, by lewde and ill-disposed people, in cuttinge the bankes

[21] Milton is at PRO LR 2/35 (4/9/1615); Salzman 273. Hugh Myddelton himself paid £2 a year for the supply to his house in Bashishawe Street: PRO LR 2/41.

and letting out the said water, to the inconvenience and prejudice of the tennantes, casting in dogges and filth, and lettinge in sewers and other fowle and unclean water, to the annoyance of the said water; breakeinge and carreinge away the bridges, vaultes and rayles standinge in and upon the river; taking and carryinge water out of the said river in lickquer cartes, tubbs or barrells, and stealing branches and cockes from the pipes without any composicion, together with many such like abuses and annoyances: these shalbe therefore to will and require yow, and in his Majesty's name to charge and comaund yow and every of yow that, upon informacion given unto yow by the said Hugh Midleton yow cause the offenders to be ymediatly brought before us, to answere in their misdemeanours in that behalfe, whereof they may be assured his Majestie wilbe very sensible, beinge to the prejudice of soe worthie a worke, wherin his Highnes is soe deeply interessed. Hereof yow may not faile.[22]

In order to increase the income, attempts were made to put pressure on the citizenry to take the New River water. In December 1616 the Privy Council wrote to the City reminding them of Myddelton's achievement and stating that he 'did expend greate summes of money in purchasinge the ground through which the water was to passe'. This assertion is totally false; it will be recalled that the basic statute required 'the inheritance' of the land to be left in its owners, and the scores of compensation receipts surviving prove beyond doubt that only a wayleave was sought and given. But the seeds of confusion as to the ownership of the land through which the river runs were already sown. The letter then recalls the political opposition described above and goes on to remonstrate with the City:

Unlesse his Majestie had ben graciously pleased to favour and supporte his undertakinge, he [Myddelton] had suncke under the waight of that burthen and never ben able to have brought it to that passe as now it is; whereunto his Majestie was the rather moved at the humble suite of yow, the Aldermen, as wee well remember, for passage of that water through his parke for the use and benefitt of that citty. Forasmuch as the only scope and ende of those lawes was the generall good and profitt of that citty, aswell in the use of sweete and holesome water, as for the preservacon of the same from casualty and dainger of fire, whereof there hath ben good experience three severall tymes this last somer, and that his Majestie and the Boarde are informed

[22] APC 1615–16, 212–13 (abridged).

that but few, in respect of the generallytie and such for whome it was principally intended, doe take that water, and that it is not to be thought that such a suite was made for the obtayninge of two severall Acts in twoe sessions of parliamentes, nor yet an act of Common Councell made in a busines soe much concerning the health and safety of that citty, to noe use or purpose other then the hinderance and prejudice of such as were by yow deputed to undertake the same; his Majestie hath comaunded, and accordingly wee do require you to order and provide either by Comon Councell or otherwise that the said water may be taken into all such houses within that citty and the liberties, as either out of necessity or conveniencie may make use of the same: which beinge the only motives to induce the parliament to make those lawes, it is held very expedient that accordingly the citty be in all partes furnished and provided, as shalbe most behoufefull for the publicke.[23]

This document is less than candid; it affects to be concerned only with public welfare and omits all mention of the King's pecuniary interest; and it put the City in a dilemma. They had transferred the statutory powers together with all the profit to be made by their exercise to a private citizen at a time when they could hardly have foreseen that His Majesty would become financially involved. Now they were being instructed to use such authority as they possessed in order to enforce the compulsory purchase by their citizens of the new water. Further, the great magnates who counted on royal support in their struggles with Parliament were being ordered to forward a monopoly in which they had no stake. The letter was received and duly noted by the City but no attempt was made to implement it. A further complication was the interest shown by would-be competitors. In 1617, for instance, a number of brewers offered to take over the cost of maintaining the Dowgate conduit if they might lay pipes into their breweries. The City's committee ascertained that they were ready to take in 'Middleton's water' for other purposes and to pay reasonable rents, and recommended acceptance. Someone, however, informed the Privy Council of the proposal and another letter issued to the City explaining that

since the said new stream, brought at great cost from the springs of Chadwell and Amwell, was of great consequence to His Majesty's

[23] APC 1615–16, 99–100 (abridged).

service, and deserved all due encouragement, they had deemed it expedient to require that stay should be made of the intended water-works &c at Dowgate, the more so since the brewers could so conveniently be supplied from the new stream.[24]

James I made several attempts to secure some return on his investment. On 19 January 1618 he appointed Edward Ball to be 'surveyor' of the New River for life at an annual salary of £100 to be deducted from the King's share of the profits; the accounts show that this was paid punctually, no doubt as the price of Ball's countersignature each half-year. James then considered both selling to and buying out the Adventurers and appointed a committee (which included Coke) to advise 'what course they thinke fitt to be settled for his Majesty's best profit'. The outcome was a compromise which produced a new, and quite unique, juridical person: the New River Company.[25]

[24] APC 1617–18, 54; *Remembrancia* 557–8.
[25] CSPD 1611–18, 517; APC 1617–18, 158; PRO LR 2/31–3.

CHAPTER 3

Incorporation and After

3.1 Incorporation

THE Charter of incorporation of 1619 is printed in Appendix F. It recalls that the enterprise 'hath not hitherto yeilded such profitt as was hoped for partlie by reason of the Expences dailie arisinge farre greater and heavier than . . . was expected and partlie for want of power to settle the carriage and Government thereof'. It then distinguishes two moieties in 'the said Worke and the profitts and comodities thereof': the first is 'to the use of us the King our heirs and successors all necessary charges deducted'; the second is 'to the use of the Adventurers their heirs and assigns for ever'. The twenty-nine Adventurers are then incorporated under the name of 'The Governor and Company of the New River brought from Chadwell and Amwell to London'. They include Hugh and seven other Myddeltons, Sir Henry Montagu (by then Lord Chief Justice of the King's Bench), Sir Henry Neville (who, as we have seen, held two shares), Sir Laurence Hyde, Samuel Backhouse (owner of the site of the New River head) and his son John, and Peter Vanlore (whom Tawney calls 'the ubiquitous cosmopolitan, at home wherever he caught the smell of money'). The fledgling company is given the usual incidents of corporate life: perpetual succession, power to litigate, and a common seal. It is empowered to acquire and dispose of land, though this is presumably intended only for the purpose of the waterworks, since later in the instrument permission is given, 'the Statute of Mortmaine notwithstanding', to acquire one house in London as a head-quarters 'so as the same be not holden of us . . . by knight's service in capite'. This last precaution was presumably inserted to prevent the loss to the Crown of the appropriate incidents which fell due on the death of a human tenant in chief; after all, the new and vigorous Master of the Court of Wards and Liveries was none other than Lionel Cranfield. As we shall see later, the Company read its birth certificate with a generous spirit and diversified into landholding quite unconnected with the New River.[1]

The Charter deals also with the governance of the Company. It provides the means for appointing the officers and for a committee of five (one being the Governor or his deputy) to lease the water for a term not exceeding twenty-one years or three lives, appoint clerical staff, and make by-laws. A larger annual meeting of at least seven (including the Governor or his deputy) was required to elect the three principal officers of Governor, Deputy, and Treasurer at a meeting on 'the Tuesday next after the feast of All Saints or within ten daies thereafter'; and a meeting of at least twelve was needed to remove them during their term of office and elect a replacement. Other provisions make it clear that Hugh Myddelton had kept his covenant with Sir Henry Neville and there were only thirty-six shares in the Adventurers' moiety. At the moment of incorporation these were held by twenty-nine Adventurers and were transferable. The Company itself, however—or, in modern parlance, the voting membership—was restricted to the number of twenty-nine. If a member parted with his share he was removed and in his place there was elected another holder 'to whom a thirtie sixth parte or share of the benefitt or profitt of the said worke shall appertaine'. Thus, until this century the 'Directors' of the company were limited to twenty-nine with a qualification of one entire Adventurers' share. Only twenty-four of these shares remained whole, the others becoming much divided; the problems caused thereby will be discussed in Chapter 6.2.[2]

One provision is so important as to require special emphasis. It is cast in the familiar phraseology of the conveyancer:

> Wee have given and graunted and by these presents for us our heires and Successors (for the consideracons aforesaid) as much as in us is Wee doe give and graunt unto the [Company] and their successors the said new River cutt and streame with the appurtenances and all manner of profitts Advantages and Comodities thereof or by reason thereof in any sorte to be made raised or gotten To have hould and enjoy the said new River cutt or streame with the appurtenances to the [Company] and their successors for ever accordinge to the true

[1] Tawney 82. Clifford ii 79 n. 1 is mistaken in several respects.

[2] To this day the Annual General Meeting occurs at the appointed time.

meaninge of these presents: *To be holden of us our heires and successors as of our Mannor of Eastgreenwich in our Countie of Kent in free and comon Socage by fealty only and not in chiefe or by knights service.*

This provision is a commonplace in the royal grants of land acquired by the Crown on the dissolution of the monasteries; in fact by a happy coincidence, though a quite different title, the Company later came to own much of Clerkenwell by 'Greenwich tenure' (see Chapter 5.3). It is also found in the early colonial charters of Newfoundland, New England, and the like and in that of the Yarmouth Saltmakers of 1636. All these, however, concerned possessory interests in land—corporeal hereditaments. The New River Company held only a servitude; and further, the power to obtain such an interest, and its actual acquisition, were the work of Hugh Myddelton alone: strictly speaking, the King had nothing to grant. In fact at no time in the history of the Company (and despite several attempts) did it obtain a formal transfer of the statutory powers. Yet on the face of the charter it looks as if the Company holds its capital asset *and its future profits* by socage tenure. It will be seen in the next chapter how this provision led to the almost unanimous view that, if the profits were held in tenure, then the shares in those profits must themselves be realty.[3]

The Letters Patent of incorporation also provide that on the death of a shareholder there should be taken into the Company 'such heire or person unto whom the Inheritance of such part porcon or share shall come'. This clause is relied on by late nineteenth-century doctrine (but by no one else) as the reason for the strange status of the shares.[4]

After incorporation the King's interests were still being looked after by Edward Ball, although he played no part in the governance of the Company. In November 1619 James I created a sinecure duplicate of this office at £200 a year and conferred it upon Giles Mompesson, who held it until, in 1621, he had the distinction of being the first subject to be impeached since 1449. The Company adopted as its seal the device of a

[3] The cautious 'as much as in us' is rare: see Carr, *Charters* xv. For the saltmakers see ibid. 155.

[4] The first two editions of Challis, *Real Property*, aver that New River shares are realty by statute (1885, 33; 1892, 38). Charles Sweet, the learned editor of the third edition, was persuaded by L. L. Shadwell that they were realty because of the clause quoted (1911, 58).

hand over a city and as its motto the phrase from the Vulgate *Et plui super unam civitatem* (Amos 4: 7). The oath of office as the first Governor was administered to Hugh Myddelton by Baron Bromley in the following terms:

You shall sweare that you shall be Faithfull and true to our Soveraigne Lord the Kinge and his heires and successors Kinges and Quenes of this realm and all the lawful ordinances made and to bee made by the Governor and Companie of the Newe Ryver brought from Chadwell and Amwell to London you shall kepe and meyneteyne to your power.

You shall honestlie behave yourself in the place of Governor of this Companie and justlie and indifferentlie shall order the matters and causes of this Companie according to right and conscience and no singular profitt to your owne person nor take whereby the common profitt of this Companie or the particuler benefitt of anie member thereof shall or may be damaged.

You shall admitt no person into this Companie nor shall refuse to admitt anie into the same but according to the purport of the Kinges Majesties Letters Patentt to the said Governor and Companie granted and the orders and constitutions lawfullie made and to be made according to the same and all other thinges perteyning to your office to the uttermoste of your power and skill You shall well and trulie doe and perform. So help you God.

According to a later copy of the Minutes, the first meeting was held on 2 November 1619 (i.e. the first Tuesday after the Feast of All Saints, as required by the Charter) at Sir Henry Montagu's chambers in Serjeants' Inn. Twenty-one Adventurers were present and it was agreed that their moiety was divided into thirty-six shares; twenty-two of them held one and the following held two: Hugh Myddelton, Sir Laurence Hyde, Sir Henry Neville, Nicholas Hyde, Samuel Backhouse, his son John, and Peter Vanlore.[5]

3.2 The Company

The curious features of the Company's juridical nature have already been pointed out. Additional misgivings were created by several factors. Firstly, there were still attacks on the process

[5] CSPD 1611-18517; 1619-2391; F. W. Maitland, *Constitutional History* 246; Original Oath and copy Minutes at NR.

by which the City had transferred its public powers to a private citizen. Secondly, even if this were accepted, it was Hugh Myddelton who was the City's lawful deputy and he seems never to have attempted a transfer of his powers to the Company. Thirdly, even if the Company had somehow acquired the powers by the approval inherent in its incorporation, was it a private or a public body? On the answer to this question depended, as will be seen in Chapter 6.4, the vital issue of whether *mandamus* would lie. Fourthly (as explained in the next section), the Company was illegally abstracting water from the Lea. And finally, the Charter of incorporation had attempted to confer a monopoly. A passage which begins harmlessly enough by prohibiting pollution or private sale of the new supply goes on to equate with such malefactors anyone who should

> attempt or goe about to bring to the said Citties of London and Westminster and to the borough of Southwark or to either of them anie other river or pipe for conveyeyinge or bringinge of water from anie place whatsoever without the lycense and assent of the said Governor and Company.

With Mompesson's impeachment over the gold thread affair, and a Statute of Monopolies on the horizon (it arrived in 1624), the Company's position must have seemed far from safe.

For all these reasons, the Adventurers wanted to secure Parliamentary approval of the Company's existence. Their first attempt in 1621 did not get beyond a first reading. Three years later their Bill did at least reach the Committee stage and earn the approval of Sir Edward Coke, who pronounced it 'a very good Bill. Prevents one great mischief that hangs over the City—*nimia potatio: frequens incendium*.' The third Bill came on the eve of the Civil War, and it was not till 1737 that the Company was recognized by Parliament. Its entire constitution was not so endorsed until 1904, by which time it no longer held the New River in socage tenure.[6]

[6] CJ i 611, 745; ii 554; Byde Act 1737; New River Company's Act 1904.

3.3 The Source of the Water

By the date of incorporation the number of the Company's tenants was over 1,000 and the water provided by the springs was becoming insufficient. The obvious solution—though not permitted by either the statutes or the Charter—was to tap the River Lea, and the accounts for 17 June 1620 show expenditure of 10*s*. 'for twentie piles to make a damme in the Ryver [Lea] toe turne in the [New] Ryver at vjd a pce'. The result may be clearly seen to this day. The spring water flows eastward and alone for only a few yards before being joined by a cut running north-west about half a mile to the Lea. So began a dispute which persisted for 200 years and may as well be briefly described. The Lea was very important as a waterway for bringing produce to London, and its navigation had engaged Parliament as early as the reign of Henry VI. The bargemen protested against the Company's dam and removed it, whereupon it was promptly rebuilt.

Disputes simmered and in 1670 Charles II, by Order in Council, appointed a Committee to consider the 'complaint of the Inhabitants and Bargemen belonging to the towns of Hertford and Ware shewing that the Company have derived much of the ancient navigable River of Lee (which supplies the City with great quantities of corn and provisions) into their own River, thereby rendering the former incommodious for passage and almost unnavigable'. The conflict of desirable aims—the supply of water and that of corn—could not have been more neatly expressed. The two active members of the Committee were Sir Robert Murray and the young Christopher Wren; after surveying the river they presented a report which is a model of lucid elegance. They made 'several sure and well grounded experiments by measuring the velocities and comparing the quantities of both streams and by other methods oft repeated and tending to the same conclusion'. These conclusions entirely exonerated the Company: 'the pipes drew off from the navigable River about one part of thirty parts, which seemed to us very little prejudicial to navigation and which could not abate the River half an inch.' The state of the New River itself was also found to be satisfactory: 'by the industry of the present officers the worke was maintained in excellent

FIG. 3. New River Source, 1809, showing the cut to the Lea curving left. It looks the same today.

repair and in divers things improved beyond the first contrivance.' The problems of navigation were, they found, caused by the millers alongside the Lea who had deepened their cuts to take more water than they needed and, when this hindered the passage of a barge, would let the water out in a 'flash' but at a price: 'they help those for money whom they have first disabled.'[7]

The report then set out the conflict of economic interests among the three groups all vital to the welfare of London: Bargemen, Millers, and the Company. It pointed to the need for malt to the extent of 200,000 quarters a year 'which quantity brought by land would ruin all the ways; but the water carriage—through the encroachments of the millers—is now as dear almost as land carriage.' On the other hand, the mills were 'of great use to the City for corn, paper fulling, and dressing of leather'. And the City's drinking water might 'indeed elsewhere be had, but with less plenty and convenience'. Wren and his colleague concluded by summarizing the problem—'to keep these three sets of men within their bounds and make them all useful to the public'—and by making specific proposals which are a mixture of regulation, free enterprise, and, inevitably, public expenditure. As to the first, they recommended that the New River be limited to its present out-take and that the millers be regulated both as to the number of wheels and the price to be charged the bargemen for 'flashes'. As to the second, they suggested that the problems of general maintenance of the Lea 'be settled by mutual agreement between the bargemen and the millers or by indifferent persons'. They end with the third: 'But when all this is done the River Lee cannot be made complete for navigation without some expence be laid out upon it by Act of Parliament in order to cut other channels, to buy out some mills and such other things as are and would in foreign parts be put in practice for the public benefit.'

It is hardly necessary to say that this last proposal was not adopted by the legislature. For the next fifty years the Company consolidated its out-take at a site between Hertford and Ware known as the Manifold Ditch; disputes persisted and lawsuits

[7] From a copy of Wren's *Report* in Robert Mylne's commonplace book at TW, Strongroom B30, box 86; see also (1753) 23 *GM* 114.

began. The settlement was embodied in an Act of Parliament of 1738/9 which gave the Company what it had long sought—complete *statutory* recognition and reinforcement of the power to litigate. The statute enjoined millers to provide a supply of water for the barges and the Company to maintain certain locks (and collect the tolls). The supply taken from the Lea was confirmed and the Manifold Ditch and its water deemed to be a part of the New River and vested in the Company; but, in conformity with the 1605 Act, the statute saved the rights and privileges of the owners through whose lands the New River ran. Despite this settlement, contention persisted until 1855.[8]

3.4 The Business

On the income side, the Company began to show a small profit soon after incorporation and at Michaelmas 1622 £433. 2*s*. 7*d*. became due to the King; but a fresh outbreak of 'plague' in 1625 had the temporary effect of reducing the number of tenants and increasing arrears.The profits recovered only slowly, and it is not until the 1630s that a small dividend begins to be paid; the first (1633) is £11. 19*s*. 1*d*., falling in the following year to £3. 4*s*. 2*d*. but then rising to sums between £20 and £30 (see Appendix I). By mid-century it is over £50 and by the next period for which detailed accounts survive the business is on a healthy footing. The abstracts of the Treasurer's audited books for 1670–84 show that the Company was employing seven rent-collectors (who took the shilling in a guinea) and had over 3,000 tenants. These included both the Fleet prison and St James's Palace, and the inhabitants of both are found, in other sources, to be protesting at the Company's threats to raise the rent or cut off the water supply. Apart from the half-yearly balances, the accounts are in single-entry form, giving meticulous details of income but only totals of expenditure. The latter was still heavy, amounting to about one-third of the income. The water rents formed by far the major source of revenue, with only trivial sums being raised by sales of spare

[8] CJ xxiii 50, 166, 186, 189, 369, 373, 375, 378; NRCD A/13; River Lee Acts 1738, 1767, 1779, 1805, 1850, 1854, 1855, 1868, 1874, 1892, 1900. The Company is recognized in a private Act of 1737 (Byde Act)—see Chapter 6.5.1; NRCD F/557, G/385.

timber and the rent of three acres at Chadwell Mead, which the Company had acquired; thus it is still far from being a landowner. The annual dividends show a steady rise from £97. 7*s.* 4*d.* in 1671 to £168. 6*s.* 4*d.* in 1683. If the estimate of the cost of a Neville share be correct at £289, then the yield is rising from 33 per cent to 58 per cent.[9]

By the mid-sixteenth century there were several rival schemes, most of which came to nothing. Sir Edward Forde's undertaking, however, deserves mention. A pamphlet published in 1641 had criticized the 'foulnesse and muddiness of Myddelton's water' and had proposed to tap the River Colne at Rickmansworth. By 1656 Forde had adopted other plans and taken a licence to dig for wells and lay pipes near St Giles in the Fields, and had also leased premises at Wapping. He went into partnership with Ralph Grey, and then granted a moiety of the Wapping business to James Hayes and Thomas Toogood. Wells were sunk and pipes laid, and in 1665 the investors obtained Letters Patent from Cromwell 'for fortifying their several titles in these projects'. Soon afterwards the business was conveyed to Edmund Hartupp and Robert Clayton, who faced the problem that they were not incorporated. The solution was the same as that adopted 150 years later by the innumerable projects threatened by the Bubble Act: the leases and fixtures were assigned to trustees and the equity divided into twenty shares, five being held by Hartupp, five by Clayton, and ten by Toogood. The trustees were bidden 'if any of the [three] were to sell all or any of their shares the trustees were to permit the vendee to receive the profits in proportion'. In 1667 the trustees and shareholders sold the whole enterprise to the New River Company for £6,100. Soon after this, as will be explained in Chapter 5.2, the fact that the Company now held a waterworks under a different title caused some puzzlement to the courts as to what effect this had on the nature of the shares.[10]

[9] CSPD 1639–40, 407; CTB 1710 xxiv pt. II 468.

[10] Foord (or Forde) 7; NRCD A/1, B/196, 197, 199, 200, 203–4. Forde was active in the supply of water, and the pumping tower he built at Strand Stairs (now Water St.) annoyed Queen Henrietta Maria: CSPD 1663–4, 655; 1664–5, 230; à Wood iii 906; Jenkins, chap. XXV; H. W. Dickinson 18 ff.

3.5 The Crown

Soon after incorporating the Company, James grew restive. In January 1622, while riding in Theobalds, he fell off his horse 'into the midst of Myddelton's water . . . so that nothing but his boots were seen'. In May he appointed another of the numerous Royal Commissions which have investigated the New River and enjoined its members to ascertain the price at which the shareholders would submit to being taken over; as usual Edward Coke was one of the investigators, and the chairman was Sir William Pitt, Commissioner of the Navy.[11]

There survive two reports made to Lionel Cranfield, Earl of Middlesex and Lord High Treasurer. It appears from the first of them, dated 20 December 1622, that the Adventurers were not disposed to co-operate. They postponed a meeting (on the grounds that many of them were out of Town) until December and then, instead of answering the question as to how much they would take to be bought out, presented a petition for further royal help. This report notes that

> the workes at present doe rather decline than advance and wee conceive that the rents and profits thereof doe hardly amount to 2,900 li. if they were all received and indeed they are not nor wilbee without hys Maties help and assistance. The chardges and repaires with fees and wages . . . cometh yearlie to about 1,100 li. soe as the cleere proffit as they now stand both to the King and Companie (if all were received) wilbee about 1,800 li.

The second Report dated 13 February 1622/3 is even more gloomy. The Adventurers had related a tale of woe:

> That their shares for the present did rise but to twentie and eight pounds a man: that they could not sell them at this rate without two great loss. That if hys Matie by regall power and proclamacon would assist them, they might then bee raised to a hundred pounds a yeere; and then they might affoord a good bargaine wch they were willing to doe, not intending to rate them higher.

The Commission wisely stated that 'wee dare not advise' use of the power of proclamation, reminded the King of his largess to

[11] Nichols iv 749; APC 1618–19, 158–9; Kent County Archives Sackville MS 621, 1177, 2422; a copy of the second report is among Pitt's papers at BL Add. MS 29974 fos. 61–4; Gough 76–7.

Edward Ball and Giles Mompesson, and expressed the view that

it may be doubted whether by anie course to bee taken without more pressure than the tymes will well beare, a saving bargain can bee made to bring the works to perfeccon and so to maintain them and wthal to answer his Mats nine thousand stocke.

Coke signed only the second Report, and it is tempting to see his hand in the piece of lawyers' law which it contains:

So the summ of all is thys: by his Mats great charge, and by his ingagemt for the halfe: and by the condicons obteined in their Incorporacon they have gotten this advantage that his Mats moitie being undevided from theirs cannot be improved without improving theirs. And they being manie, the losse of their moitie devided in manie parts is the easier to beare than his Mats which fals all upon himself. How to drive them from this hold we yet see noe means.

Charles I became even more impatient and in 1630 ordered Sir James Weston, Baron of the Exchequer, to take the accounts and to advise on the best course of action. As mentioned in Chapter 2.3, these survive at the Company's head office and recite a 'charge' of £2,580. 0*s*. 8*d*. arrears of rent which William Lewyn 'maketh oath are desparate'. By letters under the Privy Seal of 5 November 1631 the Company is discharged of the moiety of this amount due to the King. The reason given is that of the uncertainty of the royal income—'the revenue not coming one year with another in all £300 a year'—compared with what was proposed by Baron Weston and Sir Hugh Myddelton: namely that the King would sell out, not to the Company, but to Sir Hugh in return for £500 on account of the year up to Michaelmas 1630 and £500 a year for ever thereafter. This represented a yield of approximately 5 per cent and no doubt at the time seemed reasonably satisfactory; as events turned out it was a very bad bargain indeed. The annual rent charge acquired the name of 'The Crown Clog', survived until 1956, and merits a chapter to itself (see Chapter 9).[12]

[12] Lewyn's accounts at NR, and his oath at PRO LR 2/44.

Table 1. Abstract of Accounts (20 Feb. 1609 to 29 Sept. 1630)

	£	s.	d.	£	s.	d.	£	s.	d.
Received:									
King	9,262	9	6						
Company	9,262	9	6						
				18,524	19	0			
Water rents				27,142	18	4			
Arrears received				3,149	2	3½			
Fines				3,320	10	10			
Sale of elms				166	2	0			
Ware meadow rent				12	0	0			
E. Colthurst: loan repaid from dividend				76	13	9½			
Ducking pond revenue				215	5	0			
Total							52,607	11	3
Disbursed:									
Construction	28,163	2	4						
Hugh Myddelton's fee	2,500	0	0						
				30,663	2	4			
Hugh Myddelton:									
1611–19, 46*s.* 8*d.* p.w.	1,092	0	0						
1619–22 (agreed by Privy Council)	1,400	0	0						
Company bonus	450	0	0						
1622–30	8,000	0	0						
				10,942	0	0			
Wm. Lewyn (clerk): 1617–30				1,060	0	0			
A. Iremonger (bedell): 1619–30				150	6	8			
H. Jones (surveyor): lump sum				110	6	8			
Incorporation costs	144	17	0						
Survey costs	21	5	8						
Compensation to land-owners	341	2	0						
Legal fees	44	8	0						
Elm pipes	159	15	8						
Rent books	2	0	0						
Exchange of clipped coin paid by tenants	31	10	4						
				745	8	8			
Total							43,671	4	4
Balance							**8,936**	**5**	**11**

	£	s.	d.	£	s.	d.	£	s.	d.
King's Moiety				4,468	2	11½			
Less:									
E. Ball:									
24/6/1617 to 29/9/									
1630, £100 p.a.	1,325	0	0						
G. Mompesson:									
29/9/1619 to 25/12/									
1620, £200 p.a.	250	0	0						
Fees to King's officers	9	0	6						
				1,584	0	6			
Total							2,884	2	5½
Less:									
Paid to Exchequer	2,013	5	11						
Paid to Theobalds by									
Treasury warrant	300	0	0						
Total							2,313	5	11
Balance due to King							**570**	**16**	**6½**

Meanwhile, it may be useful to present the financial position as it appeared to all concerned. The accounts are still in single-entry form, so that, for instance, they show only the arrears of rent eventually received; those unpaid appear only from the 'charge' described above; similarly, it is impossible to discern if the amount entered as received on the sale of crooked elms represents the profit or the purchase price. None the less, they show that Hugh Myddleton for his expenses and, more importantly, his enterprise had taken out of the project £13,442. They are given here (**Table 1**) in a way which abbreviates and modernizes the text but preserves the form and, of course, the figures. In addition the Charge and Discharge showed that the water rents outstanding amounted to £2,580. 0*s*. 8*d*. The King wrote off the half due to him, being satisfied that it concerned 'such debts and arrearages of rent as William Lewyn . . . maketh oath are desparate'.

3.6 Hugh Myddelton

Since his first disbursement on 20 February 1609, Hugh Myddelton had been primarily responsible for all the outgoings, although from the beginning of 1612 he drew a modest personal allowance of £2. 6*s*. 8*d*. a week for himself, a man, and two geldings. Once the Company was launched, however, there was no reason for him to remain personally liable. He arranged with the Company that he would maintain the existing works—would, in modern terms, be managing director—at a salary of £800 a year, which rose to £1,000 in 1622. All further expenditure, however, was charged to the Company.

Liberated from financial commitment in London, he turned his energies further afield. He moved into a project to drain Brading Harbour in the Isle of Wight; this completed, he sold out before the sea broke in again and concentrated on his third major scheme, the silver mines of Cardiganshire. He had taken a lease of them in 1617 and may have formed a separate company—'The Mines Royal of Wales'—to handle the project; he is said to have taken out £2,000 a month. On Cornelius Jansen's portrait of him, done about 1628 (**Plate I**), appear the words *Fontes Fodinae* in canting allusion to his two greatest achievements. They could be loosely rendered 'streams of silver'.[13]

These two feats were given as the reasons for the baronetcy conferred upon him gratis in 1622. In the following year the utility of the New River in fighting London's frequent fires was demonstrated by the City's gift to him of a gold chain set with diamonds. Remembering his apprenticeship, Sir Hugh supervised its making.[14]

Three days after buying out the King's interest in the New River, Sir Hugh Myddelton made his will and within a month was dead. He appoints his wife Elizabeth to be executrix, giving her power of sale of his mortgaged realty and mining shares to be exercised, if necessary, to pay legacies. The main part of his will deals with his New River shares and, although the dispositions are curious, it is clear that the testator knew exactly what he was about. He says:

[13] APC 1618–19, 100; 1621–23, 514; Pettus 33; Scott ii 401.

[14] CSPD 1619–23, 457; Sharpe ii 26.

I doe hereby declare that the one halfe of the waterwourkes are devided into sixe and thirtye partes or shares, thirteen of which partes or shares are to my selfe belonging and are in the name of my selfe and other feoffees in trust to my use and the proffettes by me receeved.

He gives all his shares to Elizabeth for life; if the money to be raised by sale of his other assets is not enough to pay legacies, then up to four of the New River shares may be sold for that purpose. He deals with the interests in remainder after the life estate by giving one share to each of his three sons 'and his heirs', one each to his two unmarried daughters 'and her heirs', and one to the Goldsmiths for the poor of that Company. To make it clear that this is exactly what he intended, he adds:

and therefore my meaninge is that the sixe severall partes or shares hereby devised and given are sixe of the partes and shares of the said thirteene partes and noe more.

Thus—and apparently quite deliberately—Sir Hugh Myddelton died intestate as to the fee simple in remainder of seven of the shares in the Adventurers' moiety (or three, if the power of sale were exercised) and the fee simple in possession of the King's moiety which he had acquired so recently. His eldest son William was his heir, although the will recites that Sir Hugh had already given him 'the full porcon which I intended'. His two married daughters had received marriage portions (of almost £2,000), so they and their husbands were bequeathed only trifling sums 'to buy a ring' (no doubt a mourning token).[15]

Sir Hugh died on 10 December 1631, was buried in the church of which he had been churchwarden, and soon afterwards his widow proved his will. Some said, however, that this is wrong and that he lived under an assumed name until the age of 150.[16]

[15] *Wills from Doctors' Commons* 92.

[16] Milner-Gibson-Cullum 50; Smiles 116. Anderson ii 615 says 'the unhappy gentleman who began the work suffered greatly in his fortune', and Pennant 197 says he was ruined. Presumably the beliefs arose through confusion with Hugh Myddelton, eldest son of Sir Hugh's youngest son, who became a baronet in his own right and fell on evil times: Pink 55; (1809) 79 *GM* 795.

CHAPTER 4

The Shares

4.1 Introduction

IN a book on any company but the New River, a chapter on its shares would come after a treatment of the enterprise in which the shares subsist, namely the company itself. In this work, however, the shares must come first. By a series of assumptions they were thought to have a character all their own, so that in 1745 Hardwicke LC is reduced to seeing the Company as merely 'the common hand to receive the profits, and there is no other way to come at it' and by 1875 Jessel MR has come to believe 'that under the Act of Parliament of the New River Water the shares were made a fee simple of inheritance'.[1]

In order to grasp the strange nature of these shares it will be necessary to ask the question 'In what did they subsist?'; and a few preliminary matters should be emphasized. At the founder's death, the Company's fixed assets consisted of the watercourse together with the servitude *aquae ductus* (of which, at least according to its charter, it was tenant in fee simple by socage tenure), the pond at the New River Head of which, on informal trust for the Adventurers, Hugh Myddelton was tenant for years, freehold land in Amwell at the source of the water held on similar trusts, and the pipes laid in London's streets. Later on many freehold and leasehold interests were acquired and it is very important to make clear that the abundant evidence (set out in Chapters 5.3 and 6.5.1) demonstrates that these estates were conveyed to *the Company or its trustees*.[2]

We have seen in Chapter 2.4 that, in the very early days of the enterprise and a decade before incorporation, the Adventurers' moiety was divided into thirty-six transferable shares and the Company's Charter preserves this number, while providing for only twenty-nine members. The King's moiety was

[1] *Townsend* v. *Ash* (1745) 3 Atk 336 at 338; *Metcalfe* v. *Hutchinson* [1875] 1 Ch Div 591 at 594.

[2] e.g. TW terriers 2232, 2516; NRCD C/261–72.

sold to Hugh Myddelton a few weeks before his death and descended by intestacy to his heir, Sir William. At some date this interest was itself divided into thirty-six shares known as the King's shares; as will be explained in Chapter 6.2, their owners were excluded from the governance of the Company, as had been the King. It is impossible to ascertain exactly when this division occurred, but it is unlikely that it would happen while the King held the interest, and the transfer of it to trustees for him straight after incorporation, and later conveyance of both the equitable and legal estates to Sir Hugh, proceed on the assumption that it is an undivided moiety (see Appendix G). Furthermore, the 1622 Commission's description of the royal difficulties is based on the assumption that the moiety is not divided and dispersed (see Chapter 3.5).

At any rate, it is clear that by the mid-seventeenth century the King's moiety had been divided into thirty-six shares; the problems arising out of the sale of fourteen of them are discussed in Chapter 5.2. The whole enterprise was thus split into seventy-two shares and, although some were soon subdivided, there was to be no increase in their number until 1866. At first, the King's shares seem to have been of little concern to the company as such, and the Treasurer's accounts for 1670–84 present only the Adventurers' moiety as divided. Further, it was Sir Hugh and his heirs who were liable to pay the royal fee-farm, although later this obligation is discharged by the Company; the process is described in Chapter 9.3.[3]

4.2 The Nature of the Shares

For the development of the law of property in its widest sense—the law, that is, of *wealth*—the most striking feature of the seventy-two shares is that they were taken to be the realest of real property. To us today, looking back almost four centuries, it may seem clear that Hugh Myddleton and his associates were mainly concerned to create shares in the *business*. It is true that the shares are usually described as being in 'the waterworks, river, and new cut'. But the document from which this phrase

[3] W. Maitland 629; the recitals in the New River Company's Act 1904 are inaccurate: see Chapter 8.3.

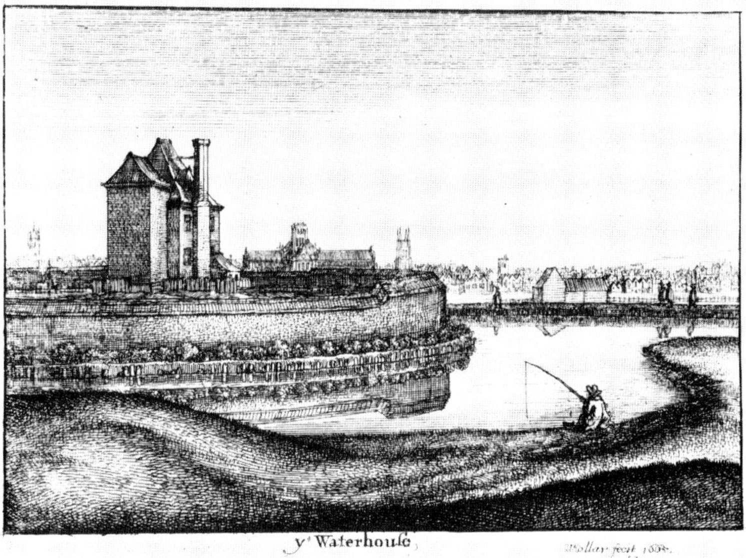

FIG. 4

is taken—the transfer of two shares to Neville in 1612 (Appendix E)—ends by emphasizing that these shares 'are entended and meant to be onlie of the gayne profitt and comoditie . . . after the halfe share of or in the profitts . . . due to the King . . . shalbe paied abated and deducted'. Similarly, the Charter (Appendix F), 'to the end that the Company shall have perpetuall Continuance', provides for membership and voting rights of twenty-nine of those holding 'anie share or shares out of the moiety of the said new River'. It looks, therefore, as if the phrase 'new river' is used to denote the enterprise, not the actual aqueduct.

4.2.1 *Techniques of transfer*

Despite the argument advanced above, it is patently obvious, and is documented in the appendix and later in this chapter, that all transactions are cast in the form appropriate to realty. Clearly the venture did not fall within the category of mere partnership. Hugh Myddelton's associates were putting in money, not enterprise, and it is in any case a durable rule of that branch of the law that no newcomer may be admitted to the firm without the consent of all existing members. None the less, as in partnership, the phrase 'a share in the New River' denotes an appreciable part of the whole business and not—as in modern companies—an abstract and arid unit of capital. At one level the selection of the category 'realty' may be the result of habit or caution. At a deeper level, however, it appears to be an almost intuitive articulation of the right response to the nature of the enterprise. In concrete terms, Hugh Myddelton and his associates—unlike the investors in, say, the Muscovy or the East India companies—could ride, or even walk, to see their assets; and these assets were immovable, sunk in the soil. The point may be made in a more abstract way by noting that the New River represented *fixed enterprise capital.* The great *trading* companies of the early seventeenth century had little that was comparable. Until 1612 the East India Company was raising a stock for each voyage or series of voyages and then sharing out the results. Of course it required ships to be built, bought, or chartered, but the capital investment therein did not provoke a need for incorporation—shipping managed perfectly well with its own scheme of unincorporate division into sixty-four limited liability shares until the nineteenth century. The existence of a distinct and permanent capital fund for the trading companies needed (apart from double-entry bookkeeping) the appearance of a stock market so that disinvestment by a shareholder did not entail reduction of capital by the company. But by its very nature the capital of the New River constituted a separate fixed asset which could not be distributed to shareholders and, until 1866, was not increased by share issue.[4]

Since, from the very beginning, the Adventurers could never expect the return of their capital, they could disinvest only by share transfer, and so the shares must be property interests of the category which is not only well known to be assignable but has an existing and sophisticated set of methods of alienation. There is no doubt whatever in the Company's Charter that the shares are assignable. Older overtones can be heard in the provision that membership of the Company is limited to successors in title of the original twenty-nine. But the requirement that the supplicant for admission possess at least one full and

[4] Heckscher i 398–400; Registration of British Vessels Act 1825.

entire thirty-sixth share echoes that in the constitution of a much older body which also held fixed enterprise capital—the Mines Royal of 1568. Prospecting licences had been granted, and the charter of incorporation of the licensees is unremarkable save in two respects. Firstly, it recites as the main reason for the wish to incorporate the many assignments of the benefits of the licences which had already occurred. Secondly, it limits membership of the new Company to those having—at least for life—one ninety-sixth or $\frac{1}{192}$ of the benefit of the licences (with double votes for the first class). Although in this respect similar to the New River, the Mines Royal showed traces of even older attitudes in that what was primarily to be divided was minerals, not money.[5]

The juridical nature of the New River shares was settled authoritatively in the great cases discussed in the following sub-section. These were, however, naturally preceded by actual share transfers—whether on sale, security, devise, or intestacy—and the outcome of the lawsuits seems to have been largely predetermined by the forms adopted. Put at its simplest, the transfers treat a share as if it were the interest of a tenant in common in fee simple absolute in possession of a corporeal hereditament. Sir Henry Neville's 'share issue' of two thirty-sixths of a moiety of the enterprise is the same in essentials as the feoffment of 20 February 1614 whereby (five years before incorporation) Hugh Myddelton, Samuel Backhouse, and two other Adventurers acquired a piece of land in Ware at the source of the stream.[6]

With some variations in detail, the *res* transferred comes to be described as a share (or part of a share) in a moiety of the watercourse, and of the ground and soil of the cut, and of the messuages and other hereditaments thereto appertaining, and in the profits thereof and in all fines and sums of money raised thereby; and this despite the fact that, by the Charter, it was *the Company* which held the watercourse and the profits and that, by later conveyances, it was always *the Company* (or its trustees) which held the land. The private forms of share transactions are the bargain and sale of a lease and release to carry the freehold (whether outright or on mortgage), the long lease

[5] Carr, *Charters* 10, 11, 14; Scott i 6.
[6] NRCD C/266.

to transfer a security interest, and the will which, after the Statute of Frauds of 1677, must be attested by at least three credible witnesses. The public forms are the Fine, the Recovery, and, from Michaelmas 1709, the Memorial in the Middlesex Deeds Register; the first two of these are cast in the style appropriate to an estate of several hundred acres lying athwart county boundaries. Further, twelve of the Adventurers' and thirty of the King's shares became subdivided, sometimes by deliberate dealings but mainly through the operation of devises to tenants in common or intestate succession by daughters as co-parceners. By similar routes, the fractions could become reunited so that, for instance, in 1780 William Hammond held six-twentieths of a King's share made up of one-eighth, one-twentieth, and one-eighth which had come to him on the deaths of three relatives. Similarly, in 1774 Peter Holford bought (for £7,500) thirteen-twelfths of an Adventurers' share made up of fractions of four original shares; he was registered in the Company's books as the owner of one entire share and one-twelfth. One hundred and twenty years later, his family sold the entire share for £96,000.[7]

Section 4.3 on the Neville holdings will demonstrate the development of the fine from near-truth to routine fantasy. To give the full flavour of the mature recovery we may select one of the last to be suffered, just a few months before the Fines and Recoveries Act of 1833 simplified the whole process. It concerns $\frac{1}{3456}$ of a share (worth about £5) and the appropriate documents are sealed for Hertfordshire, Middlesex, and London; as the only difference is in the names of the churches, an extract from the last will suffice:

LONDON to wit Joseph Todhunter in his proper person demands against Nathaniel Morphett two undivided twenty-fourth parts of one fourth part of one thirty-sixth part of a moiety of 10 messuages 100 acres of meadow 20 acres of pasture 160 acres of land covered with water and of one cut and streame of running water and water-course with the appurtenances in the parish of St Albans Wood Street All Saints otherwise All Hallows Barking All Saints otherwise All Hallows Bread Street [*and so on through all the City churches ending with*] the Minories in the Inner Temple and Middle Temple as his right

[7] NRRP A/59–60. In the nineteenth century the deeds describe the holding as an 'undivided share': GL MS 4161.

and inheritance and into which the said Nathaniel hath not entry but after the disseisin which Hugh Hunt thereof unjustly and without a judgment hath made of the aforesaid Joseph within 30 years etc. whereupon he said he was seised of the parts cut and streame aforesaid with the appurtenances in his demesne as of fee in right in time of peace in the time of our lord the present King by taking the profits thereof to the value of etc. and into which etc. and thereof he brings suit

The document then follows the established ritual with appointment of attornies, double voucher to warranty, leave to imparl, and judgment.[8]

4.2.2. *The leading cases*

The issue as to the juridical nature of a share was settled by the highest court in the litigation arising out of the will of Hugh Myddelton's youngest surviving son.[9]

Of the three sons, William, Henry, and Simon, the last seems to have been his father's favourite, a sentiment not shared by his other relatives and associates. In 1657 he persuaded his nephew Sir Hugh Myddelton (grandson and heir of the founder) in breach of trust to convey him the whole King's moiety; whether he ever paid the purchase price is uncertain, for the seller's will, proved in 1675, contains a legacy with the sad proviso that it is to be handed over 'if the debt due to me from my uncle Simon be recovered'. The acquisition of the property plunged Simon into a protracted set of lawsuits with the Clarendon family, which will be described in Chapter 5.2. Meanwhile, on the strength of this holding, he became Treasurer of the Company. In this position he 'detained the profits of divers shares and, when dismissed, refused to give up the key of the chest'. He was replaced (his *mandamus* action is described in Chapter 6.4) and in 1665 persuaded Charles II to recommend him to the humbler position of Clerk; the royal letter

[8] NR: Recovery dated 31/1/1833 (HT 4 Will. IV) in W. Worthington's title-deeds: Todhunter demandant, Morphett tenant, Perot et Ux. vouchees.

[9] *Middleton* v. *Swain* (1693) Skin 339 (which is mistaken about the testator's first name); sub nom. *Middleton* v. *Swail* (1693) Comb 201 (KB); sub nom. *Swayne* v. *Fawkener & Lane* (1696) Show PC 207 at 209, 211 (HL); BL Harg. MS 71 fo. 165; Harvard Law School MS 1169 item 2, 48 (MF H 1776-392).

to the Company cites as 'a pledge of his integrity' the fact that he held the King's moiety in fee-farm. This provoked a furious reaction: the entitlement to the moiety was precisely the subject of the complex and costly litigation and, besides, Simon 'was once mad, and spoke traitorous speeches, and would be apt to relapse; also that the office is beneath his estate and dignity'. Simon replied with a letter pleading 'a violent fever' and blaming a conspiracy among the shareholders. When this was produced at a company meeting the Governor (Sir Richard Neville) said that such letters 'were to be had for 5s. each, declared . . . that it was false, and would hardly let it be read through'.[10]

Simon died aged 67 in 1680 'seised in fee simple', as his will expressed it, of seventeen of the thirty-six shares in the King's moiety subject to the Crown Clog. He had married four times and was survived by a widow and four children by his second wife—Hugh, Sarah, Hannah and Anne—and four by his third—Elizabeth, Rebecca, Benjamin, and Hezekiah. His only other asset was a leasehold house in Hackney, and he used his shares to provide for his children in a way whose function resembles that of the settlement of land—to transfer the lion's share to his heir apparent but to burden the inheritance with provisions for the younger children. He devised ten shares 'to Hugh . . . and his heirs' but imposed on him the obligation of discharging the Crown Clog (and another family charge) on three shares which were devised to the heir's full sisters so that they obtained one each by the words 'to each of them and their heirs'. To each of the four children of the second marriage 'and his or her heirs' was devised a share subject to the Clog, and Hezekiah's share was charged with an additional sum of £150 to pay for Benjamin's apprenticeship. If any of the seven younger children died under 21 and unmarried then the will gave 'that part or share, with the profits thereof . . . to the survivor or survivors, share and share alike'. Thus, this disposition alone omitted the words of limitation (survivor 'and his heirs') necessary to pass the fee simple in the case of realty.

Rebecca died an adult and Hezekiah was drowned in 1688 while still an unmarried infant. This left five younger children,

[10] CSPD 1664–5, 303, 315, 324; Milner-Gibson-Cullum 52; HMC xvii (HL) 223. At the end of his life, however, Simon Myddelton appears as auditor of the Company Treasurer's accounts: BL Harl. MS 3604 fo. 113.

PLATE I. Sir Hugh Myddelton, 1628

of whom Anne, by lease and release, settled the fifth part of her dead half-brother Hezekiah's share on herself and her future husband Bennet Swayne, with remainder to their children and an ultimate remainder to the right heir of the spouses; she married and died childless. It will be recalled that the cross-remainder contained no words of limitation; if, therefore, by application of the rules of real property, such were needed to pass an absolute interest, then her entitlement ended on her death and the remainder vested in the right heir of Hezekiah—i.e. his only brother of the whole blood, Benjamin. In the litigation between him and Swayne, the King's Bench found for Benjamin, holding—as reported by Skinner—that the word 'share' is 'to express the thing which he devised and not the quantity of the estate' and—as reported by Shower—that 'the five survivors became tenants in common and each was seised of a fifth part only for life'. The judgment was upheld in the Lords after an attempt by the appellant to convince the House that a 'share' meant a person's *interest* in a thing and not the thing in itself—'as much as if a person being seised in Fee of Lands should say in his Will he devises all his Estate to JS, it could be no question but such a Devise would convey the said lands to such Devisee and his heirs'. The Upper House, however, affirmed that '*totam illam partem* carried only the Thing devised not the interest which the Devisor had therein'. In none of the three printed and two manuscript reports are the statutes or the Letters Patent cited, as 'it is well known and agreed that a Part or Share of the New River is an Inheritance'.[11]

It is evident that Simon was employing the familiar, and sophisticated, techniques for dealing with an asset as a family endowment worked out by conveyancers long before, and he is careful—save in the phrase litigated—to use words of limitation appropriate to the grant of the fee simple. To some extent, moreoever, the testator, in switching the burdens, was utilizing the shares as interchangeable investments. In his hands they were subject to a charge by title paramount—the Crown Clog—and to a family charge; but his will purports to remove these incumbrances from three of the shares and transfer them to those devised to his heir. In a sense, he is attempting a kind of 'real subrogation'. The King's Bench and House of Lords

[11] Skin 339, 5; Show 211.

apply the strict requirements of real property law, the former saying, according to Skinner's report, 'though it might be his intent was that they should have it to them and their heirs yet [the Court] could not collect such intent out of the words of the will; and therefore without sufficient words they would not disinherit the heir which in this case is the eldest son by the second venter'. The courts also decide that the word 'share' in this context does not signify the same as 'estate'. In a decision of considerable importance both to company law and to the use of shares in family settlements, they hold that a share is a separate *res* in which may subsist the complex of estates worked out long before in relation to land itself.[12]

Now in the plain case of land, the 'thing' in which the estates inhere is some corporeal or incorporeal hereditament; in either, the physical object itself can be readily identified. What does not emerge from the reports of this case—and, indeed, seems not to have been consciously perceived as a problem—is the counterpart physical object in the New River. The life estates, remainders, and reversions subsisted in the share which is itself agreed to be realty. But what is it a share *in*? The answer could be: in the freehold land by then acquired by the Company; in the bed of the river if, as do the courts, one ignores the words of the 1605 Act—the shares are agreed to be 'an Inheritance' but the founding statute expressly reserves 'the inheritance' to the landowners; in the water which flowed along that bed—both the testator and the King's Bench refer to shares 'in the New River water' and—although there is good authority for the proposition that running water may not be the subject of ownership—that is the phrase used in the later taxing statutes. Yet to the modern mind it seems that what made the shares worth acquiring, devising, and litigating was that they subsisted in a *fund*—the 'profitts advantages benefitt and comoditie' of the undertaking; a fund which, to cloud the matter further, the Company, according to its charter, held of the Crown by socage tenure. It would be the natural view of a bookkeeper that the object of inherence of the shares was a fund. There was, however, to be no conscious articulation of that view by English lawyers until many decades, and as many lawsuits, had come and gone.

[12] Skin 339, 5.

Meanwhile the seventy-two shares—in whatever they subsist—are readily accepted as pieces of real property. This has three main consequences. Firstly, it brings to the shares themselves the whole complex of the rules governing realty, both beneficial—such as the county vote—and dangerous—such as the trap into which Simon Myddelton fell. Secondly, it raises profound problems as to the legal relationship of the shareholders to the fixed assets of the enterprise. But thirdly it means that, with care, the shareholders have at their disposal an investment which, while ensuring them a far better yield than land, can yet be moulded into the elaborate refinements of strict settlements and secured transactions at a period when the law of personal property was not adequate for those purposes. This last feature will be illustrated later in sections 4.3 and 4.4 and in Chapter 9.2.

The application of the strict rules for realty can be shown from three other cases. The headnote to *Drybutter* v. *Bartholemew* (1723) reads 'Baron in right of the wife seised in fee of a share of the New River water, baron and feme make a mortgage by way of lease for 1000 years by deed, without fine, reserving a peppercorn rent'. Now for spouses to deal with the wife's realty in this way a fine was necessary, as the lender discovered when, after the husband's death, he sought to foreclose. It was argued on his behalf that the widow's payment of interest affirmed the mortgage, but the court held that the husband's death ended the lease, so that there was nothing to foreclose. The case was heard by Sir Joseph Jekyll MR (who fourteen years later was to permit the belated enrolment of the 1619 Charter), and he made two observations on the nature of the shares. He considered that, had the widow accepted rent under a lease, she would have affirmed the estate: 'but here is no acceptance and the lease is of an incorporeal thing, out of which rent could not well be reserved.' The authority for the last statement is Coke on Littleton at 47a, whose reason for the rule is that 'a rent must be reserved out of lands or tenements, whereunto the lessor may have resort or recourse to distresse'. The exception (which saved the fee-farm forming the Crown Clog) is that the Crown may reserve a rent; although Coke does not say why, the reason is presumably that the Crown has other means of enforcing payment. At least, however, Jekyll MR accepts that the shares, while realty, are incorporeal; it was later judges who thought the shares themselves corporeal. The second statement was that 'a fine may be (and usually is) levied of New River shares by the description of so much land *acqua coopert*' and in this case there ought to have been a fine, it being the inheritance of the wife'. It is undoubtedly true that the shares were usually transferred by fine or recovery, as will be shown in section 4.3. The case was reported in the second volume of William Peere Williams and a note added in the first (1740) and all subsequent editions, which reads thus:

And wherever a fine and recovery are necessary for the cutting off of the entail and remainder of such shares, in regard the New River runs through three counties, viz. Hertford, Middlesex, and London, there must be three several fines and recoveries as to any of these shares, viz. a fine and recovery in each county.

This statement rapidly becomes part of the English *corpus juris* finding its way into Cruise on Fines and Recoveries, Viner, and several cases. It may be worth pausing, however, to reflect on the chasms beneath it. It assumes that the shares are the same thing as the river. It refers to three counties—but the New River ran through only Hertford and Middlesex; it was the pipes which distributed the water into London. In fact all that this meant in practice was that the attorney's clerk paid a special fee at the Cursitors' Office to have a precipe addressed to each sheriff; they were then engrossed on the same parchment, although the recoveries demanded entry on a separate roll for each county. Finally, even if all the preceding problems are ignored and it is assumed that a shareholding conferred some direct right in relation to the river itself, it is doubtful, to say the least, whether a fine is the appropriate way of transferring an interest in running water. As has been frequently stressed, the basic statute reserved 'the inheritance' of the subjacent land to the landowners.[13]

In 1745 the relation between the shareholders and the fixed assets gave rise to the very difficult case of *Townsend* v. *Ash* in which Lord Hardwicke LC had to wrestle with the problems of seisin and disseisin of a share. By a deed of 1698 two shares

[13] *Drybutter* v. *Bartholemew* (1723) 2 P Wms 127; Viner, *Baron & Feme* Z pl. 18, *Fine* X 5 pl. 1; Cruise, *Digest*, *Deed* 2, 30, *Fine* 5, 37; *Stafford* v. *Buckley* (1750) 2 Ves Sen 171 at 182; *Attorney's Practice Epitomized* 64.

in the King's moiety had been settled by limitations appropriate to land: a life estate to the settlor's daughter-in-law, then to the husband for life, then to trustees to preserve contingent remainders; then entails to such children of the marriage *who were not his heir* as the husband should appoint, with remainders in default of such children to other branches of the family and an ultimate limitation to the husband's right heir. The husband survived the wife and died leaving only a daughter—she was thus, as his heir, excluded from the mesne remainders. None the less—perhaps assuming that she took under the last limitation—the daughter and her husband, by bargain and sale enrolled, conveyed the shares to *A* and his heirs so that by that deed, and by fines to be levied, he might become tenant to the precipe and start the process of barring all claims by a recovery. Fines were levied in Hilary Term 1733, soon after the death of the life tenant and *before* the daughter had received any dividends on the shares. Trustees for the other members of the family filed a bill for discovery of the deed of settlement, meaning to produce it in an ejectment action. It was admitted, of course, that a disseisor could levy a fine, for he has an estate if only by wrong; but what counts as *disseisin of a share*?

Lord Hardwicke's notebooks reveal that much time was spent in arguing the precise juridical nature of the shares and of the Company. Counsel, for instance, liken the former to *vestura terrae*, by a grant of which 'the land itself shall not pass' (Coke on Littleton 4b), and the latter to the hospital described in Littleton 657. In the end, the Lord Chancellor accepts that a New River share 'is a legal estate and a corporeal inheritance'—thereby differing from Sir Joseph Jekyll MR, who, as we have seen, had considered it realty but incorporeal. He insists, however, that 'no one proprietor could receive the profits himself, but the Company or their officers are the common hand to receive the profits, and there is no other way to come at it'. 'The Company', he says, 'are a kind of stewards, a common hand to receive and pay the proprietors.' At this stage, therefore, the shares are perceived as conferring a direct right upon the fixed assets, with the Company as some sort of reeve or rent collector. Now the would-be disseisors had received no dividends (the report also uses the words 'rent' and 'profits') before levying the fine. Lord Hardwicke thus has to decide what actions would amount to disseisin of a share: 'Consider then what kind of possession the defendants had of these water shares which are admitted to be real estate: they had made no actual entry nor had they received any profits.' He then assumes that, as shareholders, they could have 'cut a turf, taken up some of the water, or used a like ceremony'—in other words, that the shares confer direct possessory rights against the fixed assets—but concludes that even that 'would not have been sufficient to enable them to levy a fine so as to operate by disseisin'. The only thing that would have sufficed—which the defendants cannot show—would have been prior receipt of the dividends. Thus, the Lord Chancellor first treats the share as an interest in the river itself but then concludes that, since the only revenue inherent in shareholding is the dividends, it is perception of those which counts as adverse possession. He is still faced, however, with the issue of jurisdiction: for if the shares confer a right of possession in the river itself and the defendants are trespassers, then his Lordship's court is not the appropriate forum. He resolves this by saying 'though the legal estate is in the proprietors it would be absurd to send the plaintiffs to law, for it would be difficult to bring ejectments for a 36th part and bits of land in several counties, and to bring actions of trespass against the tertenants would be very extraordinary as the management is in the company'.[14]

It is clear that the Lord Chancellor accepts in principle the notion that the shareholders could bring ejectment, and, indeed, the whole machinery of fines and recoveries assumes that the shares confer the right of possession; or, to put it in the language of the time, that a *precipe quod reddat* would lie. Until this century the two cases just described are cited almost mechanically as establishing the juridical nature of the New River shares. In neither of them is the law of watercourses discussed. Since 1502 it had been well, and unsurprisingly, settled that

[14] *Townsend* v. *Ash* (1745) 3 Atk 336 at 338, 339; BL Add. MS 36056 fos. 100, 106; Linc. Inn Misc. MSS 384 VIII 563 (MF H 1787-C383); Cruise, *Digest*, *Fine* 5, 37 (taken from another MS but with a printer's repetition at the end of the statement of fact), *Fines and Recoveries* i 107. For the difficulties over enforcement, see BL Add. MS 36063 fo. 130; *Townshend* v. *Windham* (1750) 2 Ves Sen 1 and Ves Sen Supp 243. Co Litt 4b is to the effect that 'if a man hath 20 acres of land, and, by deed granteth to another and his heires *vesturam terrae* . . . the land itself shall not passe'. Litt 657 says 'Also, if the master of an hospitall discontinue certaine land of his hospitall, his successor cannot enter but is put to his writ of *de ingressu sine assensu confratrum et consororum &c.*'

one who owned the land on which water stood or flowed could maintain an action of ejectment: '*on poit aver precipe quod reddat unam acram cum acqua cooptam.*' If one owned merely the water-course, however, the King's Bench had held unanimously in 1608 that ejectment failed if brought for running water 'for *rivulus seu acquae cursus* doth not lie in demand neither doth a precipe lie of it, nor can livery of seisin be made of it; for *non moratur* but is ever flowing; nor can execution by *habere fac' seisinam* be made of it.' And the report in Yelverton (who was the successful counsel) adds: 'If the land under the river or water does not belong to the plaintiff but the river only, then on a disturbance his remedy is only by action on the case & non aliter. *Quod nota.*' This last instruction was obeyed by Viner and the same point is made in his title on Watercourses. The title is very brief, however, and no one ever seems to have taken the point that the 1608 lawsuit concerned a natural river; the rule as stated by Yelverton and Viner, and the reasons given in support, appear to be applicable to 'Myddelton's water'.[15]

In 1778 it was agreed in *Sandys* v. *Sibthorpe* 'that New River shares are real property and descendible to the heir'; the issue has now become so settled that the report contains only the one sentence, although the Company's own documents show that the ruling was required to establish the entitlement of a putative shareholder.[16]

However frail their foundations, the great New River cases left several legacies. The first was the assumption that the shares themselves were realty, which was usually explained by reference to the socage clause in the charter. The second was the belief that they conferred a right of possession in the fixed assets of a public-utility company. Whether the second was the consequence or the cause of the first is never clear; but the last chapter must be devoted to the effect of these notions on perceptions of property and company law. The third—which will be examined in Chapter 6.6—was the effect on the Company itself. If its shareholders have some direct rights over its fixed assets, how on earth is the Company to sell a plot of land without their joining in the conveyance? And—what became in practice much more important—how is money to be raised

[15] YB 12 Hen. VII 4; *Challenor* v. *Thomas* (1608) Yelv 142; Viner, *Watercourse.*

[16] *Sandys* v. *Sibthorpe* (1778) Dick 545; NRRP A/34.

on mortgage without the consent of either the proprietors or Parliament? The early Adventurers, however, were unconcerned with these mysteries. From their point of view they held an investment which was producing a good yield and, being taken to be realty, could be moulded into the familiar patterns of endowment. We must now turn to some examples of the use of the shares for this purpose. The history of one share is traced from 1612 to 1904 in somewhat tedious detail, in order that it may be used as an example in later treatment of the Company itself.

4.3 The Neville Holdings 1612–1904[17]

Sir Henry Neville of Billingsbear in Berkshire was the son of the courtier and diplomatist of the same name. As we have seen, he was one of the pre-incorporation investors and an Adventurer named in the charter. The document of 8 May 1612 by which he acquired two shares is printed in Appendix E and has been described. It will be recalled that each share cost £100 plus a liability for 'calls' amounting, as events turned out, to a further £189; and that Hugh Myddelton conveyed to him 'his heirs and assigns for ever two full and intire six and thirtieth parts of the said water . . . and of the profit benefit and comoditie of the moiety' with a covenant for further assurance that Sir Henry would have 'a good and absolute estate and interest in the premises'. The subsequent history of these shares reveals a good deal of information about the way in which they were used as investment, endowment, and security exactly as if they themselves were plots of land.

The Neville family. The shares remained in the Neville family for almost a century. Sir Henry's will executed on 24 June 1629 does not deal with the property specifically but leaves 'all other lands tenements and hereditaments' to the testator's son and

[17] Based on: PRO CP25(2) 763 (33 & 34 Chas. II HT), 899 (10 Will. III TT), 1260 (25 & 26 Geo. II TT), CP43 Index 17194; Rolls 255, 256, 257 (1 Geo. II PT); MDR 1794/4/197; 1888/24/560, 561; NRRP A/165, B/75, 77, C/189, F/430, 454, H/433; Water Stock Distribution Accounts of Adventurers' Shares 1905, Dividend Lists 1633–1903 (all at NR); TW, Strongroom B30, box 79, indentures and examined abstracts *re* Ruck's title.

heir Richard in tail male, remainder to his son Henry in tail male, with remainders over. Richard barred the entail, became Governor of the Company and, by a codicil to his will made on 4 October 1676, left the two shares specifically to his son John and his heirs charged with the payment of £100 a year to his younger son Richard for life. John died intestate and without issue, so that Richard succeeded to the shares as heir at law.

For the next twenty years, Richard (a friend of the Clarendons and MP for Berkshire) used the shares to raise money—the annual dividend on each was by then some £170—beginning with a mortgage of 19 November 1681. The question of how to mortgage a share presented no problem: the shares were leased. In return for an advance of £1,000 by one Andrew Duffield, the lender was granted a 500-year lease at a peppercorn rent with a proviso for avoidance on payment of £1,060. The borrower also covenanted (and kept his promise) ere the end of the next Hilary Term to 'levy a fine sur conusance etc.' of the two shares to John Noune (i.e. a nominee) to the use of Duffield his executors administrators and assigns for 500 years and thereafter to the use of Richard Neville and his heirs for ever. The fine itself, although flawed, is almost truthful. Translated from the abbreviated Latin, its specification of the property runs:

> two thirty-sixth parts of two acres of land covered with water and one watercourse with the appurtenances in Islington and Clerkenwell in the County of Middlesex and two thirty-sixth parts of one watercourse with the appurtenances in the parish of St Sepulchre in the County of London and two thirty-sixth parts of one watercourse with the appurtenances in Amwell and Chadwell in the County of Hertford.

By 1681 the Company had indeed acquired between two and three acres at the New River Head and about the same at the sources—the story is told in Chapters 5.3 and 6.5.1—although it was not covered with water. The fine is cast, however, in terms which make it clear that the property is a waterworks, and although St Sepulchre's church was in the City the parish extended north of the walls towards St John's Street. It also contains an error which is not repeated in later records—the omission, after the specification of the shares, of an indication (by the word *medietatis*) that they subsist only in a moiety.

Three years later the capital was still owing but the interest was being paid promptly, and Duffield lent a further £500 in return for a release of the equity of redemption in the 500-year term subject to a proviso for avoidance on payment of £1,575. The following year, in consideration of repayment, Duffield assigned to one James Hays 'the said two shares and all his estate therein . . . for the residue of the said 500 years'. It appears that the assignee was trustee for the borrower.

Certainly, a decade later, he complied with Richard Neville's directions as to a refinancing scheme in which each share was treated separately: thus, although the original term of years remained entire, its substratum was divided. One share was assigned for the remainder of the term to Josiah Bacon in return for £3,000 paid to Neville; the other was assigned for the remainder of the term to Richard Webb, who paid £2,000 to Neville and declared himself a trustee of a fifth part of his leasehold estate for the other lender, Bacon. The deed contains the usual provisos for reassignment of the term to Neville or his nominee on repayment of the capital plus 5 per cent interest. The interest of £250 a year would be covered by the dividend, which for 1694 was £199. 6*s*. 7*d*. on each share, although the disastrous year of 1696, when competition from the York and Hampstead waterworks brought it down to £113. 7*s*. 6*d*., must have caused a slight problem. In any case the two lenders had secured themselves on making the loan by taking a separate indenture to which they, Neville and Thomas Darwin, treasurer of the Company, were parties and which authorized this last to make interest payments direct to the mortgagees out of the 'profits' on the shares.

In 1697 Richard Neville borrowed another £500 from Webb, secured by a further mortgage and a bond with a penalty of £5,000; a year later Bacon assigned his mortgage term to the Hon. Peregrine Bertie in return for £3,090. The borrower and the two mortgagees then decided to create a trust term and bring in George Stanlake as nominee. The documents demonstrate that the parties are not distinguishing between fixed assets and future profits. Neville covenants to levy a fine of the two shares 'of the New River waterworks or watercourse and the cutt or streame . . . and of all pipes and conduits thereto belonging and of all rents profits and advantages by reason thereof'. The fine is 'to enure to the use of George Stanlake his executors administrators and assigns for a term of 1,000 years in trust as to one of the said shares for Peregrine Bertie his executors [etc.] and as to the other for Richard Webb . . . and after the expiry or sooner determination thereof to the use of Richard Nevill his heirs and assigns for ever' with the usual provisos for cesser on redemption. A fine was levied and, after another advance by Webb, he assigned his mortgage term to Henry Penton, and Stanlake assigned the residue of the 1,000-year term to Henry Cherry. The foot of the fine shows the process of stereotyped inflation of the property, which becomes a regular feature of dealings in New River shares: the subject-matter (in translation) is now:

two thirty-sixth parts of a moiety of one messuage and 150 acres of land covered with water and of one gorce (gurgitis) and watercourse with the appurtenances in Amwell Magna Amwell Parva . . . Hoddesdon . . . Wormley . . . Cheshunt and Theobalds in the County of Hertford and two thirty-sixth parts of a moiety of one messuage and 150 acres of land covered with water and of one cut and watercourse with the appurtenances in the parishes of Marybone . . . St Giles in the Fields St Giles without Cripplegate St Leonard Shoreditch St Mary Newington St Mary Islington St Mary Whitechapel . . . St Clement Dane . . . St Margaret Westminster St James Westminster in the County of Middlesex and two thirty-sixth parts of a moiety of one watercourse with the appurtenances in the parishes of St Alban Woodstock [*and many other City churches*] in the County of London.

Unlike the earlier fine, the description now starts at the source of the river but, as will be seen from the acreage alleged to be covered with water, has become a pure formality; the fact that the bed of the river—according to the statutes—does not belong to either Company or shareholders is conveniently ignored. The only concession to reality shown by the draftsman is that he refrains from asserting that most of the City of London was 'land covered with water' (later recoveries are not so pusillanimous). Further, although the Hertford parishes are those which follow the course of the river, those in Westminster and the City are the site of the water mains. It looks rather as if every time a new street was opened up, the name of its parish church was added to the 'share transfer'.[18]

The Allen family. When, in 1707, Edward Allen (then Treasurer of the Company) decided to buy one of the shares he was faced with a title showing the freehold in Richard Neville and two outstanding legal terms, one of 500 years in Henry Penton and one of 1,000 years in Henry Cherry. In order to convey the first of these estates Neville bargained and sold a lease for a year on 26 May with a release the following day: the takers are Edward Allen and his trustee, William Murvell, and the fee simple in the one share is released charged with the money owing to Penton. On the same day the buyer repaid the loan and got in the outstanding terms. He paid £3,240 to Penton and £660 to Neville and, in return, Penton bargained and sold the residue of the 500 years to John Gerrard, and Cherry did the same for the longer term in favour of John Blunt; each of the assignees holds his estate in trust for the buyer and to attend the inheritance; the terms themselves now secure nothing. The share with a clear title has cost the buyer £3,900 plus the legal fees on a lease, a release, and a bargain and sale of the terms. During the five years in which he held it the dividends averaged some £160, giving a yield of just over 4 per cent, so that he is buying at twenty-five years' purchase.

It will be recalled that Allen was the Company's Treasurer and so in receipt of its income. To secure his fidelity in this office he and his trustee joined in another lease of the share, this time to the Company itself. The charge is to secure the revenues received by the Treasurer and the term granted is of 400 years at a peppercorn rent, with a proviso for avoidance if the officer 'gives a just account of all moneys by him received'. This condition must have been satisfied because in 1711 the Company, by deed poll, surrendered the term 'to the intent to merge and extinguish the said tenure'. The notion that there was something problematic about a Company taking a lease of its own share surfaced only among the scruples of a later cen-

[18] The precise reason for creating the 1,000-year trust term does not emerge from the documents. It may have been to bar dower or to create a personalty interest available for creditors at the debtor's death: see Nottingham 232–4. (The writer owes these suggestions and references to Mr John Kaye of The Queen's College, Oxford.)

tury. Meanwhile, however, Allen had died, leaving the share to his wife for life with remainder to his son John and his heirs, and the widow bargained and sold her 'estate for life in the said share' to the remainderman.

The Sambrooke family. In 1712 the dividend was £164. 8*s*. 5*d*., so that the acquisition of a clear title to the share by Sir Samuel Vanacker Sambrooke at a cost of £7,000 represented optimism as to future earnings. In fact, in the following year the dividend rose above £200 and was to average more than this for the next two centuries. In any event, there had to be the usual transfer of freehold and leasehold estates. The former passed by a lease and release in which John Allen and his father's trustee William Murvell conveyed the fee to Samuel and his brother Jeremy (the latter being trustee) with the usual covenants as to freedom from incumbrances and for further assurance. The two terms were assigned to separate individuals to attend the inheritance. In execution of a Chancery decree of 1706 this after-acquired property now had to be brought into the Sambrooke family settlement. By lease and release of 29 and 30 March 1713 Samuel and Jeremy granted the share to George Wright and his heirs on a set of uses, so that the Statute of Uses carried legal estates to the members of the family as follows:

(1) Samuel for life without impeachment of waste;
(2) Wright to preserve contingent remainders;
(3) the first and other sons of Samuel in tail male;
(4) Jeremy for life without impeachment of waste;
(5) Wright to preserve contingent remainders;
(6) the first and other sons of Jeremy in tail male;
(7) John (third son) for life with the same remainders;
(8) The settlors' mother and her heirs.

A clause is added requiring any male beneficiary to take the name of Vanacker.

After Samuel's death the entail to his eldest son John (hereafter referred to as JVS) vested in possession and, in 1727, he bargained and sold the share to the use of one Henry Cranmer his heirs and assigns to the intent that Henry might become tenant to the precipe in a common recovery whereby one Edward Dearing would be demandant and JVS vouchee to warranty. The recovery was suffered in the same year, leaving JVS with the unincumbered fee simple in the share, with the appropriate records being drawn for each county. Unfortunately, JVS was also in debt and no less a person than Wriothesley, Duke of Bedford, had obtained judgment against him. James Colebrooke, later Deputy Governor of the Company, came to his rescue, having first prudently obtained from the Duke's executor an assurance that he would not attempt to enforce the judgment against the New River share. In 1732 he bought the share along with two others for £5,000 each, the freehold being vested in the familiar way in the purchaser and a trustee, and the mortgage terms assigned to other trustees.

The Ruck family. Colebrooke may have retained the other shares, but that whose title is being traced was conveyed in 1733 by bargain and sale of a lease and release to his partner James Ruck for £5,000. At that date, despite some fluctuations, the yearly dividend was of the order of £200 giving a yield of 4 per cent. The outstanding terms remained vested in Colebrooke's nominees but as trustees for the new purchaser. By a will valid for realty, Ruck left the share to his daughter Mary her heirs and assigns and appointed his three sons executors. They proved the will in 1736; the eldest brother then died, having left everything among his three siblings, and letters of administration *cum testamento annexo* were granted to his brother George. The other brother died unmarried and George cautiously perfected his sister's title to the share by lease and release in 1743.

In 1752 Mary married James Gambier, a naval captain. The marriage settlement conveyed her share to her brother George and another on trust for her husband for life with remainder as appointed among the children, in default to all equally, with an ultimate remainder in fee to the survivor of the spouses; the appropriate fine was then levied. Among the bundles of mid-eighteenth-century Feet of Fines for mixed counties, those dealing with New River shares stand out by their size. In this case the property is described as

> one thirty-sixth part of the moiety of 10 messuages one hundred and sixty acres of land covered with water and of one cutt and streame of running water and watercourse with the appurtenances in the

parishes of St. Andrew & All Saints in the town of Hertford and in Chadwell Great Amwell Little Amwell [*etc.*] in the County of Hertford and of one thirty-sixth part of the moiety of 10 messuages 160 acres of land covered with water and of one cutt and stream of running water and watercourse with the appurtenances in [*some thirty parishes ending with Lincoln's Inn and Gray's Inn*] in the County of Middlesex and of one thirty-sixth part of the moiety of one stream of running water and watercourse with the appurtenances in [*the City parishes ending with the Minories and the Inner and Middle Temple*] in the County of London.

Gambier, however, ran into debt and had judgment entered against him. His brother-in-law came to his aid but Gambier was often at sea and in 1757 the couple separated. (He went on to help capture Louisburg and Guadaloupe, become a vice-admiral, and command Jamaica.) The marriage settlement, however, was amicably overridden by an indenture to which the spouses were parties, which resulted in the trustees holding the share for Mary in fee simple.

Six years later she died, having appointed her brother George executor, and left the share on trust for sale to pay her considerable legacies. He died before completing his duties, and letters of administration to his sister's estate *cum testamento annexo et de bonis non administratis* were granted to his executors, William and Samuel Smith. Under the authority of a Chancery decree the share was advertised in the *London Gazette* in 1768 and bought by Samuel Smith for £6,700. This was part of a family arrangement, for in March of the following year he conveyed it by lease and release to two sisters as joint tenants: Mary Smith and Elizabeth Ruck, a widow, who both lived at the same address.

In June 1794, for reasons which are not clear, the sisters executed a lease and release whereby the share was conveyed to Elizabeth's son-in-law Benjamin Keene, so that by operation of the Statute of Uses each took the legal estate in a moiety as tenants in common. The parcels clause continues the practice of treating the share as inhering in the company's fixed assets and income, describing it as a thirty-sixth part of a moiety of the New River and the profits thereof, a thirty-sixth share in a moiety of all hereditaments etc., of all profits advantages and commodities, and of all sums of money raised. The sisters continued to live together and, by a certificate dated 27 February

1801, Miss Smith took advantage of the recently introduced statutory power to redeem the land tax (of £50 per annum) on the whole share at a price of £1,833. 6*s.* 8*d.* payable in instalments. The annual dividend was by then averaging some £450. In May 1804 each made a will leaving her half to the other for life with remainder to Elizabeth's son-in-law Benjamin Keene in fee simple, and by a codicil Mary added the benefit of the redemption of land tax. The sisters died within a few months of each other in 1811 and Benjamin—who proved their wills—succeeded to the fee simple in the entire share, the two moieties becoming united.

In 1821 Benjamin's son, The Revd Charles Edmund Ruck Keene, was about to marry Rebecca Shiffner. By lease and release the share was transferred to the bride's brothers in trust for the groom's parents for their lives, then to trustees to preserve contingent remainders, with a 200-year trust term to the brothers to provide for the bride, then to the groom for life with remainder as he should appoint. Benjamin survived his wife and died in 1837, when Charles's life estate vested in possession and brought him an income of some £650 a year.

In 1845 the annual dividends had risen to almost £850 and the couple had produced eleven children. By deed poll, Charles appointed the share, subject to his own life estate, to his son and heir apparent Edmund on a determinable fee simple: if the son were to die without male issue during his parents' lifetime then the other ten children were to take equal shares. By 1877, however, when Charles made his will, he had either forgotten about this appointment—unlikely because of the endorsement on his marriage settlement—or had decided that, as the dividends were now over £2,000 a year, his other children ought to be given some part therein. Among the latter, those with most claim to his attention must have been the four unmarried girls whose very names suggest that they are the daughters of a Victorian clergyman: Mary Augusta, Henrietta, Charlotte Maria, and Emily. In any event he purported to give them an income of £150 a year in fee charged on the share and protected by powers of entry and perception of dividends. Three years later, when his wife and one of his other children had died, he executed a codicil attempting to increase the girls' rent charges by £50 and to impose on his son Edmund the duty to charge the share to raise a capital sum of £9,000 so that each younger child would get £1,000. In that year the gross dividend was £2,369 and such few shares as came on the market were fetching prices of about £60,000.

On Charles's death in December 1880 the fee simple absolute in possession vested in his eldest son Lt.-Col. Edmund Ruck Keene, and the records do not disclose whether he carried out the wishes in respect of his siblings expressed in the ineffective second exercise of the power of appointment. He was a widower with three young sons and was about to marry again. The settlement gave the usual trust term (1,000 years without impeachment of waste) to brother and brother-in-law to provide for his second wife and younger children and limited the fee simple on a contingency: to the first son to attain the age of 21. By that time the institutional investors were greatly interested in the New River and in 1888 some kind of bargain was struck with the Royal Exchange Assurance Company. Edmund, however, died shortly after and the Company retransferred their interest to his executors and his eldest son, who had satisfied the contingency by becoming 21 the year before. In August 1888 these three conveyed the share to trustees for Admiral Sir Leopold Heath and his heirs at a price of £95,000, and the latter remained owner until 25 July 1904 when, by operation of the Metropolis Water Act 1902, his share as regards the water supply business was transformed into water stock to the value of £67,931. 6*s.* 7*d.* and, as regards the landed estates, was about to become a holding in the new New River Company Ltd.

During the 292 years of its first life the dividends paid on the share before poll tax and land tax, but after income tax, amounted to approximately £158,300. The estimated maximum which the share cost Sir Henry Neville was £289. If this be deducted from the redemption value and the result added to the dividends, we find that the 'profits advantages and commodity' accruing to the initial investment and distributed amounted to £225,942 which is an average of almost £774 a year, giving an annual yield of over 267 per cent. In addition, the shareholder received 1,365 fully paid £1 shares in the new New River Company, whose story will be outlined in Chapter 8.3.

4.4 The Myddelton Holdings 1631–1904[19]

It will be recalled that Sir Hugh's will left his thirteen shares in the Adventurers' moiety to his wife for life with remainder in fee as to one each to his three sons, two spinster daughters, and the Goldsmiths' Company. He died intestate as to the remainders in seven of the shares and the whole of the King's moiety; the fate of the latter will be recounted in Chapter 5.2.

Succeeding generations did not display Sir Hugh's abilities, a fact which afforded much opportunity for moralizing among later writers. It means, however, that it is difficult to trace their shareholdings beyond a couple of generations. Sir William Myddelton, Hugh's eldest surviving son and heir, was Governor of the Company in succession to his father and, although he sold the King's moiety, he kept at least some of the Adventurers' shares acquired by descent. His daughter Elizabeth acquired four of them on his death in 1652 and married John Grene, who, through her, obtained both the shares and the office of clerk to the Company. (In this position he both acquired land as trustee for the Company and constructed at the Cistern House in Islington the beautiful oaken room which is probably the work of Grinling Gibbons.) His wife died in 1673 and, by lease and release, he settled the four shares on himself for life and then to a trustee in fee on the following trusts: to each of his children William, Elizabeth, and Katherine and the heirs of their bodies £60 a year from the dividends with remainders over on their death without issue to such person as he should appoint to take the annual sum; the balance of the income to his eldest son Giles for life, with remainder to his sons successively in tail general, remainder to Giles's daughters in tail, remainder on the same limitations to William, remainder as to a moiety each to Elizabeth and Catherine for life with remainders in tail and cross-remainders, and an ultimate limitation to the right heir of the founder, Sir Hugh Myddelton. The £60 annuity to the daughters was to cease if they received certain marriage portions. The 1674 dividend was £129. 4*s*.

[19] Based on: Milner-Gibson-Cullum 270; CSPD 1667, 471; HMC xvii (HL) 3–5; BL Harl. MS 3604; *Grene* v. *Grene* (1710) 1 Bro PC 143; the appellant's printed case therein at TW, Strongroom B30, box 86/37; NR dividend list; NRRP A/36.

7d., so that the total income in the settlement was £516. 18*s.* 4*d.*

In the following year Grene married his servant Joanna, who bore him four children. A decade later the income was amounting to almost £800 a year and John Grene began the process of trying to break the settlement. Having failed to obtain the trustee's consent, he attempted to alter the trusts by deeds of 1685, which were set aside by the Lord Chancellor. In 1694, when his second son William was an adult, father and son entered into a deed of variation which was a pale shadow of the normal resettlement of entailed land. In consideration of £50 down and £100 a year for life out of the his father's income as life tenant, William relinquished his own life estate in £60 a year and the fees tail, which, it will be recalled, were in remainder on his elder brother's issue's entail. That brother died childless, so that, had there been no purported variation of trust, William would have benefited from both remainders. His father promoted a private Bill to secure his power of disposition over the shares but, after reference to a House of Lords Select Committee in 1697, nothing more is heard of it. John Grene died in 1705, leaving his widow Joanna with an income from the shares of some £735 a year. Had it not been for the deed of variation, William would then have held the life estate in possession with the power, when his own child reached majority, of joining in a recovery.

Consequently, he filed a bill to have the variation set aside. At this, his stepmother produced a bond of 1693 on which she had him imprisoned in the Fleet (where, no doubt, he drank New River water). He was later released but his suit before Cowper LC failed to provide him with an income, although the decree saved the rights of his issue. Before the House of Lords his counsel argued that the variation was the result of parental threats. On the other side, however, counsel pointed out that, at the time it was entered into, each party had balanced bargaining counters: under the original settlement William was entitled to nothing while his father lived, and his elder brother Giles was then married and in good health, so that his 'future interest was of little value and consequently the consideration of the agreement (an immediate payment of £50 and entitlement to an immediate income of £100 a year) was both fair and adequate'. Their Lordships declined to disturb the decree, so that his stepmother kept the substantial residuary income of the shares. On her and William's deaths, however, they vested in his only child Jane under the original entail. She married The Revd R. Ellacombe and two of the shares remained in that family until this century. Over the years, each acquired its own proper name, one being known as the Thynne share, the other as the Maynard. On the retransfer of the water supply into public ownership their holders suffered the ignominy of seeing the interest transmuted into personalty, but were compensated by the issue of water-stock to the value of almost £70,000 per share, shares in the new Company, and, in the case of The Revd H. N. Ellacombe, a seat on the Board.[20]

The rest of the Myddelton holdings in the Adventurers' shares were dispersed, though there are traces in the recitals of a mortgage of 1718 recorded in the Middlesex Deeds Register of a Myddelton 'merchant of Smyrna'. By the early nineteenth century most of his descendants were of humble station. The Company itself at that time was, as we shall see, attracting a good deal of public attention and somehow the notion took hold that it held a vast sum waiting to be claimed by a Myddelton. The Minute Books record several sad and fruitless appeals to the Company, such as that of Mrs Elizabeth Rabeth 'residing at Mrs Wilshere's academy' and claiming descent from the founder. The City, however, appears to have been rather more generous. In the back of the Guildhall Library's copy of an extremely rare little work published in 1613 to celebrate the opening of the river and written by 'T.M.' (presumably Thomas Myddelton) is a manuscript note that on 28 July 1818 the sum of £50 was voted to one Jabez Myddelton 'in consideration of his distressed situation'.[21]

[20] NR: Directors' Report 1905; NR Water Stock Distribution Account 1905.

[21] MDR 1718/5/221, 222, 261, 1719/4/144; (1781) 51 *GM* 256, (1782) 52 *GM* 73–4, (1784) 54 *GM* 643, 723, (1792) 62 *GM* 720, (1809) 79 *GM* 795; M 12/11/1812, 7/3/1882; 'T.M.' at GL (Strongroom with pageants).

4.5 The Goldsmiths' Share 1631–1904[22]

The remainder in fee of one share left by Sir Hugh Myddelton to the Goldsmiths' Company caused some initial embarrassment. In late 1643 Sir William was denying the Company its right to the share until his father's debts were paid and was also anxious to settle the issue of apportionment of the dividend. Over dinner, however, both sides agreed that the previous dividend could be used for his mother's funeral and that from Ladyday 1644 dividends were to be paid direct to the Goldsmiths. The latter appointed as their trustee one of the original Adventurers, Gabriel Newman, who was also of their Company but not of the Myddelton family, and he took pains to see that the New River rendered proper accounts. The Goldsmiths were paid the dividends for the first two years (of some £27 and £32) but the founder's family seemed to consider that they had a right to nominate the recipients of the charitable fund. In July 1647 Sir William's widow Eleanor 'pressed so vehemently' the case of one applicant that the Goldsmiths gave in but minuted that 'she is to be told that this act shall not be taken as a precedent'. Two months later they had to remind the New River Company to send their dividend direct 'because the last half-year's dividend was paid to Lady Myddelton, which occasioned the Wardens to go to her in person for it, and with much difficulty they obtained payment thereof'. In 1694 the Goldsmiths decided to appoint a trustee of their interests and followed the pattern usual in the Company of transferring the share to Bartholemew Soames 'for ninety and nine years if he shall so long live in trust for the [Goldsmiths' Company]'. His family were related to the Myddeltons by marriage and remained connected with the New River for many years. Although the dividends were later amalgamated with the Goldsmiths' other charitable funds, the old New River share remained theirs until the transfer into public ownership of this century.

[22] Prideaux i 214, 217–18, 236, 244–5, ii 168, 172, 179–80; Herbert ii 250, 251, 277.

CHAPTER 5

The Clarendon Connection

AMONG the manuscript sources for this work, the bulkiest coverage is that of the relations between the Company and the Backhouse, Clarendon, and Lloyd families. The disputes lasted well over a century and must be recounted, at least in outline, because of the light they throw both on the nature of the 'King's shares' and on the process by which the Company developed from being concerned only with the supply of water to being, as it is to this day, a substantial proprietor of valuable landed estates at Clerkenwell. In order to make sense of the story, a few words should first be said about the person who formed the connection between the three families.

5.1 Flower Backhouse

It will be recalled that among the original Adventurers were Samuel Backhouse (1552–1626) and his son and heir apparent John (1584–1649). The father was a man of considerable wealth, both inherited and acquired, who owned Swallowfield in Berkshire as his country seat and over 70 acres in Clerkenwell and Islington, the major part of which was known (with countless variants of the spelling) as 'the Commandery Mantles'. It was here that the New River head was constructed and, in modern terms, is very roughly the area between Rosebery Avenue and Pentonville Road bounded by Percy Circus to the west and St John's Street to the east. He died in 1626, leaving four sons and four daughters, Sir John being his heir. The three elder sons, however, died childless and the family property descended to the youngest, Sir William Backhouse (1593–1662), the alchemist who taught Elias Ashmole 'in Silables the true Matter of the Philosopher's Stone'. William's son predeceased him without issue and in 1662 his younger child and only daughter Flower succeeded to the Backhouse fortune.[1]

[1] Ashmole ii 643; à Wood iii 576; Russell 125; NR: Case to Counsel (J. Booth) 1743. Elias Ashmole was a close friend of the Backhouse family, and his MSS contain

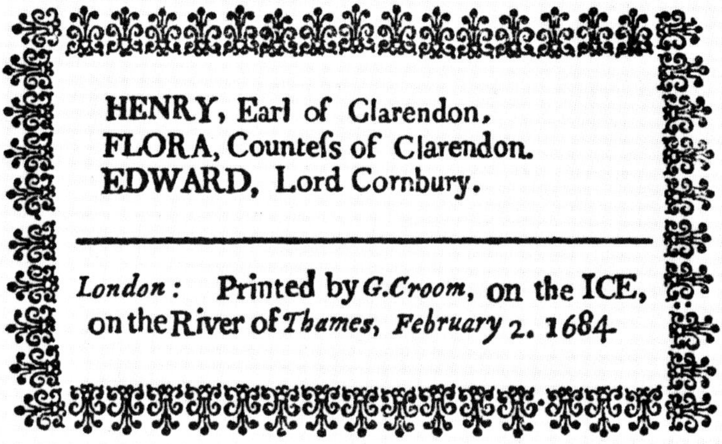
HENRY, Earl of Clarendon.
FLORA, Counteſs of Clarendon.
EDWARD, Lord Cornbury.

London: Printed by *G.Croom*, on the ICE, on the River of *Thames*, *February* 2. 1684.

FIG. 5

She was born in 1641 and formed a close friendship with her brother's tutor, William Lloyd, who later became successively Bishop of St Asaph, Lichfield, and Worcester, was one of the seven Bishops sent to the tower by James II in 1688 for opposition to the second 'Declaration of Indulgence', and died in 1717 at the age of 90. When she was 15 years old Flower married William Bishop; by him she had first one child then a second, but they both died babies and she never bore another. Her husband died in 1660 and two years later she married her cousin Sir William Backhouse, thus acquiring her maiden as her married name. He died in 1669 and the following year she was wedded (in a ceremony performed by Dr William Lloyd) to a widower with one son: Henry Hyde, Viscount Cornbury, heir apparent to Edward, first Earl of Clarendon.[2]

Flower was thus sister-in-law to the Duchess of York, and aunt to two future Queens, Mary and Anne. Four years after her marriage she became Countess of Clarendon, and from 1682 to 1687 the Earl was Governor of the New River Company. According to Sarah, Duchess of Marlborough, she 'looked like a madwoman and talked like a scholar' but John

horoscopes of several members. References are given in Josten, though at page 2 there is an error as to Samuel's date of birth.

[2] M. Ashley, *England in the Seventeenth Century* 173; Ashmole ii 667; Kenyon 244; Russell 137.

Evelyn thought her 'of a comely countenance, clad very plaine but cleane and tight' and much admired her garden, 'my Lady being so extraordinarily skilled in the flowry part'. Along with Bishop Lloyd, she was an ardent anti-Catholic, believing that Charles II's child was smuggled in in a Jesuit warming-pan and—more interestingly for our purposes—that Papists had got control of the New River in order to prevent its use in fighting the Great Fire. The legal history of the Commandery Mantles before its acquisition by the Company in 1744 is much complicated by the pecuniary difficulties which beset her and the extravagant second Earl. She died in 1700.[3]

5.2 The King's Shares

As explained in Chapter 3.6, Sir Hugh Myddelton died intestate as to the King's moiety which he had purchased from Charles I a few weeks before his death (see Appendix G). This interest descended to his heir Sir William and became divided, like the Adventurers' moiety, into thirty-six shares known until 1904 as the King's shares, though always held by subjects. In 1646 he transferred the legal title to his brother Henry and three others on a straightforward set of trusts: William and his wife for life, his debts and portions for his daughters then to be paid out of the rents and profits, with an ultimate remainder 'to permit Sir Hugh Myddelton [*the settlor's heir*] and his heirs to take and receive the rents and profits of the premisses'.[4]

Sir William died in 1652 and five years later the trusts had not all been carried out, for his daughters were entitled to various portions 'at several great sums'. In order to meet these commitments Hugh—the equitable tenant in fee—contracted with William Bishop (who had married Flower the year before) for the sale of fourteen of the King's shares free of the Crown Clog at a price of £7,000; £250 was paid at once and the balance was to be expended towards the portions as Hugh and the trustees directed. The contract was made in June 1657 but

[3] Evelyn iv 481, 482–3; Russell 135, 143.

[4] *Dame Flora Backhouse* v. *Simon Middleton and others* (1670) 1 Chan Cas 173; 2 Freem 132; 3 Chan Rep 39. *The Lord Cornbury & Dame Flora his wife* v. *Simon Middleton and others* (1671) 1 Chan Cas 208. Nottingham 263, 292.

not followed by a conveyance. Instead, six months later Hugh succumbed to the persuasion of his uncle Simon, the founder's youngest son. Other adventures of Simon Myddelton are described in Chapters 4.2.2 and 6.4; here the point is that he persuaded Hugh to sell him in fee the entire King's moiety at a price of £15,100, and his contract with Hugh was followed by a conveyance to which Hugh and his uncle Henry (described as 'the only active trustee') were parties. It is unlikely that Simon ever paid the purchase price.[5]

The litigation lasted from 1658 to 1671, by which time the dividends had increased from about £60 to almost £100 a year and the Company's post-Fire prospects were excellent. Bishop began a suit against Hugh for specific performance of the contract for the sale of fourteen shares; the defendant filed an answer and Simon a cross-bill, witnesses were sworn, and then Bishop died. His will left the benefit of the contract to Flower and her heirs, so she brought a bill of revivor to restore the action; however, on her second marriage this suit abated. Simon then got judgment in his favour on his cross-bill but Flower's new husband petitioned to have this set aside and the spouses brought another bill of revivor to restore the original specific performance action. Under this bill witnesses were examined and their depositions taken but the bill itself was then dismissed for failure to join all necessary parties. Having failed to revive the earlier suit, the spouses then brought an original bill for specific performance which abated when the second husband died. Flower brought her own bill of revivor and made several attempts to persuade the court to permit her to use as evidence the depositions obtained in the earlier stages. 'Upon long debate and after several formal arguments' it was ruled in 1669 by Sir Orlando Bridgeman, Lord Keeper, that this was not permitted. Meanwhile, he ordered the legal title to be conveyed to the Six Clerks to await the outcome of the lawsuits.[6]

Nothing daunted, Flower led fresh evidence towards establishing the crucial issue: that when Simon took his conveyance he had *notice* of the earlier contract. She succeeded in this endeavour and added, for good measure, the argument

[5] 1 Chan Cas 173.

[6] Ibid. 175.

that the trustees had no power to sell the shares to raise portions since these sums were to be met only out of the 'rents and profits'. Bridgeman, however, could well see that the portions trust was to raise *capital* on certain events, such as a daughter's marriage, and that therefore the trustees were not confined to distributing income but must have power to sell the shares themselves (he was followed on this point by Jessell MR in 1875). Simon's defence raised a subtle and elegant argument. Firstly, the *res* contracted to be sold by Hugh Myddelton to William Bishop was merely whatever might be left after the debts and portions were paid; secondly, there was no conveyance even of that *res* but only a contract to convey; and thirdly, Flower took the benefit of that contract only under her first husband's will. In a brilliant summary his counsel described her interest as 'at the best a devise of an Equity on an Equity'. The Lord Keeper was much impressed by this, believing, in the then state of the evidence, that all four trustees had conveyed to Simon, and was minded to dismiss Flower's case. He said, however, that he would 'think farther of it' and while he was doing so she married again.[7]

Her lawsuit of course abated by this event and so she and Viscount Cornbury filed yet another bill of revivor. Their cause was heard twice in 1671 before Bridgeman, who was assisted by Wyld J. and Windham B. afforced, after they all disagreed, by Sir Harbottle Grimstone MR and Rainsford J. At this stage evidence was led showing that Simon had taken a conveyance from only one of the trustees. Without a sight of the original transfer upon trust of 1646 (which cannot be traced) one cannot know for certain whether Henry and the other three took the legal title jointly or in common, although centuries of precedent would suggest the former course. The court does not assume that the conveyance by one alone was ineffective to transfer the legal estate; instead (if we assume the trustees held jointly) they take it to have worked a severance: Bridgeman LK says that the conveyance to Simon 'carries no more from Henry than his fourth part' and Wyld J. says that 'three parts of the four were vested' in the other trustees and that Henry's transfer was merely 'for one tenant in common which passeth but his own share'.[8]

[7] Ibid. 175, 176; *Metcalfe* v. *Hutchinson* [1875] 1 Ch Div 591.

[8] 1 Chan Cas 211, 212.

In his defence Simon advanced four main arguments: they were addressed to the substance of the interest contracted to be bought by Flower's first husband, to the question whether the benefit of the contract was assignable at all, to the issue of mutuality, and to the very nature of New River shares. The first we would now describe as the problem of certainty of subject-matter of a trust, it being contended that Hugh was entitled in equity only to whatever might be left over after debts and portions (themselves contingent on marriage) were satisfied and that this was 'but a meer possibility contingent'. This argument persuaded only Windham B., the others agreeing that 'Sir Hugh had an equitable interest'. The second line of defence was that, even if this were so, 'the breach of the agreement was not deviseable', but Wyld J. sensibly held that 'if this be an interest it is deviseable; and it is but circuity of action to bring in the heir', thus persuading Rainsford J. and the Master of the Rolls. Bridgeman LK was much more doubtful but, as Bishop's heir was party and consented, he did not press his misgivings. The third objection was that Simon could not have forced Flower to pay and so, in turn, could not be specifically enjoined to convey: 'if the City which was lately burnt had not been rebuilt, or any other loss had befallen the water-work, the said Sir Hugh could never have compelled the Lady Cornbury to pay the money.' Only Windham B. in his dissent takes this seriously, saying 'cases that rest in privity are to be carried on in privity and strangers not to be engaged in it'. The others do not meet the point head-on but merely emphasize that conscience is on the side of the plaintiff.[9]

The fourth defence argument is very interesting for the light it throws on contemporary notions of the nature of a share. Chapter 3.4 described the process by which the Company had acquired the Forde waterworks, which, of course, it held under a title quite different from that of the New River itself. This occurred after the contract to sell fourteen shares to Bishop, and so Simon argues that the *res* in which these shares are held has changed 'and that no distinct account could be taken and so it was impracticable to decree the performance of the agreement with Bishop'. As reported, only the Lord Keeper deals with this. The majority agree that the conveyance by the one

[9] Ibid. 210, 211, 212.

trustee to Simon 'carries no more from Henry than his fourth part and carries Sir Hugh's equity no further' and decree 'that out of the three parts remaining [i.e. those of the other trustees] fourteen shares of the thirty-six parts shall be conveyed by the Six Clerks to the Lady Cornbury and her heirs'. But Bridgeman adds a rider that 'as to Forde's water-work if it can be severed it cannot be taken into the decree; but if it cannot there must be an allowance for it'. Thus, exactly like the Adventurers' shares, those in the King's moiety are taken to confer direct rights over the fixed assets. Finally, since the fourteen shares were contracted to be sold free of the Crown Clog, despite Simon's argument that this was a mere personal covenant by the vendor, the decree ordered the seven-eighteenths of the rent charge of £500 a year to be borne by the remaining twenty-two shares. Chapter 9.3.3 will explain how the exact incidence of this charge was finally determined—in 1911.[10]

As was recounted in chapter 4.2.2, Simon died seised of seventeen of the shares left him by the decree, and his will altered still further the incidence of the Crown Clog. It may be mentioned in passing that his daughter Sarah, devisee of one share, married Robert Harley, Speaker of the House of Commons and later first Earl of Oxford. His papers contain a good deal of correspondence with Clarendon and others about the affairs of the New River.[11]

5.3 The Commandery Mantles[12]

The disputes over the property at the New River Head began soon after Sir Hugh Myddelton's death in 1631 and lasted until the middle of the following century. Before the Dissolution of the Monasteries the land belonged to the Knights of St John of Jerusalem and acquired its first name from the word *commenda* used by the Order throughout Europe to denote a subdivision of its organization; the second word may be a corruption of Mandeville. In 1560 Elizabeth granted the Mantles to Thomas,

[10] Ibid. 210, 212.

[11] HMC 29 (Portland MS) iii 561, 580, 592, 609, 640; iv 51, 52, 76, 77.

[12] Based on: BL Harl. MS 3604; TW terriers 2035–6; NRCD B/193, C/233, G/128, and Case to Counsel (J. Booth) 8/3/1743.

Duke of Norfolk, to hold of her as of her Manor of East Greenwich in common socage and not *in capite*; it is thus of the same tenure as the fixed assets and profits of the Company itself. Five years later Norfolk enfeoffed Nicholas Backhouse, whose marriage settlement, after the usual life estates, gave the land to his right heir. That heir was Samuel Backhouse and in 1581 he paid to the Crown the feudal incidents (two years' value of the estate) due as the price of a special livery under the Great Seal.

The southern part of the Mantles was some 80 feet above the Thames to the north of the City and ideally situated as the site of the pond into which the New River would run; from there the force of gravity would help its water through the pipes. Agreement was reached and Appendix C.5 prints the receipt of 1614 signed by Samuel Backhouse for £65 paid by Hugh Myddelton for the right to lay the last 100 yards of the trench and to build a brick wall and cistern house. Presumably Samuel also invested money in the scheme, for both he and his son John are among the original Adventurers and, on incorporation, held two shares each. Hugh Myddelton made a store pond surrounded by 'a fair brick wall' with waste ponds for seepage and also built a brick dwelling for his overseer. Enriched by John Grene in the 1670s and restored by Robert Mylne in 1782, its most beautiful features are incorporated in the present Thames Water building on Rosebery Avenue.

The full agreement between Hugh and Samuel is unknown and was probably informal. On their deaths, however, it became a matter of dispute between their heirs, Sir William Myddelton contending that his father had bought the freehold of the pond and cistern house and, at the first General Meeting, had transferred it to the newly incorporated Company, while Sir John Backhouse

> does now make title unto the said house and pond pretending that the ground was not granted to Hugh Myddelton and goes about to take the same and refuses free passage over his land to the pond whereby the waterwork is liable to be overthrown and the City deprived of the benefit of the water.

Moreover, said Sir William, the ascertainment of the truth was difficult because all Sir Hugh's papers were with either his widow or William Lewyn the Company secretary (in fact a perusal of the expenditure ledgers would have revealed that Sir John was still receiving rent). Sir William therefore began a lawsuit in the Court of Requests against his mother, Sir John Backhouse, and William Lewyn (see **Plate II**).

At the first hearing in May 1637 the court ordered production of such documents as were to be found, suggested a compromise—a conveyance by Sir John Backhouse but at a fee-farm rent—and advised the parties 'to treat together and reconcile their differences'. They did so, and in the following Michaelmas term the court had before it the document printed at Appendix C.5 and described above. As a consequence of this it ordered a gratuitous conveyance of the inner pond and a conveyance at a rent of £10 of the waste ponds 'except only of the soil of the said trench or cut whereby the said water runneth . . . as in the said Act of Parliament is provided'. Thus the court may have read the statute as forbidding the owners to transfer the fee in the ground itself, or may simply have suggested the minimum for a compromise with the maximum of efficiency: for if the enterprise were to fail it would be highly inconvenient for Sir John to be bereft of a narrow strip across his land. The Order also deals with the details necessary to placate the parties, reserving Sir John access for his cattle and fish and stipulating a restrictive covenant that the Cistern House be not used as a tavern.[13]

In compliance with this decree, Sir William in 1639 executed a deed poll by which—as his father's heir, not as Governor of the Company—he disclaimed to Sir John any rights he might have in the pond, wall, and house. Two days later an indenture was executed between Sir John of the one part and, of the other, the Company and certain trustees, including several Adventurers and the Secretary. After reciting the court order, Sir John conveys to and to the use of the named trustees and their heirs the inner pond and house and the watercourse thereto together with the right to lay pipes to carry the water to the City, but 'except and always reserved unto the said Sir John Backhouse the inheritance of the soyle of the said Newe Cut or Trench according to the purport of an Act of Par-

[13] For the rent payments see PRO LR 2/32 (24/6/1620). For the lawsuit and settlement, see PRO Req. 1/76 fos. 260, 310; NRCD B/193; TW terriers 2035–6.

liament'. The consideration for this grant is said to be the £65 paid to Samuel in 1614 (Appendix C.5). He goes on in the same way to convey the nearby waste ponds at a fee-farm rent of £10 a year with the usual proviso for re-entry in default. The deed contains no express declaration of the trust, but after the words of conveyance the trustees drop out to be replaced by the corporate name. It is to the Company that the grantor gives a right over his retained land to enter and repair the watercourse and it is the Company which covenants to pay the annual rent and gives Sir John and his heirs the right to keep fish in the waste ponds. The final clause provides that

> It is the true intent and meaneinge of all the said parties to these presents that this Graunt and every clause article and sentence therein contayned shalbe taken expounded and construed onely for the better improveinge and advancement of the said Water works.

Thus, the deed sets a pattern which alters only by becoming more explicit: all future conveyances are to the Company or its trustees and, if the land is let, the rent finds its way into the Company's revenue account.

Sir John Backhouse was still, of course, seised of the rest of the Mantles together with other estates inherited from his father, and in 1647 he set up a trust thereof which was to play a part in the development of the Rule against perpetuities. In the case of freehold, the utility of the entail as a means of tying up the succession to a particular piece of land had long been undermined by the devices of the recovery and fine. In its turn, the Statute of Uses of 1535 had ensured that a conveyance of the fee to feoffees to the use of successive beneficiaries carried to the latter the appropriate legal estates encumbered with the various rules devised by the courts to resolve conflicts over alienability. By use of the appropriate formula it was indeed possible to create a trust of freehold property, but an alternative was beginning to be appreciated in the early seventeenth century: the scheme whereby a freeholder conveyed to trustees not the fee simple but a long lease on enduring family trusts. Since the Statute of Uses took effect only where the feoffee was *seised*, it had no impact whatever on this transaction; consequently the family interests subsisted behind a trust and under the protection of the Chancery, from whom a greater leniency might be expected.

Sir John therefore demised the land to trustees for 99 years on the following limitations of the equitable interest:

(1) to himself and his wife for life;
(2) to pay his debts and legacies;
(3) to his brother Nicholas for life, remainder to his sons successively in tail male. Nicholas died childless in John's lifetime.
(4) to his brother William (Flower's father) for life;
(5) to his nephew John (Flower's brother) for life, remainder to John's sons successively in tail male. John died childless in his father's lifetime.
(6) to his uncle Rowland for life, remainder to his sons successively in tail male. One such son survived and was the father of Flower's second husband William Backhouse.
(7) to his sister's son Samuel Bellingham in tail male;
(8) to the settlor's right heir (i.e. retainer of the ultimate reversion).

It should be noted that the vesting of the entails was not made contingent on the death without issue of prior tenants in tail during the lifetime of existing members of the Backhouse family.

The settlor died in 1650, having confirmed the trust in his will. This was proved by his widow and on her death letters of administration to his estate *cum testamento annexo* were granted to Flower's father, who was by then Sir John's only living brother; he was also administrator of the estates of his other brother and of his own only son. He then conveyed whatever interest he might have in the Mantles to William Lloyd and Francis Turner as trustees, and died in 1662; his will did not dispose specifically of the Mantles. Flower obtained letters of administration to her uncle John's estate and proved her father's will.

The validity of the trusts of the Mantles was challenged in a lawsuit reported under the name *Backhouse* v. *Bellingham* by Pollexfen along with a case which he described as following the same rule, namely *Wood* v. *Saunders*. In fact, Bellingham did not defend the Backhouse claim, which proceeded against the executrix of the last trustee of the 99-year trust term. The decision was no doubt sensible, since on any view of the con-

PLATE II. Sir John Backhouse in 1637, at the time of the lawsuit with Sir William Myddelton. The disputed property is depicted in the picture under his right hand and is the earliest surviving representation of the New River Head.

temporary law Bellingham could not win. As has been said, the essence of the settlor's scheme was to utilize the then popular device of carving out a set of estates behind a trust of a term of years. Initial difficulties had once been felt in reconciling the sanctity bestowed on the freehold—which carried seisin—with the term of years which did not. According to Coke, 'any estate for life . . . is a higher and greater estate than a lease for years, though it be for a 1000 years or more . . .'. The flaw lies in the word 'any'. Certainly out of a lease there cannot be carved a freehold carrying seisin, but it does not follow that the leasehold interest cannot be held by *A* for life; and if this be so there may be a remainder after the life estate. While there are early Tudor difficulties with this reasoning, Coke himself reports the great lawsuits of *Matthew Manning* (1609) and *Lampet* (1612), which not only accepted the gift by will of a lease to *A* for life but prevented *A* from destroying the gifts over in remainder. Further, the latter might validly be made to vest on some contingency such as birth, and the modern Rule against perpetuities was born of a need to control just such dispositions.[14]

In the Mantles trust, however, the life estates were followed by entails and in the 1660s the relationship of this estate to the lease was far from settled. The aim of an entail—that of welding the generations to the property and vice versa—had long ago been frustrated for freehold assets by the fine and the recovery. But both of these depended ultimately on enforcement by the sheriff's livery of *seisin*, and so were not available where only a leasehold was involved. However, a similar result could be achieved by refusing to permit entails to inhere in terms of years and giving the 'tenant in tail' the term absolutely; but if gifts over on the failure of his issue were held valid then the effects of *De Donis* would reappear as settlors' advisers utilized the long lease to attain their clients' aims of tying their property to a family. The problem was foreseen in *Child* v. *Baylie* (1618): 'Such an entail of a term is not allowable at law, for the mischief which otherwise would ensue if there should be such a perpetuity of a term.'[15]

[14] *Backhouse* v. *Bellingham* (1664) Pollex 33; *Wood* v. *Saunders* (1669) ibid. 35; Co Litt 46a; *Anon* (1536) Dyer 7a; *Matthew Manning's Case* (1609) 8 Co Rep 94b; *Lampet's Case* (1612) 10 Co Rep 46b; *Cotton* v. *Heath* (1638) 1 Roll Ab 612 pl. 3; *Eyres* v. *Faulkland* (1697) 1 Salk 231; Nottingham 223–31.

[15] *Child* v. *Baylie* (1618) Cro Jac 459 at 461; Cruise, *Fines and Recoveries* i 105, 310; Sheppard, *Touchstone* i 14.

The action brought by Flower and her second husband William Backhouse could have been resolved in two ways, either of which would have defeated the 'entail' to Bellingham. In the first method it would be held that the limitation of a term of years in tail destroyed all subsequent remainders even though that entail never vested in interest. Thus, the first entail to the son of Nicholas—who was never born—would be sufficient to avoid the gifts over but, as that gift never vested at all, Flower would take under the ultimate limitation as right heir. The second method would be to hold that once an entail vested, all later limitations in a trust of a long lease were destroyed, even if that entail then failed for want of issue. In that case Flower's husband, at the date of the action, would be the tenant in tail, although on his death childless the property would go to Flower as right heir.

In 1664 the case came before the Lord Chancellor, who was none other than the Earl of Clarendon, although he could hardly have known that his son and heir was to marry the female plaintiff. The report tells us only that he decreed the limitation of the remainder to Bellingham to be void and ordered the trust estate to be conveyed to Lloyd and Turner 'for the benefit of the plaintiffs'. It seems likely that it was the first line of reasoning which prevailed, and this is the view of later doctrine—although, in the interests of strict accuracy, it should be pointed out that both *Backhouse* and *Wood* v. *Saunders* concerned *inter vivos* trusts of terms and not gifts by will. Fearne, for instance, assimilates the two, saying of *Backhouse*

> it formerly was held that wherever the first executory limitation was in such words as would convey the whole interest, then any subsequent limitation was void notwithstanding the preceding limitation never took effect: as where a term was limited to a man for life and afterwards to his first and other sons in tail successively and for default of such issue remainders over; this remainder was held void though no son was ever born; because the first remainder to the sons in tail was an executory devise of the whole interest; so that, whenever an executory devise would if it had vested have carried the whole interest, no limitation over could be good even though the preceding never vested.[16]

If this had remained the law then Bridgeman and Not-

[16] Fearne (10th edn.) i 517.

tingham would have argued in vain and we might have been denied the Rule against perpetuities in its classic form. And although Pollexfen follows his report of *Backhouse* with one said to be 'to the same purpose', the seeds of the crucial distinction are sown in *Wood* v. *Saunders* (1669). Put simply, this was a case where a lease of salt-water boileries was held on trust for *C* in tail if he or his issue survived two living persons; if he did not, then for *D* in tail with remainder to *E*. *C* died childless during the lives in being and Bridgeman as Lord Keeper, together with Twisden, Rainsford, and Wild JJ, held that *D*, who did outlive the life in being, took the term and that the fact that *D* then died without issue did not avail *E*. Thus, the last point emphasizes that the vesting of an entail in a term of years destroys gifts over; the first point, however, upholds the validity of a subsequent entail which, if it ever does vest, is bound to do so on the failure of the prior entail during the lifetime of a living person. The stage is set for the *Duke of Norfolk's Case* in 1681 and 1682.[17]

The regime at stake in that lawsuit and devised by Bridgeman in 1647 for the Earl of Arundel was similar to, but more strictly drafted than, those in the two cases just discussed. A 200-year lease was demised to trustees and this asset was then settled on the client's second son in tail male, remainder to the third son in tail male if the first son died without issue in the lifetime of the second. The common-law judges, in their opinions against the validity of the gift over, state in blunt terms their views as to the incompatibility of entail and lease: 'if there be a trust of a term to a man and the heirs of his body, no limitation can be over' (Montague LCB) and 'the whole term is swallowed in the estate-tail' (Pemberton LCJ). Nottingham, however, draws the vital distinction between *Backhouse* and *Wood* v. *Saunders*. As to the first, he says:

> if a term be limited to a man for life and after to his first, second, third &c. sons in tail successively and for default of such issue the remainder over, tho' the contingency never happen yet the remainder is void, although there were never a son then born to him; for that looks like a perpetuity and that was Sir William Backhurst [*sic*] his case in the 16 of this King.

[17] *Wood* v. *Saunders* (1669) Pollex 35.

He then says, however, that *Wood* v. *Saunders* 'was a fuller and flatter case' since the contingency on which the gift over was to occur was 'wearing out in the compass of two lives in being'.[18]

The *Backhouse* case is usually distinguished by later judges on the ground that the gifts over were not limited to failure of issue of prior donees within the perpetuity period, and the result is neatly summarized by Fearne:

> It seems now to be settled that whatever number of limitations there may be after the first executory devise of the whole interest, any of them which is so limited that it must take effect (if at all) within 21 years after the period of a life in being may be good in event, if no one of the preceding limitations which would carry the whole interest happens to vest. But when once any preceding executory limitation which carries the whole interest happens to take place, that instant all the subsequent limitations become void and the whole interest is then become vested.

The litigation on the Mantles, then, was part of the process by which the distinctions between freehold and leasehold lost their functional significance, as landowners—who were almost invariably freeholders—utilized now the fee and now the term of years to create an asset capable of being moulded into the desired pattern of commercial investment and family endowment. Nottingham put the point vividly:

> Oh yes, terms are mere chattels and are not, in consideration of law, so great as freeholds or inheritances. These are words, and but words, there is not any difference at all but the reason of mankind will laugh at it. Shall a man . . . be disabled to provide for the contingencies of his family which are within his view and prospect, because it is a lease for years and not an inheritance of a freehold? There is that absurdity in it which is to me insuperable.[19]

The next stage is interesting, for with the growth of other fields of investment which, like land, were both permanent and income-producing, settlors began to devise very similar regimes to provide for their families; but the asset settled was stocks and shares. This development will be described in Chapter 10.6.

For the moment, however, we must return to Flower. In

[18] *Duke of Norfolk's Case* (1682) 3 Chan Cas 1 at 17, 22, 29, 35.

[19] *Stanley* v. *Leigh* (1732) 2 P Wms 693; Fearne (10th edn.) i 517 and cases there cited; Gray 361 and cases there cited; *Duke of Norfolk's Case* (1682) 3 Chan Cas 1 at 50.

pursuance of the Lord Chancellor's decree the legal term was assigned to her family trustees, Lloyd and Turner, and in 1669 she and her husband, by demise, mortgaged the Mantles to Seth, Bishop of Sarum, to secure a loan of £2,000. She was widowed shortly afterwards and in 1670 sold to the New River Company (for 5*s.*) an acre 'which now is wasted away by the water' just north-east of the ponds which it had bought from her uncle John in 1639; the mortgagee joined in to release his interest. On her marriage to Henry Hyde, Viscount Cornbury, the marriage settlement conveyed to Lloyd and Turner in fee the rest of the Mantles, other London property, and New River shares and fractions of shares. The trusts were for the spouses for life and then as she should appoint, in default to her and her heirs. In 1676 the Clarendons, the mortgagees, and the trustees all joined in a sale to the Company (for £200) of another 2 acres just north-west of the ponds at the head of the river.

The story during the next 68 years is of Clarendon's debts and of disputes with the Company. The mortgage was assigned, others created, and further advances made; in the last year of her life Flower was using what remained of her equity in the Mantles as collateral for a loan of £600 secured primarily by a pledge of her pearl necklace. Her brother-in-law the Earl of Rochester had found a buyer for six of the shares which she had recovered in the litigation described in the preceding section. The price offered was £3,500 a share, but shrewdly Flower declined to sell, and her husband conceded that 'in truth I cannot much blame her, for it is visible that revenue does daily more increase than land can do'. Occasional plans were made to sell the Mantles and pay off the family debts, but these were never executed, although after the Earl's death in 1709 the mortgages thereon were redeemed by the sale of other land. The legal title to the freehold devolved eventually on John Lloyd, grandson of Bishop Lloyd.[20]

Meanwhile, the Company's need for land at the New River Head had been growing as the business expanded. In particular, about 1708 the Company began to make use of another storage point for water, the 'Upper Pond' on the northern edge of the Mantles. It may be seen today in the shape of the covered

[20] *Clarendon Letters* i 198–200.

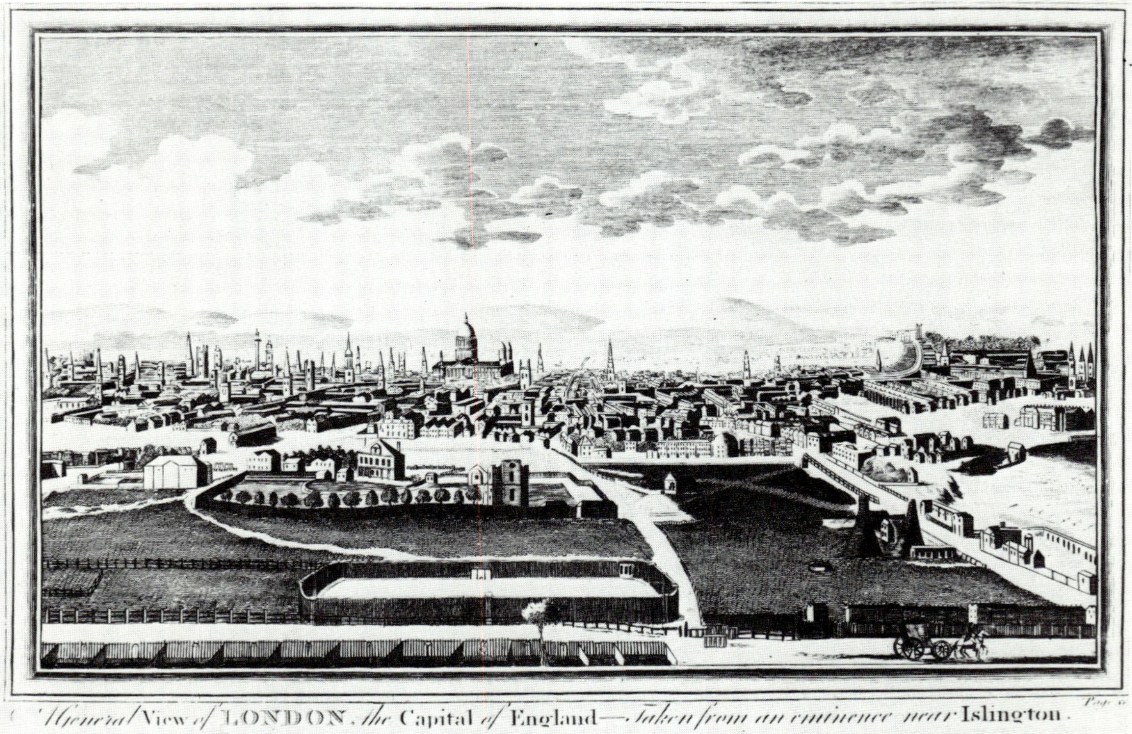

FIG. 6. New River Head with Upper Pond in foreground, *c.*1720

reservoir at the corner of Pentonville Road and Amwell Street. John Lloyd began proceedings which came before the Lord Chancellor; although the case does not seem to have been reported, it is clear from Lord Hardwicke's careful notes that the Company was successful on all counts. The plaintiff's first complaint—as to the laying of pipes across the Mantles—was defeated by the grant of such a right in the feoffment of 1639. His second was that the trench of the river was by now twice as wide as the ten feet prescribed by the 1605 statute; to this Hardwicke recalled a reported case of 1701 which had held that 'the Act is to be taken in a liberal sense that the town in general might be supplied with water' and noted that for this reason he would 'extend the words beyond their natural meaning'. The final and much stronger ground of complaint concerned the construction of the Upper Pond; but this, Hardwicke thought, was 'mere trespass' and so Lloyd was left to his remedy at common law. He promptly began an ejectment action, which spurred the Company to reach an agreement with him in the Autumn of 1742. Before that arrangement could be embodied in a formal indenture, however, the Company needed to be satisfied as to his title. Flower had executed, revoked, and remade several appointments of the beneficial fee simple; she had certainly given 10 acres to John Lloyd, but the rest might well have been claimed by the Clarendons.[21]

The Company's counsel was happy with the legal title to the fee simple and the trust terms, since it held no flaws that could not be cured by a recovery, a fine, and perhaps an Act of Parliament—which would, he advised, be 'the safest way of all'. He had greater doubts about the equitable estate, thinking that the Clarendons might have claims the possibility of which would be known to the Company and warning that 'notice reduces a purchaser to the situation of a volunteer'. The Company, however, seems to have been prepared to take the risk and, although they made Lloyd both levy a fine and suffer a recovery, decided to dispense with an Act of Parliament. In 1744 Lloyd, the trustees of outstanding terms, and Lloyd's brothers and sisters joined in a conveyance by lease and release of over 30 acres of the Mantles to Robert Holford and others as trustees for the New River Company. The transfer also ex-

[21] BL Add. MS 36051 fo. 153; *NR Co* v. *Graves* (1701) 2 Vern 432.

pressly included 'the soil of the Cut or Channel of the said New River . . . the inheritance of which said soil was reserved' in the feoffment of 1639. The consideration was the payment of arrears of rent for the use of the Upper Pond, and a perpetual rent charge of £362. 10*s*. 0*d*. which was not redeemed until 1948.[22]

[22] The Company paid the rent charge punctually (M 1/11/1770). MWB 45th Annual Report (1947–8) 35.

CHAPTER 6

The Company (I) Governance and Finance

6.1 Introduction

On Christmas Day 1769 an emergency committee meeting was held at Peel's Coffee-house in Fleet Street; present were Peter Holford the Governor, Henry Berners the Treasurer, and two Adventurers. Their task was to cope with the effects of the fire which, on the day before, had destroyed the Head Office at Bridewell Precinct. Earlier that year they had paid £50 for a fire engine, but that was kept at the waterworks at Islington, and their first need was to reconstruct the day-to-day business. Immediate instructions were given to call in the collectors' books and compile a list of customers, to reconstruct expenditure from the Treasurer's own documents, and to make a claim on the insurance policy with the Hand-in-Hand Fire Office.[1]

During the following weeks the Treasurer presided over a committee on Tuesdays, and on Thursdays the Governor took the chair at a meeting attended by some dozen Adventurers. They arranged temporary accommodation and the surrender to the City of the lease of the remains of their office. The Company also held a lease of land at Dorset Yard and it was decided to use the £1,000 proceeds of insurance to build new offices there. The first stone was laid in June and the Company remained there until the move to Islington in 1819; in 1861 the Dorset Yard lease was sold and the proceeds later divided as a bonus among the shareholders (see Appendix I).[2]

At the General Court of 15 February, attended by the officers and eleven others, it was reported that the minutes, receipt books, and orders for payment had all been burnt. The Company seems to have assumed that everything was lost for, at the next Annual General Court held as prescribed by the Char-

[1] M 25/12/1769, 28/12/1769, 2/1/1770, 7/1/1770.

[2] M 25/12/1769, 7/1/1770, 28/6/1770, 19/4/1819.

ter in the following November, new forms of the Oath for the Governor and other officers were approved; yet Hugh Myddelton's oath survived and is given in Chapter 3.1. Indeed, the whole attitude to the original documents is puzzling. Throughout the nineteenth century the 1769 fire is given by the Company as the reason for the loss of all its records as, before that Christmas Eve, it had blamed the Great Fire of London. Yet there is preserved among the Guildhall Manuscripts an Inventory dated 26 June 1686 of the documents 'lockt up in the Company's indenture chest'. All of them have been traced by the present writer, save a few leases and copyhold surrenders; and probably even these could be tracked down among the Thames Water terriers. However, although the foundation documents survive, it is the case that Minute Books, annual accounts, and detailed evidence of the day-to-day life of the Company are missing for the first century and a half of its life. The records which begin after the fire are prefaced with abstracts of such by-laws and the like as could then be traced, but for some parts of the story any account must be derived from other sources.[3]

6.2 Governance

As will be seen from the Charter (Appendix F), there were twenty-nine original corporators. Twenty-two of them owned one entire share in the Adventurers' moiety and seven held two, making the total of thirty-six. The shares were freely alienable and divisible, but the Charter goes on to stipulate that in order to be one of the twenty-nine who were 'of the Company' a member had to hold 'a full thirtie sixth parte'. Only such a person was qualified to stand for office as Governor, Deputy Governor, or Treasurer, or even to vote for the officers (the quorum was seven), to remove them (quorum of twelve), or to make by-laws (with a quorum of five). Thus, there were excluded from membership of the company all holders of King's shares and, potentially, up to seven holders of Adventurers' shares. In fact (although early documentation is lacking) it seems that this last exclusion caused no problem since, with

[3] M 15/2/1770, 8/11/1770. GL MS 4883.

some persons owning two or more Adventurers' shares, there were never more than twenty-nine individuals (and frequently fewer) in the class of potential members. Certainly, there is no record of all twenty-nine ever attending a meeting.

Greater difficulty was caused by the division of shares, either by act of the owner or the operation of the laws of intestate succession among daughters who took as co-parceners; although this was, in its turn, sometimes cured when the fragments of a share became reunited by devise or descent. An example, given in Chapter 4.3, occurred when in 1794 two joint tenants of one of the Neville shares severed *inter se* but each then devised her half to the same person. Even worse problems arose when one person held one thirty-sixth or more of the moiety but made up of fractions of different original shares. In 1821, for instance, there were thirty whole Adventurers' shares while in 1904 there were only twenty-four, but there were four other holdings of fractions equalling the amount of the original shares. It is said that in the early eighteenth century the matter came before the Chancery and that Cowper LC made a decree that the holders of fractions of a share could together appoint a deputy to represent them. Whether this merely solved a particular dispute is not known; the decree is not mentioned in later papers on voting rights, and a list of members of about 1745 gives the names of twenty-three 'proprietors'. The Company, however, refused to fragment its dividend payments but required the holders of fractions to agree on a recipient of the total sum. The King's shares—perhaps because there was no hope of a holder being a member of the Company—were more frequently divided, so that by 1904 only six remained whole.[4]

Further complications were caused by the fact that shares were often held by trustees or proxies. The method of appointing the latter was by demise of the share for a term of 99 years if the grantee should so long live with a proviso for avoidance on tender of 6*d*. This was the form used by the Goldsmiths' Company in 1694 (see Chapter 4.5) and it persisted until this century to cause some ponderous amusement to the last Court of Arbitration. One cannot, therefore, be certain (though one

[4] W. Maitland 629; PP 1821 v 241; S. Lewis 428; NR: List of Proprietors, Officers, and Employees (undated, *c*.1745).

can sometimes guess) from the Minute Books which of those present were merely proxies—for instance the Samuel Smith who attended meetings in the late eighteenth century may well have been sitting for the Neville share held by his two female relatives, as recounted in Chapter 4.3. Another difficulty is caused by the strong family connections with the New River: the Berners held seats and offices for 200 years, as did the Holfords. Finally, the Adventurers' families often intermarried, and the sitting members are always male, so that some may well have been sitting in right of their wives.[5]

By 1800 the word 'Board' is being used where the charter spoke of 'the Company' and the word 'Director' of those holding one of the twenty-nine places; resignation on sale of the qualifying share is said always to have occurred without dispute. It should be stressed, however, that the sitting members were not 'Directors' in the modern sense but were the entire Company. In 1888, on the sale of the Neville share by the Ruck-Keenes, Counsel had to advise that the limitations in the charter meant that a person holding a whole Adventurers' share, where there was no other such holder who was not a 'Director' and where the present number was under twenty-nine, could not be excluded from the Board.[6]

Transfers of Adventurers' and King's shares were reported to the Board—though no price is recorded in the minutes—and the Treasurer was advised on the appropriate recipient of the dividend: depending on the trusts of the share, this would be the tenant in fee simple, trustees, tenant for life, or the husband of such a person. On 26 February 1778, for instance, the meeting decided to pay the dividends on two King's shares to W. B. Daniel for the life of his wife. This led to a strange sequel, for in 1811 the husband published a twisted, though obsessively meticulous, account of the shares, a rectory, and a revenue cutter 'whilst under the superintendence and management of a learned solicitor'. According to his story, he had mortgaged the shares to Mansfield LCJ and another, and later spent time in a debtors' prison. The book is dedicated to his solicitor, who is blamed for all the writer's grief.[7]

[5] M 20/7/1775; Fry Arbitration Transcript (1905) 10, 11. TW, Strongroom B6, No. A207 (2 vols.).

[6] NR: Case to Counsel (R. E. Webster A-G & V. Hawkins) 9/7/1888.

[7] M 26/2/1778; W. B. Daniel.

The nearest approach to a modern Register of Shareholders is the Company's Register of Proprietors, which runs from 1770 to 1888; presumably there was an earlier version which perished in the fire of 1769. Entries were made only when shares changed hands and consist of an abstract of the title to the share, a memorial of the deed or will which transferred it, and a certificate as to who may safely be paid dividends. Thus, the Company is taking notice of trusts of shares and seeking to ascertain the responsible trustee whose receipt for the dividend will be good. An example can be taken from the latter days of the Neville share (Chapter 4.3). In 1821 C. E. Ruck Keene became tenant for life with a power of appointment. On his death in 1880 his will and codicil were presented to the Company, which was about to act on the gifts therein when there was produced an earlier deed of appointment of 1845; the Register notes that the testamentary disposition is therefore ineffective. The volumes also record relevant decrees of the Chancery such as, in connection with a dispute as to entitlement on intestacy, the confirmation by the Lord Chancellor in 1778 that the shares were realty and so descended to the heir at law.[8]

Despite the great wealth and importance which the New River Company attained, its governance seems generally to have caused few problems. With a voting membership limited to twenty-nine electing a Board of the same number, no doubt problems could be resolved informally. As will be shown in Chapter 9.3.2, the only attempt by the owner of the Crown Clog to intervene in the Company's affairs failed decisively. Further, there is no trace of resentment from the holders of the King's shares that they were entirely excluded from control, although by the late nineteenth century, on the rare occasions when shares of both classes came on the market, the entitlement to so-called Directors' fees provoked higher prices for the Adventurers' shares. In fact, these were received only for attendance at meetings and were modest. In 1741 the sum of 5*s*. 'for coach hire' was being paid and this was later raised to one guinea, then five. In 1904 the special Arbitration on the amount

[8] NRRP vols. A–I; *Sandys* v. *Sibthorpe* (1778) Dick 546; NRRP A/34, 37, 71, 123.

due as compensation awarded only £76,917. 17*s*. 10*d*. for the three officers and twenty-two others.[9]

In short, the governance of the New River was more like that of a partnership than of a large Company. Every Thursday some fifteen or so Adventurers held their weekly meeting, made rules for collectors and workmen, agreed the sums to be paid in compensation for the innumerable street accidents caused by their pipes and excavations (5*s*. an ass was the standard figure), noted share transfers, received the accounts, and decided on capital expenditure and dividends. In 1852—to cope with the pressures decribed in Chapter 7—they set up committees for Estates and Legal Business, Works and Contracts, and Finance, dividing the work among the twenty-one members then sitting. About once a month they transformed themselves into a General Court (with, from 1817, its own Minute Book) which received reports, ratified decisions taken at the weekly meeting, ordered the sealing of deeds, and passed the resolutions necessary for the issue of new share or loan capital. The Annual General Court for the election of officers was held every November from 1619 to 1903. In none of the records of the many Company meetings is there sign of serious contest or indeed of any formal voting whatever.[10]

6.3 The Business

After the Great Fire of 1666, the number of customers began the growth which, with occasional pauses, it was to maintain until this century, making the New River indisputably the greatest water company in Europe and an enterprise whose assets (although all situated in south-east England) were not insignificant even in comparison with the better-known names of the South Sea, East India, Levant, Africa, and Hudson's Bay companies. The Round Pond was a subject for Hollar's beautiful etchings of the post-Fire period and in 1667 John Dryden raised a laugh in his play *Sir Martin Mar-all* with a reference to 'the New River, dearer by six pence the pound

[9] M 11/3/1771, GCM 10/2/1820; Revelstoke Arbitration Transcript (1904) (TW, Strongroom B6).

[10] M *passim*; GCM 13/3/1817–21/7/1904.

FIG. 7

than ever God Almighty made it'. Along with the great trading concerns, the Company subscribed to William Morgan's fine 1682 map of London and was rewarded with an acknowledgement and a depiction of the New River Pond in a prominent position under the main title.[11]

The accounts which survive for the period 1670–84 show (in round figures) that in the year beginning Ladyday 1670 the Company had seven collectors (who were personally responsible for arrears), an income of just over £12,500, and expenditure of £6,287; the balance divided among the seventy-two shares gave each some £86. In 1683 there are eight collectors and the figures are: income £21,000, expenditure £8,775, dividend £168. The disbursements over this period average about £7,000 a year. There are no surviving detailed accounts which might show how much of this is capital expenditure, and a good deal must have been spent on renewing the elm pipes, whose useful life varied—depending on the soil—

[11] John Dryden, *Sir Martin Mar-all*, Act IV, scene 1, line 220 (there is a variant reading of the text: see *Works* ed. J. Loftis, vol. ix (1966) 441); Pepys thought the play very funny: *Diary* viii 387. William Morgan, *London &c Actually Survey'd* (1682).

from four to twenty-five years. We know the figure up to 1631 was £18,500 and that Forde's waterworks were bought in 1657 for £6,100, and it seems reasonable to assume that about £3,000 a year was permanent capital investment. In 1695 the population of London had grown to about half a million and (according to Scott) the three bodies with the largest capital were the East India Company (£1,212,000), the Bank of England (£720,000), and the New River (£288,000). From other sources (see Appendix I) it appears that the total distributed in dividend that year amounted to almost £15,000.[12]

In addition to the collectors and small office staff, the Company's full-time employees included 'walksmen' to conserve the river, turncocks to control the supply, a foreman of the pipe borers, an overseer of the yard, paviours, smiths, founders, and plumbers. Its activities naturally attracted the attention of the Company of Plumbers, which in 1644 attempted to ensure that the Company give it the administration of the work involved in connecting houses to the mains. The New River plumber's lengthy and detailed reply persuaded the officers that to take such a step would be 'raishly to throw [the] worke into the very jaws of a confused and distraicted posture'.[13]

Because of the 1769 fire there is little original source material for much of the eighteenth century, but the later fortunes of the Company are amply documented in its records and in the papers of the Select Committees, Royal Commissions, and the like which from 1821 began to take a keen interest in the London water supply. From these we learn that in 1800 the Company was supplying water to almost 55,000 houses (farming the rents to the owners of the larger tenements at 25 per cent) and that its prices had not increased greatly since the earliest days: the average per house was still 26*s.* 8*d.* a year. Thanks to the increase in population, however, demand had increased enormously and the company's gross income was £61,000, of which just over half was distributed giving a dividend per share of some £464. After the heavy capital expenditure and disastrous competition of the next two decades the Company's fortunes recovered dramatically; the effect on dividends can be seen in Appendix I, and the reasons for the

[12] BL Harl. MS 3604; M A/1; Scott i 335–6.

[13] BL Stowe MS 796 fo. 45b.

prosperity will be explained in Chapter 7. The policy of employing tradesmen had of course continued, and there were nine company plumbers in the mid-eighteenth century, although later the much greater use of metal installations led to some arrangements with independent contractors. The Company also showed a sound grasp of cost-benefit analysis. When a surgeon drew attention to their habit of not covering the holes in the ground at the mains connections and complained that this caused many accidents to animals, he was told 'that they have a donkey's leg to pay for now and then; this is less expensive than keeping the plug holes covered'.[14]

Undoubtedly the heaviest recurrent expenditure was on the elm pipes. The exact ratio of outgoings to income depended on the soil of the district, but, for instance, it was estimated that around Shoreditch 53 per cent of the water rents was spent on maintenance. Yet, until the early nineteenth century, the Company financed its acquisition of land and heavy investment in waterworks and other installations entirely from net income. After receiving the half-yearly accounts of past, and estimates of future, expenditure, the General Court decided what sum should be withdrawn from dividend. Thus, on 31 January 1771, on learning that the new offices would cost more than the insurance money for the old, the Court determined 'to withhold £10 from every share, making a total of £720', and another £25 per share was deducted from the dividend declared for Midsummer. Four years later £15 was deducted so that 'a new main be drove from Islington to the West end of Town toward St Mary le Bonne'. And in January 1811, as the figures for expenditure were not complete, it was resolved 'that £10 per share be reserved in the Treasurer's hands in aid of paying the same; but this is not intended to be adduced as a precedent'. In modern terms, this whole process can be compared with making calls on, or issuing new shares to, the original holders.[15]

But the water supply was still not continuous. With the assistance of the Boulton & Watt pumping engine, the great mains which led into the City, Soho, Marylebone, and Westminster were filled from the original or the upper pond

[14] PP 1821 v 165 and Appx. C; NR: List of Proprietors, Officers, and Employees (*c*.1745); PP 1828 ix 89; M 11/1/1810, 22/6/1820, 7/12/1820, 11/4/1867.

[15] M 28/4/1814; M/GC 31/1/1771, 25/5/1771, 20/7/1775, 31/1/1811, 28/9/1815.

FIG. 8. New River mains at Bagnigge Wells, *c.* 1800

for a certain period every week, usually for seven hours on alternate days as the supply was switched from one area to another, and the water was delivered to the basement or ground floor of the houses, where it was collected into cisterns. The use of wooden pipes was unsatisfactory and very expensive. About a quarter of the water was lost, it was easily contaminated by gas and other substances, the maximum diameter of the largest main was seven inches, it was difficult to increase the pressure, and if as the water was pumped along a main the turncocks closed one set of branch pipes before opening the next, the main blew up.[16]

Pipes of cast iron suffered none of these disadvantages and, after the invention in 1785 of the spigot and socket joint, their widespread use became feasible. The price, however, was double that of wood—11*s.* 3*d.* per yard of four-inch pipe as opposed to 5*s.* 2*d.* a yard for elm. In 1811 the Company decided to replace their 400 miles of piping and so, faced with a probable outlay approaching £½m., were, for the first time in 200 years, forced to raise capital; the process is described in section

[16] PP 1821 v 35, 211.

6.6. Their foresight did, however, save the Company from the public pressure (and rise of piping prices) occasioned by section 12 of Michael Angelo Taylor's Act, which, in 1817, ordered that all new mains be made of iron.[17]

6.4 Judicial Control and Perfecting the Title

Despite the efficient governance and profitable business described in the preceding sections, two types of problem beset the New River. The first—judicial control of its activities—was one shared with the other emerging business corporations; the second—its weak title to the statutory powers and the fee simple in the river bed—was peculiar to this Company.

The New River began when the powers conferred by Parliament on the City of London were transferred to a citizen to be exercised at his sole risk but for his own benefit. The Company formed by the Charter granted to Hugh Myddelton and his associates continued to wield the powers (though these were never formally transferred) and to reap the rewards. The important question which arose is whether it was a public or a private corporation, for its powers fell into the former and its profits into the latter category. Up to the nineteenth century the assumption persisted that all corporations were formed for public purposes. From this it could be argued that the remedies available to ousted officers and disgruntled shareholders were those which are nowadays clearly classified as part of public law: in particular the prerogative writ of *mandamus* issued from the King's Bench to compel the performance of public duties. As we have seen in the preceding sections, the New River's shareholders were on the whole well content; but the great exception, once again, was the black sheep of the family, Simon Myddelton, the founder's youngest surviving son.[18]

Having, in breach of trust, bought the King's moiety (with the consequences described in Chapters 4.2.2 and 5.2), Simon became Treasurer to the Company and promptly 'detained the profits of divers shares'. On being dismissed from office he not only kept the key to the Chest but in 1663 brought *mandamus*

[17] PP 1821 v 242; MWB, *London Water Supply* 25; Metropolis Paving Act 1817.
[18] Kyd ii 291, 319; Grant 271; Impey 38–9; Tapping 170 ff.; Shortt 286 ff.

to be restored to his position. The three printed and three manuscript reports of the case are brief but serve to illustrate the difficulties felt by the law in disentangling notions of private property from public powers. Many an office was a piece of property which, like land itself, could be held for life or in fee and recovered by the procedures available for realty (the appropriate 'assize') or protected against interference by a process ('case') which was not unlike a nuisance action. If, however, the duties and emoluments did not rank as property, then the appropriate private remedy was be to found in the emerging law of contract, while *mandamus* lay to compel performance of a public service on the grounds not merely of an injury to the applicant but of some detriment to the common weal. Simon's application for the writ was supported by Maynard, Attorney-General, on the grounds of the public nature of the company's activities. According to Siderfin (translated from his Law French),

> it was said that was a public office (*lieu de publick*) concerned not only in relation to the King but also to several of his subjects. 1. In relation to the King because this treasurer is accountant to the King for £500 a year as his, being parcel of the profits of the New River which belong to the King. 2. In relation to his subjects, that is citizens or inhabitants of the City of London which is Camera Regis, and experience has well shown of what great advantage this river is to the City.[19]

Counsel for the Company accept that the writ would issue where the office 'concerns any publick administration' but contend that this is merely a private matter and say (as reported by Keble) 'the Court may as well send mandamus to admit one in the Corporation of Mercers'. The court seems to have felt grave doubts. One reason for these was that the application did not disclose whether the office of Treasurer was awarded by private contract or (as is in fact the case) was mentioned in the Charter. A more fundamental difference of opinion was over the public nature of the office. Kelyng J. felt that *mandamus* should lie to restore officers of any corporation. Hyde CJ, how-

[19] CSPD 1664–5, 303, 315, 324; *Middleton's Case* (1663) 1 Sid 169; 1 Lev 123; 1 Keb 625; Kelyng, Linc. Inn Misc. MSS 501, 8 (MF H 1786-582); Cremer, Gray's Inn MSS 34, 499 (MF H 1792-15); Anon., Linc. Inn Misc. MSS 497 (case No. 62) 143–4 (MF H 1786-552).

ever, inclined against the remedy; as reported by Keble, he equated the New River with other 'private corporations for commerce, established by a private Act of Parliament'. Windham J. (according to an anonymous manuscript report) was even more vehement:

> He said he had often heard the judges say that some bound ought to be set to their discretion in granting *mandamus* and the bounds which he had proposed to himself was [*sic*] that whensoever a man was by wrong turned out of any office or franchise that concerned some public work or the administration of justice, he might properly be restored by *mandamus* but for any officer or member of any private corporation to have it would extend so far that he should not be of the opinion to grant them.

Twysden J. appears to have resolved the dispute by proposing that the writ issue so that at a later stage the true nature of the New River and its Charter might be determined. Kelyng J.'s own manuscript note ends by saying 'the writ was granted *de bene esse* to see what they would return but never heard more of it'. Certainly we know that Simon was not restored to the treasurership, for we find him seeking the humbler position of clerk.[20]

After the 1660s the public-utility argument did not become of first importance again until raised by the political scientists of a later age. In fact the very argument that the powers were for the public benefit was used to strengthen the Company's private-law powers. Thus, in 1701 a dispute was litigated between the Company and the freeholder of a field. Earlier the Company had laid pipes through the land and paid the tenant compensation, but on the expiry of the lease the landlord removed them. His defence was based on the words of the statute conferring the powers: they permitted the water to be brought in a trench or vault but said nothing of pipes and provided for supply to London, not to adjacent districts. The court held that

> the Act is to be taken in a liberal sense, that the Town in general might be served with water without regard to its being within or without the liberties of the City; and although a trunk or trench of ten foot wide is mentioned in the Act of Parliament, yet the intent of the act was to give power *in alieno solo* not exceeding ten foot wide

[20] Keb 625, 630, 631; Anon., loc. cit. (above, n. 19).

and therefore decreed a commission to issue to ascertain the damages and the plaintiffs to be quieted in the possession of their pipes.

Similarly, Lord Hardwicke's notebooks show that his attitude to the Company in the Clarendon litigation described in Chapter 5.3 is quite consciously influenced by the fact that the water supply was for the public good.[21]

Simon Myddelton's case found its way into the Abridgments and was occasionally raised in argument in later litigation on the control of companies. In 1695 and 1703 Holt CJ refused to be swayed by the precedent, and denied *mandamus* to a water-bailiff and the clerk to the Butchers' Company; but in 1732 the City's Clerk of Works relied on the case successfully, at least to the extent of obtaining *mandamus* so that the public nature of his office might be determined on the return to the writ. In later years the tide turned and both company officers and shareholders found the courts refusing them this remedy: the most cogent reason was that given by Best J. in 1819—'if we were to grant this rule, we should make ourselves auditors to all the trading corporations in England.'[22]

Despite this reassuring treatment by the courts, the Company was uneasily aware of two further problems: firstly, that it had not expressly been granted the statutory powers transferred by the City to its founder; and secondly, that under the Act it did not strictly own the fee simple in the whole channel of the river. For a while it attempted to obtain Parliamentary recognition of its Charter, but its third and last Bill was thwarted by the Civil War. In 1725 the Company laid its title before Thomas Lutwyche and J. Browne of counsel, and asked their opinion as to whether it would be perfected by a fresh grant from the City of its statutory powers. The junior thought that Hugh Myddelton must have conveyed to the Company

[21] *New River Co* v. *Graves* (1701) 2 Vern 432 (quotation abridged); BL Add. MS 36051, 153.

[22] Viner, *Mandamus* G 5; Nelson, *Mandamus* A 16; Bacon, *Mandamus* C; Comyns, *Mandamus* p. 28. *R* v. *Lee* (1690) 1 Show KB 251; SC sub nom. *Mr Leigh's Case* 3 Mod 332; *Cudmore* (*or Shepheard*) v. *Tripe* (1695) Comb 347; *White's Case* (1703) 6 Mod 18, 3 Salk 332, 2 Ld Ray 1004 (which says that *mandamus* issued); *R* v. *Mayor etc. of London* (1732) 2 TR 182(b); *R* v. *Bank of England* (1819) 2 B & Ald 620 per Best J. at 623. The 1695 case says that *mandamus* was granted to restore the *surveyor* of the New River water and this is repeated in *Turner's Case* (1728) 1 Barn 123 at 135 and by Kyd ii 319, Tapping 170, and Shortt 286. There is no trace of any such litigation and the string of later assertions probably stems from an error in *Tripe's Case*.

the benefit of his powers and recommended a search. Lutwyche had graver doubts: firstly, because the initial grant to Hugh and his heirs was subject to conditions as to time and 'though in equity and justice it may be a sufficient foundation for enjoyment of the same privileges by the Company' it was not impregnable at law; and secondly, because, as the bed belonged to the owners and the powers to Hugh Myddelton, 'I do not see how the *Charter* could vest the New River and the benefit of the water in the Company.' He advised that, as the statutes gave the powers to the City, if 'the City granted them to the Company it will be a sufficient conveyance' but—and then follows what might have been taken for a disreputable hint—'if the grant to Hugh Myddelton by the City appears, I conceive it takes away the force of any subsequent grant by the City.' Both counsel concur that, as the inheritance of the river bed was left with the owners, any action to protect the river must sound in case and not trespass; or, in less technical jargon, be concerned not with an injury to land one owns or occupies but to a right one has over another's land.[23]

The Company followed this advice and in 1726 petitioned the City's Common Council to make

> a new and further grant of the stream and premisses in such terms and on such covenants and agreements as are contained in former grants thereof already made and complyed with.

The City Lands Committee called for an abstract of the Company's title and submitted it to the Recorder and the Common Serjeant for their opinion, but appears to have done no more.[24]

The second problem became acute in dealing with unauthorized use of the water. In 1741 the Company again took counsel's opinion on the question of how to deal with a customer who had opened a brewery in his house, taken more water than he was paying for, and responded to complaints by shutting off sluices which controlled the supply elsewhere. The normal method of dealing with such conduct was to cut off the water, but the house in question abutted the river. The point was specifically raised that

[23] CJ i 611, 745, ii 554; M A/19.

[24] Sharpe ii 27–8; City Records, Jo. lvii 143b–144; City Lands Committee xix 28, 39b.

Fifty Pounds Reward.

WHEREAS the PLUGS on the NEW RIVER PIPES in HOLLOWAY, have frequently been drawn without the knowledge of the Company, or their Servants, which has prevented many of their Tenants from receiving a regular supply of Water: The NEW RIVER COMPANY, hereby, offer a

Reward of Fifty Pounds

to any one, who will give information against such Person, or Persons, by whom they may have been drawn, so that he or they may be prosecuted to Conviction.

I. P. Rowe, Sec.

New River Office.
Aug. 1, 1811

Printed by T. Woodfall, Villiers St. London.

Fig. 9

the Company seem only to have a right to the running of this stream of water, but the soil under the river and the banks and the heritage thereof seem to be reserved in the proprietors.

Counsel (Edward Bootle) advised that the correct form of action was not trespass but 'a special action on the case'.[25]

Apart from Parliament, the City, and the courts, the other authority that might be used to secure the Company's status was the Crown. The advisers to James I had been wary of exercising the power of proclamation, and he proclaimed only

[25] TW Strongroom B30, box 86: Counsel's Opinion (Ed. Bootle) 30/4/1741.

that he 'did exceedingly approve and commend the bringing of the New-Streame'. His grandson, however, was happy to favour a company whose Governor was the Earl of Clarendon. The Proclamation of Ladyday 1685 recites the merits of the river, the providence of his grandfather, and the great abuses daily committed, and continues:

> We therefore taking it into our princely consideration that the preservation of the said river is of so great and special consequence are graciously pleased by this our Royal Proclamation with the advice of our Privy Council strictly to charge and command that all the grants clauses and restrictions in the said Acts, letters patent and other our orders and proclamations be carefully observed obeyed and performed
>
> And we strictly prohibit and forbid all and singular the inhabitants of London Hertford and Middlesex and likewise all the plumbers, paviours, and other artificers that without permission they presume not to intermeddle with the said works or pipes nor shall fetch or carry the said water out of the said river or otherwise hinder waste consume disturb infect abuse or corrupt the said river by fishing watering of cattle keeping of geese or ducks casting of carrion therein
>
> And that the Company have liberty in the daytime in the presence of a constable to search any houses where they shall suspect any breach
>
> Upon pain of our high displeasure and of such pains penalties and punishments as by the laws or our prerogative royal can and may be inflicted.

The substance was repeated in the following year and in 1689 by William and Mary, in 1704 by Anne, and in 1716 by George I. None of these Proclamations, however, solved the problem that the Company found itself running an enterprise that was certainly a public utility but was always very vulnerable to theft, nuisance, vandalism, and improper use.[26]

[26] Larkin, Proclamation 152; NRCD B/182 (quotation abridged), A/33, 35, B/200; GL Proclamations (large) 15/2/1703/4; HMC 6th Rept. ix 18b.

6.5 Fixed Assets

6.5.1 *Land*

Naturally the Company was interested in acquiring land along the route of the aqueduct, and it will suffice to describe certain transactions selected for their particular legal interest. At the very beginning of the project, Hugh Myddelton took a lease of the land at the head of the river; the story of how the Company ultimately acquired the fee is told in Chapter 5.3. At the source of the water, freehold was acquired early. By a feoffment dated 20 November 1613 Hugh and others took an acre of land in the parish of Amwell, and in 1635 his son and heir, Sir William Myddelton, released the estate to certain of the Adventurers,

> yet upon special trust and confidence that they . . . their heirs and assigns shall and will from time to time and at all times hereafter permit and suffer the rents issues and profits thereof to be had taken and enjoyed by the [Company] and its successors for ever for the only proper use and benefit of the said [Company].[27]

Similarly, in 1670 John Grene (whose problems are described in Chapter 4.4) was admitted as copyhold tenant of three acres in the manor of Little Amwell and the following year executed an indenture with the Company by which he acknowledged that 'the sum of four-score pound paid by him was the proper money of the Company', confirmed that his admission was in trust for the Company, and covenanted to surrender to them on request the copyhold title. Likewise, in 1699 he took a conveyance by lease and release of 2 acres at Chadwell Mead and expressly declared himself trustee for the Company.[28]

On many occasions, however, the title is transferred direct to the Company, whether it be the 800-year lease of Lady Meadow near Ware which it bought from John Leonard in 1670 or the innumerable purchases made in the latter half of the eighteenth century of land along the route of the river. On one occasion (in 1737/8), when the owner was an infant, a private Act of Parliament was required. The statute secured for the Company a vital advantage in its claims to access to the River

[27] NRCD C/261, 266; GL MS 2884/23.
[28] NRCD A/71, C/269.

Lea and incidentally was the first parliamentary recognition of its corporate existence. After prudently taking counsel's opinion in 1736 that it was proper for a company incorporated by charter to take a conveyance by lease and release, the Company began to acquire more land, including many acres of the prebendary manor of Stoke Newington, and by 1825 was able to construct the reservoirs which now cover the area. The N. & E. Railway, however, insisted—as late as 1845—on conveying its unneeded land to the Company by feoffment with livery of seisin.[29]

Not all the land so acquired was essential for the purposes of the waterworks and the members of the Company also seem to have had an eye for a good bargain. This was particularly true of the Holford family, three of whose members were Governors for some eighty years between the 1720s and 1827. When, for instance, the South Sea Bubble burst, Robert Holford showed a keen entrepreneurial spirit. Statutes of 1720 first forbade the officers to leave the country and then provided for the forced sale of their assets. Holford, encouraged by Jasper Bull, the energetic company Secretary, bought a number of houses near the Strand and Fleet Street, though their acquisition was hardly necessary to improve the water supply. He died in 1753 and his son and heir Peter, also Governor, acknowledged that the purchase price had come from New River funds 'and the name of Robert Holford was made use of only in trust for the Company' and conveyed the legal title to the latter. Similarly, soon after the Commandery Mantles were finally acquired in 1734 (Chapter 5.3), Robert Holford used corporate money to acquire eleven houses in St James's, Clerkenwell, which he then held for the Company.[30]

Thus, the Company's property holdings began to fall into two categories: that used for the ever-increasing needs of the largest water supplier in Europe and the separate 'landed estates'. For the reasons given earlier (section 6.2) the decision was taken in 1811 to use iron in place of the traditional elm for the water-pipes. The incidental effect on the Commandery Mantles is vividly described in the words of the Company Engineer, W. C. Mylne:

29 NRCD A/35, 100, 110, 119, 152, B/202, D/330, E/290, 312, 603, F/127, 557; TW, terrier 2232; Byde Act 1737; Stoke Newington Prebendary Act 1830.

30 South Sea Acts 1720; NRCD A/100, C/212–14.

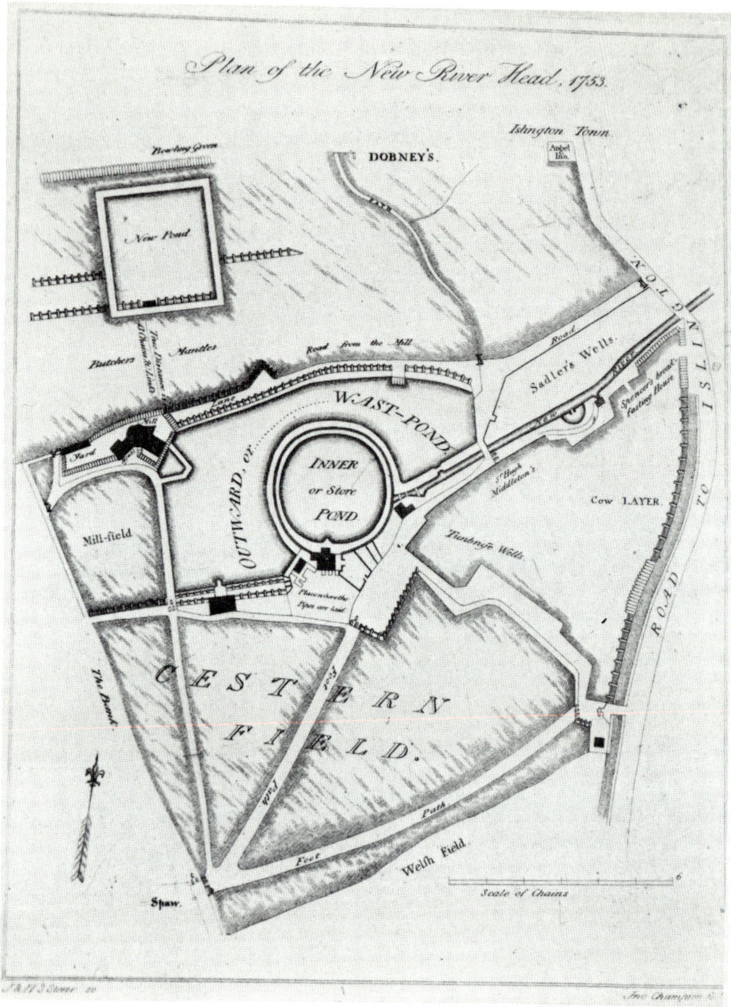

FIG. 10

Around that little centre [the New River Head] the Company were compelled to buy 50 acres of land, Sir Hugh Myddelton not having secured sufficient . . . The pipes multiplied very rapidly, none of them being larger than seven inches in diameter; there were hundreds of them and they covered those 50 acres like the threads of a garment almost. When we came to use iron, that land only let as grass land at about £500 a year. When I was enabled to put it into iron, I took care to carry the trunk mains along the land in the lines in which streets could be laid out; the whole of that ground which we had been compelled to buy, producing £500 a year, is now let at ground-rents, producing a return of £4,000 a year.

This origin of the Clerkenwell development can be read in the street names to this day: Myddelton Passage, Myddleton Square, Amwell Street, and so on. Mylne administered the whole scheme of building-leases, usually of 99 years, and for this reason the Company, on giving the site for the church in the square, explained how gratified they would be to see him its architect. The ecclesiastical authorities took the hint and he designed St Mark's.[31]

The Company divided the increased income along with its water rents, although it did show some signs of using the fund for special purposes (see section 6.6). As will be explained in Chapter 7.7, however, the Metropolis Water Act 1871 enjoined separate accounting, and the results will be seen for the years 1872 onward in Appendix I. Other landholdings on the route of the river which turned out not to be required for the water-works were also developed, and here the Company had a particular advantage: in the early nineteenth-century building plans it was thought that the gravel strata generally determined the site of all but the poorest housing because that marked the limit of natural springs of water; and certainly the development along the New Road (in Euston and Marylebone) coincides with the edge of the 'Taplow terrace', where the river gravel gives way to London clay. But of course the Company's sites did not need to depend on springs for they had the New River itself near at hand.[32]

The Company's own land, if suitable, was also used to sink the dozen or so wells which helped the New River to satisfy the ever-growing demands of nineteenth-century London. In this endeavour the anachronistic structure was of great assistance. The competitors—entirely the creature of statute—found their powers of abstracting underground water limited; but, so long as the well could be sunk on its own land and financed without recourse to Parliament, the Company could exercise the privi-

[31] PP 1851 xv Q 11848; M 21/11/1822. St Mark's is now open only on Sundays at 10 a.m.

[32] Tindal 111; Garnett 110.

leges of an ordinary landowner. The Board therefore rejoiced at the decision of the House of Lords in *Chasemore* v. *Richards* (1859) which held—distinguishing the earlier cases on merely statutory powers—that the landowner exercising his common-law rights need have no regard for their effect on his neighbours' water. A year later this precedent was sufficient to protect the Company against a plaintiff whose well had run dry because of their Hertford drainage works. The inhabitants of the area were much aggrieved by both these rulings and even dreamed of their reversal by Parliament.[33]

6.5.2 *Installations*

The details of the pipes, engines, tumbling-bays, and other devices installed by the company do not belong in a book of legal history, and only a few points need be made. In the first place, the Company had the wisdom to acquire the services of excellent engineers. Edward Pond, whose name appears as witness to the 1613 receipt printed at Appendix C.3, was a mathematician and compiler of almanacs who worked for Hugh Myddelton (at £2. 6*s*. 8*d*. a week) from 1611 until 1613 and showed great skill in surveying the course of the river so that it fell only between 2 and 5 inches a mile; his Almanac was amended to describe him as 'the sole Artist' of the scheme.

Later the New River was served by engineers (called 'surveyors') who combined great ability with long life. Under John White (*c*.1691–1720) was built the Upper Pond at the northern edge of the Mantles, and a small pumping station to drive the water to it from the Round Pond. This was powered first by wind, then by horses, later by engine; the stump of what is clearly a windmill may still be seen. He was followed by Henry Mill (inventor of a typewriter), who held the position until 1762 and was succeeded by Robert Mylne, FRS, winner of the Prix de Rome and designer (to the great disgust of Dr Samuel Johnson) of Blackfriars Bridge. The Minute Books show how he rebuilt the New River Head and took control of the engineering, installing Boulton & Watt pumping engines which not only enabled the water to be forced to higher levels but

[33] *Chasemore* v. *Richards* (1859) 7 HLC 349; *New River Co* v. *Johnson* (1860) 2 El & El 435; PP 1900 xxxviii pt. 2, 597.

kept a record of the quantity supplied; it is also clear that he started the tradition which spread to all the London companies, namely that the 'engineer' was in reality the commercial manager. He died in 1811 aged 78 and was succeeded by his son William Chadwell Mylne (the middle name shows the family loyalty), who lived until 1862.

William's was the technical mind behind the replacement of the old elm pipes with those of iron, the construction of the Stoke Newington reservoirs, improvements in the course of the river, and many other innovations both of engineering and enterprise. In addition he found time to defend the water against the Fenians (as had his father against the Gordon rioters), give evidence to several Parliamentary Committees, and to win the contract and finance to supply water to the City of Paris; but for this last project, as he frequently complained, he could not get a signature on the necessary official papers. The skills were continued in his sons: Robert succeeded to his father's office as trustee of some of the Company's copyhold land and William became its river engineer.[34]

The second way in which the Company acquired installations was by taking over the stock of defeated competitors. Forde's waterworks were the first to fall when in 1657, with the approval of the Privy Council, the Company bought (for £6,100) the powers under Cromwell's Letters Patent and the pipes in the streets around the Strand, Drury Lane, and Bow Street, and took over the leases of the warehouses; the legal implications for the nature of the shares of this increase in the Company's fixed assets are discussed in Chapter 5.2. In 1691 the York Buildings Company was formed as a water supplier with first twelve and then forty-eight shares. It diversified into mining, ironworks, and Jacobinism and competed, with dwindling success, until in 1810 it raised extra capital with the idea, as their secretary put it, that they 'could make a fortune as the New River had done'. The scheme foundered, small dividends

[34] Gough 50–1; S. Lewis 430 is wrong about Mill's length of service; Boswell i 351; Stringer 30–7; M 15 and 20/10/1758, 17/3/1769, 11/8/1769, 4/7/1777, 25/7/1811, 25/1/1816, 14/12/1867; PP 1851 xv 810. Robert Mylne is buried in St Paul's crypt, near Christopher Wren. For much of his period of service, W. C. Mylne's salary was £830 a year. About John White (surveyor *c.*1691–1720) little is known except his epitaph in St Andrew's, Enfield, which begins 'Here lies John White who, day by day, / On river walks did use much clay; / Is now himself turning that way.'

were paid out of capital, and in 1818 the New River took over its mains, fixtures, and of course its customers, in the Strand. Its reservoirs now lie beneath Charing Cross railway station.[35]

The London Bridge waterworks (begun in 1579) fell in 1822, giving the New River virtually a monopoly of the City supply, and the Company added a pumping engine at Broken Wharf in order to use the Thames if their own sources failed in time of drought. The Hampstead Aqueducts Waterworks had begun when, in 1692, the City leased its statutory powers under the Act of 1543 (see Chapter 1.1) to a group which included William Paterson, better known as a founder of the Bank of England. In the 1850s the New River was anxious to extend its own supply into the area from Camden Town to Hampstead and came to an arrangement under which it would provide the aqueduct owners with a redeemable annuity of £4,200 and buy the leasehold interest in the reservoirs. The takeover was formally completed in 1861 and the Company attempted to acquire the freehold from the City; when this failed, the Adventurers consoled themselves with the thought that at the end of their term they would relinquish merely empty reservoirs. The lease expired in 1936 but the Hampstead ponds remain.[36]

6.6 Loan Capital

In the early nineteenth century, faced with the need to raise the capital required to change 400 miles of piping from wood to iron, the Adventurers' first instinct was to borrow from themselves and the King's shareholders. In 1811 and 1812 the General Court decided to raise first £1,000 and then a total of £28,800 at 5 per cent, secured by bond, with the principal being repaid out of a fund set up from the Clerkenwell ground rents and some miscellaneous sales. The total figure is easily divisible by 72 and we then find bonds being sealed showing that each owner of an entire share could lend up to £400, or up to £100 for holders of a quarter. The Holfords, the Berners,

[35] NRCD A/1, B/196, 197, 208, F/674, 824; M8/2/1815, 29/1/1819, 8/7/1819; GCM 24/11/1818; PP 1821 v 55, 1828 ix 56, 1851 xv Q 11513. The effect of competition by the York and Hampstead rivals can be seen in the dividends from 1693: Appendix I.

[36] M 25/5/1820, 23/5/1822, 30/5/1822, 18/12/1849, 29/4/1852, 15/5/1852; GCM 21/11/1861.

and the Goldsmiths all lent the maximum, but the total authorized by this method was quite inadequate.[37]

No outside investor would lend at favourable rates without security. There was naturally no provision in the Charter for the issue of debenture stock, but we have seen that by 1810 a great deal of land had been acquired and, as has been amply demonstrated in Chapters 5.3 and 6.5.1, had always been conveyed to the Company or to its trustees. Yet, from the juridical point of view, the New River was a strange creature. Its oddities would not perturb a seller who would simply convey as directed and take the money. Mortgagees, however, can afford to be even more punctilious in their examination of title than buyers, and in the heyday of the Industrial Revolution there were plenty of other outlets for capital investment. Now the shares themselves were real property and, as has been demonstrated at length, were taken to confer rights over the land itself. It was quite possible, therefore, that a prudent lender would want to peruse the title both to the land and the shares, and would insist on there being joined as parties to his mortgage every holder of each King's and Adventurers' share and—worse still—of every fraction of a share, including those who, like William Hammond, held six-twentieths made up of one-eighth, one-twentieth, and one-eighth acquired under three different titles, and Mr and Mrs Perot, who owned $\frac{1}{3456}$ of a share worth about £5. Given the inevitable cluster of infancies, entails, insanities, errors, fear of incurring personal liability, and simple obduracy, the transaction costs would have been vast.[38]

The Company therefore sought the advice of learned counsel, namely Samuel Romilly. They explained that the projected expenditure could not possibly be defrayed from income and that they proposed to borrow on mortgage, invest the loan in capital improvements, pay the mortgage interest out of revenue, and, since the commitments of a capital nature which had always been financed out of income would cease, invest a further part of the revenue in a sinking fund to pay off the principal advanced. Their question was simply

> Whether the New River Company under their Corporate Seal can make a good and effectual mortgage of their lands for raising money

[37] M/GC 12/12/1811, 30/1/1812, 16/4/1812, 28/5/1812; GCM 18/1/1821.

[38] Above, Chapter 4.2.1.

for the above purpose, and if so whether it will be justified not only in keeping down the interest but in retaining a reasonable proportion of the annual profits to form an accumulating fund towards discharging the principal for otherwise there will be no possible means of doing this but by actual sale of the mortgaged estate or submitting to a foreclosure;

Or cannot such purpose be effected without the express consent (were it possible to acquire it) of every individual proprietor as well of King's shares as of Adventurers' shares;

Or can any means be devised . . . without the aid of Parliament?

The Opinion received was short, straightforward, and exactly what the Company wanted:

The Corporation has a right to sell or to mortgage its estates in order to raise money for any purposes that it may think proper and it would not in my opinion be incumbent on a purchaser or mortgagee to enquire for what purposes the money was raised.

A conveyance under the corporate seal affixed to it by those who have lawful authority to do so would give an effectual title to a purchaser or mortgagee and I think that by the charter the Board have authority so to affix the seal.

I am also of opinion that the Board acting in the making such sale or mortgage bona fide for the benefit of the Company according to the best of their judgment will not be liable to be called upon as for a breach of trust by any individual proprietors in respect of such conduct and I think that the Board will be justifiable in not only keeping down the interest of any mortgage they may make out of the annual profits but in retaining a further part of the profits as an accumulating fund towards discharging the principal.

It does not occur to me that there is any other mode by which the plan that has been suggested can be carried into execution than that of mortgaging or selling part of the Company's estates.

Saml Romilly
Lincoln's Inn
Nov 4 1811[39]

Armed with this advice the Company was ready to borrow, and found an unexpected ally in the Chancellor of the Exchequer. Towards the end of the Napoleonic Wars, the Government

[39] NR: Case to Counsel (Samuel Romilly) with Opinion endorsed 4/11/1811; M/GC 16/6/1811, 7/11/1811.

were growing perturbed at the slump in business of the iron foundries, particularly in Staffordshire. W. C. Mylne met Vansittart, who 'failing to have the money, gave us an introduction to the Bank of England'. This led to an arrangement which, save that banks now open credit lines instead of discounting bills of exchange, is in essentials of the same structure as those widely used today throughout the Western world. Details of the scheme were put to a General Court on 13 December 1816 and the necessary approval and authorities to officers were conferred. The Bank of England agreed to finance the project to a limit of £150,000. The suppliers (mainly Fereday & Co.) drew bills on the Company which were accepted by the Treasurer on its behalf; the Bank discounted the bills, provided they were certified to be issued 'for iron castings as per invoice transmitted', and agreed to delay presenting them to the Company for payment so long as interest was paid and security given. On 13 February 1817 the Company sealed a penal bond for £300,000 and executed a mortgage to the bank. Three holdings were transferred as security. The Commandery Mantles (see Chapter 5.3) and the land in Hertford acquired under the Byde Act (section 6.5.1) were conveyed by Robert Holford (the third of the family to be Governor), who was then trustee for the Company; and the latter assigned the residue of the 1,000-year lease which it had taken in 1757 from the Duke of Dorset of its head office premises at Dorset Yard. The mortgage deed permitted the Company to retain possession and gave it powers of leasing for terms of up to twenty-one years; the Bank had power to appoint a receiver of the rents and profits in case of default. The loan was to be paid off by instalments over ten years beginning three years after each bill discounted fell due, and interest on the sum outstanding was computed and discharged yearly. The scheme worked perfectly smoothly and in 1830 the mortgaged land was reconveyed to the Company and the seal torn off the bond.[40]

Twenty years later, as will be explained in Chapter 7, the supply of drinking water was being accepted as merely part of a whole complex of services which included drainage, sanitation, and sewage. The Company wished to widen parts of the

[40] NR: Bond and mortgage of 13/2/1817; M/GC 5/11/1816, 13/12/1816; PP 1851 xv Q 11776.

river, to install filtration plants at Stoke Newington, build other reservoirs in Islington and drains in Enfield, and construct a communication network. To acquire the requisite compulsory purchase powers a special Act of Parliament was needed, and the New River Company's Act received the royal assent in 1852 on the same day as a batch of statutes dealing with the other water companies. The statute deemed the share capital to be £1,519,958, and the crucial significance of this special Act will be explained in Chapters 7 and 8. Here we are concerned with the sections, added merely to facilitate the new works, which authorized the Company to borrow up to £250,000 for that purpose and up to another £150,000 for 'the general purposes of the undertaking'. The only method authorized was by bond, and the point to be emphasized is that (although there was a standard saving clause for the rights under the Charter) the Company did not rely on any general common-law power it might have but obtained specific statutory permission.

In 1854 (for reasons explained in Chapter 7.6), the Company obtained a Hertford (Sewage Diversion) Act and again added a section enabling it to borrow on bond up to another £100,000. In the same session an Act authorized the construction of other Middlesex reservoirs and the raising of a further £20,000 on bond. Both these statutes incorporated the Lands Clauses Consolidation Act 1845 and parts of the 1847 Waterworks Clauses Act, and were subject to the general Metropolis Water Act 1852; but neither they nor any subsequent statute expressly saved the Company's position under its Charter.

So far all three of the Company's statutes have been mainly to acquire compulsory powers to carry out public works, with the borrowing powers added because it was no doubt simpler to point a lender to the legislation than to rehearse the charter and the long history. Its 1857 Act, however, is expressed to be 'to enable the New River Company to raise a further sum of money'. It recalls that the earlier statutes authorized the raising of £700,000, recites that 'it is expedient that the company should be empowered to raise a further sum of money for the purposes of their undertaking', and states that the proposed new sewers in Hertford will cost £2,000—this must be a misprint for £20,000. The preamble ends 'But the objects aforesaid cannot be effected without the authority of Parliament.'

The statute then permits the raising of an additional £30,000 on bond. It also enables the Company to issue debenture stock in lieu of the bond debt, allocate it primarily to the lenders thereof, and offer any residue on the market. Section 9 contains a clause which was commonplace in legislation affecting purely statutory enterprises:

To the extent of the total amount of the debenture stock for the time being created, the powers of the company for borrowing or reborrowing money shall be extinguished.

The problem with this ill-drafted sentence is that it is not clear whether it merely abolishes the previous *statutory* borrowing powers or whether it does away with all those powers under the Charter which had been affirmed by Romilly and utilized so successfully. The Company's Act of 1879 (followed by others in 1896 and 1897) somewhat disingenuously recites that the section quoted extinguished the '*special*' powers of borrowing and they go on to authorize the issue of more debenture stock. Meanwhile, however, the Company decided to appeal to another type of investor.

6.7 Equity Capital

The statute of 1866 which authorized a new share issue was short and simple. It recited that the £1m. authorized by the legislation described above had been borrowed and spent and that the raising of share capital required an Act of Parliament. The present structure of the company was described—with thirty-six 'original shares' in each of the two moieties and a capital (as declared by the 1852 Act) of £1,519,958, giving a value per share of £21,110. 10*s*. 6½*d*. The Company was authorized to raise £500,000 in £100 shares, to be first offered *at par* to holders of the original shares and then on the market. The new shares were subject to calls (for £80), for which the company could 'sue . . . in any court of competent jurisdiction', ranked for dividend equally with the old, were evidenced by share certificates registered in the usual modern way, and were declared to be personalty, not realty. Their holders were not given votes, but this proved no deterrent and within a decade all the new equity capital had been paid up and the shares were standing at over £200.[41]

As will be explained in Chapter 7.10.2, the Company's Parliamentary attempts to raise capital in the last two decades of the century found themselves subject to financial control. The Attorney-General's opinion was sought as to whether the New River could not return to the days of Romilly and raise money by mortgage at common law. Whatever might have been the legal position, however, economic and political pressure prevented this simple solution. Thus, at the end of its life as a public-utility company, the New River's equity capital comprised the nominal value of the original shares declared by the 1852 Act to be £1,519,958 and the new shares of £500,000. Its loan capital was by then all in statutory debenture stock of just over £2m.; and other debenture stock had been issued jointly with other companies to finance the Staines Reservoirs and intercommunication works.[42]

6.8 Taxation

6.8.1 *Poll tax*

The poll tax statutes of the early Stuarts levied the sums due on the nobility, office-holders in the Church, the Law, the City, the twelve great, and then the lesser, City companies, and the mysteries, and on everyone who could 'dispend £100 of his own'. On the accession of William, however, the new forms of corporate enterprise are recognized. The statute of 1688 begins with a list like that given above but then adds:

> Every member in the East India Company shall pay for his share or shares which he hath in the joint-stock of the said company four shillings for every £100 according to the first capital of the said stock.

The tax is thus at 1*s*. in the £ on an assumed return of 4 per

[41] New River Company's Act 1866 (the statute miscites the Company's 1857 Act). Fry Arbitration Transcript, Table of Net Profits.

[42] NR: Case to Counsel (R. E. Webster A-G & V. Hawkins) 23/11/1891; Fry Arbitration Transcript, Table W.P.1.

cent; payment is to be made by the Company's officers and deducted from dividends. The Guinea and Hudson's Bay companies are treated in the same way, so that a proportion of the nominal value of the share is used as the basis of calculation. Once again, the New River is an anomaly, for (until 1852) no figure can be given as the value of each of its seventy-two shares. Consequently, the statute, after dealing with the trading companies, clears up the position of the merchant stranger and the Jew, and ends its charging provisions with:

> Each and every person and persons having any share or shares or interest in the fresh stream of running water brought to the North parts of the City of London commonly called the New River, or any rents or profits arising thereby, shall pay for the same two shillings for every twenty shillings of the yearly value thereof.

It is thus a tax assessed directly on income but, curiously enough, there is no provision for payment by the Company and deduction from dividends, so (despite the nature of their shares) the shareholders fell under the general clauses for personalty requiring assessment by the Commissioners for the taxpayer's place of abode. As will be demonstrated in the next subsection, the Land Tax Act passed six weeks later adopted exactly the same basis of assessment, which continued (at varying rates) until this century or earlier voluntary redemption. Under the latter statute, however, payment was to be made initially by the Company and then deducted. The same technique was then adopted in the second and all later poll tax Acts of the reign, and the section on the New River, the other waterworks, and the King's Printing House is virtually identical in the two different sets of legislation. The trading companies continued to be treated in a separate section, so at least the New River escaped the tax on their joint stock levied by 4 & 5 William & Mary, c. 14.[43]

The use of the poll tax as a fiscal instrument lasted only until 1698 but gave rise to events which are worthy of brief mention. The first concerns Thomas Vincent, who had been patiently waiting for Elias Ashmole to die, having been promised the latter's office as Comptroller of Excise. When Ashmole died

[43] Poll tax: 16 Chas. I, cc. 3, 8; 1 Will. & Mar., c. 13; 2 Will. & Mar., c. 2; 3 Will. & Mar., c. 6; 4 Will. & Mar., c. 15; Dowell ii 46, iii 6. Land tax: 1 Will. & Mar., c. 20; sess. 2, cc. 1, 5; 4 Will. & Mar., c. 1.

(aged 75) in 1692, the lucrative position was bestowed on another and Vincent compensated by a grant of £1,200 out of the New River tax, which had been assessed at £1,800. The second is the natural protest of the Adventurers at what they saw, with some justification, to be double taxation. The surviving notes for a brief on their behalf point out that the East India, Guinea, and Hudson's Bay companies

are appoynted to be taxed for their share in the joynt stock of the said Company. But all sharers in the New River water are to be taxed in respect of their shares. If it be intended that it should be only in respect of their shares, pray it may be so expressed. If it be intended that each sharer shall by the Poll Bill be rated for the yearly revenue arising by fynes and rents reserved upon leases this seems unreasonable

1 Because they have been rated for their yearly revenue upon every land tax
2 There is no other revenue besides this intended to be rated upon the Poll Bill.[44]

The final curiosity is *Margaret Webster's Case*. The litigant lived in London and was there assessed on the three shares which she owned. Having paid, she then found herself assessed by the Middlesex Commissioners at £1,800, which was approximately 2*s*. in the pound of the Company's entire dividends. At this stage, the only printed report (by Skinner) records that she was held liable to pay but for only her proportion of the dividend. This is bad enough, but the manuscript note of Dodd CB suggests that the Attorney-General argued that the New River shareholders were jointly liable, so that any one of them might be made to pay the whole sum. The Court of Exchequer held that she was liable, but decided to consider further before any enforcement process issued, and this decision was affirmed in the Exchequer Chamber. The State Papers contain her petition to have this ruling reversed in Parliament, endorsed with a note by Samuel Dodd and William Cherry ('we consider this judgment to be erroneous'), and the Solicitor-General later granted the petition.[45]

[44] Dowell ii 46; Ashmole iv 1862, 1870, 1894; CTB 1693–6 pt. ii 565, 6277; PRO SP 16/487 No. 76 (undated; calendared at CSPD 1641–3, 233 *sed quaere*).

[45] Skin 640; Viner, *Taxes* C 1. The MS references are: BL Harg. MS 71, 168; Harvard Law School MS 1169 item 2, 50 (MF H 1776-392); Linc. Inn MSS Misc. 540 and 559, 49 (MF H 1786-844, 869); PRO SP 44, 238, 398–9. See also CTB 1693–6, 627; CSPD 1699–1700, 390–1.

6.8.2 *Land tax*

The 'land tax' introduced on the accession of William and Mary was imposed not only on land but on offices, stock, merchandise, and specie; the name was acquired because land—which could not be concealed—became the principal subject of assessment. An Act (c. 20) of the first session of William and Mary's reign contains the charging clauses at the rate of 1*s*. in the £: the tax falls on, *inter alia*, the 'true yearly value' of land as assessed by the Commissioners (s. 4); and s. 15 provides that

> all and every person having any share or interest in the fresh stream of running water . . . called the New River shall pay for the same the sum of one shilling for every twenty shillings of the clear yearly value thereof.

The value was to be assessed by the London Commissioners, paid initially by the Company but then 'deducted at and out of [the] next dividends'. The scheme does not impose a double tax burden with the Company paying a kind of 'corporation tax' on its assets (under s. 4) and the shareholders an 'income tax' on their dividends under the later section quoted. For the purposes of this tax the Company is indeed a kind of 'reeve or bailiff' liable to nothing itself save the chore of deducting and forwarding land tax at the sums assessed on the dividends. This was assumed to be the situation for centuries and was (in 1904) confirmed to have been correct. There is thus a distinction between the generality of property chargeable under s. 4 which was taxed at an equal rate in the pound so as to make up the quota imposed on each district, and the New River shares which were taxed at a flat rate in the pound.[46]

The charging sections remained virtually unaltered, although the rate was soon increased to two, three, and finally four shillings. The 1692 statute which imposed this last figure also fixed the quotas for each district within the jurisdiction of the several Commissioners at an amount which was rarely altered thereafter. The tax was imposed by annual statutes at rates which varied up to 4*s*. throughout the eighteenth century. In 1798, however, Pitt paused between increasing dog tax and introducing income tax to make land tax perpetual but re-

[46] 1 Will. & Mar., c. 20; *MWB* v. *New River Co* (1904) 20 TLR 687 (HL).

deemable, and this was followed by a consolidating statute of 1802 which, *inter alia*, made it clear that New River shareholders, like the more commonplace landowners, could redeem. The charging sections and district quotas thus prolonged were those of 38 Geo III, c. 5, s. 4 of which was the general, and s. 57, the New River clause. The tax soon dwindled but survived until 1963.[47]

The original Act empowered the owner of land to deduct tax at the appropriate rate 'out of every fee-farm rent and other annual rent or payment charged upon or issuing out of the premises'. This provision formed section 6 and was repeated in some section of all later Acts. Consequently, the Company always deducted land tax from the Clog at the prevailing rate; during the greater part of the centuries after 1689 this was at 4*s*., so that the owner of the Clog received £400. This did not mean, however, that the £100 deducted was transmitted to the Revenue; it was simply set off against the land tax assessed on the shareholders represented by the Company.[48]

In 1692, when the assessment of the 'clear yearly value' of the shares settled into its standard pattern, the dividend on each was just over £255, giving a total for the seventy-two shares of £18,360. At 4*s*. in the £ (and with no allowance for necessary expenditure because this was deducted before declaring the dividend) this would lead to an assessment of £3,600, and indeed the figure did reach this total a hundred years later—though for most of the eighteenth century it was rather less. When documents become available again—for the period after the 1769 fire—the sum assessed is £3,300, and its increase by £300 in 1794 provoked the Company to seek counsel's opinion as to the feasibility of an appeal. They told him, however, that the annual profits were in fact over £30,000 (which, if disclosed, would have led to an assessment of £6,000) and he told them that the Commissioners might administer an oath which it would be 'impolitic to decline'; no appeal seems

[47] 1 Will. & Mar., sess. 2, cc. 1, 5; 4 Will. & Mar., c. 1. Sabine correctly states that the original statute is 1 Will. & Mar., c. 20, and not, as is often supposed, that of 1692 (4 Will. & Mar., c. 1). His account of the rise in the rates from 1*s*. to 4*s*. differs a little from that in the text: Sabine, *Income Tax* 103–7. 38 Geo. III, c. 16 (dogs etc.), c. 60 (land tax); 39 Geo. III, c. 13 (income tax); 42 Geo. III, c. 116 (land tax consolidation); Finance Act 1963, s. 68.

[48] See Chapter 9.3.2.

to have been made. Thereafter the total assessment was always £3,600, with slight additions when the New River took over its rivals (for example, in the 1850s it was £3,627).[49]

The sum of £3,600 is easily divisible by 72, and from 1794 until 1904 (or earlier redemption) land tax at £50 a share was deducted from each annual dividend. But of course the dividends grew progressively larger, so that the standard figure represented an ever smaller percentage, while the remorseless application of arithmetic forced the owner of the Clog to bear the tax always at the full rate. The Company thus deducted £100 from the annual £500 and set this against the assessment of £3,600. The unfairness of this led the tenant for life of the Clog to Lord Eldon's court in 1805, with the result recounted in Chapter 9.3.2.

The statutes of 1798 and 1802 provoked redemption of the tax by many holders of full shares and fractions. The scheme required the person redeeming to contribute, by instalments, the amount needed to buy 3 per cent Consols yielding 110 per cent of the land tax. Thus, as each share was assessed at £50, the capital required to produce £55 was fixed at £1,833. 6*s*. 8*d*. The Acts also contain provisions enabling the land tax to be sold, and indeed they attempt to set up a kind of national mortgage market for dealings in the annual sums secured by the charging clauses of 38 Geo III, c. 5. In the New River documents there is no trace of this actually occurring, so that possible problems created by the section which declared the land tax redeemed or bought to be personalty did not arise.[50]

So far we have considered only the land tax imposed on the notional income accruing to shareholders. It will be recalled however, that the Company acquired land along the route of the river which fell under the general charging clauses, being assessed at its net yearly value for tax by the appropriate local Commissioners. After 1798 the Company redeemed much of this tax, but seems never to have done so for the tax on the river bed itself. For the assessment of the Company's landed estates it was treated like any other landowner, but it proved much more difficult to see how the property used for the water

[49] NR: Case to Counsel (Samuel Marryat) with Opinion endorsed 25/11/1794; case cited below, n. 51.

[50] 38 Geo. III, c. 60; 42 Geo. III, c. 116; NR: Redemption Certificates.

supply should be dealt with, since it could be argued that this suffered its tax burden under the section charging the shares. The Commandery Mantles, for instance, on which stood the major works for the distribution of the water, was never assessed by the Middlesex commissioners. In 1854, however, the Hertford commissioners, for the first time ever, assessed the river running through Great Amwell. By then the Company owned about 15 acres in the district, but had redeemed the tax on most of the area.

A special case was stated which came before the Exchequer Division in 1857; the court was asked the simple question of whether the river was rateable to the Hertford land tax and, if so, to how much. Serjeant Byles, for the Company, recalled what had long been forgotten: that the founding statute (Appendix A.1) conferred power to acquire only the 'use and liberty' of the watercourse, leaving the inheritance in the owners, and therefore 'in respect of the bed of the river, the company has only an easement'. He then cited the great lawsuits (see Chapter 4.2.2) which established that the shares were realty, and argued that therefore 'the individual corporators have the property, the corporation having only the management of it' and that property was already being taxed at 4*s*. in the £ by the section devoted to the New River Company; thus, if the Hertford assessment stood 'the property will pay a double tax'. In reply it was argued, rather faintly, that the shares were taxed as personal property but the land itself, though covered with water, was to be taxed under the general clauses; Pollock CB intervened to say that if this were correct 'it has taken a century and a half to find it out'. Counsel for the Commissioners also objected to the suggestion that the Company held a mere easement by recalling the socage tenure provisions of the Charter (see Chapter 3.1) and Martin B. interjected the comment that 'the case of the New River is quite peculiar: it is a chartered company the members of which are held to be seised of the property; I believe that there is no other corporation in the Kingdom similarly circumstanced.'[51]

After deliberation, the court's judgment was delivered by Pollock CB. He held that all the Company's property held in

[51] *New River Co* v. *Herts Land Tax Commissioners* 26 LJ (Ex) 281 at 84; (1857) 2 H & N 127 at 138, 139, 140, 141.

1798 (including, of course, the river) was taxed only by the special section in the charging clauses of the Act of that year which was then made perpetual; but that property bought thereafter was taxable where situated. Thus, the difficult question of the assessment of the local value of the land used to supply London with water did not require an answer, but the Chief Baron had earlier indicated his view that 'the land is worth nothing except as a waterway and as a waterway it is assessed in London'.[52]

6.8.3 *Income tax*

The first 'duties on income' statute of 1799 (39 Geo III, c. 13) does not expressly include waterworks in Schedule A I, which is where one would expect to find it among the rules in case 12 dealing with mines. They were not added in the amending Acts which followed (39 Geo III, cc. 22, 42, and 72), although the first of these added to mines (in what had become case 10) 'insurance offices from fire'. They may be comprised in the final phrase of those cases, namely 'other profits of uncertain annual amount', but in any event it was left to the taxpayer to make a general declaration of his income.[53]

Addington's Act of 1803 changed the system from being a tax on income received to one imposed at the source of the income. 'Water works and streams of water' are charged (at 1*s*. in the £ of the annual value) along with other land in Schedule A. This provision, however, is appropriate to the private landowner, so ss. 101 and 102 enact that income from water supplies owned by a company should be assessed by the Commissioners for the company's head office as profits of a trade under case 3 of Schedule D. The principle of deduction at source was set out in s. 208 and has changed little ever since. Similarly, the ancestor of the modern tax return is to be found in Schedule G 6, where the form to be delivered by the taxpayer lists income according to its sources and includes that from 'streams of water'. The 1806 Act brought all waterworks under Schedule A, charging the tax (at 2*s*. in the £) on the company,

[52] (1857) 2 H & N at 143.
[53] Sabine, *Income Tax* 30.

and allowing it to be deducted from dividends. This method lasted until 1815 when, with the French wars over, the taxation of incomes came to an end.[54]

In 1842, Peel reintroduced the tax (at 7*d.* in the £); it was, he said, 'for a time to be limited'. His legislation is a close copy of the 1806 Act, which, thus revived, has been with us ever since. Companies were charged to the tax and allowed to deduct from dividends (ss. 40, 54) with the annual profits of waterworks and streams being classed under Schedule A III and assessed in the district of the Head Office on a preceding-year basis. The dividends in Appendix I are given after deduction of income tax.[55]

6.8.4 *Rating*

Like many substantial landowners, the New River Company was involved in frequent disputes about the imposition of that form of property taxation known first as 'the poor's rate' and later, when this instrument came to be used for other purposes of local improvement, simply 'the rates'. It will suffice to deal only with those problems whose solution contributed to a development of general principles of this branch of the law.

Innumerable local statutes dating from the fifteenth century and enduring until 1925 imposed liability to contribute to such facilities as those afforded by sea defence, river maintenance, surface drainage ('sewers'), bridges, gaols, and the like. It was, however, the Poor Relief Act of 1601 (which lasted until 1967) which imposed a kingdom-wide and relatively uniform liability. On this was then grafted most of the taxation for other amenities of local government, especially in the field of public health and safety. The introduction of the special water rate assessment in the 1880s will be discussed in Chapter 7.9; here the main point to be made is that the 1601 Act merely required the authorities in a parish 'to raise . . . by taxation of . . . every occupier of lands . . . competent sums of money for and towards the necessary relief of the lame, impotent, old, blind and . . . poor'.

[54] 43 Geo. III, c. 122; 46 Geo. III, c. 65; *Exposition, passim*; Sabine, *Income Tax* 118.
[55] 5 & 6 Vict., c. 35; Inspector-General . . ., *Guide, passim*; Sabine, *Income Tax* 122–3; M 20/10/1853, 5/10/1854.

With no statutory guidance whatever as to how the 'competent sums' were to be assessed, the courts gradually deduced the principle that it should be based not on the profits of the land raised within the rating area, but on its annual rental value as a base from which profits might be made elsewhere. It is this principle which enables houses near London to be rated more highly, even though the accommodation they afford and the services with which they are provided are similar to those in the provinces. This emerges clearly from the 1813 case of *R* v. *New River Company*. The Company had long owned some two acres at the source of the river; their land formed the basin surrounding the Chadwell spring and held the early stages of the watercourse itself. They were rated for Little Amwell on an annual value of £300. It was accepted, however, firstly that the land itself, disregarding the water, had an annual value of £5, and secondly that the Company took no benefit *within the parish* from the water. None the less, the King's Bench unanimously and unhesitatingly held that the assessment was correct. A passage from the judgment of Bayley J. is worth quoting for, as will be shown in Chapter 10.5.2, his argument is evoked in the later leading cases which settled the modern notion of a company share:

> I think it is clear that the company are liable to be rated for the spring, which is part of the produce of the land. The company have the means of carrying this produce to market, where it affords a beneficial return; and it can make no difference whether they convey it along a canal or in carts and waggons or by any other mode. It is still the produce of the land which, when brought to market, produces a profit.[56]

Neither counsel nor the Bench, in any of the rating cases, trouble themselves with the problem that it was the shareholders and not the company which owned the land. The importance of the case just quoted is that, by detaching the assessment of the rateable value from the profit produced in the rating district, it leads to the conclusion that the true basis is the estimated rental value of the land. It is this view which informs the principle made statutory in the Parochial Assessments Act 1836 that the 'net annual value' of land for rating purposes is

[56] (1813) 1 M & S 503 at 512, 513; Ryde 268–9.

the rent at which the same might reasonably be expected to be let from year to year, free of all usual tenants rates and taxes . . . and deducting therefrom the probable annual costs of repairs, insurance and other expenses . . .

An even more difficult problem arose just before the Company lost all interest in water. As explained, they had long been taking water from the River Lea and, by the statute of 1738, acquired the Manifold Ditch and permission to divert thereby a certain quantity of water. Under that statute, and various later ones, appropriate payment was made to the Lea Trustees. For decades the rateable value had been assessed at £650, computed by an estimate of the cost of the land and buildings thereon. In 1900, however, a supplemental valuation added a further £3,180 to the rateable value. This was an estimate of the worth of the water to the Company worked out on the basis of the sums payable to the Lea Trustees. In argument before the Divisional Court, the rating authority argued that the right to take the water was part of the value of the land and the question to be asked was what would the New River Company give as a tenant for that right. The court disagreed, distinguishing the 1813 case discussed above on the ground that there the spring was part of the land itself.[57]

This decision was reversed by the Court of Appeal and returned to quarter sessions for an assessment which would take into account the right to abstract water but would not base it on the sums payable under the River Lee Acts. Armed with this, the assessment committee contended successfully that, had the Company not owned the water rights, the capital cost of sinking wells and installing pumps would have been so great that they would gladly have paid £3,180 for the intake from the Lea.[58]

[57] *New River Co* v. *Hertford Union* [1901] 2 KB 620 (Div Ct).

[58] [1902] 2 KB 597 (CA); Ryde 269–72.

CHAPTER 7

The Company (II) The Nineteenth-century Water Question

7.1 Introduction

THE nineteenth century saw four Royal Commissions, dozens of Select Committees, scores of unsuccessful Bills, and over a hundred Acts of Parliament devoted to the metropolitan water supply; at the end of the century it was still in private hands. The matters involved are extremely complex. Firstly, there was the problem of the sources from which the growing conurbation was to obtain so vital a necessity. Secondly, there was the issue of the quality of the water. Epidemics killed thousands in 1832, 1838, 1849, 1853, and 1866; it was not until 1849 that the link between cholera and the water supply was established and only twenty years later was the true mode of propagation of typhoid understood. Thirdly, the disputes about the supply of water raged in committees and lawcourts throughout the century: the two main questions were whether a householder was entitled to demand water at all and whether he could have it all the time or merely for an hour or so each day—only in 1899 did the New River Company provide overall constant supply. Fourthly, assuming that the householder was satisfied with the water delivered to him, the problem of what he was to do with it after use was one which the water companies declined to handle: W. C. Mylne repeatedly told Parliamentary Committees that the New River Company 'never regarded the want of drains as a reason for not laying on water'. The resolution of this conflict introduces the fifth problem: Sir Edwin Chadwick. It was he and his few faithful Benthamite colleagues (such as Southwood Smith, to whom the master bequeathed his corpse) who fought for a scheme now taken for granted: that *water* should be used not merely for household and industrial purposes but also as the motive power for cleansing away human excrement and other refuse. Chadwick's public career was destroyed by this great, if prosaic, cause whose victory was long delayed by its champion's own manner: he displayed, as Finer puts it, 'a glorification of the public official and a contempt for national habits that is extreme even among civil servants. As an administrator he might typify Prussia; in England he is unique.'[1]

Another set of problems concerned the financial control of the water companies as to the capital raised and expended, the revenue earned by water charges, and the dividends declared. And the possibility of public control was greatly hindered by the chaotic state of the administration of London and its suburbs. In the early part of the century the City, of course, had its ancient government which appointed its own Commission of Sewers. Outside that jurisdiction there was no administrative unity whatever. The 'metropolis' meant 300 parishes with their vestries and, operating under some 250 local Acts, innumerable boards, commissioners, trustees, and committees dealing with paving, cleansing, bridges, lighting, and so on. The main drainage was administered by Crown-appointed commissions numbering over 1,000 people and the improvements introduced by Chadwick in 1848 were said by one anonymous pamphleteer a few years later to have 'gained the notoriety of accomplishing nothing'. Even the last twenty years of the century show that the City and the LCC were mutually hostile and the surrounding counties were at odds with both. The final complication is the fact that at crucial moments in the history of the London water question the Government fell: the 1851 bill for amalgamation died with the Whig majority, the plans for public purchase struggled to failure after Gladstone replaced Disraeli in April 1880, as did the City's and LCC's attempts when the Tories took over in June 1895.[2]

Parliament's positive contribution was to enact over a hundred statutes of different classes, almost all of which were passed with no thought for their effect on the others. As a rough systematization, we may distinguish the following:

[1] PP 1850 xxii 141; Finer 235, 301, 475. Charles Dickens complained of 'a blue mountain of Parliamentary inquiry' on the Water Question: *Household Words* 13/4/1850, 49.

[2] Jephson 10; Finer 306; R. A. Lewis 151; *How long is London to be Victimised?* 9; PP 1834 xv *passim*; PP 1842 xxvi 309 ff.

A. PUBLIC AND GENERAL ACTS

1. Statutes covering the whole country which incidentally affected the metropolitan water supply: examples are the Parochial Assessment Act 1836 s. 1; Lands Clauses and Companies Clauses Consolidation Acts 1845; Nuisances Removal Act 1855 ss. 23–8; Sanitary Laws (Amendment) Act 1874 s. 50; Public Health Act 1875 s. 343(5)(3); Conspiracy Act 1875 s. 4; Rivers Pollution Prevention Act 1876; Local Government Act 1888 s. 40(8).

2. Statutes on the water supply of the whole country: Waterworks Clauses Act 1847; Waterworks Clauses (Amendment) Act 1863; Limited Owners' Reservoirs [etc.] Act 1877; Water Companies (Regulation of Powers) Act 1887.

3. Statutes on the metropolitan water supply: Metropolis Water Act 1852; Metropolis Water (Amendment) Act 1871; Water Rate (Definition) Act 1885; Metropolis Water Acts 1897 and 1899.

4. Metropolitan statutes incidentally affecting the water companies: Metropolis Management Act 1855 ss. 109, 111, 114, 115; Metropolis Management Act 1862 s. 67; Metropolitan Fire Brigade Act 1865 s. 32; Metropolis Subways Act 1868 ss. 4–9; Thames Navigation Act 1866 ss. 59–70; Thames Preservation Act 1879 s. 18; Public Health (London) Act 1891 ss. 48–54.

5. City of London Acts incidentally affecting the water companies: Sewers Acts 1848 ss. 55, 56; 1851 s. 48.

B. LOCAL AND PRIVATE ACTS

1. Statutes on rivers: River Lee Acts 1855, 1868, 1874, 1892, 1900; Thames Conservancy Act 1894; London Water Act 1892.

2. Eighty statutes of the metropolitan water companies.

This chapter will attempt to recount the story from the point of view of one enterprise, and it should be said at once that there is a considerable body of evidence to show that it was in many respects a great deal better than its rivals. Both lay and medical opinion approved of the New River water, and the fact that the round pond was drained only every twenty years and the upper pond at the northern edge of the Mantles was never cleaned at all was of little consequence beside the clarified sewage which the other companies brought from the Thames to their customers. Within the Company's district only a third of households received no water at all, which in the first decades of the century was no worse than the rest of London. Further, as we have seen in the preceding chapter, the Company was managed very efficiently since all its corporators were 'directors' and its engineer—in reality its commercial manager—was the extremely able W. C. Mylne. Its charges were by no means the highest and its control of waste the best: for instance, the customers' habit of dealing with defects in their drains by tying down the lavatory chain was prosecuted upon discovery. And the Company invented a durable feature of English plumbing: the overflow pipe from a cistern used to lead into the sink or water-closet; in the latter half of the century, however, the Company insisted that it be fixed so as to project over the back door in such a way that the householder could hardly fail to notice any waste of water. Indeed one can hear the note of pure pleasure in the tone of the Government auditor of 1897 who told the fourth Royal Commission that 'it is marvellous, in going through the accounts to notice the control that is exercised over expenditure'.[3]

7.2 Competition 1805–1815

At the beginning of the nineteenth century the main suppliers of water to London north of the Thames (who had themselves swallowed up many smaller undertakings) were as follows. The New River Company was by far the largest, covering part of the City and Islington and areas west and east thereof. The London Bridge Waterworks supplied the City until it fell to the New River in 1822. The York Buildings Company brought Thames water along the Strand until they were bought up by the New River in 1818 and their owner dissolved by Parliament in 1829, and the Hampstead Aqueducts which provided for the district below Hampstead to Camden Town were finally acquired by the New River in 1861 (see Chapter 6.5.2).[4]

[3] *New River Co* v. *Restall* (1884) and *New River Co* v. *Cole* (1884); *Water* 22/3/84, 9; PP 1852 xii Q 3922; *Water* 16/2/84, letter signed 'Aquarius'; PP 1900 xxxviii pt. 1 Q 14205.

[4] PP 1821 v 23 and Appendices.

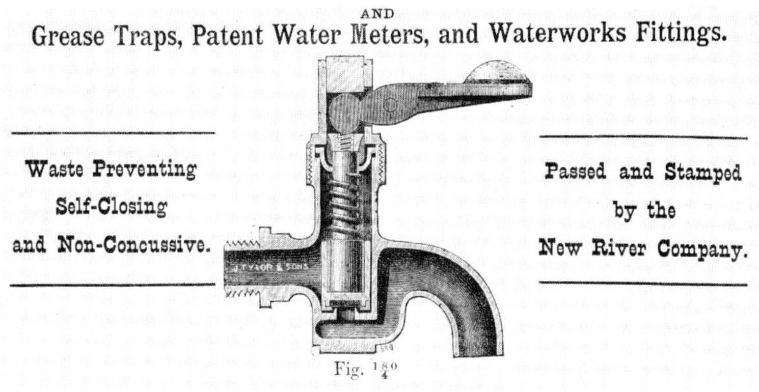

FIG. 11. Advertisement, 1884

The only early undertaking to survive takeover by the New River was the Chelsea Company. Its charter of 1722 was authorized by a statute of the preceding year which simply recited the need to furnish water in Westminster; the incorporation created a company whose structure—compared with that of its older rival—was modern. A capital of £40,000 was to be raised in £20 shares which could be transferred (but not split) by entry in the company's register. Officers were to be elected under a system which awarded one vote for every five shares held and the charter concludes with a standard saving clause for the rights, titles, estates, and so on of the New River, the York Buildings, the City, and any other waterworks, while enjoining them not to damage the new enterprise. The company constructed reservoirs in Green Park, filling them with water taken from the Thames at Chelsea and distributed in Westminster and St James's.[5]

Adam Smith himself had stated that the corporate form was appropriate for only four commercial activities, but had conceded that one of them was 'bringing water for the supply of a great city'. Several bodies, then, began the nineteenth century with permission both to be and to do—to be perpetual corporations and to carry out waterworks—but only the New River and the Chelsea survived. However the growth of popu-

[5] Chelsea Waterworks Act 1721; Charter 8/3/1722 GLMS 173/1. More capital was raised by the Company's 1809 Act.

lation and increased demand for water led to the creation by statute of the West Middlesex Company in 1806 and the East London in 1807, and in the following year the latter bought other works from the London Dock Company. In 1811 a waterworks company was created (of course by statute) to exploit the water supply rights vested in the Grand Junction Canal Company under their earlier Act. South of the Thames were formed the Kent, the Lambeth, and others which later amalgamated into the Southwark & Vauxhall.[6]

It very soon became an article of faith with reformers that, in permitting the creation of these new bodies, Parliament was inspired by a belief in the beneficent effects of competition. No doubt there were many MPs who took this view, but it is suggested that the evidence of legislative intent is not as clear as is often supposed. In the first place, the economics of competition are not obviously applicable. To have the enormous capital investment of two or three companies duplicated in the the same locality seems wasteful, and the opportunity thereby given to householders to change suppliers every few months is a cost not only for the companies but for all who must endure the incessant excavation of the streets. And in ordinary cases competition ought to adjust supply to demand by the freedom of sellers to go out of the market as well as to come in. But the provision of water involves large capital expenditure to furnish something which can be sold only on the spot; and if the newcomer is to take custom from the old, since there is relatively little difference in the good he offers, his only hope is to lower his charges below those of his rival. Thus, the competitors will be forced into a price war to the point of ruin since it is better to be paid too little than to receive nothing for a good which, having been brought to market, cannot by its very nature be taken away.[7]

A second argument is to be found in Parliament's own actions. There is nothing to the point in Hansard, but the statute of 1806 which created the first new company suggests that competition was not the legislator's aim. The preamble merely

[6] Adam Smith ii 390; The Waterworks Companies' Acts are listed in the Table of Statutes.

[7] In this chapter all references to the Company's Minutes are (unless otherwise indicated) to nineteenth-century dates. M 5/3/18; PP 1821 xv 25–6.

recites the need for increased water supply caused by the growth of population in parts of Chelsea, Kensington, and Hammersmith 'west of a line hereinafter described' and the act then goes on to incorporate the West Middlesex Waterworks Company with a capital of £30,000 in £100 shares, and powers to raise more by share issue or 'mortgage'. The provisions dealing with the governance are standard and there is nothing to stop rival companies buying shares save the general limit that no one could hold more than five shares or have more than five votes. In conferring the powers to take from the Thames and to carry out the necessary works, however, the statute carefully limits the area, and s. 35 provides that the company is not to lay pipes east of a line stretching (roughly) from the Thames to the King's Road, nor (with one limited exception) in Westminster. The purpose of this restriction becomes clear when we read (s. 35) that, if it is transgressed, the *Chelsea* company is entitled to an annual sum of £10 for every house supplied. Finally, it should be noted—since the issue became extremely contentious in later decades—that the charge for the water was to be such sum 'as mutually agreed upon' (s. 59) with power to cut off supplies in default of payment. A customer who brought an action and lost was to pay double costs to the company (ss. 80, 81).[8]

The East London Company's statute of 1807, while not so unambiguous, hardly supports the view that competition was Parliament's will. Again, the preamble merely recites the need for water and the Act incorporates the company with a capital of £60,000 in £100 shares and powers to raise more. These provisions, and those dealing with governance and charges, are similar to those of the West Middlesex. The new company is then given powers to take from the Lea and carry out the necessary works. There are no territorial limits, although its district overlapped the New River's area, but there is a section providing that nothing in the act 'shall be construed or taken to hinder the [New River Company] from exercising all such right title estate [etc.] as they have' (s. 53).[9]

It may, however, be possible to detect in the West Middlesex's statute of 1810 a policy of deliberately fostering com-

[8] West Middlesex Waterworks Act 1806.

[9] East London Waterworks Acts 1807 and 1808.

petition. The company was given powers to raise another £160,000 either in share or loan capital and to extend its works. The Act recites that the supply might be beneficially extended to certain named parishes in Westminster, Soho, and Covent Garden, which were in Chelsea and New River territory—the two older companies, of course, had no specification in statute or charter as to their parishes. Further, s. 13 forbade the West Middlesex Company to sell or dispose of its powers to any other water company; it was, instead, 'to take and demand such sums as shall be reasonable for the water supplied under the provisions of this Act'. (This may have meant that the company was to sell to its rivals, for the notion that it controlled charges to *consumers* was to astonish Lord Eldon, as will be explained in the next section.) On the other hand the Act contains a section (s. 18) which repealed so much of the founding statute as might be construed to permit supply outside the parish boundaries listed in the two Acts; and s. 22 was the standard saving clause for the rights of the New River, York Buildings, Chelsea, and the City.[10]

Whatever the intentions of the legislator, there is no doubt that the newcomers sought actively to compete. A director of the Grand Junction stated boldly that the object was 'to crush the old companies'. Capital was lavished eagerly upon them—the East London shares jumped immediately to a price of over £150 and in many ways the 'water mania' of the time foreshadowed that for railways in the 1840s and, a little later, for those companies formed in order to work mines on the Stock Exchange. Further, the new companies had the enormous advantage of new plant and, above all, of the chance to start in iron. In October 1811, when the necessary works had been completed, the West Middlesex began its advertisement campaign to attract the New River's customers in Marylebone and neighbourhood. Their product, they promised, would be 'water of the purest quality, unlimited in quantity and delivered, if chosen, in the upper stories of the loftiest houses in London'. Their charges would be 'at lower rates than those adopted by

[10] West Middlesex Waterworks Act 1810; below, section 7.3. A more obvious threat to the New River appeared in the Holloway Waterworks Act 1810, which, without even the standard saving clause, incorporated the business of one George Pocock, who had sunk a deep well near what is now Eden Grove, N7. The New River hastily laid pipes nearby and Pocock went bankrupt in 1815.

any existing establishment'. This 'spontaneous reduction' was, they alleged, the 'provident design of the legislature' to whom they attributed the insight that 'the price of every article of consumption naturally regulates itself by a comparison of the supply with the demand . . . by competition as the supply must, of course, increase, a corresponding diminution could not fail to take place in the price of the commodity.'[11]

The New River, with its back to the Thames, thus found itself threatened on its left flank by the West Middlesex and on its right by the East London, which advanced into Whitechapel, Shoreditch, and Islington, supplying the main houses and taking care never to go into the back streets. The Minute Books of the period abound with reports from the battlefield. The East London company's men tore up New River pipes and its secretary denied having received the (hand-delivered) letter of reproach. On being told in person that the older companies had an understanding whereby a customer was not connected until the new supplier had ascertained that he did not owe money to the old, he replied that 'as a new company they were not acquainted with this practice'. By night the West Middlesex connected the New River's tenants to its own mains and they expected to be restored to the New River free of charge. Legal action was threatened but a more effective redress was the rumour spread by the New River's collectors that the West Middlesex was on the verge of insolvency and that customers who had changed to them would be reconnected to Myddelton's water at three times the old price.[12]

The Company's counter-attack was carried out by four tactics. The first was to forgo the annual dinner. The second was the modernization of the system by borrowing from shareholders and then, with the aid of Vansittart, from the Bank of England, as described in Chapter 6.6. The third was a publicity campaign to secure a favourable image:

> The present opposition to the New River company, and the unjust representations of their conduct, have rendered it a duty to make this appeal, and to show their claims upon the public for support.
>
> They have served the metropolis with water nearly two centuries at

[11] PP 1821 v 93, 107, 113.

[12] M 5/7/10, 7/6/10, 12/7/10, 14/2/11, 21/2/11, 31/10/11; M/GC 12/12/11; M 9/4/12, 30/7/12, 24/3/13, 6/5/13, 3/6/13, 23/9/13.

> rates which have at no time yielded them above six-and-a-quarter per cent. The property of the company has advanced less beyond its original value than any species of real property.
>
> The absurd report that their shares (seventy-two in number) originally cost only £100 each needs no refutation. The formation of their works at the time of Sir Hugh Middleton cost, according to the best authorities, £500,000.

The West Middlesex replied with advertisements suggesting that the original New River shares had cost only £12,000 each, while 'A Friend to Truth' wrote to *The Times* to reveal that they had cost a mere £6,000.[13]

The fourth tactic to be used against competitors was the Board's melancholy resolution that 'it has become a duty to oppose them by rendering our water at a price that will induce our tenants to remain'. Wherever a new company appeared and offered a lower rate, the New River matched it and their average charges were cut from almost 30*s*. a building supplied down to 24*s*. and then 20*s*. The East London joined in the war and made extravagant promises that water would soon be as cheap as beer. The results of this competition were disastrous for all three. The West Middlesex divided no profit at all from 1807 to 1819, although the East London was somewhat more successful. The New River's income dropped from £82,456 in 1810 to £68,372 in 1813, and out of this it had to service the interest on the shareholders' bonds. The effects on the annual dividends are shown in Appendix I. Well over £400 had been paid on average every year since 1788 but in 1811 the figure drops to £282, then £220, then £113. In 1814 the nadir is reached with the sum of £23.[14]

[13] M 25/1/16; PP 1821 v 107–9 (abbreviated); *The Times* 14/3/1816.

[14] M 21/2/1811; PP 1840 xii QQ 506–9; PP 1851 xv Q 11765; PP 1900 xxxix Appx. D4. The effects of competition on the Crown Clog are mentioned in Chapter 9.3.1.

SIR,

BEING ordered by the NEW RIVER COMPANY to wait on you to counteract mis-representations that are industriously circulated to their prejudice, I take the liberty of requesting, you will have the goodness, if any applications should be made to induce you to change your supply of Water, not to consent thereto until I have had an opportunity of seeing you: I am directed also to say, that whatever apparent advantages may be held out to you, the NEW RIVER COMPANY are determined to make a sacrifice, and meet their opponents on any terms they may offer.

I am,

SIR,

Your obedient humble Servant,

Collector.

7th November, 1811.

Printed by T. Woodfall, Villiers-street, Strand, London.

FIG. 12

7.3 The Aftermath of Competition 1815–1840

7.3.1 *Peace treaties*

It soon became obvious to the rivals that all were losing by the war. The New River was fighting the East London for Islington, Shoreditch, and Whitechapel, and the West Middlesex for

Bloomsbury, Covent Garden, Soho, and St Marylebone. Mylne devised a plan to secure exclusive occupation of an area forming, very roughly, an oblong with its base at the Thames between Charing Cross and the Tower; the western boundary ran up Haymarket, Tottenham Court Road, and Hampstead Road on to Highgate, and the eastern line went from the Tower directly north to Stamford Hill, thereby including the site of the company's planned reservoirs at Stoke Newington. The essence of the scheme was to ensure that no portion would be too far from the main waterworks on the Commandery Mantles. The first step was to put pressure on the rivals by laying iron mains only up to a certain point in their district:

> I laid out as fast as I could in substituting iron for wood; then I was enabled to meet them upon their own ground, and supply as high as the new companies could do; and when I abandoned my extremities, it threw such a demand for water upon their works which they had not calculated upon; their engines were not equal to meet it, and then came a truce.[15]

The right flank looking north from the New River Head was secured by an agreement with the East London company signed on 9 November 1815 and later described as being 'as decisive as the battle of Waterloo'. The heart of the New River's tactic was to cede wood and gain iron. Having worked out that maintenance costs on its elm pipes to the east were 53 per cent of the gross income, the Company was prepared to yield over £2 of rental from tenants on the wooden mains for every £1 paid by one connected to iron. In the bargaining process a certain amount was given up, so that the final net figures showed a loss of £400 a year, but that was considered infinitely preferable to continuing the war. The substance of the treaty was as follows:

(1) A demarcation line was agreed.
(2) Each relinquished to the other its right to supply water in the other's territory.
(3) Each ceded the plant in the other's territory with a small financial adjustment.
(4) Each covenanted not to supply in the other's territory and agreed, on breach, to pay the other double the

[15] PP 1851 xv QQ 11766, 11776, 11790–2.

annual water charge of the relevant building, such sum being 'by way of liquidated damages and not of penalty'.
(5) Within its own area, each promised to supply the other's old customers; on breach the other could move in.
(6) The New River Company guaranteed performance of the agreement by any successor in title.[16]

Having severed the territory, the parties did not need to reach any agreement on the price of their product. To protect its left flank the New River Company first persuaded the West Middlesex to join in promoting a Bill to merge the two enterprises. When this was dropped, the rivals entered into an agreement which was similar in substance to that described above, but differed in that it was not formalized because of doubts about the effect of the 1810 Act's prohibition on the sale or disposal of statutory rights. Instead the Board meeting of 21 May 1818 minuted in lengthy detail the precise territorial boundary agreed upon. A copy was sent to the West Middlesex, whose secretary, in acknowledging receipt, added that his letter was official confirmation of the agreement. Similar understandings were reached with and between the other undertakings so that by 1818 the area north of the Thames was effectively carved into districts where each company enjoyed a monopoly which lasted until this century.[17]

7.3.2 *Public outcry*

The effects are no surprise. At Christmas 1815 to the east and 1817 to the west, the New River simply stopped supplying its old customers in what was now ceded territory, and the number of its tenants dropped from 60,000 in 1809 to 52,000. In 1818 the other undertakings raised charges to their captive consumers by up to 25 per cent, although the New River Company merely restored the price to the 1810 pre-competition level. Refusal to pay the increase was countered by cutting off the water—which was perfectly licit—and the householder found that no other company would supply him. The public reaction produced publications, complaints to the Press, vestry petitions

[16] M/GC 28/9/15; NRCD D/105; PP 1821 v Appx. C; PP 1868–9 xxiii para. 115; PP 1900 xxxviii pt. 1 Q 1298 and xxxix Appx. A6, U2 (ii).

[17] (1816) lxx CJ 43; M 23/4/16, 21/5/18, 4/6/18.

to Parliament, and a Bill to freeze charges promoted by Michael Angelo Taylor. The Bill failed by one vote in Committee, but he did achieve the 1817 Metropolis Paving Act, which contained over 100 pages of precise instructions affecting, among others, the water companies and which, according to Chadwick, was universally ignored.[18]

In the House of Lords in April 1818 the Earl of Grosvenor revealed that his tenants were complaining about the partition, which provoked the sententious Eldon to observe that

> if the objects of the legislature in passing the different bills for the supply of water in the metropolis, which must be supposed to be that of creating a competition, had been defeated by the different companies joining together to establish a monopoly, he trusted their lordships would not separate without its being distinctly understood that it was perfectly within the competence of Parliament to set that matter right.

At this point it should be made perfectly clear that the legislature never again managed to establish competition for the supply of water.[19]

The carve-up of London also provoked litigation. James Weale lived in Marylebone and, like many of his neighbours, took the New River water. At Christmas 1817 they found themselves in West Middlesex territory; the Chadwell spring ceased to reach their doors and the new supplier connected them to his mains demanding a rate 25 per cent higher than that charged by the New River during the tranquil days before the price war. Three hundred and seventy householders refused to pay and were cut off. Weale's bill in Chancery contains a great deal about the inhabitants as a whole, making it clear that he is really attempting what is today called a 'class action'. Eldon LC is, of course, adamant that 'according to the established rules of this court, Weale can only come into it on the footing of his own contract and his own equitable right'.[20]

The plaintiff's case rested both on representations made by the West Middlesex Company and on the words of their Acts

[18] PP 1821 v Appendices K and M; PP 1840 xii Q 509; PP 1842 xxvi 280. The effects of Michael Angelo Taylor's Act were felt mildly by the Company in the end: *New River Co* v. *Mayor etc. of Westminster* (1904) 20 TLR 507.

[19] Hans. xxxvii 1183.

[20] *Weale* v. *West Middlesex Waterworks Co* (1820) 1 Jac & W 358 at 370.

At a Meeting of Inhabitants of ISLINGTON and STOKE NEWINGTON, held at Canonbury Tavern the 12th of May, 1810, for the Purpose of taking into Consideration the most effectual Means to prevent the Practice of indecent Bathing in the New River,

MR. INNES in the Chair,

RESOLVED,

THAT the Custom of bathing in the New River between ISLINGTON and STOKE NEWINGTON has long been highly indecent and offensive; and to prevent this intolerable Nuisance in future, that this Meeting do co-operate with the Magistrates in bringing to Justice all Persons who may be found to offend by bathing in the River between the above Places; and that Hand-Bills, declarative of this Resolution, be printed, and circulated in Islington and Stoke Newington, and the Neighbourhoods thereof.

THAT the Thanks of this Meeting are due to the Magistrates for their Exertions in suppressing the above evil, and for their Aid and Assistance in the Prosecution of a Man who during the last Summer was found offending by bathing and exposing his Person in the Fields between Islington and Stoke Newington, and who in the Month of December last was convicted and sentenced at the Middlesex Quarter Session to Two Months Imprisonment in Newgate for this Offence.

THAT this Meeting do expressly declare, and are anxious to have it clearly understood, that they do not feel the least Inclination to diminish the Comforts and innocent Recreations of the Public, or to prevent any Person from bathing in retired Situations; but with the Rights of the New River Company they do not interfere.

THAT this Meeting do adjourn to Saturday, the 19th Day of May, at Seven o'Clock precisely, when they will again meet at this House, for the Purpose of appointing a Committee to carry the foregoing Resolutions into Effect; and that any Inhabitant of Islington and Stoke Newington, who may feel the necessity of remedying the above Evil, be requested to favour the Meeting with his Attendance.

THAT a Subscription be now opened to defray the necessary Expences, and that a Book be provided, and left with Mr. BAGSTER, at Canonbury Tavern, for the Purpose of receiving Signatures.

(B. Clarke, Printer, Well-Street, London.)

FIG. 13

of Parliament. He alleged that the statutes were obtained by promises of lower costs which were repeated in advertisements to the locality. Further, the 1810 Act which forbade the Company to cede its statutory powers enjoined it to 'take and demand such sums as shall be reasonable' (s. 13). The bill asked for a decree that the Company continue to supply at a reasonable price and an injunction against cutting off the water. The defence pointed to the 1806 statute, which provided for such payment 'as shall be mutually agreed' and argued that 'the court has no jurisdiction to interfere . . . it might as well be called upon to fix the price of any other article. Under the first Act, contract was the medium by which persons are to obtain a supply of water; it is not repealed by the second.'[21]

The Lord Chancellor refuses, as has been said, to consider the inhabitants as a class, but states the issue before him to be whether the plaintiff 'has a right to have it giving a *reasonable* price as distinguished from that which may be settled by mutual contract'. Against the former interpretation he sees that it might lead to a court's being asked in every individual case 'what is a reasonable price quoad that inhabitant'. Even assuming, however, that the this is the legislature's intent, he declines to afford a remedy to the plaintiff because 'where is the mutuality? Could I under this Act compel any one inhabitant to take water?' He grasps, of course, that a common-law remedy would be precisely what the plaintiff did not want, but is content to say

> if it turns out that the courts of law can give nothing but damages and a court of Equity cannot interfere to compel a specific performance . . . it is a defect which, whether it proceed from mistake on the part of the legislature or, if I may presume to say so, from negligent inattention, no court of justice can supply the remedy.[22]

Having failed before the Lord Chancellor, Weale turned to other methods, and it was the Marylebone Vestry petition (along with those of the companies for more powers) which led to the hearings before the Select Committee of 1821, whose report is of such crucial importance for the New River's capital account and balance sheet for the rest of its life as a water company. The Committee heard graphic accounts as to the years of competition and the subsequent division of the spoils. James Weale himself gave evidence and put forward a view that took decades to find acceptance. Water, he argued, was a necessity of human life and so 'ought not to be the subject of

[21] Ibid. 367–8.
[22] Ibid. 371, 373, 374.

free trade nor any kind of trade'. It should be supplied free to the poor with cost met out of local revenue, as was done for drainage, paving, and the police. The Romans grasped this but 'the salutary principle of this system was first broken in upon by the assignment to Sir Hugh Middleton of the privileges granted to the corporation of London and afterwards in the establishment of a succession of joint-stock companies for the supply of water'. The Committee accepted that the service had improved but considered that the charges required legislative attention 'where the subject matter is an article of the first necessity and the supply has, from peculiar circumstances, got into such a course that it is not under the operation of those principles which govern supply and demand in other cases'. They recommended a Bill fixing charges for four years. This was never enacted, but the Report formed the basis of all subsequent treatment of the water question, and every statute thereafter, beginning with that of the Grand Junction in 1826, provided that water charges should be fixed not by agreement but by reference to scales.[23]

For the New River, the vital importance of this Report lay in the acceptance and publication of the Company's own estimate of its capital. From this quite lengthy and detailed document, we may make a rough initial comparison with the accounts audited for the King in 1630 and abstracted in Chapter 3.5 (**Table 2**).

Of course the figures given here do not represent capital at the same moment of time. They are used merely to show that the value of the undertaking is, after 200 years, estimated at about twenty times its initial cost. Apparently Mylne simply calculated the older works of the springs, conduits, installations at the Lea, reservoirs, and pipes at current prices. The Company never appeared to know of the existence of the accounts abstracted in Chapter 3.5, and the books of expenditure were buried among the Land Revenue papers in the Public Record Office. It is rather more surprising that the officers did not inspect the terriers of their own land, which they must have known they had and which would have revealed at a glance the initial purchase price whether by lump sum or rent charge.

[23] PP 1821 v 102; Grand Junction Act 1826 s. 27; East London Act 1829 s. 79; Vauxhall Act 1834 s. 18; Southwark Act 1834 s. 86; Lambeth Acts 1834 s. 11, 1848 s. 37. All the special Acts of 1852 fixed a scale; see section 7.6.

Table 2[24]

	1815			1630		
	£	*s.*	*d.*	£	*s.*	*d.*
Springs and making river	369,600	0	0	18,524	19	0
Inner pond land and construction	12,000	0	0	65	0	0
Outer pond land and construction	16,000	0	0	200	0	0*
Upper pond land	12,500	0	0			
Mantles etc.	6,000	0	0	7,350	0	0†
Mains etc. added	—	—	—	—	—	—
TOTAL	846,640	7	0	43,671	4	4

* Denotes the rent charge of £10 at 20 years' purchase.

† The sums paid for small parts of the Mantles plus the 1745 rent charge at 20 years' purchase; see Chapter 5.3.

Looked at from another angle, however, the 1815 calculations seem remarkably accurate, even modest. We know that for two hundred years the New River had been financing capital expenditure out of net income, although no detailed records have survived for most of that period: as the Company put it, 'the income of the proprietors has been applied to increase the capital employed in the public service'. But from the dividends listed in Appendix I we can calculate that for the years 1633–1814 the total distributed among shareholders amounted to some £2,472,358. The capital value estimated by the Company at £846,640. 7*s.* 0*d.* is just over one-third of that sum, which implies that, over the lifetime of the New River, a quarter of its net income had been reinvested in capital expenditure.[25]

To this 1815 total the Company added the heavy expenditure on modernization in iron of the years to 1820, deducted over £113,000 for the 257 miles of wooden pipes left to rot, and arrived at a total capital for Christmas 1820 of £986,868. 13*s.* 0½*d.*, giving a value per share of some £13,706, which the Company rounded up to £14,000. In fact a King's share was

[24] PP 1821 v Appendix C(10). Details of mains outlay omitted.

[25] PP 1834 xv Appendix 1.6.

Copy

I agree to Purchase Lot 1 - as described in the Particulars & agreeably to the annexed Conditions, & to give for the same, the Sum of Eight Thousand, Seven Hundred & Forty Pounds

[illegible]

John Miles

Witness [illegible]

NEW RIVER COMPANY'S SHARES.

PARTICULARS

OF

A King's Share, and One Half of an Adventurer's Share,

In the New River Company,

WHICH WILL BE SOLD BY AUCTION,

BY

Mr. HOGGART,

At the Auction Mart, opposite the Bank of England,

On FRIDAY, the 10th of AUGUST, 1821,

AT TWELVE O'CLOCK,

IN TWO LOTS.

Particulars may be had at the Auction Mart; ~~and of Mr. HOGGART, No. 62, Old Broad Street,~~ Royal Exchange.

LOT 1. A KING'S SHARE in the NEW RIVER COMPANY, now producing a Net Sum of £337 : 10 : 8d. per Annum, with every Expectation of further Improvement.

LOT 2. ONE-HALF of an ADVENTURER'S SHARE, now producing a Net Sum of £164 : 15 : 4d. per Annum.

The above SHARES being FREEHOLD PROPERTY, entitle the Holders to VOTES for the COUNTIES of MIDDLESEX and HERTS.

CONDITIONS OF SALE.

I. The highest Bidders to be the Purchasers; and if any Dispute arise between Two or more Bidders, the Lot in Dispute to be immediately put up again.

II. No Person to advance less than £20. at each Bidding for Lot 1, and £10. for Lot 2.

III. Each Purchaser is to pay down immediately a Deposit of £20. per Cent. in Part of the Purchase-money, and sign an Agreement for Payment of the Remainder on or before the 25th Day of December, 1821.

IV. The Purchasers shall have proper Conveyances, each at his own Expense, on Payment of the Remainder of the Purchase-money, agreeably to the Third Condition, and be entitled to the Dividends from the 25th of December, 1821. All Attested or other Copies of Deeds, or other Documents, required by the Purchasers, are to be at their Expense.

V. There being a Duty on all Sales of Estates, &c. of Seven-pence in the Pound, the Lots comprised in this Particular are to be Sold subject to the Seller paying One Moiety of the said Tax, and the Buyers the other, exclusive of the Sums the said Lots shall sell for.

VI. If through any Mistake the Lots should be improperly described, or any Error or Mis-statement be inserted in this Particular, such Error or Mis-statement shall not vitiate the Sale thereof, but the Vendor or Purchaser, as the Case may happen, shall pay or allow a proportionate Value, according to the Average of the whole Purchase-money, as a Compensation either way.

Lastly.—If the Purchasers shall neglect or fail to comply with the above Conditions, the Deposit-Money to be forfeited, and the Vendor shall be at full Liberty to re-sell the said Lots, and the Deficiency, if any, by such second Sale, together with all Charges attending the same, to be made good by the Defaulter or Defaulters at this present Sale.

FIG. 14

sold at auction the following summer and fetched £8,740. However, the dividends of the previous disastrous decade had averaged only £153; as events turned out, the price was more than recouped within nineteen years.[26]

7.4 Health and Sanitation

Although discontent about prices simmered on, the dominant feature of the next decades was a concern with the state of the London water supply from the point of view of health and sanitation. The full story is recounted in the many works on public health and in the biographies of Chadwick; here only a brief account will be offered from the point of view of one partisan in the conflicts. The source of most of the capital's water was the sewage-laden Thames; in this respect the New River was more wholesome, although its out-take from the Lea took in Hertford's sewage and the water then ran almost 40 miles in an open channel which was used by the neighbours for many purposes. An example is the complaint to the Company dated 10 April 1800 and signed by many inhabitants of Colebrook Row in Islington about the conduct of Baron Ephraim de Aguilar, whose stables had been 'long converted to the sole use of feeding, or rather starving, bulls, cows, calves, hogs, dogs, geese, and so on, the filth from which collection of animals drains into the River'.[27]

The round pond into which ran the New River consisted by then of an outer ring about a yard deep and an inner pond about ten feet deep. The water flowed for distribution through an orifice about 18 feet from the top and, when the accumulated sludge had almost reached that point, the pond was emptied and cleaned out. This occurred about once every twenty years. The water was then pumped up to the upper reservoir at the north-west of the Mantles in order to take advantage of its elevation. That reservoir had never been cleaned since it was built in the early eighteenth century. It was not until about

[26] Full details are in PP 1821 v Appendices C(10), C(11), and M. The figure in the text includes the York buildings purchase price.

[27] TW, Strongroom B30, box 86/292. Since the Baron was of a distinguished Sephardic family, it is difficult to believe that he knew about the hogs: see Yogev 45, 126, 171, 296.

1830 that filtration was carried out (by the Chelsea company) and the New River built reservoirs at Stoke Newington, where the contents were allowed to settle for a while. The water flowed along the mains for an hour or so each weekday or on alternate days—but never on Sundays, when those of the poor who could afford supplies no doubt would have wished to wash—and was delivered to the customers at ground level. They had then to store the water in whatever receptacles they could; as the Medical Officers of Health put it: 'In inspecting the courts and alleys of the City one constantly sees butts for the reception of water, dirty mouldering and coverless inviting filth from insects, vermin, sparrows, cats, and children. There is disease and death in the tanks, wells and water-butts.'[28]

The supply of water could be carried on for reward, but its removal after use was not a service that any individual would willingly pay for. Consequently, any water which was drunk then found its way through the customer's body either directly into the New River or into a cesspool which often lay, boarded over, under the feet of the family. Solid excrement went the same way, or into the ancient rectangular sewers through which flowed an occasional trickle of water, or into heaps to be conserved, ripened, and sold. The polite name for this substance was 'dust'.[29]

These and other problems led Sir Francis Burdett in 1828 to propose to the Commons public ownership of the water supply. Peel told him quite firmly that water 'ought not to be provided by government, nor the expense defrayed by the public. If so, the supply would never again be procured at so cheap a rate.' Hansard reports that 'here the conversation dropped'.[30]

However, a Select Committee then heard abundant evidence that the Thames was filthy, that the New River had recently been raising its rates, and that the West Middlesex's statute contained a provision that if a customer sued and lost he had to pay double costs. Its recommendation of a Royal Commission was followed and Telford was one of the members. The Commission suggested 'a scientific study' of the water question,

[28] M/GC 2/6/1774, 22/9/1852; PP 1850 xxii 38–9; PP 1851 xv Q 11617; PP 1852 xii Q 1152; Jephson 52, 107 (abridged).

[29] M 14/12/O9; PP 1842 xxvi 64; Jephson 52.

[30] Hans. (New Ser.) xix 773–4.

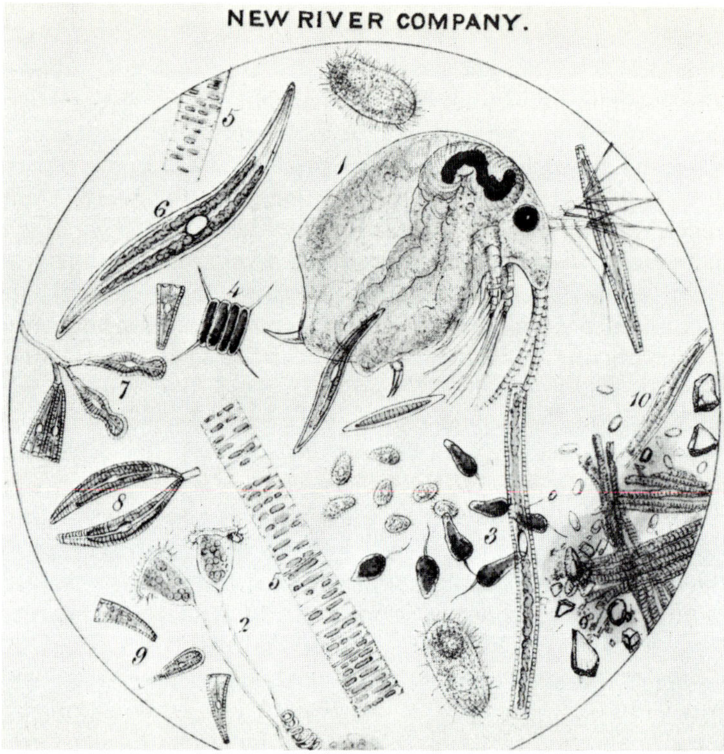

NEW RIVER COMPANY.

Entomostraceæ.

Fig. 1. Lynceus longirostris.
2. Vorticella nebulifera.
3. Bodo, species of.

Desmideæ.

4. Scenedesmus quadricaudatus.

Diatomaceæ.

5. Fragilaria pectinalis.
6. Gyrosigma Hippocampa.
7. Gomphonema truncatum.
8. Cocconema cymbiforme.
9. Gomphonema minutissimum.

Dead organic matter.

10. Decomposing vegetable matter, infested with monads.

FIG. 15. A. H. Hassall's microscopic examination of the inhabitants of the New River, 1850

which Telford carried out, and in 1834 he urged that new sources be tapped in the River Verulam. He also singled out the New River for especial praise, referring to it as a 'magnificent work' with 'pure water' which was 'maintained with great care and expense'. The Governor of the time was the energetic and able Robert Percy Smith, ex-Attorney-General of Bengal, and elder brother of Sydney, Dean of St Paul's. The House of Commons produced a rather desultory commentary on the enterprise, while the House of Lords Committee, after hearing from a resident that 'there cannot be such water that the people of London ought to drink and drink it again and again', devoted most of its attention to a lengthy dispute over charges between the New River Company and Thomas Tubbs, a cow-keeper of 6 Palace Road.[31]

In the 1837–8 epidemic of typhoid, however, a particularly fatal outbreak occurred near one of Shoreditch's stagnant ponds and the movement grew which culminated in the famous Sanitary Report of the Poor Law Commissioners of 1842. Its powerful pages describe how the customers 'merely pass dirty linen through dirty water [with] no way of getting rid of waste water but by throwing it out of the door', argue the economic case for lowering the incidence and cost of illness, disability, and death by improving sanitary conditions, detail the chaos of administration then reigning and the inefficacy of existing legal powers, and propose the engineering needed to coordinate the whole system, using the power of water as the motive force. Chadwick's humanitarian concern and his practical logic fired him with one great ambition: to consolidate the supply, drainage, sewage, and street-cleaning of the whole metropolis. For a time the economic arguments persuaded him that such a body should be in private hands and he involved W. C. Mylne in his Town Improvement Company. Eventually, however, he settled for the view that the best answer lay in a public authority, whose case was put in the second report of the Health of Towns Commission. His proposals, as much as his manner, aroused intense opposition from the water companies, the Parliamentary agents whose living depended on the flow of private Bills, and a section of political opinion well represented in the House of Commons debates: 'the reason why

[31] PP 1834 xv 1 and li 285–6; PP 1840 xii QQ 309, 694 ff.

the condition of this country was at the lowest ebb and, he might say, sink of filth was that this House had passed laws which affected the labour and the industry of man. Away with this mawkish philanthropy.'[32]

7.5 The 1840s Clauses Acts

During this complex and heated debate the flow of private Bills for public purposes increased. Up to the 1840s the Bills were examined by Parliamentary Committees in order to ascertain two different things: what the applicant might do and what he might be. The first required evaluation of the works proposed—railways, mines, docks, turnpikes, gasworks, cemeteries, waterworks, and the like—which usually involved the compulsory acquisition of land. The second concerned the corporate status applied for, since a long tradition had assumed that incorporation was bestowed only on bodies set up for the public benefit. Its consideration entailed quite different problems regarding the structure and governance of the projected company and the protection of prospective shareholders. Naturally enough, a large number of the clauses had become standard. Many of those in the first category were governed by Standing Orders of each House while those of the second had evolved from the deeds of settlement used to circumvent the Bubble Act before its repeal in 1825.

In order to utilize the decades of experience already gained and to save Parliamentary time, a number of 'clauses' Acts were passed in 1845, their purpose being to provide a model to be used in subsequent private statutes. The Companies Clauses Act was to be incorporated in legislation which created companies formed 'for carrying on undertakings of a public nature' (a phrase which demonstrates the tenacity of the link between incorporation and public benefit), but the major statute was that which governed the acquisition of land for such purposes: the Lands Clauses Consolidation Act contained an elaborate regime governing such powers with provisions for arbitration which were scrupulous in point of form if vague in that of

[32] PP 1842 xxvi 60, 64; PP 1845 xviii Rec. 17; Hans. (3rd Ser.) xcviii 710; Finer 235–6; R. A. Lewis 41 ff.

substance. Two points need to be borne in mind. The first is that an undertaking's Bill might well incorporate both statutes. The second is that the Acts were facultative, not mandatory. Although they did not require to be expressly incorporated by the private Act, they could be excluded or varied by its provisions—provided, of course, that the proposals passed the scrutiny of the appropriate Parliamentary Committee.[33]

The only specific activity dealt with in the 1845 batch of clauses Acts was that for which regulation was urgently needed, namely the railways, and it had the immediate effect of reducing private Bills on the topic from over one hundred pages to about a dozen. But Bills for other purposes showed no signs of abating and in 1846 a House of Commons Select Committee was instructed to consider the whole topic in the light of the report of the Health of Towns Commission. Chadwick's evidence, and that of other witnesses, repeated the message of that body: that no more competition like that of the water companies should be given Parliamentary sanction and that the whole complex of sanitation services should be under the control of a Local Authority. The experience of the past years, said Chadwick, had led to 'double capitals, double machinery, double establishments, double sources of water, and double collection of rates. The competing companies always end by coming to an agreement and making the public pay for the whole amount of the previous waste.' The petition to the Committee of the Metropolitan Working Classes Association insisted that the Bills currently presented provided only for the upper and middle classes, as was clearly shown by the extra charge imposed in all of them on the owner of a water-closet. Finally, an apparently technical point was made which was ultimately to cost the New River Company some £5m. (see Chapter 8.2). The senior Parliamentary draftsman, J. E. D. Bethune, who described himself as 'legislative counsel to the Cabinet', complained that the Lands Clauses Consolidation Act applied automatically to any special statute giving power to take land and did not need express incorporation. 'I think', he said, 'that that is a mistake and I called the Government's attention to it at the time, but my opinion was overruled.'[34]

[33] Lands Clauses Consolidation Act 1845 ss. 16–68.
[34] PP 1846 xii QQ 321, 638 and Appx. 15.

The 1847 Waterworks Clauses Act does not tackle the thorny topic of public ownership but does go much further than the provision of a simple model statute. Firstly, the Parliamentary draftsman had his way and it applies

> only to such works as may be authorised by any Act of Parliament hereafter to be passed which shall declare that this Act shall be incorporated therewith and all the clauses of this act, save so far as they shall be expressly varied or excepted by any such act, shall apply to the undertaking authorised thereby so far as . . . applicable (s. 1).

Section 2 defines 'undertaking' to mean the works 'by the special Act authorised to be constructed' and s. 3 defines 'waterworks' in a similar way. Section 6 applies the Lands Clauses Acts to any compulsory acquisition of land. As will be seen in Chapter 8.2, this apparently harmless material was to present the courts of all three instances with grave problems in the twentieth century.

The Act then settles down to business. After straightforward sections dealing with powers to dig up streets and duties to fill them in again, it lays down a number of provisions which gravely threatened the water companies. The three most important are as follows:

1. *Supply*. Section 35 orders the companies to lay mains and provide water in their districts on the request of that number of occupants whose annual payments would amount to not less than one-tenth of the cost of providing the pipes and who would promise to take for at least three years. The first condition reflects the feeling of the legislator that 10 per cent was the right return on capital invested in waterworks; the second is to prevent the changes of capricious householders which cost so much in the days of competition. The section could, of course, be excluded or altered by the special Act.

2. *Water rates*. Sections 68–74 attempt to limit the charges imposed on consumers. The old principle of freedom of contract had not, in fact, been enacted since the earliest legislation of the century. Instead, the general rule now provides for charging by rates fixed in the special Act by reference to 'the annual value of the tenement supplied with water' (s. 68). Disputes are to be referred to two Justices of the Peace, but the Act neglects to define the meaning of 'annual value'.

3. *Company profits.* Having limited the revenue, the Act then sets out to restrict the dividends payable to shareholders. Sections 75–84 provide a scheme which, in essence, forbids the companies to divide more than a 10 per cent return on their 'paid-up capital' unless 'a larger dividend be at any time necessary to make up the deficiency of any previous dividend which shall have fallen short'. It should be noted at this point that the New River Company had no 'paid-up capital' and that, if it had and were subject to the Act, the question as to whether it could make up dividends back to 1619 or only to 1847 depends on whether the phrase 'shall have fallen short' is the future perfect of the indicative mood (1847) or is a clumsy use of modal 'shall' with imperative force in order to designate a present condition (1619).

Any excess of profit over the 10 per cent is first to be invested in Government stock to provide a reserve fund but, once this has reached one-tenth of the paid-up capital and all back dividends below 10 per cent have been made up, the extra revenue is to be used to reduce the rates paid by consumers for the water. It should be said at this point that only one supplier (the West Middlesex) ever reached this stage, but an immense amount of effort and ingenuity was expended by all the companies in postponing its arrival.

7.6 1852: General and Special Metropolis Water Acts

The cholera outbreak of 1848 roused all London and, when the Registrar-General's returns showed that the New River's customers had escaped relatively lightly compared with those who drank the Thames, a host of schemes was promoted to bring water from fresher sources. Chadwick's 1850 report on the London water supply contrived to offend the vestries, the Commissioners of Sewers, and, of course, the companies.[35]

But some action was urgently needed, and in April 1851 Lord John Russell's Whig Government introduced a far-

[35] PP 1850 xxii; Finer 392, 395. Among more weighty matters, the Report criticized Hugh Myddelton's plain river, which 'did not have the elevating effect of architectural decorations'; a witness called it 'a rude and vicious conduit' (304, 470).

reaching Bill which announced a continuous supply of pure water from, if necessary, new sources, at reduced rates, and under Government control. Public ownership was not promised; instead all the undertakings were to be amalgamated and their property vested in one great company. Their shareholders were to be recompensed with that amount of stock in the new company which, at a dividend of 5 per cent, would give them the same income as their previous holdings. Any future excess over that percentage was to be used to reduce water rates; and the company was to be subject to audit, control, and direction as to sources under a Secretary of State.[36]

Opposition came from Chadwick at the Board of Health (because of the divorce between supply and disposal), from the vestries (because the Bill did not propose control by a representative body), and, of course, from the Parliamentary agents and counsel, and the water companies. The latter bought the support of the *Daily News* and *Morning Chronicle* and a hundred Parliamentary votes, although the New River's man in the Commons—Sir John Johnstone—was moderate in debates which posed no great danger as long as the House was engrossed—as it was made to be—with the problems of Thomas Tubbs, cowkeeper. Sir George Gray had courteously sent advance notice of this Bill to the Company, and Thomas Mills, the Governor, drafted a reply. The Board decided, however, to send a deputation to wait upon the Home Secretary with a list of questions, one of which asked how the Government could contemplate 'converting that which is now real estate and possessed of all its privileges into personal property to the great injury of all those who have interests under settlements'. The meeting took place on 28 April 1851 and its results were reported to the Board. The gist of the answers was that all would be settled by arbitration but the Company, not unnaturally, had asked in vain for an explanation of the principles on which compensation would be evaluated. A resolution was passed that the New River 'offer no assistance to the Government bill', a petition against it was approved, and the Adventurers were urged to use their influence with members of both Houses, especially those who were shareholders.[37]

[36] Hans. (3rd Ser.) cxvi 309; PP 1900 xxxix Appendix X1.

[37] M 10/4/51, 24/4/51, 30/4/51, 27/5/51, 12/6/51, 19/6/51.

The Whigs—with many other problems engaging their attention—yielded on amalgamation, procrastinated on health measures, and delayed the Bill until it collapsed in Committee, whereupon the Adventurers followed the advice of their solicitor, who wrote 'you may congatulate yourselves upon the defeat of the present government measures'. Russell's administration lasted only until February 1852 and, in the uneasy coalition which followed, the notion of amalgamating the water suppliers was dropped and a much more cautious measure became the law.[38]

The Metropolis Water Act 1852 abandoned all attempts at amalgamation or limiting dividends and merely laid down a number of precautionary measures. Those companies which used the Thames were not to take from below Teddington lock after 1855, within five years the reservoirs in London were to be covered (though nothing was said about the householders' water-butts), and the companies were to filter before distribution. Audited accounts were to be kept available for the public and the Board of Trade was empowered to appoint inspectors to deal with complaints and initiate prosecutions. Subject to their own special Acts, the suppliers had five years within which to prepare to provide a *constant* supply at the request of four-fifths of the householders on a main. This provision never worked and the century was ending ere all the New River's mains were filled around the clock. The Company minuted that the Act contained 'nothing which can damage the interests of the London water companies whilst on the other hand the settlement of a long agitated question will be of material service in restoring public confidence in their investments'.[39]

Special Bills were numerous. The New River was forced to fight off the Lea trustees' proposal to form a company to supply the whole of London north of the Thames and to go itself to Parliament for powers to widen the conduit, construct reservoirs, and lay drains; it added to these a statutory provision for loan capital in addition to its common-law powers. The Company had great difficulty in drafting its Bill, but had learned from the 1847 Waterworks Clauses Act and the 1852

[38] Hans. (3rd Ser.) cxvii 459 and cxviii 834; PP 1851 xv; M 24/7/51; Finer 407–12.
[39] M 1/7/52 (abridged).

Act that it would be politic to add clauses dealing with constant supply and rates of charges. It circulated all members and succeeded on second reading by 80 to 54. The Bill was then considered by a Select Committee of the House of Commons, along with the Government Bill and those of other companies. All the companies petitioned against the Government Bill but no company objected to another's. To forestall any stricter terms which the Committee might be minded to impose, they called Mr Alfred Bell to give evidence. A solicitor in Parliamentary practice, he was also Lord Eldon's executor and held strong views on constitutional principle. 'All local and personal Acts are', he declared, 'contracts between the legislature and the company', and he had long advised his clients that 'they would run no risk whatever in advancing their money on the faith of that Act'. The Committee was thus warned that it should do nothing to restrict the existing statutory privileges of the other companies.[40]

Since the New River was relatively good in the practical areas concerning the supply and quality of its water, the main political pressures which the Company had to face were for financial control of both income and dividends. In these matters, its ancient corporate structure was an anachronism in a world of juridical persons whose anatomy could be defined by arithmetic: so much paid-up capital and so many thousand shares of a fixed nominal value. It lacked the former, its seventy-two shares, like any other piece of real property, had no par value, many were split into tiny fractions, and only twenty-nine of one moiety of them counted as the Company.

The first task, therefore, was to persuade the Committee to accept the Company's valuation of its present capital. The evidence offered took as its datum the figure of £986,868 presented to the 1821 Committee, with Mylne explaining that 'the land was valued at the prices of that day; all the documents have been burnt; we have no records whatever to guide us.' To this was added the scrupulously audited figures for capital expenditure ex income for the years 1821–51: they show a total net revenue of almost £2m., from which something over a quarter had been added to capital. The Committee made a

[40] M 20/11/51, 18/12/51; GCM 30/12/51; M 1/7/52, 2/12/51; PP 1852 xii QQ 1443–52.

minute examination of the figures, was impressed by the honesty of an accounting system which, for instance, charged a new boiler to expenditure and then deducted from capital the scrap value of the old one, and was finally convinced by the Company's estimate that its current capital value was £1,519,958.[41]

As to the rates to be charged to customers, the Company was made to follow the current legislative trend in proposing a scale based on the 'annual value'. When asked how this would be assessed, however, the reply came that they 'would look at the house and put a value on it . . . estimate what it would let for'. They would not 'take the actual rent, nor the rating in any book, but measure the size, the number of rooms and so on'. It was thirty years before the House of Lords put a stop to this, as is explained in section 7.9. They also promised—what was very important in municipal politics—that they would continue the favourable terms agreed with the City when the London Bridge waterworks was taken over in 1822; the importance of this concession is dealt with in section 7.10.1. On winning the Committee over, the Company minuted their satisfaction 'in securing themselves by Act of Parliament the property and privileges which they have previously held only by Charter and as not only delivering them from virtual confiscation but as confirming and strengthening their position'.[42]

The New River Company's Act 1852, which enshrined this triumph, was later ascribed by Lord Fitzgerald to 'malicious ingenuity', while Lord Macnaghten LC, with more restraint, observed that 'if the object had been to render it as difficult of construction as possible, success could hardly have been more complete'. Despite these warnings, however, if we are to follow the later legal and financial history of the Company we must pay close attention to at least some of the statute's provisions.[43]

1. *Incorporations.* The Act (unnecessarily) incorporates the Lands Clauses Consolidation Act of 1845 in respect of the new property required and new works authorized and (quite unnecessarily) excludes its operation in regard to old activities. It then incorporates the Waterworks Clauses Act 1847 (except its section 35 on supply and its sections on the obligation to

41 PP 1852 xii QQ 3885–994, 8212.

42 Ibid. QQ 8232, 8244–52; M 1/7/52.

43 *Cooke* v. *New River Co* (1889) 14 App Cas 698 at 699, 703.

connect householders from the mains, which are dealt with later in the special Act) and continues 'provided that the clauses with respect to the construction of waterworks, lands adjoining and mines shall not apply to any waterworks constructed or lands acquired previously to the passing of this Act'. Now, unlike the 1845 statutes, the 1847 Waterworks Act (which, among milder provisions, limited dividends to 10 per cent of paid-up capital) did not take effect automatically but needed express incorporation; and the special Act incorporated the whole but then excluded as to past works certain sections *but not those limiting dividends*. On the other hand, by its very terms, the 1847 Act once incorporated applied 'only to such waterworks as may be authorised by [the special] Act' (s. 1), so that the Company's proviso was logically absurd. The special Act did not, of course, incorporate the Companies Clauses Act since that dealt only with companies to be newly formed by statute.

2. *Capital.* Section 3 of the Act provides that 'the capital raised and expended so far' shall be deemed to be £1,519,958. It does not use the epithet 'paid-up', which would have been even more incongruous than the notion that such a sum had been 'raised'.

3. *Old territory and new works.* The New River Company's Act lists all the places currently supplied (s. 5) and authorizes new works. Part of these would involve abandoning sections of Myddleton's aqueduct, and the Lands Clauses Act stipulated that such superfluous land was, if possible, to be offered to the owner of the land from which it was severed (s. 128). The special Act prudently deems such owner to be untraceable, the founding statute's provisions reserving him 'the inheritance' being ignored (s. 8).

4. *Borrowing powers.* The Company was given power to borrow on bond up to £250,000 for the works authorized by the Act and up to another £150,000 for 'general purposes'—for the cost, that is, of complying with the requirements as to filtration, coverage of reservoirs, and the like imposed by the Metropolis Water Act of 1852. Interest on the loan was of course to be paid in preference to dividends (ss. 14–27).

5. *Supply.* The section of the 1847 Act which was expressly excluded provided for mains to be laid at the request of householders in the district whose payments would amount to 10 per

cent of the cost, as explained in section 7.4. The Company's version (s. 34) followed the same pattern (with connections at the consumers' expense) but added the tell-tale proviso

> that the Company shall not be bound to furnish any such supply of water, or lay down any pipes for such purpose, in any part of the district, which part is for the time being supplied with water by any other company.

This clause was copied by all the companies north of the Thames, with the result that none of them could be made to compete with any other.

6. *Charges.* For water used in dwelling-houses within their district for domestic purposes the Company laid down a scale: the maximum was £4 per cent 'where the annual value of the dwellinghouse shall not exceed £200' and £3 per cent above. Baths, water-closets, and supply more than 10 feet above the ground floor were charged as extras; 'domestic purposes' were defined to exclude flushing sewers and baths, although by this last word the Company presumably meant public establishments (ss. 35–8).

For non-domestic purposes within their district, the Company's charges were to be fixed by agreement (s. 40) but the next section gave 'any consumer of water for purposes other than [those] in respect of which rates . . . are hereinbefore provided' the right to demand a charge by meter. This provision, which would appear to empower a bone-boiler in Carlisle to call for a metered supply of Myddelton's water, was to cause a great deal of trouble.

7. *Savings.* Section 75 of the special Act saved the Company's rights under the Charter, statute, or prescription 'except so far as the same are necessarily altered by this Act'.

Part of the price of Committee approval of the special Act was a pledge to do something about the Hertford sewage which flowed into the Lea above the New River out-take. A Bill to redeem this pledge was thrown out by the House of Lords Committee in the next session for failure to comply with Standing Orders and the Company was pained to receive a letter from Lord Palmerston complaining about the state of their water. In 1854 the Company procured two statutes, one to enable it to construct new reservoirs in Middlesex and raise money on bond, and the other to deal with Hertford's sewage. One solution to this problem would have been to move the out-take; but, partly for the sake of improving relations with the town, the Company chose instead to divert the sewage to an outlet downriver. When a Select Committee pointed out to W. C. Mylne that this meant that 'the East London Waterworks Company will catch it all' he replied: 'No doubt.'[44]

As explained in Chapter 6.7, the next capital raised by the Company was under its 1866 Act, and took the form of £500,000 in £100 shares. They were personalty and voteless, but commanded an immediate premium and were offered to the original shareholders *at par*.

7.7 1860–1879: Cholera and Commissions

During the 1850s the New River Company's dividends were held steady at about £850 per share. In the next decade, however, they began a healthy rise which was to take them to £1,625 by 1870 and, a decade later, to £2,330. There were several reasons for this prosperity. The first was the growth of the population: the number of customers increased from 52,000 in 1820 to 121,000 in 1872. The second was the adoption by inhabitants of modest means of the benefits of household deliveries of water and the use of baths and water-closets; and the third (which outstripped both) was the rise in rateable value. The Company's 1852 statute allowed it to charge a percentage of the annual value, and the disputes about how this last figure was to be reached will be described in section 7.9. Meanwhile, it is sufficient to note that, however measured, with the growth in municipal services, the annual value of London houses was increasing for reasons which had nothing to do with the supply of water.[45]

The Company coped with the increase in demand by taking extra water from the Lea (the River Lee Act 1855 vested all the river water, save that necessary for navigation, in the New River and East London companies in return for annual pay-

[44] M 27/7/54, 10/8/54; PP 1851 xv Q 11879.
[45] PP 1884–5 lxxi 18.

ments to the Conservators), by constructing new works paid for by debenture stock under statutory powers, and by sinking wells under the common-law powers of a landowner. In the distribution of its water the Company introduced strict and successful measures against waste and, although the 1852 general Act had enjoined continuous supply within five years, the supply throughout most of the New River district remained intermittent. The Company was always reluctant to provide constant supply because of the problems of peak-time consumption and overloading the system; where, for special reasons, it was provided, double rates were charged.[46]

The popularity of the water-closet meant that even more fecal matter flowed into London's rivers. The cholera of 1866 was caused by the East London Company's neglect to filter its water from the Lea, and the outbreak had the familiar results: 5,548 deaths followed by the appointment of a Royal Commission. Its function was to consider fresh sources of water for London's growing needs, and the best means of utilizing those which already existed. To the modern reader of its pages, the most striking impression is that of the self-confidence of the projectors and their engineers, who put forward bold plans to supply the entire metropolis with water collected in the mountains of Cumberland and Wales and conveyed in covered aqueducts. The Commission reported against these schemes and concluded that the Thames valley could provide enough water if only it could be cleansed before use. The most important recommendation, however, was that the cost of the whole supply both for private and public use should be met by levying a general rate; and, since 'no trading company could be permitted to levy or expend such compulsory rates, that therefore the future control of the water supply should be entrusted to a responsible public body with powers to buy the existing works and levy the rates'.[47]

The concrete result of this proposal was the Metropolis Water Act of 1871, which was hardly a far-reaching measure. Indeed its enactment was almost a replay of the scene of twenty years before, with a Government Bill including a clause to purchase

[46] River Lee Act 1855; New River Company's Act 1857 (the Company's 1866 Act gives the wrong reference to this statute); M 23/5/1822, 1/7/1852.

[47] PP 1868–9 xxxiii para. 263; Jephson 191.

the companies being withdrawn in favour of merely sanitary measures. The 1852 general Act had failed to produce a constant supply of clean water and the 1871 Act had no greater success. It empowered the City or the Metropolitan Board of Works to require a constant supply subject to appeal to the Board of Trade, but they never effectively did so. Similarly, it forbade the companies to supply to any house without a cistern; so builders would buy one cistern for their whole new street and move it from house to house as each was built in order to produce it to any inquisitive Company. The Act also provided for the appointment of water examiners, for a supply on Sundays, and for an independent audit of the companies' books; but the New River succeeded in inserting a section excluding from this control their landed estates (s. 47). Thereafter they declined to answer Parliamentary enquiries about the Commandery Mantles on the grounds that 'the estates and houses in question are private property'.[48]

7.8 1879: The Tory Offer

Disraeli's Government was continually being urged to act on the London water question. There were several pressure-groups: the Medical Officers of Health, to whom, in a crowded city, 'dirt was as dangerous as dynamite'; the Churches, for both Cardinal Manning and the Bishop of London were agreed that the present supply 'was injurious to the cleanliness and, consequently, to the temperance, the morals, and, in the last resort, the religion of the population'; the ratepayers, who found the cost of water rising, especially since the statute of 1869, which provided for quinqennial revaluation of their properties; and, within this group, the City magnates, still benefiting from the lower prices agreed by the New River in 1822, but uneasily aware of the courts' view of the New River's statutory powers to charge for their clerks' use of a washroom by reference to the annual value of their counting-houses.[49]

The Tories' embarrassment was increased when the Metropolitan Board of Works introduced two Bills to enable it to go

[48] PP 1884–5 lxxi 1013; PP 1900 xxxviii pt. 1 para. 182, Q 621.
[49] Hans. (3rd Ser.) cclxiv 109; Valuation (Metropolis) Act 1869.

into the water supply business and to buy out the companies. The proposals did not reach a second reading, but the Board then discovered that it had no powers either to legislate on the water question or to incur costs in an attempt to do so. In August 1879, therefore, an indemnity Act was rushed through, followed by a money Act to widen the Board's powers. During their passage, on a private member's motion calling on the Government to act, the Home Secretary, Assheton Cross, promised to buy out the companies, by compulsion if necessary but preferably by agreement.[50]

Although the water undertakings are frequently depicted by their contemporary critics and modern historians as obdurate and rapacious traffickers in a prime necessity, there is no doubt whatever that the New River Company was perfectly willing to sell—at the right price. Negotiations on the terms were entrusted by the Government to E. J. Smith, a distinguished civil engineer, whose task was, to put it mildly, rather difficult. He dealt, as he plaintively explained, '*en amateur* entirely at my own cost'; the Board of Trade's experts on the physical plant of the waterworks, although directed to collaborate, were unwilling to do so in writing; he knew little either of the law or of the stock market; he had to deal, individually and in confidence, with all eight companies and could do nothing unless all consented; and he had no money to buy them with.[51]

Within four months he had secured agreement with all eight companies, and a Bill to enact the purchase had gone through eight revisions. He himself attributed the speed of his success to his warnings to the sellers that the Tories might not be long in office, but the stock market told a different story: within days of the price he was offering becoming known, the stock in all the companies began to rocket. In any event, when Gladstone succeeded Disraeli in April 1880 and sent the question to a committee chaired by his future Chancellor of the Exchequer, Sir William Harcourt, it became obvious that the offer was uncommonly generous. On paper, the equity capital in the New River was worth £2,019,958; on the market the original shares were selling (occasionally) for about £95,000 and the

[50] Metropolitan Board of Works (Indemnity) and (Money) Acts 1879; Hans. (3rd Ser.) ccxxxviii 1217 and ccxxxix 917.

[51] PP 1880 x QQ 16, 56, 61, 67.

new shares stood at £350, making a total of £8,590,000. Its draft contract with E. J. Smith took over the debenture liability and secured the company £6m. down (in $3\frac{1}{2}$ per cent water stock) and another £3m. in deferred annuities; in addition the Company was to keep the Clerkenwell estates, whose building leases now covered the Commandery Mantles and were reaching the last twenty years of their terms. The price represented the value of the existing assets, the expected increase in revenue from the growth of population and in rateable values, and a handsome sum for the right to distribute 'back dividends' from future income. The Company had argued, and Sir Henry Thring, the Parliamentary counsel, had advised, that the New River was not subject at all to the limitation on dividends contained in the Waterworks Clauses Act 1847; but that if they were they might make up dividends back to 1619. E. J. Smith estimated that this might be worth £15m. and discounted it for present purchase at a little over £2m. The Harcourt Committee declined to buy at these prices but, like the Royal Commission of 1868, strongly recommended the introduction of a Bill to vest the capital's water supply in a representative public body.[52]

The only step which Parliament took in relation to this scheme was to acquire during the next decade sporadic returns comparing the actual income of the water companies with those which Smith's offer would have brought. These brought much satisfaction at the benefits of inactivity and provoked Mr G. J. (later Viscount) Goschen—who had been responsible for the quinqennial revaluation Act—to reflect that 'Parliament never does make a bargain except it is more or less of an improvident nature; that is an unfortunate habit that Parliament has.'[53]

7.9 The Charges Controlled

Up to the last quarter of the nineteenth century the water companies were charging by scales based on an 'annual value' which they calculated themselves. For general rating purposes there were two ways of estimating this figure. The lower result

[52] PP 1880 x Recs. 1–5, QQ 590–610, 896–9, 1841–74, Appx. 5.
[53] Hans. (3rd Ser.) cclxxxv 1235; PP 1884–5 lxxi 1012–13, 1025.

would be achieved by taking the method for the poor rate codified in the Parochial Assessment Act 1836: that is, in simple terms, to estimate the rent which would be paid by a tenant who himself did the repairs. The higher figure would be reached by using the 'gross value' as defined in the Valuation (Metropolis) Act 1869—that is, the rent that could be obtained by a landlord responsible for repairs and insurance. The New River Company (which maintained that the only complaints about the cost of water stemmed from milkmen) was quite happy to use the latter figure until challenged by a pugnacious customer.

The case of *New River Co* v. *Mather* (1875) began quietly enough with a successful action in the Clerkenwell County Court for 16*s*. water rates, based on a gross value of £22. The defendant, however, knew the statutes and contended that the correct figure was the net sum of £18 given in the local valuation list. The Divisional Court held that, under the relevant statutes, the correct forum for adjudicating on such a dispute was the Magistrates' Court.

This jurisdiction was invoked on the same question in *Dobbs* v. *Grand Junction Co* (1882), in which the magistrate's ruling that the correct figure was that of the gross value was reversed by the Divisional Court, restored by the Court of Appeal, and reversed again (for varying reasons) by the House of Lords. Bramwell's solution was the simplest: 'value means net value; net value means value' and land is worth to a landlord 'what he gets minus what it costs him to get it'. (The result was confirmed by statute in 1885.) The New River Company estimated that this decision cost them £12,000 a year, and for the next ten years held their dividends at £2,520 per old share. For failure to pay the correct sum they preferred to cut off the water rather than go to law, but were deprived of the exercise of this remedy for the poorer tenements by a statute of 1887.[54]

The Company expended much ingenuity in mitigating the effect of *Dobbs*. The first reaction was to issue demand notices based on the gross value, but with a note added promising rectification of any error drawn to their attention. They then, for the first time, began to seek information as to the extent of

[54] *New River Co* v. *Mather* (1875) LR 10 CP 442; *Dobbs* v. *Grand Junction Co* (1883) 9 App Cas 49 at 55; Water Rate (Definition) Act 1885; Water Companies (Regulation of Powers) Act 1887.

WATER RATES.

HOUSE OF LORDS DECISION.

ARCHD. E. DOBBS, Esq.

Will Address a Meeting of the

RATEPAYERS

AT

HOLLOWAY HALL, HOLLOWAY ROAD,

On Wednesday Evening, December 19th, 1883.

Convened by the Committee of the Islington Branch of the Water Consumers' Defence League.

Members of the Committee and other Ratepayers will also address the Meeting.

Chair to be taken at EIGHT o'Clock by

MR. J. H. MOTE.

Admission by Ticket: To be obtained of the Hon. Sec. Mr. R. J. SUTTON, 15, Hilldrop Crescent, N., or at

ISLINGTON COMMITTEE ROOM,
HAMILTON HOUSE, LORAINE ROAD, HOLLOWAY, N.

FIG. 16. Advertisement, 1883

the accommodation supplied, so as to form their own estimate. Then, although stabling and the like were taken into account in assessing the rateable value, the Company claimed a percentage of that figure plus non-domestic charges for the stable. Finally, they underestimated the rateable value of better houses if there was a danger of their moving from the 4 per cent to the 3 per cent bracket.[55]

Outside the field of domestic supply, the New River resisted all pressure to abandon the principle of freely negotiated contractual agreement. The 1847 Waterworks Clauses Act, which the Company had injudiciously incorporated in its own statute of 1852, required water to be supplied for public purposes at a

[55] PP 1880 x Q 2346; *New River Co* v. *Barham* (1884) *Water* 5/1/84, 6; *New River Co* v. *Wilson* (1884) *Water* 23/2/84, 4; *The Times* 29/5/84 (letter signed 'W').

price to be settled by the parties or a Justice of the Peace. But the 1852 Act also provided for a metered supply for non-domestic purposes. By agreement with the Metropolitan Board of Works, the Company was selling its water for cleaning Victoria Embankment at a price which would be halved if controlled by meter; and the Board tried unsuccessfully to persuade both the Divisional Court and the Court of Appeal that 'the powers given by the [private] Acts of 1852 create a monopoly and if there be any doubt in the construction of these powers the public, whom the plaintiffs represent, ought to have the benefit of it'. The appellate court did not even require the assistance of the Company's counsel to conclude that the price was to be fixed by agreement.[56]

From 1886 to 1889 the meter supply section of the Company's special Act of 1852 (s. 41) came before all three instances in the extraordinary case of *Cooke* v. *New River Co.* The provision's oddities are here emphasized:

> That the Company *shall*, at the request of *any consumer* of water for purposes other than the purposes for or in respect of which the rates or charges are hereinbefore provided or limited, *or at their own instance*, afford a supply of water by means of a meter . . .

and the section then went on to give the rates of charge. The plaintiffs had a carpet warehouse in Friday Street; it was six storeys high, and the water was used for operating the hydraulic lift and by the employees in the daytime. For the supply to work the lift there was no question but that the price was to be fixed by agreement; but the Company was classifying the employees' use of water as domestic and charging for it by reference to the building's annual value at a figure four times higher than would have been obtainable by meter.

The plaintiffs succeeded before Kekewich J., who stated that the 1852 special Act was 'in fact a contract between the company on the one hand and the . . . public on the other, that in consideration of large powers of taking land compulsorily and otherwise conceded to the company, they shall be under obligations under which they did not previously lie'. Reading the statute in this way, he held that it imposed a duty on the company to supply water to a non-domestic consumer and, if required, to charge for it by meter.

[56] *Metropolitan Board of Works* v. *New River Co* (1877) 37 LT (NS) 124.

The Court of Appeal reversed this decision by reasoning which can only, if respectfully, be described as labyrinthine. Cotton LJ read the 'shall' and the 'at their own instance' as meaning that the Company 'may if they like . . . but they shall where required to do so by any consumer'. The last phrase cannot, he held, mean anyone who wants to consume; it must mean someone actually consuming water; but to fall within this category the plaintiffs must accept that they are consuming for domestic purposes and so must meet the higher rates. Bowen LJ rewrote English grammar and stated 'that "shall" is only the future tense and colourless'. The House of Lords devoted some time to criticisms of the statute, but affirmed the Court of Appeal. Lord Macnaghten stressed that originally the Company was not bound to supply water to anyone and presumed that Parliament in 1852 might enjoin a supply for domestic purposes, but would otherwise 'leave them unfettered'.[57]

The chairman of the Royal Commission which reported in 1900 (himself a lawyer) described *Cooke* v. *New River Co* as 'the most extraordinary decision I ever heard in my life'. Its importance in the politics of the water question lay in the fact that it exposed the City offices to the threat that the New River might go back on its 1822 concession and begin to bargain.[58]

7.10 The Last Campaigns

In the final twenty years of the century, the water question becomes extremely confused with disparate, and often conflicting, proposals being put forward for consideration by the legislature and with two Royal Commissions in the last decade alone. The fortunes of the New River Company as a water supplier become entwined with those of the other companies and therefore, in order to make sense of the story, some form of classification must be imposed.

[57] (1887) 36 Ch Div 641 at 643; (1888) 38 Ch Div 56 at 61–5, 69; (1889) 14 App Cas 698 at 704.

[58] PP 1900 xxxvii pt. 1 Q 13593.

7.10.1 *Local Authority projects*

The public bodies most involved in the issues were the City; the parish vestries; the Metropolitan Board of Works, whose functions, from 1889, were transferred to the London County Council; the Board of Trade, whose powers were vested in the Local Government Board in 1872; and the local governments of the outlying counties and towns. The Metropolitan Board of Works had controlled London's main drainage since 1855 but had learned to its cost that its statute gave it no power to supply water; and the Public Health Act 1875, which did enable Local Authorities to do this, did not apply to the metropolis. None the less, many of London's Authorities proposed schemes and promoted Bills for the transfer of London's water to public control, but the one consistent feature of their ventures is the way in which each opposed the others.[59]

An example is the City Bill of 1884, which was aimed at the New River Company. This proposed that charges be made by meter, a method obviously in the interests of those many establishments whose use of water ceased when their staff went home in the evening, but one condemned by Lord Randolph Churchill as 'the wildest Socialistic doctrine'. A further clause required the Company to bring into their accounts the value and income of their Clerkenwell estates, at the time producing ground rents of about £4,000 but soon to be enriched by the rack-rents. Churchill thought this 'robbery' and, as the Metropolitan Board of Works declined support, the Bill never received a second reading. Six years later the Common Council voted funds for a public enquiry, which began at the Guildhall, adjourned to Manchester and Glasgow, and reported in favour of public acquisition on the lines practised in those towns. The water companies declined to participate and the City's plan was dropped, although it did engage in confidential, and unsuccessful, negotiations with the New River Company.[60]

Similarly, in early 1890 the newly elected LCC energetically set up a Water Committee only to discover later that they had no powers either to spend money on enquiries or to promote Bills. Their Bill to empower them to do both of these was

[59] Public Health Act 1872 s. 35; Public Health Act 1875 s. 343; Public Health (London) Act 1891 s. 142(5).

[60] Hans. (3rd Ser.) cclxxxv 1223, 1225; PP 1900 xxxviii pt. 2 QQ 6799–805.

considered by a Select Committee of the House of Commons along the with City's Bill to vest the supply in a London Water Commission and the vestries' bill to set up a representative Water Trust to buy out the undertakings. None of the three supported the other two and all were faced with opposition by the suburban authorities, the Thames Conservators, and, of course, the companies.[61]

The only tangible result was the London Water Act of 1892, which merely enabled the LCC to introduce Bills. This power was frequently, if unsuccesfully, employed to bring in Bills in batches of eight to buy out each of the companies. The most important issue was the terms of arbitration. The City seems to have been fairly content with the standard form under the Lands Clauses Consolidation Act 1845, which, with its case-law gloss, was relatively generous. The LCC, however, was anxious to authorize the arbitrator to ignore the potential growth in the companies' income represented by the unflagging increase in rateable values and, most importantly, the New River's claim to be able to go on for ever distributing this enormous income by way of dividend, which meant that their customers—one-fifth of London's households—could never expect a reduction in their water rates. Although for a while in the 1870s the Company had prudently kept the return on the new shares at £9. 19*s.* 11*d.* so as to be under the 10 per cent ceiling, it was by this time dividing at a rate approaching 13 per cent. Various versions of the desired instructions were put forward, the most extreme being authority to the arbitrator to act 'as fully and effectively as might be done by Act of Parliament'. The slight hope that these Bills might have had of passing vanished with the safe Radical majority after the LCC elections of 1895, followed by the return to power of a Tory Government headed by Salisbury. None the less, as the LCC thought they were votes in the water question, it spent the next decade opposing all other Bills in the interests of its own scheme to bring water from Wales.[62]

Thus, by 1900 the public control over the supply and cost of water was still slight. Certainly the quality had improved; but

[61] PP 1890–1 xii.

[62] Hans. (4th Ser.) xxxix 41; PP 1900 xxxviii pt. 1 para. 25 and refs., and Q 4799; Shadwell 5, 136–8, 152.

a number of households had no running water at all, which provoked the Public Health (London) Act 1891 to declare them a statutory nuisance. Of those which did have it, a large number in the New River's territory had only intermittent supply, the Local Authorities did not exercise the statutory powers conferred on them, and there is almost a note of desperation in that provision of the Metropolis Water Act 1897 which allows householders to complain about their water to the Railway and Canal Commissioners.[63]

7.10.2 *Financial control*

In the last two decades of the nineteenth century over a score of private Bills were enacted, usually after considerable alteration by a Parliamentary Committee, and a larger number were withdrawn or rejected; their usual purpose was to tap new sources, construct new reservoirs and other works, and raise more money. Control of the companies' income was effected by tying the scales to the net rateable value in the 1885 enactment of the rule in *Dobbs's* case (see section 7.9). Control of their capital and the return thereon was a more complex matter which can be best explained by a simplified scheme.

7.10.2.1 *Share capital*

The earlier assumptions as to share capital are clearly seen in the New River Company's Act 1866. In the first place, there is no Parliamentary objection to raising money by this means—the water supply of London is still perceived as a business involving investors in risk. In the second place, the new issue could be, and was, offered *at par* to the holders of Adventurers' and King's shares, thereby enriching them to the extent of the more sanguine expectations of the market.

By the last quarter of the century the notion that investment in the water supply was hazardous had been quite dispelled by events. Furthermore, it was expected, in some quarters with confidence, that all the undertakings would shortly be taken into public hands; and so means were sought of ensuring that the capital of the companies—for the acquisition of which com-

[63] Public Health (London) Act 1891 ss. 1, 49; Metropolis Water Act 1897 s. 1; PP 1900 xxxviii pt. 1 para. 155 and refs.

pensation would have to be paid—was subject to some form of restraint. The solution devised by the Metropolitan Board of Works and inserted in the Grand Junction's Act of 1878 was then converted by a Standing Order of the Commons into a general curb. This was the 'auction clause', which ensured that new stock was sold on the market. There were slightly different versions of this provision, but the main effect was twofold: firstly, a company could not raise more than the sum authorized by the statute, for it could sell only so much new stock as, with the premium, would reach that figure; secondly, while the entire price paid was carried to capital, dividends were declared only on the nominal value so that the 10 per cent ceiling would be reached the more quickly since the return would actually be that produced by the greater capital invested. This clause was one reason why the New River Company was reluctant to issue new shares. The market in the original shares became extremely active (see Appendix I), many of the old guard sold out at prices between £95,000 and £125,500, and the 1866 issue stood at about £350. In 1895 the Company presented a Bill permitting it to raise new share capital without the auction clause. The Commons Committee estimated, however, that the 1866 shares issued at a nominal value of £½m. had commanded a premium of over £370,000, and insisted on the clause. The Bill was withdrawn.[64]

The final stage of control of equity capital can be seen in the fact that, in effect, after 1886 no company was permitted to raise money by new share issue, and in 1896 the New River was forbidden to convert debenture stock into share capital.[65]

7.10.2.2 *Loan capital*

The early Acts of the companies permitted money to be raised either by issuing shares or by borrowing. When, in 1857, the New River first acquired power to issue debenture stock this was issued at par and the difference between the 4 per cent interest due and the return which the borrowed capital produced went into the general profits of the Company; and since,

[64] PP 1900 xxxviii pt. 1 QQ 43 ff., 2254–7, 2267–78, 2352–4, Appendix C2. From 1880 Alfred Lass, the accountants, published an annual analysis of the water companies' accounts.

[65] New River Company's Act 1896 s. 23.

as it claimed, there was no limit on the income which it could divide and the debentures were irredeemable, there was no end to its enjoyment of the difference.[66]

Parliamentary control of loan capital moved through several stages. The first was the requirement (which the New River evaded until 1896) that, like shares, the debenture stock be sold on the market in such a way that the nominal amount offered, together with the premium, equalled the sum authorized by the statute. The second (in the Company's 1896 Act) was the requirement that the interest offered on the stock be that recommended by the Bank of England as best calculated to ensure that the stock was taken up at par; any premium none the less acquired was not distributable as profits, nor did it form part of the capital on which dividends might be paid. The third was the provision that the debentures be redeemable, so as not to fetter any possible public acquirer with perpetual debt. The fourth was the ingenious sinking-fund clause which was imposed from 1886 onwards, but only on the metropolitan water companies.[67]

There were several editions of this scheme, but that applied to the New River Company was as follows. After three years, the difference between the interest payable to the debenture holders and the average return on the whole capital was, after deduction of 1 per cent for management costs, to be paid to the Chamberlain of the City of London and used for buying New River shares and investing the dividends thereon with a view to extinguishing the capital of the Company. Since the average return was over 12 per cent and the normal rate of interest on debentures under 4 per cent, this was potentially a large sum and was the main reason why the Company discussed with counsel the prospects of reviving those common-law borrowing powers which had been so trenchantly confirmed by Sir Samuel Romilly in 1811 (see Chapter 6.6). Before the Select Committee, the Company fought hard but in vain against the imposition of the sinking-fund clause: their main argument was their ancient structure, which made 'in every respect, the property in the New River Company as unlike an ordinary share in a commercial undertaking as can be conceived'. Un-

[66] New River Company's Act 1857 ss. 4–15.
[67] New River Company's Act 1896 ss. 23, 25.

fortunately, their mid-century statutes made it perfectly possible for the Government Auditor to assist them in applying the scheme: a nominal value of £1½m. had been ascribed in their 1852 Act to the King's and Adventurers' shares and the 1866 Act added £½m. in new shares of the normal modern type. Similarly, their loan capital had been issued in easily calculable permanent debenture stock. The clause was applied, but the revenue from the separate landed estates was not taken into account.[68]

There were several flaws in the new sinking-fund scheme. The use of the Chamberlain—who was not a corporation sole—caused some legal purists to raise an eyebrow, but the main weaknesses were financial. In the first place, the transfer of the difference between net profit and interest paid merely postponed the day when the other companies would reach their maximum level of dividend and begin to reduce charges to the consumer. In the second place, the Chamberlain had to buy stock in the very company which had accounted to him for the difference. Now of course the sellers knew exactly when this occurred, how much was in his hands, and that he was obliged to buy; the effect on prices can be easily imagined. As the City Remembrancer put it, he was 'forced to make a market against himself'.[69]

The other device to restrain the growth of the Company's private wealth—the 'sterilization clause'—was to insist, as in the New River's 1896 and later Acts, that, if the undertaking were acquired by a public authority, the 1 per cent which it had been allowed for managing the debenture stock was not to increase its capital or be subject to compensation. An even stronger version of the same principle was applied when the New River joined with two other companies in the Staines Reservoir scheme, for the Act provided that if, within seven years, the companies were bought by a public body otherwise than by agreement, they could claim nothing for any advantage conferred by the Act. Schemes to make the Company separate old and new capital were also proposed but, not suprisingly, proved too complex.[70]

[68] Ibid. s. 31(1); PP 1896 xi QQ 2778–896.

[69] PP 1900 xxxviii pt. 1 paras. 64–5 and refs.

[70] New River Company's Act 1896 s. 31(2); Staines Reservoir Act 1896 s. 84.

7.10.3 *The Royal Commissions*

One way of breaking the companies was to provide a competitor who could supply water from elsewhere. This was among the reasons for the setting up of the Royal Commission of 1893 with a warrant to enquire into the problem of sources. The Commission reported, however, that with careful management the valleys of the Thames and the Lea should prove sufficient for the foreseeable future. Of course the scores of private Acts had ensured that the companies held almost all the sources of that area, and, as we have seen, the New River had exercised its common-law powers as landowner to sink over a dozen large wells in the chalk along the Lea.[71]

The second Royal Commission was appointed in May 1897 under the chairmanship of Viscount Llandaff, who, as Henry Matthews, had enjoyed a long career as lawyer, Tory politician, and public servant. Their task was to inquire whether the water undertakings should be acquired by a public authority. Having initially decided to exclude counsel, they then relented and met throughout the drought of 1898, which prompted an interim Report recommending intercommunication of supply. The three-volume Final Report appeared in 1900.[72]

The arguments rehearsed in favour of public acquisition were by now well known. It had been recommended by the 1869 Commission and many Select Committees; it had occurred elsewhere in the country without ill effect; it was particularly appropriate to the metropolis, where the competition assumed to have been intended by Parliament had long settled into truce; the London system of quinqennial revaluation had swollen the charges for water by factors quite irrelevant to the merits of the supply, and the average rateable value within London had risen from £37 in 1851 to £73 in 1896; finally, the recent imposition by Parliament of auction, sinking-fund, and sterilization clauses showed that that body contemplated public ownership.[73]

Against this scheme were advanced the economic argument of the efficiency of private enterprise, which at times amounted

[71] PP 1893–4 xl pt. 1.

[72] Interim Report PP 1899 xli; Metropolis Water Act 1899; Final Report PP 1900 xxxviii and xxxix.

[73] PP 1900 xxxviii para. 10 and refs.

almost to proposals for the canonization of Hugh Myddelton; the complexity of the whole issue; the sanctity of the contracts embodied in the private Acts of the last decades; and—a new contention—'that it is inexpedient that any representative body, largely elected by the working classes, should by taking over the water supply become large employers of labour'.[74]

The Llandaff Commission declined to enter into these delicate political matters, but confined itself to setting out the arguments for the financial expediency of purchase in the interests of ratepayers and the companies. Their report deals meticulously with the cost of purchase and the problems of reaching a figure by arbitration. One factor which is stressed continually is the position of the New River. The West Middlesex Company had reached its 10 per cent, paid off its back dividends, and reduced its charges, and the other companies were nearing that position. As to the New River, however, the Llandaff Commission states frequently and with confidence that the Company was not subject to the restrictions on dividend imposed by the 1847 Act: consequently, without public acquisition none of its consumers—one-fifth of the population of the metropolis—could ever expect lower charges.[75]

The Commission is firm in its recommendation that, if the companies are to be acquired, this should be carried out not by the LCC—who were eager to do so—but by a new Metropolitan Water Board. Similarly, the LCC's views on the crucial issue of compensation were rejected. The Report states:

> The companies have, upon the whole, performed their duties to the public satisfactorily and well. Most of them have gone though periods of struggle and difficulty, during which the shareholders ran considerable risks and received inadequate returns for their money. Some have now reached, and others are approaching a more prosperous condition, by the help, no doubt, of the great privileges which Parliament has given them. We see nothing which leads us to suppose that, if these undertakings are compulsorily purchased for the public advantage, Parliament will sanction any exceptional provisions, or depart from the terms of arbitration usual where the property of private persons is taken from them against their will.[76]

[74] Ibid., Q 5755.

[75] Ibid., para. 38, QQ 2360, 2374.

[76] Ibid., para. 48. The Commission did, however, suggest that 'it would be improper for an arbitrator to give any kind of compensation in the nature of a solatium for the deprivation of water shares' (para. 55).

CHAPTER 8

The Company (III) The Twentieth-century Takeovers

8.1 Metropolis Water Act 1902

SPACE does not permit of an account of the 1901 Bill to resolve the water question, nor of the lengthy and acrimonious debates in both Houses and their Joint Select Committee on the 1902 version which finally received the Royal Assent on 18 December. In basic terms, the Act followed the recommendations of the Llandaff Commission, and its general structure may be briefly outlined. Section 1 sets up a Metropolitan Water Board (MWB), a body corporate whose members were to be appointed by the Local Authorities within the area supplied by the old companies and by the Thames and Lea managements. At Midsummer Day 1904 for the other companies and 25 July for the New River their 'undertaking' vests in the MWB together with liabilities on debenture stock and mortgage debts 'and all other debts, liabilities and obligations of such company' (s. 2(1)). The existence of *irredeemable* debentures was an embarrassment overcome by providing for their conversion into water stock with a guaranteed life of sixty years (s. 7). Redeemable stock and mortgage debt were subject to the terms agreed when they were issued or incurred but were generally to be paid off within a century (s. 8).[1]

Following the precedent of the Local Government Act 1888, the statute creates a Water Fund of the MWB's revenue from the various rating districts and confers borrowing powers. On this fund is charged the 3 per cent Water Stock (a trustee investment) raised to discharge obligations to the water companies and their incumbrancers (ss. 16, 17). In the absence of agreement with the companies, compensation is to be settled by a special Court of Arbitration presided over by Sir Edward

[1] PP 1901 iii 351; PP 1902 iii 265, 297, 343, 389; PP 1902 vi 259. A competing Bill was introduced by the LCC: Hans. (4th Ser.) cii 339. The Water Act 1973 vested the undertaking in the Thames Water Authority.

Fry. As he had recently retired from the Court of Appeal, it was provided that any case to be stated should go to that body and not, as normally, to the High Court. In fixing the sums the court is to follow the traditional pattern of the Lands Clauses Consolidation Act assessments but to make no allowance (the 'solatium' of about 10 per cent) for compulsory sale. On receipt of final compensation, the companies—with the inevitable exception—wind themselves up and die (s. 29).[2]

Needless to say, the New River required special treatment and a complex clause was agreed with the Company at the hearings before the Joint Select Committee; it was then further amended before becoming s. 9 of the Act. Firstly, the landed estates and their terriers and accounts are excluded from the operation of the statute. They are also exonerated from any liability in respect of debenture stock transferred to the MWB, and the latter takes free of incumbrances on the landed estates. Secondly, sufficient accommodation for the Company was saved for it at the New River Head; and it should be mentioned in passing that, though the Company moved out and the MWB rebuilt after the First World War, the Oak Room installed by John Grene and occupied by Henry Mill and the two Mylnes from the late seventeenth century was lovingly preserved and may still be admired. Thirdly, at the Company's own request, the compensation was to be paid only in stock and not cash—a provision necessary to deal with the complex trusts affecting the original shares and fractions thereof. The Arbitration Court was to apportion the stock among the holders of King's, Adventurers', and new shares.[3]

There remained two crucial problems stemming from the nature of the original shares. In the case of the other companies it had been grasped for over half a century that ownership of a share gives no title to the assets on the other side of the balance-sheet. But, as we saw in Chapters 4.2.2 and 5.2, the Adventurers' and King's shares were taken both to be realty in themselves and to confer some direct rights over the river and land. Consequently, s. 9(6) provides that

> The transfer of the undertaking . . . to the Water Board shall include the transfer of all interest and estate of any shareholder of the company

[2] Hans. (4th Ser.) ci 1389.

[3] Ibid.; PP 1902 vi 259.

in any land or property forming part or used for the purposes of the undertaking of the company and not excepted by the provisions of this section.

Thus, the seventy-two shares continue to contain some kind of proprietory rights over the landed estates.

As initially agreed, the clause then declared that both these shares and any stock issued in compensation were to be considered as *land* and held on existing trusts. No time limit was provided for their conversion into personalty, an omission which aroused heated criticism in the House of Commons at the Committee stage—not because of the juridical oddity involved, but because the shareholders would still be entitled to the county vote of the 40*s*. freeholder. The Attorney-General's explanation to the House repeated the ancient wisdom: 'a share or portion of a share in the New River Company gave a person who held it an interest in the land covered with water', and amendment was promised in another place. Three days before the Royal Assent, Lord Balfour explained to that other place that 'the property was vested in the owners of the Adventurers' and King's shares and that the Company only administered the property for the owners', and the clause was altered to provide that the shares and stock were to remain land only until (after the appointed day) they were sold or devolved on a holder who was *sui juris* and absolutely entitled or had a general power of disposition (save as trustee, tenant for life under the Settled Land Act 1882, or mortgagee). Finally, the Company was bidden to introduce a Bill to implement the arbitration and to make provision for its own death or rebirth.[4]

8.2 The Arbitrations

Two separate arbitrations were required to implement the Metropolis Water Act 1902. The first need not detain us: carried out by Lord Revelstoke, it fixed the compensation for loss of office to the twenty-five 'Directors' (i.e. the corporators) at £76,917. 17*s*. 10*d*. They had claimed £396,255.[5]

[4] Hans. (4th Ser.) cii 1307, cxvi 271–2, 674, 1177, 1290–1; PP 1902 vi 259.

[5] Revelstoke Arbitration Award (19/12/04) transcript; Fry Arbitration (1903–5) transcript Table T (TW, Strongroom B6, No. A207).

The Fry arbitration was important, prolonged, and difficult. Three shareholders were appointed to represent the particular categories of Adventurers', King's, and new shares, and five points of law were stated to the Court of Appeal, four of them going to the House of Lords. In the end, all of Sir Edward Fry's rulings were accepted.

Three of the points can be dealt with quite briefly. The Arbitration Court held that the land tax was a burden on the shareholders and not an expense of the Company—this had always been the view of those concerned, as explained in Chapter 6.7.2—and, though reversed by the Court of Appeal, this ruling was restored by the House of Lords. The decisions that the Company ought to be valued as subject to the sinking-fund and sterilization clauses explained in Chapter 7.10.2.2. were upheld by the Court of Appeal.[6]

The real battle concerned the 10 per cent limitation on dividend imposed by the 1847 Waterworks Clauses Act and, as a minor corollary, the question whether, if that Act applied, the separate profits of the landed estates should be included in computing this sum. The New River was the only company to claim immunity from the 1847 Act, and we have seen that its view was shared by Sir Henry Thring (Chapter 7.8) and accepted without hesitation by the Llandaff Commission (Chapter 7.10.3). If the Company were not subject to the limit, then at the heart of its claim for compensation lay the 16 per cent profit in 1904 capitalized by a multiplier of just over 36. That profit was almost £340,000, giving a capital figure of almost £12½m. If it were bound by that limit, then it could capitalize only about £202,000 at something over £7m. Further, although the 1847 Act, if applicable, would have allowed back-dividends at least to 1852, the date of the special Act in which it was incorporated, the Company had in fact been dividing almost 10 per cent averaged over the last half-century, leaving a derisory sum of £400,000 to be allotted under that head.[7]

Three silks and a junior appeared for the New River and, for the MWB, four silks and a junior headed by Fletcher Moulton KC (whom we shall meet again in Chapter 9.3). The crucial s. 75 of the 1847 Act limited 'the profits of the undertaking to

[6] (1904) 20 TLR 245 (CA); ibid. 687 (HL).
[7] Fry Arbitration transcript Tables T and T.A.

be divided among the undertakers in any year' to a percentage of 'the paid-up capital'. The Act, however, required express incorporation and then applied, according to its first section, 'only to such waterworks as may be authorised by any Act of Parliament hereafter to be passed'. It should be said at once that this provision becomes meaningless when new works are mingled with old, and it would be strange if the sections (61–7) which forbid fouling the water were to apply only to that running in new installations.

The New River Company's Act 1852 had incorporated the 1847 Act, excluded from effect on old works certain of its provisions (but not s. 75), and deemed the capital raised and expended to be just over £1½m. Sir Edward Fry and his colleagues declined to distinguish between 'paid-up' capital and that 'raised and expended' and held the King's successors to be 'undertakers' within the meaning of s. 75. They were pressed with the clause in the special Act saving the Company's ancient privileges, but that itself contained a declaration that it took effect only where consistent.

To the delight of the Company, a unanimous Court of Appeal held that the statutory limit did not apply. Collins MR observed that Fry had assumed that the 1847 Act, once incorporated, applied to the whole undertaking, whereas that Act itself limits its own effect to new works authorized by the special Act. Romer LJ agreed and, pointing out that before the 1852 Act the Company had the undoubted right to divide all its profits, insisted that a heavy burden lay on one who would argue that the legislature intended to take away the private rights of individuals. Matthew LJ fastened on the word 'undertakers' in the 1847 Act and doubted whether it could apply to the King's shares, which stood quite outside the Company as created by its Charter.[8]

Although the Earl of Halsbury LC dissented, the rest of the House of Lords restored the limit. Lord Macnaghten described the Company's special Act as 'a careless and slovenly piece of work' into which had been pitchforked the 1847 Act. He dealt with the arguments drawn from the very words of the 1847 Act as to its own operation by saying that this was simply a difference in machinery from the 1845 Clauses Acts, which ap-

[8] (1904) 20 TLR 307, 308, 309.

plied without express incorporation (see Chapter 7.5). The main thrust of his speech, however, represents a particular attitude towards the interpretation of private statutes:

> My Lords, from the time of Lord Eldon, Acts of this class have always been held to be Parliamentary bargains between the promoters on the one hand and Parliament on behalf of the public . . . on the other. How can the promoters escape from their bargain by proving that their offer construed literally is unintelligible and illusory? If the language of the Act of 1852 can be construed so as to give effect to the bargain as understood or meant to be understood at the time, it is the duty of the Court so to construe it.

Armed with this attitude, His Lordship found it easy to read the £1½m. as 'paid-up capital' and 'the undertakers' as the holders of both types of share. Further, he found no difficulty in including the income of the landed estates—'there has only been one undertaking of the New River Company throughout its history'.[9]

Lord Lindley agreed that the 1847 Act was more readily applicable to companies of the modern type, but insisted that it must be adapted 'so as to give effect to the intention of the Legislature in passing the special Act, and not so as to frustrate such intention'. Lord Halsbury alone was more cautious in his approach to statutory interpretation and declined to 'do violence to the language of the Act. I think that there is neither an "undertaker" nor a "capital" nor a "dividend" in the sense in which those words are used in the Waterworks Acts.'[10]

The result of the imposition of the dividend limit was that, where the Company had claimed £13,260,144, the sum finally awarded for the takeover was £6,000,534. This was to be distributed in proportion to the nominal value of the three classes of share: £½m. being the 1866 issue and £759,979 for each class of the original shares. The compensation for loss of the office of 'director' was spread over all the Adventurers' shares and, out of the Fry award, the holder of an entire share (often, of course, a trustee), having proved the title, received water-stock with a cash value of almost £67,800, and 1,365 £1 shares in the new Company, while the owners of fractions received a proportionate amount. Deductions were made from those shares

[9] Ibid. 689, 690.
[10] Ibid. 692, 693.

and fragments subject to the Crown Clog (see Chapter 9.3) and in relation to the few holdings still subject to land tax. As water-stock was below par, the nominal amount awarded was £6,534,000. The Company set aside some for expenses (including its heavy costs on the appeals against the dividend limit) and divided £6,500,000 in stock among its shareholders.[11]

8.3 The New River Company Limited

Ten days before the old Company died, its past proud history engaged the attention of the Chancery Division and its title—over which there had been centuries of misgiving—was cured by default. Henry VIII's Statute of Bridges of 1530 imposed on their makers a duty to repair the approaches, and numerous cases encrusted around the Act had held that this meant a distance of 300 feet. Hertfordshire County Council sued the Company and sought to apply this limit to its bridges at the places whose names occur so often in Hugh Myddelton's ledgers—Broxbourne, Stansted St Margarets, and Wormley. Swinfen Eady J. held that the Tudor statute (as interpreted by its cases) was overridden by the Act 'passed so late as the reign of James I' which 'empowers *a company* to cut a highway and imposes on it a liability to make and maintain a bridge'. Consequently, the New River had to maintain its bridges and approaches but not necessarily to the extent of 300 feet. The case is hardly significant, save that all assume that the Company has rightful title to the powers conferred upon the City by the statute of 1605.[12]

Meanwhile, the Company had been busy with the much more important task of drafting the legislation which was to transform it into a modern property company. The recitals in the New River Company's Act 1904 are insouciant but protective. The story is outlined and it is said (emphasis added) that the Letters Patent of incorporation '*in effect* provided that . . . the "adventurers' shares" . . . as well as the King's moiety

[11] Directors' Report presented at first Ordinary General Meeting 28/9/05; Water Stock Distribution Accounts 1905 (at NR). In addition, the MWB took over debenture debts of £1,258,000.

[12] *Hertfordshire CC* v. *New River Co* (1904) 20 TLR 686 and 687.

should be of the nature of real estate'. The division of the King's moiety is said to have been carried out by Simon Myddelton and 'Sir Hugh Myddelton the son of the said Simon'—in fact, the Hugh in question was the eldest son of the founder's heir, Sir William. It then announced that 'the New River Company keep no register of the persons who are entitled to the fee simple of the adventurers' and King's shares and do not know in whom the same is vested'.

The Act then provided the machinery of a modern property company. On registration under the Companies Acts 1862–1900 the enterprise was to continue under the name of the New River Company Limited and its charter and all previous statutes (save, of course, that of 1902) were to cease to apply. The memorandum and articles were scheduled to the Act, its authorized capital was £240,000 in £1 shares, and its main objects were to acquire, develop, manage, and sell realty. One new share was allotted as fully paid in respect of every £50 of water-stock held by the holders of Adventurers' shares, King's shares, and old new shares, so the owner (or trustee) of an entire original share would receive about 1,360 new shares. As a result only 130,000 were actually issued; the higher figure of 240,000 had been inserted in the special Act at a time when it was hoped that the dividend limit question would be resolved in the Company's favour, resulting in a much larger award of water-stock. The crucial figures in the first balance-sheet were therefore the liabilities of £130,000 forming the new shares, and the assets of the landed estates which were represented nominally by the same figure.[13]

The problem of the juridical relation between liabilities and assets still had to be dealt with; or, in terms long familiar to the New River, the fact that its shares had always been realty. The 1904 statute solved the problem in two parts. Firstly, as to the nature of the shares in the hands of their holders, it was enacted that the new £1 shares issued in respect of Adventurers' or King's holdings were to remain land and be held on the same trusts until they were sold or vested in someone *sui juris* and absolutely entitled beneficially in possession (s. 16). Secondly, as to the relation between such shares and the

[13] Directors' Report 28/9/05.

Company's fixed assets, the Act provided (s. 31) that, after registration of the new Company,

> all interest and estate (if any) of any holder of an adventurers' or King's share or any part [thereof] in any land or property forming part of the undertaking of the Company . . . shall pass to and vest in the Company . . . for all the estate and interest (if any) of any holder . . .

Thus, there may well have been a time after registration of the Company but before sale of a share when the latter would still be realty but would confer no rights at all on any land.[14]

The Company began its new life with twenty-one directors (the old corporators), a gross income of almost £10,000 from ground and rack-rents, and dividend prospects of about 5 per cent, but with bright hopes for the future. It owned over 600 houses in Clerkenwell whose long-term building-leases were beginning to fall in—about two-thirds were to expire within the decade. In addition there were over 150 houses in the more distant suburbs; as their development had begun later, the long leases were not due to end until the mid-twentieth century. There seems little point, however, in tracing its fortunes as a modern property company. The old magic has gone.

8.4 1974: The Second Takeover[15]

After the First World War most of the occupants of the houses built on the New River's land became tenants protected by the Rent Acts, and the glittering prospects of the early 1900s never materialized. In the early 1960s a subsidiary of London Merchant Securities (LMS) began to acquire equity and loan capital in the Company, and the two collaborated in lengthy and largely fruitless negotiations with the Local Authority over the redevelopment of Islington.

In 1972, the Company's freehold assets were revalued at £9m.; its gross rental income was some £250,000 per annum,

[14] The sections are copied from the Metropolis Water Act 1902 s. 9(6) and (7) including the provisions about a general power of disposition (see section 8.1).

[15] J. Henry Schroder Wagg & Co Ltd., *Recommended Cash Offer* 29/10/74; London Merchant Securities PLC, *Report and Accounts 1983*, 8; personal communication from Mr N. G. E. Driver of London Merchant Securities PLC, 11/11/83.

its pre-tax net profit £155,000, and its gross dividend some 13½ per cent. The authorized capital was £2m., but of this only £800,000 was issued as stock, into which the share capital had been converted. Shareholders' funds also included a capital reserve of £7.4m., which arose mainly as a result of the property revaluation. In addition, almost £3m. convertible unsecured loan stock had been raised. In 1973 the Company reconverted the stock into £1 shares. Discussions with the Borough of Islington continued both on the subject of redevelopment of the three-acre site at the Angel intersection and in response to the Borough's desire to acquire the Company's residential holdings.

In 1974 these resulted in the sale to the Borough of a substantial part of the Clerkenwell estate for a price of over £4m. By this time, Sir Max Rayne (as he then was) either personally or through LMS subsidiaries held an effective voting interest in the equity share capital of 39.4 per cent, together with 45.9 per cent of the convertible loan stock. In October of that year shares were being quoted at £3; LMS offered £4.50 and the New River Company Limited was taken over.

Since that time the Clerkenwell Estate has been improved and expanded by the purchase of new commercial premises in the vicinity, including the old Angel Corner House, which has been restored and refurbished as offices and banking hall.

In 1980, after some twenty years of discussion with the Borough of Islington, planning permission was granted for a redevelopment of the Angel site as an air-conditioned office complex of some 220,000 sq. ft. set in landscaped gardens. The building was completed in 1983, just 370 years after the Cistern House was built.

CHAPTER 9

The Crown Clog 1631–1956

9.1 Creation

BETWEEN 1612 and 1615 James I contributed £9,262. 9*s*. 6*d*. towards the expense of bringing the water to London and laying the pipes for its distribution. In return, the Crown was to have half the profit but by 1630 had received only some £4,500, which, spread over the years, represents a yield of under 3 per cent. Furthermore, annual payments fluctuated, arrears owed by householders amounted to £2,500, and there seemed no certain prospect of improvement. Sir James Weston, a Baron of the Exchequer, was instructed to take the accounts and advise; a simplified version of the accounts presented to him by William Lewyn, the Company secretary, is printed in Chapter 3.5. Weston pointed out to the King that, of the annual royal income from the river, £100 was committed to Edward Ball for life in recompense for his supervision, and advised Charles I to implement the agreement negotiated with Sir Hugh Myddelton whereby, in return for the royal moiety of the profits, the latter would pay £500 down, £500 a year for ever, and would take over the obligation to Edward Ball. As the down payment represented at least some part of the uncollected water rents and the annual sum a certain yield of 5 per cent, the King agreed and discharged the Company of his half of the arrears.[1]

The tripartite indenture which completed this transaction is printed in Appendix G. Three months after its incorporation in 1619 the Company had, at the King's request, transferred to the latter's nominees 'one full and entire moytie or halfe parte' of the profits to the use of the transferees, so that they held the legal title in trust for the King, his heirs and successors. Of the original trustees, Fulke Greville had died and Giles Mompesson had, not unnaturally, relinquished office.

The parties to the 1631 indenture are (1) the King, (2) his

[1] William Lewyn's accounts at NR (above, Chapter 3.5); APC 1617–18, 157; 1618–19, 158–9; CSPD 1631–3, 182.

trustees (Viscount Falkland, Sir Robert Naunton, and Sir Julius Caesar), and (3) the Company and Sir Hugh Myddelton. The King conveys his equitable, and the trustees their legal, title to Sir Hugh Myddelton and his heirs and the latter covenants to pay the lump sum of £500, the life annuity due to Ball, and £500 a year to the Crown in perpetuity. Charles I also promises Sir Hugh that he will not assign the rent but will 'kepe and continue the same . . . to the Kinge his heirs and successors as to their Crowne united and annexed for ever'. He also covenants with the Company, as well as Sir Hugh, that he will render further assistance, confirms the present state of the waterworks as laid in royal lands, and, to deal with vandalism and theft and enable the yearly payments to be more readily made, authorizes the issue of search warrants.

Certain features of the arrangement must be emphasized. That Sir Hugh was virtually the *alter ego* of the Company can be seen from the fact that the indenture is tri- and not quadripartite; he and the Company together form the party of the third part and take only one copy. None the less, it is perfectly clear that the royal moiety is conveyed to Sir Hugh in fee and not to the Company and that it is only he who assumes the obligation to pay the rent in perpetuity. Further, although his covenant to do so is given in consideration of the moiety, it is *not* expressly secured by any charge thereof or by any right of entry and perception of profits. When the annual payment became known as the Crown (or King's) Clog (or Clogg) cannot be ascertained—although, as the name suggests, the royal entitlement soon comes to be treated as secured by some kind of burden on some part of the undertaking and not simply to rest on a personal covenant. Bearing this in mind, it seems best to treat of the subsequent history by distinguishing benefit and burden.

9.2 Benefit

Although Charles I had promised that the rent would always be held by the Crown, his son had to pay the moral debts incurred by the Restoration. Accordingly, in 1660 we find the rent being granted for thirty-one years to one John Robinson, presumably the supporter of that name who had endured exile for his King. This grant was then cancelled and a fresh one made for the same period of years to John Buckworth. The reversion on this lease was bid for by Sir Hugh's grandson and heir, but in 1664 was given for forty-one years after the determination of the current term to Eleanor, daughter of the late Sir Edward Villiers, with a clause noting that the grant 'is to be passed as a future interest not as a reversion'.[2]

The first grant expired in 1691 and four years later we find a petition to William III by Charles II's Master of the Mint, Thomas Neale, 'shewing that he was at considerable charges in prosecuting the East India Company for the King's share of the prizes, upon promise to be allowed a third part of what was recovered' and praying for a grant—in lieu of the prize money—of forty years of the reversion on the Villiers holding. His plea was unsuccessful, however, for in 1697 the King bestowed the rent for ever on a trustee for his friend and confidant, Arnold Joos van Keppel, first Earl of Albermarle; the fee simple thus passed out of the Crown.[3]

In 1735 the trustee's heir at law conveyed the legal title to the second, spendthrift, Earl, who set about borrowing money on the security of the asset. Within two years he had raised £8,000 and in 1737—when he became Governor of Virginia—sold the equity of redemption to the lender for a further £4,000. The Clog was thus acquired by the Adair family of Flixton Hall in Suffolk at twenty-four years' purchase and was to remain in their hands for the next 219 years. It would serve little purpose to trace in detail the devolution of the property. It was used as security for advances made by the family's bankers, settled on the usual life estates and entails, disentailed by the protector of the settlement and remainderman, and by the date of its final redemption was held by a tenant in fee simple absolute in possession.[4]

In 1956 the Metropolitan Water Board (which, as will be explained in the following section, had found itself the unwilling bearer of the burden) bought out the Clog for the sum of

[2] CSPD 1660–1, 328, 522; 1661–2, 24; 1663–64, 219; 1664–5, 118.

[3] CTB 1695, 449; Conveyance under the Great Seal to the trustee (Dennis Cooling) at TW, Strongroom B30, unnumbered box.

[4] M 6/12/1770; Abstract of title deduced on 1956 sale to MWB (at TW, loc. cit. [above, n. 3]).

a View of Sadlers Wells at Islington and the New River Water House

FIG. 17

£8,230 plus the costs of the conveyance. If, for the moment, we ignore the question of land tax, the Clog had produced during its lifetime £171,230, giving a yield of something over 5 per cent. Had the Crown retained the royal moiety it would have done fifty times better, taking profits to the tune of well over £8m.[5]

9.3 Burden

It was emphasized in section 9.1 that the initial obligation to pay the perpetual rent was assumed by Sir Hugh Myddelton for himself and his heirs and was not expressed to burden the Company, or to be a charge on the moiety of which he took a conveyance. Sir Hugh died very soon afterwards, however, intestate as to this moiety and the remainders on his Adventurers' shares, as explained in Chapter 3.6. His heir, Sir William, settled the moiety in trust for his own son Hugh, and at about this time it comes to be treated as itself divided into thirty-six shares and to be subject to the burden of the annual rent. The latter was deemed a clog and yet, as recounted in Chapter 5.2, Hugh contracted to sell fourteen of the shares to William Bishop free from incumbrances. There were two of these: the Clog, whose imposition (if it occurred at all) arguably occurred on the transfer by Charles I to the vendor's grandfather and so constituted a burden paramount; and a life annuity for one of the trustees, which was clearly a charge paravail. Although the point was taken before the Lord Keeper and his brethren, the court's decree of 1671 does not distinguish between the two incumbrances:

Whereas the said 36 parts were charged with a Rent of £500 per ann. to the Crown in Fee and £100 per ann. to Henry Middleton for life; and Sir Hugh in his agreement with Bishop had covenanted to discharge the 14 shares he had agreed to sell Bishop from those Rents. It was further decreed that the Plaintiff should enjoy the 14 Shares discharged of those Rents, and that the other 22 Shares should be subject to the Plaintiff's indemnity therein, notwithstanding it was insisted that Sir Hugh's covenant to discharge the 14 Shares of those

[5] MWB Minutes (Rept. of Finance Cttee, item 5) 22/6/1956; Conveyance of the Clog to MWB (at TW, loc. cit. [above, n. 3]).

Rents was meerly personal and did not nor could charge the whole Rents upon the 22 shares.

Thus, it is accepted by the court that the royal rent is secured in some way, yet the owner of the burdened property is permitted to reallocate the charge among the shares. Similarly, we find Sir Hugh's uncle Simon shifting the incidence of the Clog among the beneficiaries in his will (see Chapter 4.2.2).[6]

The details remain obscure, however, and the New River Company's Act of 1904 simply recites that Simon and Hugh divided the King's moiety into shares and burdened twenty-nine of the King's shares and two of the Adventurers' shares with the Clog; the Act also identifies the Hugh in question as Simon's son, but this appears to be incorrect. The confusion seems to have arisen because the founder's heir's son Hugh (the defendant in the Clarendon lawsuit) inherited his grandfather's title on his father's death, while Simon's son Hugh also became a Baronet (in his own right) before dying in penury. Although in 1671 the Chancery decree leaves twenty-two of the King's shares with the burden of the Clog, the 1904 Act is basically correct in saying that twenty-nine King's and two Adventurers' shares had by then long been burdened. The truth is rather more complex, since in fact various fractions of both categories of the shares had become encumbered, so that by 1904 (by which time, as will be explained, the annual amount had been reduced to £400) the clogged King's shares contributed (by deduction from dividend) £378. 13*s*. 4*d*. and the clogged Adventurers' shares the balance of £21. 6*s*. 8*d*.[7]

It appears, however, that some time after 1631 the actual mechanics of making the annual payment were taken over by the Company, which then deducted the appropriate amount from those of the shares of whose burden it had notice. The prudence of this course of action is obvious, although it is not possible to determine exactly when it was begun. The accounts from 1670 to 1684 which have been preserved give only a total of disbursements, divide the net profits in half, and then subdivide into thirty-six only the Adventurers' moiety. Presumably the Treasurer (whose accounts they are) was con-

[6] *The Lord Cornbury and Dame Flora his Wife* v. *Simon Middleton and other* (1671) 1 Chan Cas 208 at 212.

[7] Pink 54-5; (1809) 79 *GM* 795; NR:Water Stock Accounts 1905, vols. i and ii.

cerned only with the shares of potential corporators and not with those shareholders excluded, by necessary implication in the Charter, from governance of the Company. It is this method of initial payment by the Company itself which began the doubts as to the ultimate incidence of the burden which persisted until 1911. Although, as has been demonstrated, the Clog is not in fact secured at all, this is soon lost sight of and the problem is presented as being whether it is a charge on the Company or on certain shares in the Company. Fortunately, the unanswerable question of the relation of the Clog to the fixed assets seems never to have been asked.[8]

9.3.1 *The interregnum*

In 1650 the House of Commons 'enacted' that all royal fee-farm rents were vested in trustees 'to such trusts and uses as by this Act is and by the authority of Parliament further shall be declared' with power to sell the rents (but not to themselves) at eight years' purchase or above. In the next two years other 'Acts' authorized borrowing on the security of the rents unsold, and that of 9 September 1652 found it neccssary to deal specifically with the New River. After describing the indenture creating the Clog, it continues:

> And whereas some doubt hath arisen whether the said yearly sum of Five hundred pounds be comprehended within any of the Acts of this present Parliament for that the same is not expressly reserved payable out of the moyety of the issues and profits arising out of the New River; For remedy whereof, and for clearing of the said doubt, it is hereby Enacted that the said yearly sum from the Eleventh day of March 1649 shall be and is hereby adjudged and taken to be from thenceforth issuing out of the said moyety of the issues and profits arising or accrewing out of the New River And that all and every person who shall purchase the said Rent shall have like ways and means for the recovery of the same as he might have had if the same Rent had been reserved out of the said moyety.

There is no evidence that this scheme worked; indeed, a later Act 'for the finishing of the whole affair' laments that most

[8] BL Harl. MS 3604.

landowners simply refused to pay their fee-farm rents to the Trustees or their assignees.[9]

At the Restoration the same confusion as to ultimate liability is seen in the State papers, some of which describe the rent as due from the Company while others refer to it as payable by Sir Hugh Myddelton; the two combine in the description of the rent as 'payable to the King from the Warden and Company of Myddelton's waterworks'. The Company paid the annual sums punctually and the problem slumbered until the early nineteenth century. In the lean year of 1813, the dividends on the burdened shares were not enough to cover the Clog; the Company bore the burden and deducted it from later dividends or, where the shareholder also owned unincumbered shares, amalgamated the dividends to pay the Clog.[10]

9.3.2 *Land tax*

The incidence and assessment of the 'land tax' introduced in 1689 were described in Chapter 6.7.2.[11] It will be recalled that it was charged on the 'true yearly value' of land as assessed by the Commissioners (s. 4 of the first Act); and s. 15 provides that

> all and every person having any share or interest in the fresh stream of running water . . . called the New River shall pay for the same the sum of one shilling for every twenty shillings of the clear yearly value thereof.

The value was to be assessed by the London Commissioners, paid initially by the Company, but then 'deducted at and out of [the] next dividends', and the rate soon rose to 4*s*.[12]

The original Act empowered the owner of land to deduct tax at the appropriate rate 'out of every fee-farm rent and other annual rent or payment charged upon or issuing out of the premises'. This provision formed section 6, and was repeated in some section of all later Acts. Consequently, the Company always deducted land tax from the Clog at the prevailing rate;

[9] Acts and Ordinances of the Interregnum ii 358, 412, 498, 583, 614 (quoted, abridged), 720, 1137, 1275.

[10] CSPD 1660–1, 328, 522; 1664–5, 118; M 4/8/1814, 2/2/1815.

[11] Above, p. 123.

[12] Above, p. 123.

during the larger part of the centuries after 1689 this was at 4*s*., so that the owner of the Clog received £400. This did not mean, however, that the £100 deducted was transmitted to the Revenue; it was simply set off against the land tax assessed on the shareholders represented by the Company. As explained in Chapter 6.7.2, this settled down to an assessment of £3,600 and represented an ever smaller proportion of the profits.

In 1805 some £35,000 was distributed in dividends, which means that the true tax burden was a little over 10 per cent; and even that ignores the fact that the Company's revenues were in reality far greater since it was financing very heavy investment out of income. Aggrieved at the inequality of the tax position, the Adair who was then beneficial tenant for life of the Clog brought a bill in Chancery which enabled Lord Eldon to express his views on the nature of the New River. The plaintiff asked for discovery of the Company's true income, for a declaration that the tax burden should be borne equally as between him and the Company, and for an account of arrears.[13]

The Company admitted that its profits exceeded the £18,000 on which they had been assessed to the land tax for the previous 113 years but declined to reveal the actual figure. (The gross income in 1804 was in fact over £65,000, of which £28,584 was divided.) Sir Samuel Romilly was instructed to lead for the defence with a series of arguments of varying merit. His first must have been based on the assumption that the shareholders were the landowners and the Company merely a conduit for the tax, for he pleaded want of parties and insisted on joinder of everyone entitled to a share or fraction of a share at least in the King's moiety. The Lord Chancellor agreed that this was impossible and therefore unnecessary. The second line of defence was sounder: that the statute itself enacted that it was lawful to deduct at the appropriate rate 'out of every fee-farm rent and other annual rent or payment charged upon or issuing out of the premises'. Adair's counsel recalled that the Clog rested originally on Sir Hugh Myddelton's personal covenant and advanced a more modern view of the New River enterprise, arguing that the arrangement was a matter of company law, not of real property.

[13] *Adair* v. *New River Co* (1805) 11 Ves Jun 429; 2 Ves Jun Supp 265.

This is not really a rent, though it is called so. It is derived not out of a conveyance of land but from a grant of . . . profits [and] is nothing more than a division of profits: not a rent properly which originally was confined to payment out of land.

To this Romilly replies:

upon the merits this rent-charge is a fee-farm rent payable to the Crown within the land tax acts. As between the King and the representatives of Sir Hugh Myddelton, it must upon the covenant in the grant of Charles I be considered a fee-farm rent still existing in the Crown; and then clearly upon the Acts of Parliament the land-tax is to be assessed at 4/- in the pound; that is the owner of the property is entitled to make that deduction at the same rate at which the land is assessed.[14]

The third argument for the Company is (to take a charitable view) somewhat disingenuous: 'The greatest inconvenience would arise, a total uncertainty: and a new account must every year be taken of this great adventure.' The suggestion that the New River Company—one of the most profitable enterprises in the kingdom—was not keeping scrupulous accounts is at once preposterous and impertinent. The final argument is better:

Suppose the profits of the Company reduced in consequence of any calamity by fire; the owner of the rent would not participate in the loss as long as £500 was received in the shape of profit. Whether this case is put upon mistake or fraud the plaintiff is not entitled to relief in equity: if upon fraud he comes for a proportion of the spoil; if upon a mistake giving an advantage to all the proprietors, he claims his proportion, admitting that, if the event had been different he would not have borne any loss.[15]

Although the hearing took four days, the decision did not long detain Lord Eldon. Indeed, his interventions show that he had taken the crucial point at once: 'if neither the plaintiff nor the defendants pay to the public what they ought to pay, is this Court to administer the equities between them?' As reported, his judgment contains an interesting attempt to fit the New River into modern categories:

The Company are entitled at law under the instruments to receive in

[14] Ibid. 434–46, 440; PP 1821 v Appx. C(3).
[15] (1805) 11 Ves Jun 437.

the first instance the whole profits. Afterwards, in consideration of the expense the King had been at in the work, they grant to him one moiety of the . . . rents profits and gains made. So it must be a *chose in action*. After that the King granted his moiety by an instrument to which the Company were parties to Sir Hugh Middleton who covenants to pay . . . the rent now vested in the plaintiff. The acts since done by Sir Hugh Middleton are of this nature: that moiety vested in him either expressly subject by lien or only by covenant to the sum of £500 a year had become the property of an infinite number of proprietors.

He then takes a knife to the heart of the case:

The question is whether the plaintiff, stating that he has paid no more than he ought, has an equity to call upon other persons who have paid less than they ought.

To that the answer is obvious and the plaintiff's bill is dismissed, but—no doubt in disapproval of their conduct—the Company is not awarded costs.[16]

As a result of this lawsuit, the Clog remained at £400 until it was extinguished in 1956. The recitals in the Company's 1904 Act seem somewhat surprising, for they state that the rent had been reduced from £500 a year because of 'payments made by the Company'.

9.3.3 *Takeover*

Chapter 8.1 explained the general machinery for the transfer of the various water companies into public ownership laid down by the Metropolis Water Act 1902, but for the final lawsuits rather more detail must be given. Section 2 provided that the undertaking of each water company

shall be transferred to, and shall vest in, the Water Board, and there shall also be transferred from each company to the Water Board all liabilities in respect to any debenture stock or mortgage debt of such company, and all other debts, liabilities and obligations of such company then existing.

Section 3 enacted the obvious: that thereafter the MWB might exercise the rights so vested and should '(to the exclusion of the

[16] Ibid. 441, 443–4.

company) be subject to all the duties, obligations and liabilities of the company'. Section 4 dealt with secured liabilities, saying that

> any debts, debenture stock or rentcharges or other annual payments secured on the undertaking or income of any of the metropolitan water companies, or any part thereof, shall be . . . secured in like manner on the water fund established by this Act.

The New River Company had always treated the Clog as a burden on particular shares and not on the undertaking, and its Secretary had explained to the Llandaff Commission that the Clog did not appear in the Company accounts because 'it is a deduction really from the King's shareholders' profits'. After the public takeover, the Company stopped paying the £400 a year, the once-burdened shareholders simply pocketed their (slightly smaller) compensation, but the MWB did not start to pay. Consequently, Sir Shafto Adair, who was then tenant for life of the Clog, brought proceedings against both bodies which forced the courts of all three instances to reflect, for the last time, on the juridical nature of the New River.[17]

The creation of the enterprise is now depicted in modern terms. The founding statutes are said (emphasis added) 'to confer on [the City] an *easement* of a right to construct a cut and convey water through it', and the City's transfer to Hugh Myddelton to be 'what would nowadays be called an *assignment of the benefit* of the Acts'. The Charter

> in effect vested in the New River Company (of which the only corporators were the Adventurers) the New River with the profits, and provided that the net profits of the undertaking should be paid as to one moiety to the King and as to the other to the Adventurers, and that the Adventurers' moiety should be divided into 36 equal shares. The result was that the New River Company became a trustee of the profits of the undertaking as to one-half for the King and as to the other half for the Adventurers. In 1631 there was a conveyance of the King's moiety to Sir Hugh Myddelton, his heirs and assigns, subject to a covenant by Sir Hugh. That covenant created what has since been known as the Crown Clog.[18]

That the Clog is secured is a proposition not seriously chal-

[17] PP 1900 xxxviii pt. 2 Q 22625; *Adair* v. *New River Co and MWB* (1908); *The Times* 6/6/1908 (Warrington J.); 25 TLR 193 (CA); (1911) 27 TLR 253 (HL).

[18] 25 TLR 193–4 (Headnote by J. L. Stirling, abridged).

lenged by anyone. The issue to be decided is whether it is charged on the *undertaking* so as to pass to the MWB. The Company's own Act is silent on the subject, and the definition section of the Metropolis Water Act (s. 37) is not immediately helpful, for it enacts that the word in question includes

> all rights of taking, distributing and supplying water, and all other their rights . . . and all such property . . . as may be in the possession of the company or belonging to them . . . but subject to all debts, liabilities, and obligations of the company by this Act transferred to the Water Board.

It may help to hypothesize possible extremes. At the one, a piece of land utilized for the purpose of the water supply and subject to a perpetual rent charge would pass with both its benefit and burden to the Water Board: an example would be the land surrounding the first pond built at the New River Head. The waste ponds were conveyed in 1631 at a rent charge of £10 a year (and had long since been combined into the main pond), while the outlying acres were conveyed in 1744 at a rent charge of £362. 10*s.* 0*d.* (see Chapter 5.3). The Water Board accepted these without demur and did not redeem them until the 1940s. At the other extreme, an incumbrance created by a shareholder—such as a charge on the share of a perpetual rent to be applied for certain charitable purposes—would not pass to the Board but would fall to be satisfied out of the amount of water-stock received by the shareholder as compensation for the takeover.[19]

Thanks to the unshakeable acceptance of the New River shares as realty, the position of the Clog falls between these two extremes. The Company, ignoring its previous opinion expressed to the Llandaff Commission, persuaded Warrington J. that the Clog bound the Water Board, and his decision was sustained by a majority in the Court of Appeal and by a unanimous House of Lords. The later litigation is presumably mainly concerned with costs, since four silks and three juniors are engaged. The issue, then, seems to have been fairly clearly settled; but the case deserves discussion as a revelation of the

[19] An example of the latter is the Hardwicke gift of £20 per annum charged on a share.

way in which twentieth-century lawyers rethought the juridical structure of the New River.[20]

In the Court of Appeal, the sole dissenting voice is that of Fletcher Moulton LJ, who (before his elevation to that court in 1906) had appeared as leader for the MWB in the heavy litigation on the amount of compensation to be paid to the Company. He takes the view that the £500 per annum was simply the King's proportion of the profits, payable by the Company in case of default by the heirs of Sir Hugh. He thought it 'a clear and not very difficult point'. The Clog was not a deduction which was made before arriving at net profits available for distribution; those profits were ascertained, divided by 72, and each shareholder received that dividend save that the holders of clogged shares suffered the appropriate deduction:

> a portion of the dividends . . . goes to the owners of the King's Clogg and not to the owners of the burdened shares . . . It is thus borne by certain specific and earmarked shares that . . . during centuries have been passed from hand to hand bearing this special burden from which the shares of other shareholders were free.[21]

The lengthiest analysis of the nature of the New River is that of Farwell LJ (with whom the Master of the Rolls agreed) in the Court of Appeal. He states the question is being whether the Clog is *secured on the undertaking* and so transferred under the 1902 Act, or on the shares and so to be met out of the compensation paid. He starts from the proposition that the shares are realty, citing the great cases of *Drybutter* v. *Bartholemew* and *Townshend* v. *Ash*, which were discussed in Chapter 4.2.2. His quotation, however, appears to be not from the reports of those cases but from that of Baron Alderson's judgment in *Bligh* v. *Brent* (1837). As will be explained in Chapter 10.5.2, this crucially important case on the nature of company shares is either ill-reported or else the court was misinformed about the creation of the New River Company. In any event, the effect of the punctuation in the report is that Farwell LJ says that he is citing Lord Hardwicke in *Ash* but is actually citing Baron Alderson's much later views.[22]

[20] Loc. cit. (above, n. 17).

[21] (1904) 25 TLR 193 at 195 (abridged).

[22] Ibid. 195; *Bligh* v. *Brent* (1837) 2 Y & C Ex 268. At 296 Baron Alderson's citation of Lord Hardwicke in *Ash* has quotation marks only at the beginning of a passage, most of which is not in the report in 3 Atk 336, nor in Cruise, *Digest*, at *Fine* 537, nor in Lord Hardwicke's notebook at BL Add. MS 36056 fos. 100 ff.

His analysis, however, takes full account of the curious nature of the Company's constitution:

The result is the same as if there had been a conveyance in fee of land, as to one moiety thereof to the use of the King his heirs and successors and the other moiety thereof to the use of the said Adventurers their heirs and assigns as tenants in common with a provision for the irrevocable appointment on behalf of all in perpetuity of a reeve or bailiff to manage the estate, make all necessary disbursements, and divide the net residue amongst the owners.

Farwell LJ does not expressly say *to whom* such a conveyance was made, but it cannot have been the Company since (*a*) that is the 'reeve or bailiff' and (*b*) he expressly holds that both King's and Adventurers' shares are not merely realty but *legal* estates. The conveyance of his example, then, would have been made to the King and the Adventurers as tenants in common. That this is his view is made clear by the next step in his reasoning:

The King and the Adventurers being then tenants in common in fee of the undertaking, the King owning one half and the Adventurers the other as tenants in common *inter se*, the deed of November 18 1631 was made.[23]

The 1631 transfer to Sir Hugh and his heirs does not expressly secure the Clog on anything and so Farwell LJ has to point to the covenants therein between King, Sir Hugh, *and the Company* which promise royal assistance and enjoin the Privy Council to punish vandals and thieves, saying that this is 'not only a very unusual command unless his Majesty had some interest in the property but is expressly stated to be given on the ground that it is in order to enable Sir Hugh to pay the rent of £500'. He concludes:

The effect of this deed is in my opinion to create a legal rent-charge of £500 a year issuing out of, and charged on, the undivided moiety of real estate and the profits thereof conveyed by the King to Sir Hugh. It is admitted that it makes no difference whether the property charged is an incorporeal or a corporeal hereditament because the grantee is the King, and the only question argued is whether the £500 is a mere personal covenant or a charge on or interest in a share of

[23] 25 TLR 195–6. For the deed, see Appendix G.

profits only [which was the view of Fletcher Moulton LJ] or a rent-charge charged on the fee. I am of opinion that it is a rent-charge charged on the fee to be paid by the Company as bailiffs out of the rent of the King's moiety.[24]

The learned Lord Justice then has to face the fact that, as we have seen, both Sir Hugh's youngest son Simon and his grandson and heir Sir Hugh certainly assumed that they could alter the incidence of the burden at will. (The case in which Bridgeman LK approved of this—described in Chapter 5.2 and section 9.3—was not cited to him.) He states that the the 1631 indenture

left the property of the company [*sic*] divided into two moieties of which the King's moiety was thereby subjected to a rent-charge of £500 a year. The next step is that this King's moiety was subsequently divided into 36 undivided shares, but these shares were not parts of an unencumbered estate, but of an estate subject to the rent-charge. The 36 shareholders did not create the charge so as to make the encumbrancers claim through them, but the charge was paramount to their title.

The fact that, over the years, the incidence of the Clog had been treated as altered and was finally borne by shares and fractions of shares in both the King's and the Adventurers' moieties is not decisive because

there is nothing to show that the owners of the Clogg ever released the King's moiety and accepted a substituted security, nor is there any reason why they should. The company have always paid . . .

He concludes, therefore, that 'The plaintiff's status is that of the owner of a rent-charge paramount to the interests of the holders of the 36 King's shares', and clinches the argument by pointing to the absence of any provision in either the public Act of 1902 or that of the Company in 1904 providing for redemption of the Clog.[25]

The judgment may perhaps be summarized thus. Those assets subject to incumbrances imposed prior to their acquisition carry that burden with them on takeover by the Water Board; the compensation paid reflects the value of shares in assets already diminished. The King owned half the undertaking and

[24] Ibid. 196.
[25] Ibid. 197.

the Adventurers the other; in 1631 the King charged his half with the Clog and transferred it to Sir Hugh. Although the Company itself paid the rent, it did so as a conduit, not as an owner, either at law or in equity, of the moiety. That moiety was transferred from its owners to the Water Board by the operation of the 1902 statute, but subject to the Clog, which was paramount to the owners' title.

On the Water Board's appeal, the House of Lords required the case to be argued twice, but in the end affirmed the judgment below in quite brief terms. The Earl of Halsbury remarked that 'it was difficult to define the word "Clogg" which had been variously described as a charge, a liability, an obligation, and an equity'. For the rest, however, he and the two other members simply concurred with the speech of Loreburn LC. In that short speech, the Lord Chancellor lamented the absence of guidance from Sir Edward Fry, the arbitrator appointed under the 1902 Act, seems to have approved the reasoning of Farwell LJ, and had no doubt 'as to the validity of the original charge upon the King's moiety', which was 'a charge, to use modern language, upon one half of this undertaking'.[26]

The appeal was dismissed with the Water Board paying the costs of both Sir Shafto Adair and the Company; and, as we have seen, it bore the rent charge until 1956.

[26] (1911) 27 TLR 253–4.

CHAPTER 10

The New River
Property Law and Company Law

10.1 Introduction

BY the early nineteenth century, while the *form* of legal transactions was cumbersome and expensive, the substance of the law of property had been settled, and settled by conveyancers and judges. To the basic structure of estates described by Littleton in 1481 had been added the judicial response to the need for free capital in the devices of fine and recovery; the Statutes of Uses (1535) and of Wills (1540) had been pressed into the service of ingenious estate planning; and the Restoration Rule against perpetuities had been absorbed. As far as land itself is concerned, all that remained for the courts to solve were certain problems of urban servitudes and business mortgage financing. Their main task was to apply the concepts and techniques of land law to the newer forms of wealth.

Parliament, on the other hand, having done very little in the law of private property since the Restoration, became extremely, if erratically, active. 'Free trade in land' was the battle-cry of those whose aim was to strike off the fetters binding land to its 'owner' by increasing the powers, and lowering the cost, of alienation. Their arguments were that these fetters impoverished families, injured the land itself, and starved the market. John Stuart Mill maintained that

> in an economical point of view, the best system of landed property is that in which land is most completely an object of commerce; passing readily from hand to hand when a buyer can be found to whom it is worth while to offer a greater sum for the land than the value of the income drawn from it by the existing possessor.[1]

But where a large amount of land is held as investment and endowment, the mere abolition of restraints on, and lowering the expense of, sale are not sufficient. With all the subtleties of

[1] Mill 5.9.3 (Ashley edn. 1921, 896).

the strict settlement, there were many moments at which a wealthy landowner was free to sell—accidents, as Maitland reminds us, will happen in the best-regulated museums. The occurrence of numerous and rapid sales, however, would seem to require both a psychological detachment of the owner from the land, and—interacting with this—an available alternative means of providing both for investment and endowment. The stage must be reached when most landowners feel as did the future Viscount Ossington in 1847: 'I do not think it worth while to keep a security paying 2% when I can get an equally good one paying 5%.'[2]

The wealthy man of the early nineteenth century naturally saw his land as an income-producing investment for himself and his family. To free the land from its fetters he needs, firstly, to have power to sell; such powers had long been inserted in settlements but the proceeds were almost always to be invested in *land* of equal value. Thus, the second requirement is the existence of other safe assets with an equally high yield which, for the purposes of a family settlement, can be treated as was the land. Thirdly, the transaction costs of switching his investments should be as low as possible; fourthly, there must be organized markets in the alternatives so that there can be arbitrage between land, public stock, and private shares; and finally, the landowner must realize all this.

It would be absurd to suggest, in the teeth of the evidence, that industrial development needed the joint stock company. It is, however, submitted that the reform of the *land* law became intertwined with *company* law and practice. To the development of this process, the New River—which is frequently cited in the great cases on the nature of corporate wealth—was both a help and a hindrance. The use of its shares as the substratum of sophisticated family property regimes has been amply documented in Chapter 4.3 and was well known—but of course by happy chance they were classified as *realty*. On the other hand, the notion that shareholding conferred some direct claim on a company's fixed assets (described in Chapter 4.2.2) proved an expensive obstacle to the understanding of the nature of a share. A twofold process was necessary: the law had to give juridical

[2] F. W. Maitland, 'Law of Real Property' 175; Spring 222; Evelyn Dennison quoted by Thompson 290.

expression to the accountant's perception that shares are a 'liability' of a company counterpoised to its assets; and (what proved much easier) these abstractions had to be absorbed into the class of *things* (like the seignory, the office, and the rent of earlier days) which could bear the intricate superstructure of estates, powers, and mortgages. In short, the transition is from *fundus—omne quidquid solo tenetur*—to *fund*.[3]

The theme deserves a book to itself. This chapter must, however, consider matters from the point of view of the New River and can give only an impression of the whole story. A starting-point has to be selected, and the most appropriate seems to be the year of the repeal of the Bubble Act.

10.2 1825: the Background

On 3 February 1825 Parliament assembled to hear Lord Eldon read the King's Speech at the opening of the session and was told

> that never was a period in the history of this country when all the great interests of the nation were at the same time in so thriving a condition, or when a feeling of content and satisfaction was more widely diffused through all classes of the British people.

This combination of energy and complacency was evident both in people and in things. In the Cabinet, Liverpool had been Prime Minister since 1812 and (with a short break) Eldon's tenure of the Woolsack dated from 1801. On the other hand, Huskisson had been at the Board of Trade for only two years. His presence was already liberalizing trade, and his enthusiasm for the Industrial Revolution was to take him to the opening of a railway whose lines were made of the newly patented wrought iron, where he was to be killed by the very first train.[4]

A few yards from where the Members were gathered lay physical objects that summed up both the new age and the old. An Act of the previous session had repealed legislation dating back to Edward I and ordained the use of standard measures: the 'straight brass rod' and 'standard brass weight' embodying

[3] D 50.16.115.
[4] Hans. (New Ser.) xii 1; *DNB*.

the imperial yard and troy pound were in the custody of the Clerk to the House of Commons. Overflowing another room in the Palace of Westminster was an enormous pile of legally assignable *choses in action*—the millions of wooden tallies the *stock* of which had, for seven centuries, been handed to the citizenry to signify payment into the public purse: those of the Middle Ages would go into a man's pocket, while the products of later inflation were eight feet long. A statute of 1783 had substituted paper for wood, but the things themselves could not be touched till the death of the last tally-cutter and his like in the Exchequer. A few years later the problem of what to do with them was to be solved by the use of flint and steel; a solution so effective that, in 1834, the old wooden tallies, the new brass measures, and the Houses of Parliament were destroyed by fire.[5]

Meanwhile, on that Thursday afternoon in early 1825, the tensions whose resolution is the subject of this chapter were graphically displayed. After the King's Speech the two Houses separated as usual. In the Lords, the Humble Address was rapidly agreed *nem. con.*, whereupon Eldon rose to announce that he would soon 'move for leave to regulate a system which was going on to a most mischievous extent—he meant Joint-Stock Companies'. In the Commons, on the other hand, a Member appeared to see these bodies as the salvation of everything (including Ireland) and informed the House that 'British capital, the instrument of . . . enterprise, is already insinuating its salutary juices into the exhausted veins of that country.'[6]

The tensions were visible across the country. While the old open-field agriculture was all but dead, more than half the population lived outside the towns. On the land and in trade and industry there were fewer wage-earners than self-employed; and there were more tailors and many more cobblers in England and Wales than there were coal-miners. Most 'machinery' was still made of wood, the new metal equipment was unstandardized, and the typical town-dweller 'was very far indeed from being a person who performed, for a self-made employer, in steaming air with the aid of a recently devised

[5] Weights and Measures Act 1824; Receipt of Exchequer Act 1783.

[6] Hans. (New Ser.) xii 31–3; For Eldon on companies see also Hans. (New Ser.) xi 1457, xii 1196, xiii 1021, xiv 416.

mechanism, operations which would have made his grandfather gasp'.[7]

Yet the pace of industrial development was quickening. Factories were spreading with the use, for instance, of Cartwright's power-loom in textiles, and Cort's puddling and rolling process for the production of steel. The canal age was ending as 1825 saw the publication of Wood's 'Practical Treatise on Railways', six railway Acts, and the opening of the Stockton & Darlington. The new means of transport was beginning its heavy demands on coal, steel, and labour, and a regular steamboat had begun to ply between Ireland and the Mersey. The number of industrial patents shot up in 1825 to an unprecedented 250, exports of finished goods were growing as the Navigation Acts of that year liberalized carriage by sea, and the new species of commercial traveller, selling by sample, had quite ousted from inland trade the packman merchant with his wares upon his back.

The capital required for all this enterprise was being raised by means both fair and foul, and the pattern of boom and slump was here to stay. In the spring of 1825 business was thriving on cheap credit: bank rate had come down to 4 per cent, the yield on Consols was a little over 3, and short-term money cost 2½. *The Times* published a 'Directory of Directors' and the first great eruption of joint stock companies occurred. Of the 624 schemes advertised, 143 went no further, 236 issued prospectuses but not shares, 118 saw trading in their shares before their death, and 127 were still surviving in 1827. Yet the legal structures within which this boom occurred were elderly, inadequate, and shifting, one example of this last being the fact that the 1824 statute repealing the Combination Acts was itself repealed the following year. The Factors Acts continued to widen the breach in the feudal defences of ownership by protecting mercantile dealings in goods and commercial paper, the bankruptcy laws were consolidated, and shares in ships put on a sound statutory basis; yet the usury laws were still on the statute book, their existence made tolerable only by low interest rates. During the year the Bubble Act was repealed, the Bill's moving spirit fled to Dieppe to avoid the victims of his company frauds, and the courts announced that transferable shares in

[7] Clapham i 74; Hunt chap. 3.

unincorporated companies were illegal *at common law*. Industry and business blossomed without benefit of legal form: Pilkingtons and Pickfords were not incorporated; and neither were Bradford and Birmingham.[8]

10.3 1825: The Law of Property

By far the most important feature of the law of property of 1825 was its division into realty (which bore the full weight of feudal learning) and personalty. Of course, in many cases the difference (say between a house and a horse) was obvious. And it should be made clear that legal systems often take property which is indisputably in one category and 'deem' it to fall into the other. A simple example occurs where money is to be laid out in buying land. If the regimes for the two classes of property differ—for instance in the laws of succession—it is more convenient to treat the money as land *ab initio* for otherwise entitlement might alter at some arbitrary moment of purchase. Thus, the English Chancery invented the doctrine of 'conversion' and the *Coutume de Paris* art. 93 uses a similar technique. Another reason for this process is to make certain transactions inherent in one form of property available to the other. Frequently, for example, a mortgage of land is much more developed than that of personalty. Consequently, and expressly for this purpose, the *Coutume de Paris* art. 95 deems venal offices immovable; and, in a less articulate way, the fact that New River shares were taken to be realty made available the whole range of transactions recounted in Chapter 4.3.

But the problems which confronted the nineteenth-century lawyers were not those in which all agree that property falls into one category but should be treated as if it were the other; the classification of the newer forms of wealth was to prove extremely difficult and to vary according to the purpose for which it was required. What was the status of shares in public utilities? Gas emerging from a pipe was realty, but what of the

[8] T. S. Ashton 124; Clapham i 272; EHD xix 598; Factors Acts 1823 and 1825; Combination Acts 1824 and 1825; Bubble Companies Act 1825; *Kinder* v. *Taylor* (1825) LJ Rep 68, also reported in Collyer, Appx. XI; *Van Sandau* v. *Moore* (1826) 1 Russ 441.

light it emitted when ignited? Some municipal investments were realty, others personalty, while Leicester was in the intriguing position of issuing stock which was realty and bonds which were not. Further, the legal consequences of classification might be crucial. Thus, at a time when intangible wealth was growing rapidly, and capital was not merely movable but *mobile*, the law was operating with a system designed for a world in which riches were both visible and static.[9]

There were at least thirty ways in which the legal regime governing one category of property might differ from that governing the other. On looking at a list of the major distinctions, a modern reader's first impression is likely to be that (with the exception of the durable Statute of Frauds) they have all disappeared: after all, the declared purpose of the Law of Property Act 1922 was 'to assimilate . . . the law of real and personal estate'. But further reflection may suggest a different conclusion. What has happened is that the objects of the law of property have become divided into two great classes. The first comprises all tangible things (whether land or movables) and all discrete intangible things, such as shares, copyrights, goodwill, and the like. The second consists of *funds*. A fund is an abstract segment of wealth whose identity is distinct from the objects in which it is invested. These objects may be tangible, like shops and paintings, or intangible, like stocks and shares, but, just as the changing of shareholders does not affect the legal personality of a corporation, so the switching of investments does not alter the identity of the fund.

The modern law applies to the first class a relatively simple regime of ownership, possession, and security devices. It is to the second class—the fund—that the older learning has been transferred; it is there that we find flourishing the whole complex of estates, powers, perpetuities, and (it will be argued) tenure. The pivot between the two classes is provided by the trust.

In order to demonstrate this development it is necessary to outline the main distinctions between realty and personalty as they stood in 1825.

1. *Recovering property*. In respect of the remedies available to

[9] For Leicester see Hans. (3rd Ser.) cccxxiv 713.

a plaintiff for the recovery of his property, the system assumed that personalty was essentially fungible whereas realty was unique. It is well expressed by Littleton in his account of an action for damage caused by a tenant for life: 'this action is in the realtie because the place wasted shall be recovered; and also in the personaltie because treble damages shall be recovered.' As we have seen in Chapter 4.2.2, it was assumed—though never put to the test—that, because their holdings were realty, New River shareholders could specifically recover 'bits of land in several counties'.[10]

2. *Tenure.* The first question put by the 1828 Real Property Commissioners to their expert witnesses was 'Do you consider it desirable to abolish the rule or fiction of law commonly called the doctrine of tenure?' Whichever it was, both they and most of the witnesses thought it well worth preserving. The feudal system of tenure applied only to realty. This was taken for granted by the ancient authors, but Charles Butler had celebrated his assumption of the editorship of Coke on Littleton with a lengthy and learned note demonstrating that 'real property only was admitted to be held in feudality'. By its charter, however, the New River held the business in socage. By 1825, of course, most of the feudal consequences of the doctrine of tenure had disappeared; none the less, many of the important distinctions which follow are founded upon it and it was not until 1926 that we all came to hold our houses in socage.[11]

3. *Estates.* During the nineteenth century the estate concept became finally detached from inherence in land and applied, with no essential alteration, to the fund. Propositions to the contrary mistake form for function. The following axioms occur in all the editions of Joshua Williams's separate books on Real and on Personal Property:

> The first lesson to be learned on the nature of real property is this—that of such property there can be no such thing as absolute ownership; the utmost that can be held or enjoyed in real property is an estate. With regard to personal property, however, the primary rule is precisely the reverse. Such property is essentially the subject of absolute ownership and cannot be held for any estate.

[10] Litt 492; *Townsend* v. *Ash* (1745) 3 Atk 336.

[11] PP 1829 x 87; Co Litt 191a; Law of Property Act 1922 pt. V; Administration of Estates Act 1925 Sched. 2 pt. 1.

From this last statement the author deduces that 'the settlement of [personal] property by the creation of estates in it cannot be accomplished'.[12]

This deduction, long before Littleton's day, was not true for dignities, offices, and even personal annuities—'a yearely payment of a certaine summe of money granted to another in fee, for life, or for years charging the person of the grantor only'. By the seventeenth century it was not true for leases. The next hundred years saw the Government taking great care to ensure that loans to it should be seen not merely as a good investment but as a form of property suitable for endowment, and bank stock, Consols, and the like are settled as if they were land. Shares in private companies are then treated in the same way, and the practical results were well summarized by Francis Hargrave in his note to Coke on Littleton 20a:

Upon the whole, by a series of decisions within the last two centuries, and after many struggles in respect of personalty, it is at length settled that *every* species of property is in *substance* equally capable of being settled . . . and though the modes vary according to the nature of the subject, yet they tend to the same point.

It is hardly going too far to point out that, by an extraordinary and unremarked paradox, the property legislation of 1882 and its successor of 1925 ensure in effect that the one type of property which can no longer be settled is *land*; what is settled—in the sense that the entitlement to income is dispersed among generations—is the fund.[13]

4. *Descent on intestacy*. The differing destinations of the two classes of property on the death intestate of their owner—realty to the heir, subject (unless barred) to dower or curtesy, personalty among the spouse and next-of-kin—were of profound importance in 1825. In the absence of an heir-at-law (whether in fact, or because the owner died a felon) realty escheated to the feudal lord.

This feudal learning, with its later distinctions, was applied to the New River in 1849 in *Davall*'s case. According to the

[12] Williams, *Real Property* (1st edn. 1845) 296; *Personal Property* (1st edn. 1848) 7, 299.

[13] Cruise *Dignities*, *passim*; for offices see Litt 378, 379, and *Jehu Webb's Case* (1608) 8 Co. Rep. 45b; for annuities see Litt 218. Entails of annuities caused greater problems—see section 10.6; Co Litt 144b; Fearne (10th edn. 1844) i 562 fn. (h); PP 1831-2 xxiii 5.

Company's Register of Proprietors, one-third of an Adventurers' share stood in the name of Richard Harris, but the dividends had not been claimed since 1823 and now amounted to over £6,000. Elizabeth Holford had devised the fraction to him and his brother (who died in 1808), but both men were illegitimate and so could have no heir-at-law. In 1822, by a will valid for realty (see para. 5 below) he left everything to John Hester 'in trust for purposes or legacies I shall make in any codicil'. The codicil, however, was unattested and so inapplicable to realty. Hester proved both will and codicil and died, and the New River share was now claimed by the plaintiff, whose title derived from Hester's heir-at-law. There was no doubt that the legal title had passed by devise to Hester and so to the plaintiff, but the devise itself was on a trust which had failed for want of form. Had the testator been legitimate, a resulting trust would have carried the beneficial interest to his heir. As there was no heir, the Crown would take by escheat if the property were a legal estate—but the doctrine did not apply to equitable estates until Parliament intervened in 1884; if, however, the property were not realty at all, the Crown would take as *bona vacantia*. Counsel for the Crown contended that the shares were not strictly realty. He did not, however, advance the type of argument used in the cases discussed later on the nature of shares in other companies. He accepted that a New River share conferrred some claim over the fixed assets but (rather feebly) said:

> The property belonging to the New River Company consists, in a great measure, of machinery and chattels. The New River shares are not, strictly and properly, real estate; they may be said rather to what is called 'savour of the realty' than to be realty itself. For some purposes they may be real estate, but not for all. They are like gas shares and dock shares.

In a very short judgment, Knight-Bruce VC held the shares to be realty. Since, therefore, the Crown took neither by escheat nor as *bona vacantia*, and since a bastard has no heir, the trustee's successors took the whole; the Company deducted costs, paid over the back dividends, and altered its Register of Proprietors.[14]

[14] *Davall* v. *New River Co* (1849) 3 De G & Sm 394; 18 LJ (NS) 299. The first report

The canons of descent for realty were considered by the Real Property Commissioners of 1828 to be

> far better adapted to the constitution and habits of this kingdom than the opposite law of equal partibility, which in a few generations would break down the aristocracy of the country, and by the endless subdivision of the soil must be ultimately unfavourable to agriculture and the best interests of the State.

For the next hundred years great minds—including Maitland—engaged in endless debate on the respective merits of primogeniture and partibility. The question at issue was whether, as is expressed in so many words in the Report just cited, it is the *soil* whose destination matters. By the twentieth century perceptions had adjusted to the growth of company shares so that the *hereditas* could be seen not as a collection of objects but as an abstract segment of wealth. A profound shift of values lies behind the apparently technical provision of the Administration of Estates Act 1925 s. 33(1) that an intestate's realty and personalty alike are to be turned into *money*.[15]

5. *Testacy*. In 1825 there were some ten different ways of making a will, but the prime distinction of form was between freehold property and everything else: for the former, writing and witnesses were required, for the latter nothing whatever. Realty vested instantly in the devisee, personalty passed to the executors or administrators, who, in order to pay debts and distribute the balance, had power to 'overreach' the will, sell the assets, and give a good receipt. Not till this century are these powers generalized to form the crucial pivot of the whole law of property.[16]

The most striking feature of the distinction was that wills of personalty spoke from death while those of land did not, so that a testator could deal effectively only with land owned at the date of the will and unaltered in legal form on his death. The 1837 Wills Act adopted for all property the form of testament

errs in describing the fraction as being of a one thirty-fifth share: M 2/5/1850. *Burgess* v. *Wheate* (1759) 1 Black W 623 had established (Mansfield LCJ dissenting) that an equitable estate did not escheat. This was altered by the Intestates Estates Act 1884 s. 4.

[15] PP 1829 x 7; Maitland, op. cit. (above, n. 2) 182.

[16] Statute of Frauds 1677 s. 5; Law of Property Act 1925 s. 2; Administration of Estates Act 1925 ss. 36(8), 39(1)(ii).

which had been devised for 'the funds' and made all wills speak from death.[17]

6. *Debts*. No area of the legal system in 1825 better illustrates the conflict between feudalism and commerce than that concerning the availability of the debtor's property to his creditors. In principle his realty was sacred, whether he lived, went bankrupt (if a trader), or died. The issues are strikingly set out in the debates on the various Freehold Estates Bills which began with Sir Samuel Romilly's attempt, in 1807, to make a debtor's land liable for simple contract debts. The protection of realty had, he said 'survived the reason of its original existence 500 years' and since then 'this country has become a great commercial country, and therefor it was necessary to adapt the law of property to such a situation of things'. His Bill was decisively rejected and he settled for a simple example of class legislation—an Act making the land of *traders* liable for all their debts. Later attempts by Erskine and Gray foundered on the opposition of Eldon and Ellenborough. It is interesting that when, the year after the great Reform Act, Romilly's son introduced a Bill to achieve his father's aims and make the dead debtor's land available, it was passed with little opposition. As to the living debtor, the income of half his land was available by *elegit*; the capital could not be sold by a judgment creditor until 1864; *elegit* died in 1956 at the age of 671, but curious distinctions persisted until 1979.[18]

7. *Mortmain*. The word was used to express two different ways of ensuring that land was not kept off the market. Originally, it forbade the grant of realty by deed or will to any corporation save under licence from the feudal lord or the Crown; this restriction was not entirely removed until 1960. Secondly, since 1736 the word was used to describe the statutory rule which avoided gifts of land, or the wherewithal to buy land, made to a charity within twelve months preceding the donor's death; one reason for this enactment was to protect the donor's family. It was this, more than any other distinction between land and

[17] Wills Act 1837 ss. 9, 24.

[18] Hans. viii 561–2; Debts of Traders Act 1807; Administration of Estates Act 1833; Judgments Act 1838 s. 13 allowed the creditor a charge; the 1864 Act s. 4 (which had only prospective effect) allowed sale; Land Charges Act 1900 s. 2(1); Administration of Justice Act 1956 s. 34; Charging Orders Act 1979 s. 2: see *Irani Finance* v. *Singh* [1971] Ch 59.

personalty, which, as will be shown in section 10.5.3, forced the courts to analyse the nature of shares in land-owning companies.[19]

8. *The vote.* The county vote had, since 1429, belonged to anyone who held 'freehold to the value of forty shillings by the year within the county'. The franchise thus excluded lessees and copyholders but extended to all hereditaments protected by the real actions, including some—such as the rent charge—which were merely entitlements to income. The advertisements for the sale of Adventurers' and King's shares (or fractions of them) promise the buyer the vote in the two counties through which the New River ran (see frontispiece and Fig. 14). As will be explained in section 10.5.4, this privilege also compelled the courts to consider the exact nature of a share in a company.[20]

10.4 1825: The Company Law

10.4.1 *Introduction*

John Stuart Mill (who was, of course, hardly dispassionate on the issue) saw no reason why the State should not convert landholders into fundholders; but the development of the concept of 'the fund' was faltering and inarticulate. Furthermore, it is impossible neatly to separate funds used to finance public expenditure formed by the issue of Consols, bank stock, tallies, and the like from investment in private companies since the notion that the latter were carrying out the functions of the former persisted to the mid-nineteenth century. The New River Company began with the transfer of public powers into private hands, which may have seemed unremarkable in 1609. But the Companies Clauses Act 1845 which applied to all companies incorporated by statute 'for the purpose of carrying on *any* undertaking . . . *of whatever nature*' describes itself in the long title as dealing with those incorporated 'for carrying on undertakings *of a public nature*'.[21]

[19] Charities Act 1960 ss. 38, 39; Statute of Charitable Uses 1735; it was imperfectly lightened by the Mortmain and Charitable Uses Act 1888 s. 13, amended by the Mortmain and Charitable Uses Act 1891 s. 3.

[20] Electors of Knights of the Shires Act 1429, repealed by the Representation of the People Act 1918 s. 47 and Sched. 8.

[21] Mill 2.2.6 (Ashley edn. 1921, 240).

Many excellent works have been written tracing the rise of the business corporation. They will be referred to in the following pages, but the main topic to be examined is how all shares came to be treated, like those of the New River, as pieces of abstract property. The fact that limited liability came late was of remarkably little consequence beside the crucial perception of the House of Lords in the litigation on Simon Myddelton's will described in Chapter 4.2.2: that a share is a thing-in-itself, an income-producing asset in which may subsist (and flourish) the whole complex of estates worked out long before in relation to land—'*totam illam partem* carried the Thing devised, not the interest which the Devisor had therein', as Shower prints the ruling; or, as an anonymous manuscript reports, 'a share is but a description of the thing'.[22]

In that case, of course, it was 'well known and agreed that a Part or Share of the New River is an Inheritance'. What was needed was the application of the estate concept regardless of whether the substratum were classified as realty or personalty. During the evolution of this process a number of changes in practice and rules occurred to disentangle shareholding from the following notions:

(1) that corporations exist to fulfill public functions;
(2) that monopoly and corporation are intertwined;
(3) that a share is the fruit of personal enterprise;
(4) that it could not readily be transferred;
(5) that the shareholder's liability was unlimited;
(6) that, after transfer, liability endures;
(7) that ownership of a share conferred rights over the fixed assets of the enterprise.

The New River began with (1) and (2) but, as happened with its contemporaries, the foreign trading companies, became at last a purely private venture in competition with others. Number (3) caused no problems, although traces of it can be seen in the ledger for 1626–7 when the late Edmund Colthurst's holding is valued at £76. 16*s*. 9½*d*. 'for one single share of the profitts of the waterworkes ended at Michaelmas 1626'. The

[22] *Swayne* v. *Fawkener* (1696) 1 Show PC 207 at 211; BL Harg. MS 71 fo. 165. Works dealing with the business corporation include those of Anderson (1787), Scott (1910–12), Formoy (1923), Hunt (1936), Dubois (1938), Cooke (1950), Levy (1950), Berle and Means (rev. edn. 1967).

transferability of the shares was secured by their treatment as realty—indeed it was suggested in Chapter 4.2 that this classification was prompted by the very fact that, owing to the nature of the enterprise, the Adventurers could disinvest only by selling their shares. Of the remaining items, only the last raised problems; not for the Company itself but by the use of the New River as an example in numerous lawsuits.[23]

The stories of the Bubble Act, its repeal, and the growth of transferable shares with limited liability will not be retold here. The issue to be considered is the slow progress towards the modern concept of a company share.

10.4.2 *Doctrine*

It should be made clear that, to a modern reader, the striking feature of nineteenth-century doctrine is how little today's problems seem to matter to the writer. Coke's discussion in the *Sutton's Hospital* case offered learning, authority, and above all a *list* (or rather a set of lists) which could be used to provide the framework. The abridgments largely followed his model and were, in turn, the basis for the *Treatise on the Law of Corporations* published in two volumes by Stewart Kyd in 1793. Much of the work was written while its author was a prisoner in the Tower under a warrant of commitment for high treason, and indeed reads almost like a description of that sad fabric. In measured Augustan prose it distinguishes corporations sole and aggregate, ecclesiastical and lay, eleemosynary and civil. Trading companies are briefly mentioned as being formed 'for some particular object of public policy' along with Trinity House and the College of Surgeons; and the author displays far more concern for the problems of churchwardens than for those of the Bank of England. To assist the reader to understand the governance of the great trading companies, Kyd offers the analogy of the House of Convocation of the University of Oxford. The role of the Visitor occupies over 200 pages; the Bubble Act is not mentioned; the whole country seems to be populated largely by abbots.[24]

[23] PRO LR 2/41.

[24] *Case of Sutton's Hospital* (1611) 10 Rep 1a at 29b; Kyd i 27–8. Neither William Sheppard's 1659 work on corporations nor the anonymous text of 1704 was ever reprinted.

The year 1825 saw the appearance of John George's work on joint stock companies. This does expressly address itself to the fact that 'so many new schemes for the employment of surplus capital are weekly and even daily projected' and faces the problem of the Bubble Act. It is, however, a brief and eccentric work. Treating the members of unincorporated companies as partners, George enumerates at length the appalling difficulties imposed on them by the common law, but then simply declines to deal with the Chancery side—to which, of course, the vast majority of litigants were driven—on the grounds (no doubt true) that 'proceedings in Equity are a *dernier ressort*'.[25]

A quarter of a century later, James Grant advertises more. His book is entitled *A Practical Treatise* . . ., mentioning railway, banking, canal, and other joint stock companies. The Preface, however, announces with pride that here at last is a work based on a scrupulous examination of the Year-Books; and the text shows how very true this is. The index has entries for scavage and shewage, but none for shares; for bellman and buoyage, but not the Bubble Act. Grant pounces on the innocent assertion by Kyd that civil corporations may alien in fee; recounts meticulously the authorities on the point decided between the twelfth and the fifteenth centuries; gleefully corrects a mistake in Coke's reference to the Year-Books; and concludes that corporations cannot alienate their land since it is held for corporate purposes 'or in other words [is] subject to public duties'. A casual footnote adds that 'nothing that is said in the text applies to such corporations as hold land for the purposes of trade'.[26] The whole, highly intelligent, text describes only the world that was fading.

In 1860 Lindley's work appears: it is called *The Law of Partnership, including joint-stock and other companies*, and lists the numerous general company Acts under the rubric of 'the English statutory law of *partnership*'. In later years, his work does split into two as companies come to be thought worthy of special treatment; but the last (1902) edition of the separate volume on companies is still advising the reader that, to ascertain

[25] George 17.
[26] Grant 129–37.

whether a share is realty or personalty, he must look closely at the constitution of the company involved.[27]

10.5 The Classification of Shares

10.5.1 *Introduction*

The obvious place to classify shares in a company as realty or personalty is in the instrument of incorporation. The New River charter did not expressly do so but was unmistakably cast in the terminology of realty. Later in that century the shares of other bodies are declared to be personalty, although at first this looks like an afterthought. The East India charters were silent on the subject but the Act of 1697 declares that 'the estates, interests and stocks shall be adjudged and taken . . . to be a personal and not a real estate and shall go to the executor . . . and not to the heir'. Similarly, the 1694 Act setting up the Bank of England required clarification in much the same terms in 1697, and the South Sea Company's statute includes the same provision. At the beginning of the modern law, the 1844 Act does not make the classification clear, but the 1856 Act does so.[28]

[27] Lindley, *Companies* (6th edn., 2 vols., 1902, though the first five editions were of the single book) i 630. A modest but deservedly successful exception to this type of approach is that of C. F. Wordsworth, who in 1836 first printed with comments all available statutes and certain Parliamentary Standing Orders. His work went into approximately nine editions; the reasons for the imprecision are sadly familiar today: the preface to the 8th edition (1860) reveals that 'a fresh one was prepared but the printing of it was suspended by reason of the Companies Consolidation Bill having been introduced into Parliament. It was expected [to] become law during the past session, but has been withdrawn.'

[28] East India Company Act 1697 s. 71; Bank of England Acts 1694 and 1697 s. 33 (the latter declares bank stock personalty from Midsummer 1697. Mr John Barton, of Merton College, Oxford, has drawn attention to a note in Linc. Inn MSS Hill 8 25b (MF 1787-A66). This says that in *Oldham* v. *Pickering* (1696 MT) mention was made of a case at the sittings after HT 1696 'concerning the shares in the Bank of England where Holt held that they were a fee simple so as to descend but that they had not the other qualities of a fee simple as dower etc.', and a marginal note by Serjeant Hill suggests that this prompted 7 & 8 Will. III, c. 31, s. 16 (Land Bank Act 1696). The point is not mentioned in the several printed reports of *Oldham* v. *Pickering*, and it seems strange that Holt would allow a son to plead realty for himself but to defeat his mother: one would expect so great a judge instinctively to apply the principle of *retorcutio* which heads D 2 2); South Sea Company Act 1710 s. 37; Companies Clauses

It might be thought from the above that generally there would be no problem and that the law had finally accepted the account merchant in which land is owned by the firm and appears in the books as assets, debtor to capital, while the shares are liabilities. In fact double-entry was not utilized by the Chancery until the rules of 1828 which followed Eldon's departure, and did not reach the public revenue accounts (along with the English language and arabic numerals) until 1834. Meanwhile, lawyers found the greatest difficulty in accepting that shares in a corporation whose main asset was land could themselves be personalty. A long current of the older law had held that the profits of a soke mill, turnpike tolls, and the like were real property, and that current ran strongly down the New River.[29]

Now, apart from the Bank and the great trading companies, many of the corporations of the eighteenth and early nineteenth centuries were public utilities, formed to construct and manage land used for docks, waterworks, canals, and railways. So, in a case in 1849 involving the liability of lighthouse tolls to probate and legacy duty (which did not apply to realty), we find Lord Cottenham LC, after brooding on the New River ('a question of very great nicety'), holding the *light* to be realty as a result of the following meditation:

> [I]f I send a stream of inflammable gas through a pipe and ignite it at the end, it is real property; but if I send a stream of light from the house where it originates then according to the [losing] argument it is personalty.

While the public-utility companies were clearly involved in managing land for the benefit of their shareholders, all trading and service corporations—such as banking and insurance—need some building in which to operate. So, throughout the first half of the nineteenth century we find lawyers again and again returning to the argument that if the legal entity holds land then somehow—perhaps through the medium of a trust—its shares must be realty.[30]

Consolidation Act 1845 s. 7; Joint Stock Companies Act 1856 s. 15 re-enacted in the 1862 Act s. 22.

[29] Chancery Rules of 3/4/1828 r. 61. Receipt of Exchequer Act 1834: see Hans. (3rd Ser.) xxii 199.

[30] *A-G* v. *Jones* (1849) 1 Mac & G 574 at 594–5 considering *R* v. *Coke* (1826) 5 B & C 797, where the New River's influence is decisive.

It must be emphasized, however, that the success—or even the appearance—of this contention varies according to the purpose for which classification is required. Lord Brougham LC, five years after he had set in motion the great law reforms of the early nineteenth century, is still saying from the Bench that 'nor are shares, nor the purchase of shares, things known in law'. Yet his powerful reasoning in the great case of *Keppel* v. *Bailey* in 1834 is based on the unspoken assumption that shares in a railway confer no interest in land. The shareholders sought to enforce a covenant that their line would be used to carry limestone. The action was brought against an *assignee* of the covenantor's works (who took with notice) and so raised the fundamental question as to whether such a right (perfectly good in contract) might count as a property interest and so be valid against third parties. One of the reasons given against the claim was 'There is no reversion now in the covenantees to which the right claimed . . . may be annexed . . . it is the case of mere strangers.' Similarly, Brougham was persuaded by Sugden to hold in a regrettably brief judgment that shares in a canal company were personalty and so within the bankruptcy laws.[31]

Although the question of classification was raised in countless cases and for many purposes, the New River's influence was felt most strongly in three situations. One was a matter of form—the requirement of three witnesses for a will of realty—and two were of substance—mortmain and the vote.

10.5.2 *Wills*

Arguments drawn from the New River were used in the two leading cases. In the first, the conclusion was reached that shares in a water undertaking are realty; in the second—forty years on—that they are not. In much of the later litigation it is these which are most cited, while the New River figures as a strange, almost ancestral, presence.

In *Buckeridge* v. *Ingham* (1795) the testator had disposed of shares in the Avon canal by a codicil which, if they were personalty, was valid but was not if they were realty. His family

[31] *Walbur* v. *Ingleby* (1833) 1 My & K 60 at 78; *Keppel* v *Bailey* (1834) 2 My & K 517 at 534; *Ex parte Lancaster Canal Co* (1832) 1 Deac & Chitty 411.

claimed the latter so that they would descend on intestacy to the heir, subject to the widow's dower. An Act of 1711 had given the City of Bath powers to improve navigation on the Avon and to make new cuts, build bridges, sluices, weirs, and so on. As London did before them, they transferred the powers to an unincorporate body of thirty-two persons headed by the Duke of Beaufort, and it was shares in this enterprise which the testator attempted to bequeath.

Counsel for the widow insists that 'the act 3 James I establishing the New River is just like this. Only a liberty to use the land is given, the inheritance being left in the owners.' On the other side, counsel emphasizes the oddity—'it has been considered as if the soil vested absolutely in Sir Hugh Middleton; if not, what pretence was there for a fine in each county?' Sir R. P. Arden MR holds them to be realty:

> [I]t would be strange to say, this right of making all these cuts . . . does not savour of the realty: It not only does but partakes of it: it is not the soil, which I hold would hardly pass to the grantee: but it is a right arising out of the soil. The Act establishing the New River was referred to as the foundation of the rights of that company: but that Act is vastly inferior to the powers they exercise. I cannot find anything in it but a right of making a cut of a certain length to convey water to London. That is all that is given by that Act. There must be some subsequent Act; for they lay pipes *in alieno solo* and go much further; and it is acted upon as real estate; and recoveries are suffered and fines levied upon it. There is no difference between that property and this.[32]

In *Bligh* v. *Brent* (1837) the testator owned shares in the Chelsea Waterworks Company (see Chapter 7.2) and, by a will valid for personalty but not realty, left them to his wife. The heir at law filed a bill charging 'that the shares in that company are, in their nature, real estates of inheritance in fee-simple'. Alderson B. directed a hearing before the full court in which the question is presented by counsel as being one of construction of the company's Act and charter. That statute empowered incorporation; the charter does so and provides for freely assignable shares with voting rights; no doubt with a sense of the predatory nature of the New River those rights could not be exercised by a shareholder if he, or his trustee, also held shares

[32] *Buckeridge* v. *Ingham* (1795) 2 Ves Jun 652 at 661–3; Avon Navigation Act 1711.

in any other London water company. Neither statute nor charter classifies the shares as realty or personalty.[33]

Counsel for the heir point out that many statutes declare shares to be personalty, deducing from this 'a strong argument to show what, in the contemplation of the legislature, would have been the nature of those shares without declaration'. Here, they say, the company could hold land and lay pipes *in alieno solo*; and that

> the property is vested in the shareholders as a corporation in trust for themselves individually according to their respective interests. The company has an estate vested in them and their successors for ever, which constitutes an estate in fee-simple. If so, how is it possible to contend successfully that, the company being trustee for the shareholders, the interest of the cestuis que trust is not co-extensive with the legal interest of the trustees.

As authority, of course, they cite the great New River cases and, to crown the argument, say:

> It is impossible to distinguish the nature of the property which the proprietors of this company originally acquired and that of the property belonging to the New River Company.[34]

For the company and the widow, counsel recall that the Chelsea shares have been considered personalty for 125 years. In fact they did not have to mount a very strong argument, since the court has been interrupting fairly forcefully. Baron Parke's interjections are particularly noteworthy:

> The difficulty arises from confounding the corporation with the persons who take the profits: those persons have no right to anything but the profits . . . the company is as much distinct from the proprietors as one man with another.

And—to help the defence—

> Your argument is that the shareholder has no right to the specific profits, or to the possession of any part of the realty, but only to a share of the capital according to the amount . . . subscribed.

To deal with the trust argument, he objects, 'Then whether the

[33] *Bligh* v. *Brent* (1837) 2 Y & C Ex 268; Chelsea Waterworks Act 1721.
[34] 275–7, 291–2 (abridged).

property were real or personal would depend from time to time on the option of the directors.'[35]

The judgment of the Court was delivered by Alderson B., who admits the difficulties but—although he begins by confining himself to the question of construction of the founding documents—his analysis goes much deeper.

The property is money—the subscriptions of individual corporators. In order to make that profitable it is entrusted to a corporation who have an unlimited power of converting part of it into land, part into goods.

The next step recalls the example of Bayley J. in the New River rating case of 1813, described in Chapter 6.7.4:

If [the company] thought that they could with a greater profit supply water by conveying it in carts or the like they would have a perfect right to so so. It would be strange if the nature of these shares should continually fluctuate ... Suppose a man made his will attested by two persons and at a time when the corporation held only personal estate. It is good. He becomes lunatic ... and then real property is bought by the corporation. Is his will to be set aside? And yet he cannot make another. [T]he purpose of all this is obtaining a clear surplus profit from the use and disposal of this capital. ... It is this surplus profit which alone is divisible. The land or the chattels are only the instruments ... whereby the joint stock of money is made to produce profit.[36]

The court thus produces perfectly sensible reasons for holding Chelsea waterworks shares to be personalty. It must be admitted, however, that (as reported) they cope with the problem of the New River authorities only by a mixture of confusion and assertion. The Lord Chief Baron says (italics added):

It appears that the land in that case was not vested in the corporation *of London* at all but in the individuals. The corporation was incidental to the purposes of management only and was not seised of the land. That explains the observation of Lord Hardwicke, which at first appears extraordinary, as to the possibility of the proprietors bringing ejectment. In the New River cases, the individual corporators have the property. The corporation have only the management of it.

[35] 288, 291. Counsel also cite *Weekley* v. *Weekley* (1781), a note of which is inserted at 2 Y & C Ex 283.

[36] 295, 296. Cf. *R* v. *New River Company* (1813) 1 M & S 503 at 512, 513.

Baron Parke also mixes up the two bodies: 'The Corporation *of London* took no estate but only a power, the effect of which would be vest the real property in the individual members.' And the Avon canal case, it was said, 'may be left out of the question for the Duke of Beaufort was not a corporation'.[37]

10.5.3 *Mortmain*

The problems occasioned by the inalienability of land in the hands of charities, together with a certain suspicion of clerical enterprise at the death-bed, had found expression in Magna Charta and in many later laws. The important statute was that of 1735 which, with the added aim of protecting the family, enacted that no land (etc.) 'or other hereditaments corporeal or incorporeal whatsoever, nor any . . . money, goods, chattels stock in the public funds . . . to be laid out or disposed of in the purchase of any lands' should be given for charitable purposes within the year preceding the donor's death. It seems strange today to look back on the difficulties felt by lawyers over the gift to a charity, as an investment, of shares in a company among whose assets might be land; none the less, the natural zeal of the family provoked a large number of lawsuits. A testator in 1799 left Avon navigation shares 'for the improvement of the city of Bath', declaring that this was 'agreeable to his own inclination, though perhaps not to the parties concerned'. The latter found it extremely disagreeable, prayed *Buckeridge* v. *Ingham* in aid of the Mortmain Act, and gave families a weapon they were to employ against charitably minded fathers for the next six decades.[38]

Faced with the rapid growth of these new forms of wealth, the courts began a wide and strict enforcement of the Mortmain Act and in 1823 Sir John Leach VC sharpened the disgruntled family's weapon by holding—without any reported reason—that it applied to shares in canal companies whose statutes declared the shares personalty and transmissible as such. East

[37] 284, 288–9, 295. The decision is later used as authority in other fields, such as whether contracts to sell shares in such companies fall within the Statute of Frauds s. 4: e.g. *Bradley* v. *Holdsworth* (1838) 3 M & W 422.

[38] Statute of Charitable Uses 1735; *Howse* v. *Chapman* (1799) 4 Ves Jun 542.

India shares, on the other hand, were held by the Master of the Rolls in 1835 to escape the Act; this was both because they were personalty by statute and because the company's main functions did not concern land. His successor, Langdale MR, fortified by *Bligh* v. *Brent* (the Chelsea waterworks case), applies similar reasoning to insurance policies, although the Chancery Master had attempted to work out the proportion of the companies' land to their other assets and avoid the gift *pro tanto*! In the 1840s the Chancery is using the same approach to public-utility companies whether incorporate or not, even though counsel for the family are citing *Buckeridge* v. *Ingham* and saying 'but there is a dock itself, the land covered with water, the land on which the gasometer is built'. Even so, Lord Langdale MR thought it 'a very nice question' and suggested that 'the parties will render a public service by bringing the question under the consideration of the Lord Chancellor.'[39]

That public service was rendered with a vengeance by the litigants in *Myers* v. *Perigal* (1849–52), who were forced to bring the matter before two Lords Chancellor and the Common Pleas. The testator had left his residuary estate to his wife for life and then to trustees for certain charities. The Chancery Master held a number of the assets to fall foul of the Mortmain Act, including railway shares and debentures. These were unhesitatingly classified as personalty by Shadwell VC but the shares in an *unincorporated* banking company caused great difficulty, for, although the deed of settlement declared the shares to be personalty, the bank's premises included freehold and copyhold buildings. The Vice-Chancellor held these shares to be realty, being prompted by counsel for the next-of-kin, who had insisted that the bank was 'a mere co-partnership, and every individual shareholder has an interest in the real estates and chattels real'. On appeal, Lord Truro LC adverted to the importance of the case, to the number of such investments, to the conflicting state of the case law, and to Magna Charta. His judgment is rambling and, in its handling of the cases cited, inaccurate, but finally states for the Common Pleas the question

[39] *Tomlinson* v. *Tomlinson* (1823) 9 Beav 459; *A-G* v. *Giles* (1835) 5 LJ (NS) Ch 44; *March* v. *A-G* (1842) 5 Beav 433; *Sparling* v. *Parker* (1846) 9 Beav 450 at 455; *Walker* v. *Milne* (1849) 11 Beav 507 at 516, 519.

whether the testamentary disposition of the shares was legal under the Mortmain Act.[40]

Before the Barons, Byles for the next-of-kin argues boldly:

What is the interest which a shareholder in a co-partnership, whether incorporated by charter or Act of Parliament, has to convey when he parts with his shares? An interest in land, if the corporation is possessed of lands, is conveyed by every transfer of shares.

Counsel for the charities is putting forward the modern view. The shareholders, he says, 'have an interest only in the funds of the company'. The court simply certifies that the gift is legal and the case returns to Lord St Leonards.[41]

As plain Edward Sugden, the new Lord Chancellor had appeared in many of the earlier cases on the nature of shares and his arguments were always brilliant, whether drawing on the abstruse learning of the conveyancer or proposing practical deductions from consequences. For instance, in a bankruptcy case before both Lyndhurst and Brougham LLC he had refuted the debtor's contention that shares in the Lancaster Canal Company were realty and so exempt. It was conceded that the company held the fee and so he deduced that the shares could not be real interests, even in equity, for

there must be a reversion in fee in some person. Yet these shares have no such properties; the property of them is indefinite and therefore, as it cannot be contended that they can rank higher than chattels real, they must fall in the scale of legal divisions of property and be placed under the denomination of mere personal chattels.

And as to the practical objections to the debtor's claim, he urged

in the case of every corporation that is possessed of realty, each individual corporator would be possessed of real estate. He would in right of it be entitled to vote and qualified to sport.[42]

When *Myers* v. *Perigal* came before him from the Common Pleas, he brushed aside distinctions drawn from the unincorporate nature of the firm with a number of practical reasons:

[40] *Myers* v. *Perigal* (1849) 16 Sim 533; 18 LJ (NS) Ch 185 (VC). Lord Truro's judgment is reported at (1852) 2 De G M & G 599–607.

[41] (1851) 11 CB 90 at 102; 21 LJ (NS) CP 217.

[42] *Ex parte Lancaster Canal Co* (1832) 1 Deac & Chitty 411 at 431–2 (abridged).

Suppose for example this banking company had purchased a real estate. [I]f they did sell it what were they to do with the money? Why, invest it in the funds. Therefore it is not properly real estate as regards any partner.

And, from another angle, he argued:

The true way to test it is . . . could any of the partners enter upon the lands. Suppose there was a house upon it and that the house was empty, could he say 'I will go and reside in that house. I am a partner. I have a right as a tenant in common to make use of the property'? What is his interest beyond that of its being property which represents, for the time being, a portion of the capital out of which his profit is to come?[43]

Three crucial points emerge from this decision. Firstly, the passage last quoted lays to rest that ghost of the shareholder's direct claim over the fixed assets which had haunted the law since the seventeenth-century New River cases described in Chapter 4.2.2. Secondly, in the first passage Lord St Leonards points to the essential nature of a fund: an abstract segment of wealth invested now in land, now in chattels, now in securities; the objects of inherence shift, but the fund itself is unchanged. Thirdly, in applying these perceptions to an *un*incorporate body the Lord Chancellor is at last giving juridical expression to the principle of double-entry bookkeeping.

The German economic historian Werner Sombart went so far as to wonder whether double-entry created capitalism or vice versa. Some caution is appropriate, since he also thought that double-entry contained the germs of the law of gravity, the circulation of the blood, and the first law of thermodynamics; none the less, it seems to be the case that the method appears in Italy about 1300, spreads with the growth of trade, and is essentially the same system as that first described in print by Luca da Bargo Pacioli in 1494. Sir Thomas Gresham—financial adviser to Elizabeth I—kept his private accounts in this way, and the first page of his journal is headed 'Chest oweth to Capital'. It spreads slowly, despite its entertaining advocacy by Hugh Myddelton's customer Gerard Malynes, being usually described as 'the Italian method' or—by the

[43] (1852) 2 De G M & G 599. The quotations are abridged from the fuller report of Lord St Leonards's judgment in 22 LJ (NS) Ch 431 at 433.

nineteenth-century lawmaker—as 'the form of debtor and creditor', and finally, in the 1856 Companies Act, as 'the principle of double-entry'.[44]

As its name suggests, the method requires that every relation be expressed in dual form. All assets—whatever their legal nature—owe themselves to their owner, appearing on the debit side as (in the old language) 'sundries, debtor to capital'. Consequently, tangible objects can be represented only by their exchange value, and the credit side—whether it be 'capital' which the proprietor 'owns' or the debts which the creditors are owed (and themselves own)—looks like a kind of floating charge over the the totality of the constantly changing assets. This is vividly shown in the attempt of an eighteenth-century writer to explain the feature which baffles every beginner—why the objects one starts with, such as a house and goods, are *debit* entries:

> As I am to make of my goods as much as they cost me, they are in effect the same to me as if their value was due to me . . . so I may make the goods in my possession debtor to me for their first cost.[45]

The *arithmetic* of the system is simple. All that is required is addition, plus a certain amount of mental subtraction in order to arrive at the entry needed to balance unequal sides. And—since you do not add an asset to its own value—addition is performed only vertically, never horizontally. The *algebra* was first explained to the English by Cronhelm in 1818, and goes beyond the perception of credit-debt relationships to provide the 'owner' with an abstract collection of values reduced to mathematical form. His 'profit' is no longer that realised on a single transaction, but the balance accumulating over time in an impersonal account. His worth—positive or negative—can at any moment be ascertained as that claim by or upon him represented by the balance between assets and liabilities. The notion is, of course, ancient common sense: *bona intelleguntur*

[44] Sombart ii 118–19. A photograph of Gresham's journal is in Littleton and Yamey, pl. VII; Malynes, chap. XX; Chancery Rules 1828 r. 61; Joint-Stock Companies Act 1856 Sched. Table B s. 69. The requirement is omitted in the 1862 Act's Table A s. 78 and later Acts.

[45] Benjamin Donn (1765), quoted by J. G. C. Jackson in Littleton and Yamey 297.

cuiusque quae, deducto aere alieno, supersunt. Double-entry first provides an instantaneous picture of this and then goes further.[46]

Dr. *Assets* Cr. *Liabilities*

$$(p+q+r) - (x+y+z) = \pm C[\text{apital}]$$

From this it follows that the balance of any other account may be obtained algebraically:

Dr. *Assets* Cr. *Liabilities*

$$(q+r) - (x+y+z) \mp C = -p$$

Or

$$(p+q+r) - (y+z) \mp C = x$$

The final consequence is of crucial importance to property law but in this country took centuries to seep into legal consciousness. It is inherent in the very structure of the system that, as every debit always has an equal credit entry, the books always balance and the estate itself is always exactly solvent. The person to whom it belongs is not an 'owner': he is creditor if fortunate, debtor if not; if he is neither he is nothing.

Dr. *Assets* Cr. *Liabilities*

$$(p+q+r) - (x+y+z) \mp C = 0$$

The principle of double-entry seems to bring to accounting a tool similar to that given to counting by the concept of zero.

When a person's estate or business has *its own* books in which he appears among other creditors or debtors, the fund takes on a life of its own, above and beyond mere human beings. It becomes a perpetual succession of things regarded as units of account and ever-changing. For the accountant a business is a self-owning entity. English lawyers could not (and still cannot) bring themselves to follow this, but create the artificial *persona* of the corporation or company which 'owns' the enterprise. This ownership, however, is very different from the company's

[46] D 50.16.39. In 1894 the Sadlerian Professor of Mathematics at Cambridge thought the method 'mathematically by no means uninteresting . . . like Euclid's theory of ratios an absolutely perfect one'. His logic was rigorous: 'If you throw £100 into the sea, the sea becomes your debtor for that amount . . . and you appear as neither richer nor poorer' (Cayley, preface and 19).

ownership of its assets which make up one side of its balance-sheet—over these the company has wide powers of alienation and acquisition. Its only power over its own fund is that of management. That fund—the other side of the page—is owed to the shareholders and creditors.[47]

Thus, the crucial importance of the decision in *Myers* v. *Perigal* was that it treated incorporation as irrelevant; in a way, the Lord Chancellor recognized that the nature of the shareholders' interest is not affected by whether the company exists as a legal person, since it is certainly an accounting entity.

At first his ruling was applied with some reluctance in the Grand Junction cases of 1855, but it then became accepted as worth following in its own right and not merely by virtue of the doctrine of precedent. The 1888 Mortmain and Charitable Uses Act attempted to put the whole law on a sound footing but, three years later, required amendment because of this very difficulty. To its definition of 'land' was added a phrase of cautious obscurity: 'but not money secured on land or personal estate arising from or in connection with land.'[48]

After *Myers* v. *Perigal* the New River is used as a weapon only in the last battles for the vote.

10.5.4 *The county vote*

The franchise of the freeholder worth forty shillings a year had been granted since 1429 and confirmed by the 1832 Reform Act. If a shareholder's dividends were worth that amount; and if the concern held freehold land; and if the shares were taken to confer some interest in the realty; then did he have the vote, and if so where? As we have seen, the fortunate holders of original New River shares or fractions of them could vote in the two counties through which the river ran.[49]

In about 1840 numerous inhabitants of the West Riding of Yorkshire clubbed together, bought land which was conveyed

[47] Sombart ii 119; Cory 112 ff.; A. L. Dickinson 25 ff.; Cooke 48, 185.

[48] *Edwards* v. *Hall* (1855) 6 De G M & G 92, overruling *Ware* v. *Cumberledge* (1855) 1 Beav 503. Mortmain and Charitable Uses Acts 1888 and 1891 s. 3.

[49] Electors of Knights of the Shires Act 1429; Representation of the People Act 1832 s. 26. The county vote was finally extinguished by the Representation of the People Act 1918 s. 47 & Sched. 8.

to trustees for them, and financed the construction of a mill and machinery. They did not incorporate and the partnership deed (abridged and with italics added) shows the confusion of the times as to the relation between property and company law:

And it is hereby agreed and declared that *the said lands and the mill* shall be deemed and considered as, or in the nature of, personal estate and not real estate and shall be held in trust for the parties as part of the partnership stock-in-trade in the same proportions.

In *Baxter* v. *Brown* thirty-seven of them claimed the vote in respect of their shares and the revising barrister left it to the Common Pleas to decide 'if the shares can be considered a legal or equitable estate in real property'.

Their counsel relies on the New River cases and their offspring *Buckeridge* v. *Ingham*, but one feels that the Court is teasing him in forcing him to argue that the railway shareholder who has a right to travel the line in his own carriage must be able to vote in every county through which the train runs. None the less—and despite frequent and penetrating interruptions from the Bench—Tindal CJ, in a considered judgment, holds that the shares give the vote. He answers the Chelsea waterworks case on the grounds that there the company was incorporated, and deals with other statutory companies by saying that in those cases Parliament had categorized the shares 'whereas in the case before us there is no other than a voluntary declaration by the parties themselves that the real estate shall be considered as personal'.[50]

This awkward precedent was soon distinguished into dust. In 1861 the would-be voter claims in right of a share in a milling company incorporated under the 1856 Act, s. 15 of which declares all shares personalty. By this time the notion of a company holding its fixed assets in trust for the shareholders has withered away. The Common Pleas says:

No part of the realty is held in trust for them but all that they are entitled to is that the property held by the corporation shall be used to create profits in which they have a right to participate rateably according to the number of their shares.

[50] *Baxter* v. *Brown* (1845) 7 Man & G 198 at 209, 217.

Baxter v. *Brown* is distinguished on the grounds that only the trust deed declared the shares personalty. That this is not the real reason can be seen from the fact that, on the same day, the same court dealt with the Whitstable Free-fishers Company. That ancient body had been incorporated by a statute of 1793 which certainly did not declare the interests of the fishers to be personalty. None the less, they got no vote, Keating J. holding that the effect of the Act

> was to vest the property . . . in the corporation and that the members individually had no seisin, legal or equitable, in any of the lands. [T]he right of the individual member was confined to a share in the profits when ascertained by a deduction of the expenses and did not extend to any legal or equitable interest in the land itself.[51]

Soon afterwards the same fate befell shareholders in the Manchester Corn Exchange, which had been provisionally registered under the 1844 Act, and the Sheffield Music Hall, which was unincorporated. Assimilating statutory, registered, and unincorporated companies, the Common Pleas held that a shareholder is not entitled to any interest in land, nor to any particular income, but only to a proportionate share of the profits, if any. Accounting principles had come home to the law of the constitution, leaving only the New River shareholders with not one but two votes.[52]

10.6 Estates in Shares

After the travail recounted in the preceding pages, it is a relief to find that lawyers experienced no difficulty in applying to stocks and shares the same calculus of estates (behind a trust if necessary) which they had long employed for terra firma. They may not have been quite sure what a share was, but they knew how to settle it. New River shares led the way, being, as demonstrated in Chapter 4.3, settled for life estates with shifting remainders over, both particular and reversionary estates being held jointly or in common as required. These interests were, in

[51] *Bulmer* v. *Norris* (1861) 30 LJ (NS) CP 25 at 28; Free Fishers of Whitstable Act 1793; *Acland* v. *Lewis* (1861) 30 LJ (NS) CP 29 at 33.

[52] *Bennett* v. *Blain* (1863) 15 CB (NS) 518; *Freeman* v. *Gainsford* (1865) 18 CB (NS) 185; Orme 142; Carter 29–30; Elliott 72–81.

their turn, used as security for sums advanced with the shares being conveyed in fee by way of mortgage, or charged by long lease at a peppercorn rent.

The next stage was to apply the calculus to 'the funds', and it can be traced in numerous statutes on the public revenue; two examples will suffice, one to show successive and one concurrent estates. The Act of 1692 for raising money to fight the French increased excise duties and separated the fund so raised to service loans to be advanced on a tontine scheme, whereby the dividends paid would increase as the number of lives nominated by subscribers dropped. This worked badly and the system was shifted to a grant of annuities for life at a straight 14 per cent; a similar method was adopted for part of the fund used to establish the Bank of England. Soon after, in an attempt to raise more money from investors in these two schemes, a new approach was tried. An Act of 1694 enabled anyone who, by original contribution or mesne assignment, was (italics added) 'entitled to *an estate for life* . . . in any annuity' to pay an additional £63 for every £100 originally advanced and thereby secure the choice of either 'changing or converting the *estate for life into a term of 96 years*' or of taking a 'term from the determination of such estate for life during the then residue of the said 96 years'. If he exercised the first option, then 'the present *estates for life* shall be understood to be *merged or extinguished in the said term of years*'; if the second, he took 'a good sure and absolute *estate* vested in him which shall take effect (as a *future interest*) after the determination of the *estate for life in the said term*', in which case 'it is to be understood that the present estate for life is continued'.[53]

An example of the notion of co-ownership in fee simple in 'the funds' is provided by the Acts of 1714, which enlarged the capital of the Bank of England. The first of them created a fund of excise revenue as security; the second raised a loan of almost £1m. by creating perpetual annuities at 5 per cent charged on the excise, and assured the public that 'contributors shall have good and sure estates therein for ever subject only to the proviso

[53] Tax etc. Act 1692; Government Annuities Act 1693; Bank of England Act 1694; Government Annuities Act 1695 s. 6 (abridged). For a time, the title to these annuities was deduced as if they were land: see the debate on Sir John Barnard's Bill against stock-jobbing in Hans. Parl. Hist. vii 65–7.

for redemption in this act afterwards contained'. Sections 11 and 12 (somewhat abridged) provided that the money advanced was to be 'one capital or joint-stock' in which 'every person in proportion to the money advanced shall have an interest or share in the said stock and in the proportional annuity attending the same'. These shares were personalty, transferable in the Bank's books, and 'devisable' by will attested by two witnesses. Three years later, in one of the innumerable debates on Walpole's efforts to reduce the National Debt, the Commons is warned by a member against tampering with Government annuities 'since [they] were not to be looked on as debts but as a sale of annual rents for a valuable consideration' and 'these annuities could not be touched without occasioning great confusion and disputes in private familes, by reason that most of the said annuities had been settled for portions, jointures and the like'. In 1752, however, the numerous separate annuities were consolidated in one joint stock, secured by one charge on public revenue, and confirmed to be transferable and trustee securities. This object in which so many private settlements subsisted became known in its capital aspect as 'Consols' and in its income aspect as 'the three-per-cents'.[54]

The technical objections which were raised on the grounds that such property was classified as pure personalty were brushed aside by Lord Mansfield with the words 'how common are settlements of chattels and money in the stocks, and can there be any doubt but they are good?'. Doubts which perplexed the more scrupulous Chancery mind were resolved by Talbot LC in a most revealing manner. Faced with what were, in terms of function, a set of shifting entails in bank stock, he stated a case for the King's Bench asking how the point would be decided 'if *a term of years in lands* had been bequeathed in the same manner' and his successor Lord Hardwicke followed the advice that the limitations were good.[55]

The same approach in the House of Lords saved the 'entail'

[54] National Debts Acts 1714 (the quotation is an abridgement of ss. 11 and 12 of 1 Geo I st. 2, c. 19). Hans. Parl. Hist. vii 426–7; National Debts Act 1751. There is an interesting twist to the technique of the Statute of Uses 1535 in the East India Company's Act 1773 s. 3. In order to prevent voting frauds it was provided that a transfer of stock to a nominee should vest in him both legal and beneficial interests.

[55] *Cadogan* v. *Kennett* (1776) 1 Cowp 432 at 436. *Sabbarton* v. *Sabbarton* (1734) Cas temp Talbot 55 and 245 at 250.

in bank stock which figured in the great litigation known as *William Pitts's Case* (1766) and then *The Earl of Chatham's Case* (1771), so that by 1825 John Miller could sum up the story in incisive terms:

If the common-law judges destroyed perpetual entails in real property, Equity judges have created a modified entail in personal property, of which last perhaps more than one half of the whole wealth of the country at this time subsists—one of the most glaring assumptions of legislative power which courts of justice have exercised.[56]

As shares in 'private' companies—or in those which (like the New River, the East India, and many others) had begun with a public purpose but then changed—grew more numerous, the machinery of life estates, remainders, and co-ownership was applied more or less unconsciously to all investments. It is unnecessary to rehearse the evidence in the case law since the system stands revealed in early Victorian statutes. That of 1838 which abolished arrest on mesne process allowed judgment debts to be executed on Government stock, annuities, and the shares of 'any public company *whether or not incorporated*' standing in the debtor's name or in that of his trustee. Two years later, in order to dispel doubts, it was enacted that these powers

shall be deemed and taken to extend to the interest of any judgment debtor whether *in possession or reversion and whether vested or contingent*, as well as in such stocks, funds, annuities or shares . . . as also in [their] dividends, interest or annual produce.[57]

Finally, to control the vesting of contingent interests, the Rule against perpetuities—which, as recalled in Chapter 5.3, had begun with trusts of terms and not with realty—was applied without hesitation or even reflection to all investments.

[56] *Tothill* v. *Pitt* (1766) 1 Madd 488; *Earl of Chatham* v. *Tothill and Western* (1771) 7 Bro 453; Miller 317.

[57] Judgments Acts 1838 s. 14 and 1840 s. 1 (italics added). On the issue of trusts of shares, an interesting analogy was drawn by Hardwicke LC: 'The South Sea Co. have no more right to inquire who is the true proprietor when the trust does not appear, than a lord of a manor into a right to a copyhold estate when no trust appears.' *Stockdale* v. *South Sea Co* (1740) 2 Atk 141.

10.7 Conclusion

Since Littleton wrote, five hundred years ago, the law of property has seen a gradual severance of the owner from the physical object which he owns. Even in the early days the technique of interposing between the two that abstract thing called an 'estate' testifies to detachment. But political, social, and family ties to land itself were strong for centuries and their purely legal expression may be seen in several features: in the common law's prohibition of testamentary disposition; in the principle which lasted from 1540 until 1837 that a will of land was not truly ambulatory; in the rule which persisted until 1925 that a gift of land 'to *A*' passed only a life estate. Land was seen as endowment, not just investment, and as a thing eternal counterposed to our mortality.

Of course, the legal situation was highly complex. The medieval landowner's assets included such abstract things as seignories and manors which could themselves be settled for life with remainders over, and whose tenants might change virtually at will. And the importance of pure revenue was fully realized when, in Tudor times, lessees were given a right *in rem*. The rising class of landowners was interested mainly in income because, as Baker puts it (although the evidence is controverted), 'newly enriched merchants and lawyers wanted rent; they had little desire personally to manage farms and men'. In the nineteenth century, Brougham's great speech to the House of Commons on 7 February 1828 contains a most revealing phrase. Inveighing against the antiquated common-law procedure, he instances a case of his own where he had 'a writ of right at York'. He never, however, mentions the land; the lawsuit was brought 'to try the title to *many thousands a year*'.[58]

As each new form of investment arose it was shovelled into the catch-all category of *choses in action* and the common law initially found great difficulty in applying to it the regime devised so successfully for land. The very title of this category suggests the dilemma. On the one hand these interests are, to translate the French, *things* and as such appear on the debit

[58] Litt 551; Baker 178; Hans. (New Ser.) xviii 233.

side among the assets; but the credit side is revealed in the fact expressed in the last two words, that to exchange that thing for another—to collect the money—you must bring an action. In holding that shares were not *choses in action* so as to be exempt from the reputed ownership clause of the bankruptcy laws, Lindley LJ put it in a nutshell: 'he cannot sue for the share as he has it already.' The dilemma was emphasized by his reversal in the House of Lords.[59]

At first, *choses in action* were not even alienable—unless transferability was in the State's interest, as with tallies by the common law of the Exchequer and 'the funds' by statute. Even then it was necessary for markets to arise before debts which were permanent for the nation could be liquid for the lenders. And when, with the assistance of the Chancery, more types of property became capable of transfer, the propriety of permitting them to form the substratum of estates was long questioned. Even today perfectly respectable—even excellent—academic doctrine avers that there can be no estates in chattels. Yet if a person can bail a book to another for an hour, why not for life? And if the book is part of a library 'settled with the land' then it is a constituent of a fund and all is well. Since the eighteenth century the creditors of a 'life tenant' of a chattel have been restricted by both sides of Westminster Hall to his life estate, and we are left with the empty verbalism that distinguishes the gift of a book for life from the gift of the use of a book for life and approves only of the latter. Holdsworth, while he recognized the formal distinctions, warned that 'the fundamental similarity can easily be overlooked'.[60]

The importance of the New River in the law of property lies in three features. Firstly, it proved a hindrance to the true analysis of the relation between a shareholder and the company's fixed assets. But secondly—and perhaps because of this—as its shares were assumed to be realty there was never

[59] Lindley LJ in *Colonial Bank* v. *Whinney* (1885) 30 Ch D 283 at 284. Bacon VC, Cotton, and Lindley LJJ held that shares were property and not *choses in action* (i.e. looking at the debit side), but Fry LJ and the House of Lords concentrated on the process of collecting the money (i.e. the credit side): (1886) 11 App Cas 426. All agreed that the answer depended on first principles, and the entire litigation is very instructive as to concepts of property.

[60] For estates in chattels see Goode 54–6, Holdsworth vii 478, Gray 821–6; *Hyde* v. *Parratt* (1696) 2 Vern 331; *Hoare* v. *Parker* (1786) 1 Cox 224 (Thurlow LC) and (1788) 2 TR 376 (KB).

the slightest problem with their use as the object of endowment and investment. In the case of shares in other companies, not until 1925 did English law contrive to treat them completely in the same way by applying to them the strict but empty law of entail, fine, and recovery.[61]

So far are persons now detached from objects that the modern law of property is best seen as a relation of fund to fund. All contracts are conveyances, all changes exchanges. *A* lends to *B*: the money appears on the credit side of *A*'s cash account and the same figure (now a debt he is owed) is entered on the debit side of the 'receivables' or 'sundry debtors' account' as an asset which *A* owns; his balance has not changed. *B* debits cash and credits 'accounts payable' or 'sundry creditors'—his balance has not changed. In his final accounting he appears on the same side as *A*, as creditor of his fund, only if he is solvent. If not, he is listed on the debit side as an asset owned by his books. But in either case *A* can collect his money only from the common fund of those assets so that his claim, if good at all, is good as property. The human beings—*A* and *B*—appear merely as *titulaires* of their funds: it is the disparity between the latter which gives a content to *A*'s claim.[62]

In section 10.5.3 it was suggested that the decision of Lord St Leonards in *Myers* v. *Perigal* was important in that it gave juridical expression to the accountant's treatment of a business as a self-owning entity. That discussion considered the relation of double-entry bookkeeping to the law of persons. But the technique also has a part to play in the law of property in that it sheds light on the concept of a fund. The simplest way to explain this is to borrow from a chapter of the work by Hugh Myddelton's customer, Gerard Malynes, entitled *Consuetudo vel Lex Mercatoria*, published in 1622.

Malynes begins by explaining that merchants 'make the commodities Debitor and their own Capitall or Stocke Creditor', and then devotes ten folios to the adventures of a Young Merchant who has recently inherited freehold, leasehold, cash, goods, plate, a bill of exchange, and a bond. These are ranged

[61] Law of Property Act 1925 s. 130. Of course the King's and Adventurers' shares were trustee investments.

[62] A similar view is put forward in the brilliant, if idiosyncratic, work of Noyes chaps. VI and VII.

'in so many severall Accounts of seven Debitors, and there is but one to be made Creditor for all these, which is Capitall or Stocke'. By following the author's instructions it is easy to draw up the accounts. **Table 3** illustrates how the Journal would look. On the left-hand side we have ranged seven different types of property, each with its own legal regime: a freehold manor, a leasehold house, money, household furnishing, trade goods, a mature bill, and a bond due at Ladyday; the last two are intangible. On the right hand side we have the *fund*, of which Malynes is content to say 'here you see this Young Merchant hath an estate of £5,000 to begin the world withall, consisting of the aforesaid seven parcels'.[63]

Table 3

JOURNAL

	£	£	£
Young Merchant's capital			5,000
Latham Manor		1,500	
Lease of the Golden Lion for 21 years at £20 p.a., sublet at £60 p.a., say		200	
Cash		1,000	
Plate and household stuff		200	
Warehouse:			
100 white cloths	1,200		
200 Kersies at £40 the score	400		
		1,600	
Bills receivable, viz.:			
On B.M., Mercer, by bill	300		
On N.W., Merchant, by bond due 25 March	200		
		500	
TOTAL		5,000	5,000

Since, as this example demonstrates, there is no need for the assets to be tangible, the debit side can consist entirely of intangible wealth. In other words, the *fund* can become an asset. Thus, if Malynes's hero were equal partner with another, the right-hand side of the Journal would appear as the left-hand side of the Partnership Ledger:

[63] Malynes 365.

Dr.		Cr.	
Partnership Capital	£5,000	Young Merchant	£2,500
		His Partner	£2,500
	£5,000		£5,000

In each partner's private ledger, the credit entry denoting his share in the firm appears as a debit recording his accounts' ownership of the asset, his own capital being the creditor; thus the method links fund to fund.

Further, if the partnership were incorporated and a large number of shares issued, the system would require no alteration in any fundamental. Of course, where companies are concerned, the directors possess very limited powers over the fund as a whole—the major powers are in creditors and shareholders. The officers may change the assets, but only by *ex*change. From the lawyer's point of view the accounting links in the immensely complex structure of modern corporate and private property can be seen as a relation in series, similar to that which the common law called *tenure*. Between the life tenant of a sub-mortgage of a fee simple in remainder in shares in a holding company and any physical object whatever, lies a long chain of abstract things: life interest, trustees' estate, submortgage, mortgage, remainder, trustees' estate, settled shares, the company's holding of other shares, ultimately perhaps some object perceptible to the senses. Each 'thing' is linked to the next and all are ranked in an order of priority in case of conflict—in short, in a hierarchy of degree. At every stage the asset is, for certain purposes, property in its holder's hands, conferring on him some part of the *iura utendi, fruendi et abutendi*. But each asset is more or less defined as to its duration, is burdened with provisions as to its own transformation into something else, and is subject to some exercise of the will of those *of whom* it is held. In their discussion of the nature of a company share, the modern works cite a passage from *Borland's Trustee* v. *Steel* (1901). The case concerned both the concept of ownership and the Rule against perpetuities; and the attentive reader can hear tenure in the very word the court uses: 'The contract contained

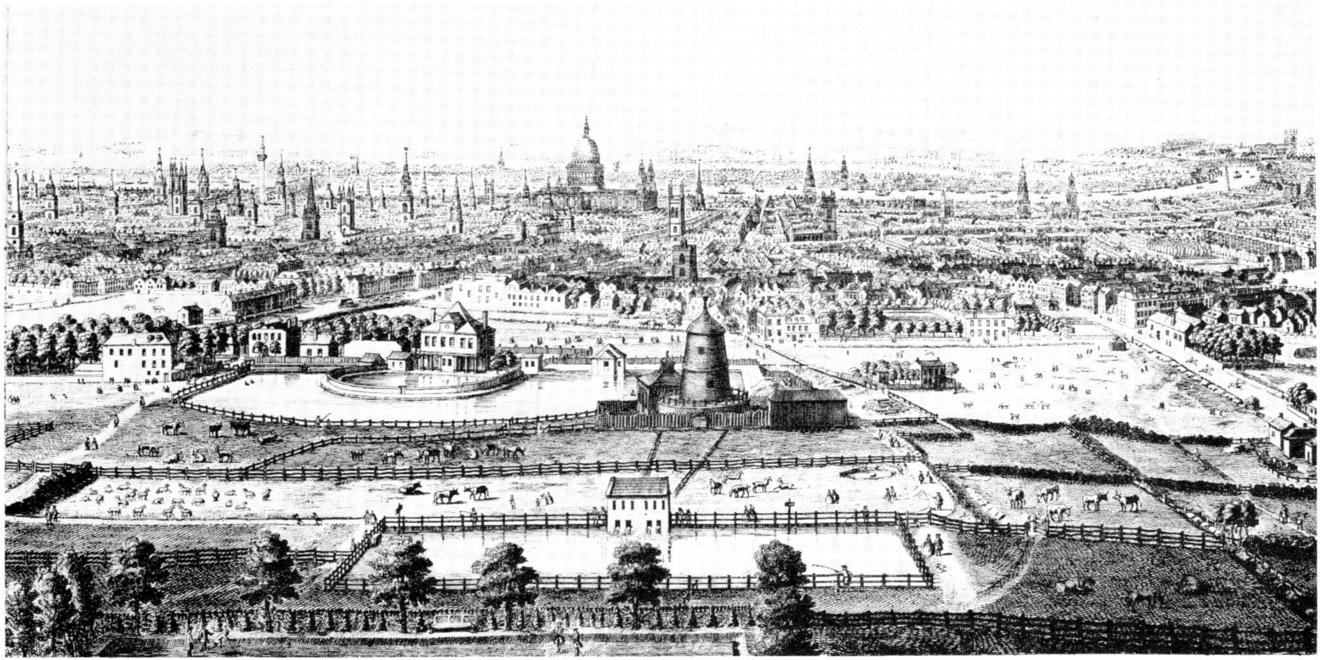

Fig. 18. Detail of view of London from Islington, 1752

in the articles of association is one of the original *incidents* of the share.'[64]

Just as the calculus of estates was instantly available to the New River shares, so the notion of tenure was explicit in the Company's charter. After three hundred and seventy years of lawsuits and legislation, it is doubtful whether we have devised a system any better than that which sustained 'our mercenary stream'.

[64] Gower 398; Sealy 370; *Borland's Trustee* v. *Steel* [1901] 1 Ch 279 at 288. Cf. Litt 131.

APPENDICES

The documents are reproduced by kind permission of the holders: (B)—original at Thames Water Authority Archives [TW], Strongroom B30, box 79; (C)—originals at TW, Strongroom B30, boxes 79 and 86; (D)—original at TW, Strongroom B30, box 79, but apparently owned by the New River Company (Pat. Roll 10 Jas. I pt. 10 no. 19; PRO C66/1952); (E)—original at TW, Strongroom B30, box 79; (F)—printed by the Company in the nineteenth century; by Sisley (1899) with many errors; by Carr, *Charters* (1913), with an omission at his p. 109; as printed here, it has been checked with the charter under the Great Seal owned by the Company (Pat. Roll 17 Jas. I pt. 16 no. 67; PRO C66/2214); (G)—original at TW, Strongroom B30, unnumbered box, but apparently owned by the Company (Pat. Roll 7 Chas. I pt. 20 no. 159; PRO C66/2579); (H)—BL Add. MS Ch. 40379; (I)—BL Harl. MS 3604 (1670–84); Minute Books (1769–1904) at TW, Strongroom B30; dividend lists of the Company, deeds, abstracts, printed information in advertisements, Parliamentary Papers, etc.

A. Statutory Foundations 1605 and 1606

A.1 3 Jas. I c. 18 (1605)

An Acte for the bringing in of a fresh Streame of running water to the North parts of the Citie of London.

For that it is found very convenient and necessary to have a fresh Streame of running water to bee brought to the North parts of the City of London, from the Springs of Chadwell and Amwell, and other springs in the Countie of Hartford not farre distant from the same, which upon view is found very fesible, and like to be profitable to many: It is therefore enacted by the Kings most Excellent Maiestie, and by the Lords Spirituall and Temporall, and Commons in this present Parliament assembled, and by the Authoritie of the same, that

[1] it shall be lawfull to the Lord Maior, Communaltie and Citizens of the Citie of London, and their Successours, at any time or times hereafter to beginne and continue the laying out of such convenient Limits of ground for the making of the Trench for the sayd River at the breadth of tenne foot and not above, as to them and their Deputies and workemen, with the allowance of the Commissioners hereafter mentioned or any seven of them shall bee seene convenient and meete for the same, And in that place that they shall find to be most apt and meet for that purpose, to have and take for the purpose abovesaid the use and libertie of such and so much ground, as shall contain Ten foot in breadth, and not above, during and by all the length, as the sayd new Channell, Cut, or River shall passe for the conveying of the said water from the sayde Springs to the Citie of London, leaving the inheritance of the New Cut in the owners thereof.

[2] And that the sayd Mayor, Comminalty, and Citizens of London, and their Successours for ever, for the consideration hereafter expressed, shall have liberty to digge the same ground to be imployed for the sayd River or New Cut, not exceeding tenne foot in breadth alongst all the sayde whole length of the sayd River or New Cut, and from time to time for ever to maintaine and preserve the same, and to lay the earth there digged or to be digged on either side of the same River or New Cutte in such places, as shall be thought meete for that purpose, and to have free Passage to and from the sayd New Cut or River with men, horses, cart and carriages at all times convenient for making of the same New Cut or Trench and for the preserving of the same, and of the Banckes thereof, from time to time

for ever, to the intent that no part of the sayde Streame be at any time after the making of the New Cut, without the consent of the Mayor, Comminalty, and Citizens of London, turned or conveyed out of the same New Cutte or Watercourse.

[3] In consideration whereof, The Mayor, Comminaltie, and Citizens of London, and their Successours shall make such satisfaction or composition to and with the Lords, Owners, and Occupiers of the same grounds, through which the Newe Cut or River shall be made, and with all such person and persons as shall sustaine any Damage, Losse or hinderance in their Mils standing upon any of the Rivers or Streames, from which the water shall be taken through the sayd New Cut or River, as shalbe to the contentment of the Lords, Owners and Occupiers of the sayd grounds and Mils, and in default of their agreement by mutuall assent such satisfaction or recompense, as shall bee limited and appoynted by the Commissioners to bee assigned for that purpose, according to the intent of this Statute, by the Lord Chancellour or Lord Keeper of the great Seale of England for the time being, by Commission under the great Seale of England, or by any nine of them, whereof foure of them to bee Citizens of the City of London.

[4] And for the better effecting of the premisses, and for the due rating of the value of the things to be compounded for by the true intent of this Statute (if the parties shall not agree,) Be it enacted by the Authoritie of this present Parliament, that at the request and charges of the Mayor, Comminalty and Citizens of London, Commission or Commissions, under the great Seale of England, shall be granted to such persons, as the Lord Chancellour or Lord Keeper of the great Seale of England for the time being, shall nominate and appoint, whereof foure shall bee of the Countie of Middlesex, foure of the Countie of Essex, and foure of the Countie of Hartford, and foure of the City of London, and every of them having lands and Tenements of the cleare yeerely value of Fortie pounds at the least: which sixteene or any nine of them, whereof two to bee of the Citie of London, shall have power to order and set downe what Rate or Rates, summe or summes of money shall be payed by the Mayor, Comminaltie and Citizens of London to the Lords, Owners, and Occupiers of the grounds, and Soyle and Milles, for which Composition is to be made by the intent of this Acte, if the Parties cannot of themselves agree, and in what manner the same shall be payed, and that for the recovery of such money, as shall be so ordered and set downe by the said Commissioners, or any nine of them, whereof two to be of the Citie of London, the partie or parties to whom the same money shall bee due to be payd by the true intent of the said order, shall or may recover

the same against the sayd Mayor and Comminaltie of London by Action of Debt in any of his Maiesties Courts at Westminster, wherein no Essoigne, Protection, or wager of Law shall be allowed.

[5] Provided alwayes, and bee it enacted, that if in the New Cutte there happen any Breaches, Inundation, or Hurts, the Mayor, Comminaltie and Citizens of London, shall from time to time stoppe the Breaches at their owne charges, and sufficiently maintaine them from time to time, and make sufficient recompense to the Partie grieved for the Damage susteined by the same Breaches rising by their default, to bee recovered by Action on the Case grounded upon this Statute.

[6] And bee it further enacted by the Authoritie aforesayd, that the Mayor, Comminaltie, and Citizens of London, and their Successours for ever, shal make and maintaine at their costes and charges from time to time convenient Bridges and wayes for the passage of the Kings Subiects, and their Cattell and carriages over or through the sayd New Cutte or River, in places meete and convenient.

[7] And further be it enacted, that untill or before a full agreement with the Lords, Owners and Occupiers of the premisses be had, or that such Order or meanes be devised and agreed upon by the Commissioners by the L. Chancellour or L. Keeper of the great Seale of England to bee nominated and appointed, or the more part of them, as shall seeme meete for the due effecting of the premisses, and the sayd Commission returned into the High Court of Chancerie, it shall not bee lawfull to the sayd L. Mayor, Comminaltie, and Citizens to put the said digging, trenching or New cutting of the said new River from the said Springs in Execution, nor to cut or take in any ground for Passage of water from the sayd Springs or any of them by force of this Statute, Anything in this Acte to the contrary not withstanding.

[8] And bee it further enacted by the Authoritie aforesayd, that after such time as there shall bee a new Cut, Streame, or River brought from the Springs aforesaid, or any of them, to the City of London, that for the better maintenance and preservation of the sayd River or new Cut, and of all the water therein running, to be brought to the Citie of London; the same shall be subiect to the Commission of Sewers, and to the Lawes and Statutes made for Sewers, as fully to all intents and purposes, as if the same River or new Cut had bene expressly mentioned in the sayd Statutes of Sewers to bee under the Survey of the syad Commissioners.

[9] Provided neverthelesse, and bee it enacted, That all such things as shall be done, at any time hereafter, for the Scouring, cleansing, amending, and conservation of the sayd new River or Cut, shall be at the onely cost and charges of the Mayor, Citizens and Communaltie

of the Citie of London; And that all Fines and amerciaments which shall bee imposed by vertue of the sayd Commission of Sewers, for any wilful annoyances and offences which shall be at any time hereafter committed to the hurt or preiudice of the sayd new River or Cut, or any thing thereunto appertaining, shall bee to the onely use, benefit, and behoofe of the sayd Mayor, Communaltie, and Citizens of Londond, and of their Successours for ever.

A.2 4 Jas. I c. 12 (1606)

An Act for explanation of the Statute
made in the third yeere of the reigne of King James,
Intituled
An Act for the bringing of a fresh Streame of running Water
to the North parts of the Citie of London.

Whereas of late in the Parliament holden at Westminster, in the third yeere of the Reigne of our Soveraigne Lord King James, An Acte was made for the bringing of a fresh Streame of running water to the North parts of the City of London, as by the same Act appeareth, Now for that sithence the making of the Law, upon view of the grounds through which the Waters are to passe, by men of skill, and upon advised consideration of the premisses, it is thought more convenient and lesse damage to the ground, That the same running water bee brought and conveyed in and through a Trunke or vault of Bricke or stone inclosed, and in some places where need is, raysed upon Arches, then in an open Trench or Sewer, which maner of conveyaunce of the same water in a Trunke or vault of Bricke or stone, is doubtful whether by the wordes of the former Law it may be lawfully effected by the Lord Maior and Communaltie and Citizens of the Citie of London, albeit they doe duely performe every part, clause, matter and thing in the said Statute conteined, which on their part are by the true intent of that Law to be performed:

[1] For cleering of which doubt. and plaine declaring of the true meaning of the sayd Lawe, Bee it enacted by our Soveraigne Lord the King, and by the Lords Spirituall and Temporall, and Commons of this present Parliament assembled, and by the Authoritie of the same, that at any time or times after the laying out of such convenient limits of ground for the making of the Trenche, or Conveyaunce of Water to the North parts of the sayd Citie of London, at the breadth of tenne foote, and not above, as to the Maior, and Communaltie, and Citizens of the Citie of London, and their Deputies, and Workemen, with the allowance of the Commissioners in the sayd former

Act mentioned, or any seven of them shall be seene convenient and meete for the same, and in that place that they shall find to be most apt and meete for that purpose, according to the true intent of the said Statute, that the Maior and Communaltie, and Citizens of the sayd Citie of London, and their Successours, Deputies and Workemen, for the consideration in the sayd former Acte expressed, shall have liberty not onely to digge the same ground to be employed for the said River, or new Cut, as in the sayd former Acte is expressed, but also in the same place, where they shall think most meete for the sayd new Cut, or Passage of Water, to frame, erect, and make a Trunke or Vault of Bricke or stone for the Passage of the sayd Water to the North parts of the sayd Citie of London, not exceeding tenne foote in bredth, in such maner and forme to be layed in the Earth or upon Arches, as to the Maior and Communaltie and Citizens of London shall seeme meete: And from time to time for ever to maintaine and preserve the same Trunke or Vault of Bricke or Stone, and for that purpose to have like liberty and free passage to and from the said Trunke or Vault of Bricke or Stone, for making, erecting, maintaining, and preserving thereof from time to time for ever, as they had or might have had by the intent of the sayd former Acte, to, and from the sayd new Cut or River, With men, horses, cart and carriages, at all times convenient, and in places convenient, for the making of the said new Cut or Trench, and for the preserving of the same from time to time for ever: Any thing in the said former Statute, or in any other Law or Statute to the contrary thereof in any wise notwithstanding.

B. Transfer of the Statutory Powers

28 March 1611

THIS INDENTURE MADE the eight and twentyeth day of Marche in the yeares of the raigne of our Soveraigne Lord James by the grace of God Kinge of England Scotland ffraunce and Ireland Defendor of the fayth That is to say of England ffraunce and Ireland the Ninthe and of Scotland the fower and fortyeth BETWEENE the Maior and Coialtye and Citizens of the Citye of London on the one ptye And Hughe Midleton Citizen and goldsmith of London on th'other ptye WITNESSETH that whereas heretofore twoe severall Actes of pliament were made and enacted [*statutes recited*]

AND WHEREAS also there were certayne Indentures heretofore made betweene the said Maior and Coialtye and Citizens of the said Citye of London of the one ptye and the said Hughe Midleton of th'other ptye bearing date the one and twentyeth day of Aprill in the yeares of the raigne of our said soveraigne Lord King James of England ffraunce and Ireland the seaventh and of Scotland the twoe and fortyeth therein reciting that since the making of the said Actes that the said Maior and Coialtye and Citizens of the said Citye of London had made ordeyned constituted and appointed the said Hughe Midleton his heires and assignes ioyntlie and severallie their true and lawfull Attorneys Deputyes and Agents in their name but to the onelye benefitt and behoofe of the said Hughe Midleton his heires and assignes to doe execute and pforme whatsoever by the said Acts of pliamente or either of them the said Maior and Coialtye and Citizens are authorised to doe or may lawfullie doe

AND WHEREAS also the said Hughe Midleton in and by the same Indentures did for him his heires executors administrators and assignes covennte and graunte to and with the the said Maio^r^ and Coialtye and Citizens of London and their successors that hee the said Hughe Midleton within two monethes next after the date of the same Indenture should and wold at his owne proper costes and charges undertake and begin the digging trenching working and bringinge of the said River or streame of freshe water from the said Springes of Chadwell and Amwell and other springes thereat or to not farr distant from the same to the northe partes of the Citye of London and would doe hys and their best indeavor at his and their owne proper costes and charges to pforme and finishe the said worke within the space of fower years then followinge

AND WHEREAS also among divers other covenntes grauntes articles and agream[ts] as well on the pte and behalfe of the said Hughe Midleton his heires executors administrators and assignes to be pformed It was finallie conditoned and agreed by and betweene the said ptyes that if the said worke shold not be effected and pformed within the said space of fower yeares next after the date of the said Indentures bearing date the said one and twentieth day of Aprill in the said seaventh yeare of his Ma[tyes] raigne of England ffraunce and Ireland and of Scotland the twoe and fortyeth aforesaid That then the said Indentures as also the Lres of Attorney or Deputacon made to the said Hughe Midleton and all covenntes and agreements had and made betweene him & the said Maior and Coialtye and Citizens concerning the premisses shold be voyd and of none effecte As by the said recited Indentures it doeth and may more at large appeare

AND FORASMUCH as the said Hughe Midleton in pte of pformance of the covennte first before recited did within two monethes next after the date of the same Indenture undertake and begin the digging trenching working and bringing of the said River and streame of freshe water And hath since the beginning thereof brought the water tenne myles or thereabouts with a purpose to have finished the same within the tyme unto hym limited by the covennte and provi[soe] or condicon in the said recited Indenture menconed But hath been stayed from proceeding therein by reason of some exhibited compleynte by divers psons of the Countyes of Hertford and Middlesex and knoweth not how long it wilbe before hee shall obteyne libertye to proceed therein ffor w[che] causes it seemeth reasonable to the said Maior and Coialtye and Citizens of the said Citye of London to give a longer tyme to the said Hughe Midleton for the pfecting of the said worke

NOW THEREFORE this Indenture witnesseth that the said Maior and Coialtye and Citizens of the said Citye of London in consideration of the surrender and giving up of the Indenture aforesaid have made constituted and appointed the said Hughe Midleton his heires and assignes ioyntlie and severallie their true and lawfull Attornyes Deputyes and Agents in their names But to the onely benefitt and behoofe of the said Hughe Midleton his heires and assignes to doe execute and pforme whatsoever by the said Actes of pliament or either of them the said Maio[r] and Coialtye and Citizens are authorised to doe or may lawfullie doe

AND THE SAID Hughe Midleton for him his heires executors administrators and assignes covennteth and graunteth to and with the said Maior Coialtye and Citizens of the Citie of London and their successors by these psntes that hee the said Hughe Midleton his heires executors administrators or assignes at his owne proper costes and charges shall and will doe his or their best indeavor to pforme and finishe the same worke within the space of seaven yeares next after the one and twentyeth day of Aprill next ensuing the date of theis psntes And that the said Hughe Midleton in digging the ground ymployed or to be ymployed for the said River or new cutt hath not exceeded nor shall not exceed tenne foot in breadth alongst all the whole length of the said River or new cutt or any pte thereof And shall from tyme to tyme for ever maynetayne and preserve the same and the banckes thereof And shall and will lay the earth their digged or to be digged on either side of the said River or new cutt in such places as shalbe most meete for that purpose

AND THE SAID Hughe Midleton doth further for himselfe his heires executors and administrators covennte promise and graunte to and with the said Maior and Coialtye and Citizens and their successors by theis psntes That hee the said Hughe Midleton his heires executors administrators and assignes shall and will make such satisfaccon & composicon to and with the Lordes owners and occupyers of the same grounds through w[ch] the new cutt or river or any pte thereof now is or shalbe made and with all such pson and psons as have sustayned or shall sustayne any damage losse or hindraunce in their mylles standing upon any of the rivers or streames from which the waters have byn or shalbe taken through the said new cutt or river as shalbe to the contentment of the Lordes owners and occupyers of the said groundes and mylles or else in default of their agreement by mutuall assent such satisfaccon or recompense as shalbe lymited and appointed by the Commissioners to be assigned for that purpose according to the intent of the said former statute And also that hee the said Hughe Midleton his heires executors or administrators shall and will well and truly satisfye and pay or cause to be satisfied or payd all such some and somes of money to all and every the ptye and ptyes to whom the same by the Commissioners assigned for that purpose in the said Acte of the third yeare of his Ma[tyes] raigne hath byn ordered and sett downe or shalbe ordered and sett downe to be payd according and as by the true intent and meaning of the same Acte of Parliament it is expressed or appointed or w[ch] thereby is menconed that the said Maior and Coialtye and Citizens of London shold or ought to pay

AND LIKEWISE the said Hughe Midleton for himselfe his heires executors administrators and assignes doth further covennte promise and graunte to and with the said Maior and Coialtye and Citizens and their successors by theis psntes that if there hath happened or at any tyme or tymes hereafter there shall happen to bee any breaches Inondacons or hurtes in the new cutt or River That then and so often the said Hughe Midleton his heires executors administrators or assignes shall and will at his and their owne proper costes and charges stoppe and amend the same breaches and at all tymes thereafter uphold mayntayne and keepe the same in sufficient repayre And also shall and will make sufficient recompense to the pty or ptyes grieved for all such damages hurtes or hindraunce as have arisen or growne or shall arise or growe to them or any of them by reason of the same breaches and inondacons and also that hee the said Hughe Midleton his heires executors and administrators hath in all places convenient where the said new cutt hath byn made and shall and will at his and their owne proper costes and charges from tyme to tyme make and maintaine convenient bridges wayes and passages for the passage of the Kinges subiectes and their cattell and carriages over or through the said new cutt or River in places meete and convenient And also that he the said Hughe Midleton his heires executors administrators nor assignes hath not nor shall not nor will putt the said digging trenching or new cutting of the said new River in execucon nor hath cutt or taken nor shall cutt or take in any grounds for passage of water from the said springes or any of them untill such tyme as there be a full agreement with the Lordes owners and occupyers of the premisses had and made or that such order or meanes have byn or shalbe devised and agreed upon by the Commissioners appointed or to be appointed by the said former Acte of Parliament or the more parte of them as shall seeme meete for the due effectinge of the premisses and shalbe agreeable to the said Actes and the said Commission to be returned into the Highe Court of Chauncery accordingly

AND FURTHER the said Hughe Midleton for himselfe his heires executors administrators and assignes doth covennte promise and graunte to and with the said Maior and Coialtye and Citizens and their successors by theis psntes That if any lawes statutes or ordennces shall happen to be made or sett downe by the Commissioners of Sewers or paynes sett downe or enioyned to be payd for the better preservacon or mayntennce of the said River or new cutt after such tyme as there shalbe a new cutt streame or river brought from the said springes or any of them to the Citye of London that then and at all tymes from thenceforth the said Hughe Midleton his heires executors administrators and assignes shall and will at once fulfill pay and pforme all the said lawes statutes ordennces and payments to be appoynted and sett downe by the said Commissioners according to the true intent and meaning of all and every the statutes and ordennces in that behalfe made or hereafter to be made

AND THE SAID Maior and Coialtye and Citizens of the City of London doe for them and their successors covennte promise and graunte to and with the said Hughe Midleton his heires executors administrators and assignes and every of them by theis psntes that all fynes and amercem^{tes} which shalbe ymposed by vertue of any Commission of Sewers for any willfull annoyaunce and offences wch shalbe at any time hereafter comitted to the hurte or preiudice of the said new River or cutt or any thinge thereunto appertayninge shalbe to the onely sole benefitt and behoofe of the said Hughe Midleton his heires and assignes forever and that hee and they shall and may quietlie have take and enioy the same to his and their owne use in the name of the said Maior and Coialtye and Citizens or in his and their owne name as shall seem best unto them or as the case shall require

AND THE SAID Hughe Midleton for himself his heires executors administrators and assignes doeth further covenannte promise and graunte to and with the said Maior and Coialtye and Citizens and their successors by theis psntes that hee the said Hughe Midleton his heires executors and administrators shall at their owne proper costes and charges well and sufficyentlie doe make suffer and pforme all and every acte and actes thinge and thinges whatsoever wch on the pte and behalfe of the said Maior and Coialtye and Citizens by the true intent and meaning of the said recited Actes of Parliament or any article proviso or clause in them or either of them conteyned is enacted limited provided or appoynted to be done and pformed by the said Maior and Coialtye and Citizens and their successors And also shall and will at his and their owne proper costes and charges at all tymes and from tyme to tyme exonerate acquite and discharge or otherwise upon reasonable notice and request to be made well and sufficyently save and keep harmeles the said Maior and Coialtye and Citizens and their successors forever of and from all charges troubles losses hinderaunces expences accons suites and demaundes that shall by any wayes or meanes growe arise come or happen by occasion meanes or reason of the said Actes of Parliament or either of them or any thinge done or to be done by vertue of the said Actes of Parliament or either of them or by vertue of any Lre of Attorney heretofore made or hereafter to be made to the said Hughe Midleton his heires and assignes by the said Maior and Coialtye and Citizens or otherwise by any thing done comitted or suffered to be done comitted or suffered by the said Hughe Midleton his heires or assignes in about or concerninge the premisses

AND IN CONSIDERACON that the said Hughe Midleton hath undertaken to doe his best indeavour to bring the said River new cutt or streame from the springes of Chadwell and Amwell and other the springes aforesaid at the sole and only charges of him the said Hughe Midleton his heires and assignes the said Maior and Coialtye and

Citizens of the said Citye of London doe for them and their successors by theis psntes fullie freely and absolutely graunte convey assigne and confirme unto the said Hughe Midleton his heires and assignes the whole entire and sole profitt benefitt comodity and advantage whatsoever that shall or may be made raysed gayned or gotten by the said River new cutt and streame and the water and benefitt of the water that may come and be conveyed thereby together with the free libertye of laying and conveying pipes for the currancye and passage of water in and through all ptes and places convenyent where the said Maior and Coialtye and Citizens have interest power and authority so to doe or to license or graunt it to be done

AND THE SAID Maior and Coialtye and Citizens of the City of London doe for them and their successors covennte graunte and agree to and with the said Hughe Midleton his heires and assignes by theis psntes that hee the said Hughe Midleton his heires and assignes shall and may at all tymes and from tyme to tyme forever have take and enioy to his onely use the whole benefitt interest profitt comodity and advantage of the said water and of the conveyance disposicon and distribucon thereof And likewise shall and may at his and their owne libertye and will bargaine sell graunte demise contracte and agree to and with all and every pson and psons whatsoever for the drawing or conveying of any pte or ptes of the said water out of the said River or streame or any pte thereof or out of any poole stayne cisterne or other place to any house or houses place or places within the said Citye or suburbes thereof or where or whether the said Maior and Coialtye and Citizens have any interest power or authority to carry or convey the same And also shall and may receave pceive have take and enioy to his and their sole and proper use the full and whole profitt rent benefitt comodity advantage some and somes of money thereby coming growing or arising or wch shalbe reserved or agreed for to or with any pson or psons without any the lett hinderaunce molestacon denyall or interrupcon of the said Maior and Coialtye and Citizens of the Citye of London and their successors or of any other pson or psons lawfullie claiming or to clayme from by or under them or by their meanes assent or procurement

AND THE SAID Maior Coialtye and Citizens of the said Citye of London doe for them and their successors covennte promise and graunte to and with the said Hughe Midleton his heires and assignes by theis psntes that the said Maior and Coialtye and Citizens and their successors at all and every tyme and tymes after the bringing of the said streame of runinge water from the said Springes of Chadwell and Amwell or either of them or other the said springes to some such fitt place of receipte as shalbe situated in the Northe ptes of the said

Citye of London and shalbe convenyent for the better conveyance and distributing of the said Streame into the partes and places of the said Citye and the suburbes thereof shall and will doe make [ac-] knowledge suffer and execute all and every such further and other reasonable acte and actes of Comon councell of the said Citye and other Acte or Actes orders or ordinaunces thinge and thinges devise and devises conveyaunce and conveyaunces assurance and assurances in the cause to and for the said Hughe Midleton his heires and assignes for the full and pfecte conveying and graunting to the said Hughe Midleton his heires and assignes of all the full whole and sole benefitt profitt rente comoditye and advantage whatsoever wch shall or may be made raysed or gayned by the said River or Streame of water or by the distribucon thereof into other ptes and places of the said Citye of London and the suburbes thereof As also of all such estate right title interest possession and clayme of in and to the said water and waterourse and of in and to such soyle or peace of ground wherein the said water and watercourse shalbe brought or whereunto the said water shalbe conveyed or kepte for the better distributing thereof in the ptes and places of the said citye or suburbes aforesaid And of the whole conveyaunce and conveyaunces of the said water as shalbe by the said Hughe Midleton his heires or assignes or by his or their Councell learned in the lawe reasonablie devised advised or required

AND THE BETTER to encourage and countenaunce this business so comendable acceptable and beneficiall to the said Citye of London and suburbes of the same and all the Inhabitantes thereof the said Maior and Coialtye and Citizens for them and their successors doe covennte graunte and agree to and with the said Hughe Midleton his heires and assignes by theis psntes that the said Maior and Coialtye and Citizens and their successors at all tymes hereafter and from tyme to tyme shall and will at the costes and charges of the said Hughe Midleton his heires and assignes be ayding helping and assisting to the said Hughe Midleton his heires executors administrators and assignes for the finishinge and effectinge of the said worke so as they be not putt to any charge or expence of money in that behalfe

PROVIDED ALLWAYES and it is condiconed and agreed by and betweene the said parties that if the said Maior or Coialtye or Citizens or their successors shalbe charged dampnified or putt to losses or expences by reason of any acte cause matter or thing that hath byn or shalbe committed done or suffered by the said Hughe Midleton his heires or assignes wch by vertue of the said Actes of pliament or the intent or meaning thereof or of any of the articles provisoes or clauses therein conteyned shall or maybe lawfullie challenged required or demaunded of the said Maior and Coialtye and Citizens or their successors And the said Hughe Midleton his heires or assignes upon notice and request in that behalfe in writing to be made and delivered to the pson of the said Hughe Midleton his heires or assignes or any of them at the Royall Exchange in London or in their absence to be there published and lefte in the usuall place or office of receipte and paym^te in or neare the same Royall Exchange To the intent that the same Hughe Midleton his heires or assignes may take notice thereof doe not within two monethes next after such notice and request made or left as aforesaid discharge and save harmeles or otherwise sufficyentlie recompense and satisfie the said Maio^r and Coialtye and Citizens and their successors of for and concerninge all the same charges damages losses and expences wch they or any of them have sustayned or shall sustayne or be putt unto or charged with and shall so notifye as aforesaid That then and at all tymes and in any such case the said Maior and Coialtye and Citizens and their succesors shall and may enter into the said waterworke and have pceave receave and take all the benefittt profitt rent comodity and advantage whatsoever wch shall rise grow renew or be for or by reason of the said runninge Streame or water And the conveyaunce and distribucon thereof into the ptes of the said Citye and the suburbes thereof or reserved to be payd to the said Hughe Midleton his heires or assignes and the same to converte and take to the proper use of the said Maior and Coialtye and Citizens and the possession of the premisses to detayne and keepe in the name of a distresse untill such tyme as the said Maior and Coialtye and Citizens shalbe fullie satisfyed and recompenced by the said Hughe Midleton his heires or assignes of all their losses charges and expences any way disbursed or sustayned by reason of or concerning the premisses or untill out of the proffitte of the same they shall or may have levyed sufficyente to satisfye and recompence themselves in that behalfe which of theis shall first happen Any thing in theis psntes conteyned to the contrary thereof notwithstanding And from and after such satisfaccon and recompence from tyme to tyme as aforesaid Then the said Hughe Midleton his heires and assignes shall have receave and take the benefitt profitt rente comodity and advantage of the said River or Streame and reenioy the same to him and his heires as in his and their former estate untill any other of the like coste charge and expence as aforesaid shall happen againe which so often as shall happen the like retayner of the profitte to be by the said Maior and Coialtye and Citizens as aforesaid

AND LASTLIE the said Hughe Midleton for himselfe his heires executors and administrators doeth covennte promise and graunte to and with the said Maior and Coialtye and Citizens and their successors by theis psntes that hee the said Hughe Midleton his heires executors administrators and assignes shall not nor will demaunde require or expecte from the said Maior and Coialtye and Citizens or their successors any manner of recompence satisfaccon or amendes in regard of the undertaking begining or progression of or in the worke aforesaid in case the same hathe or shold miscarry or not succeed well according to expectacon or that the same hath not or shall not prove fesible But that as the said Hughe Midleton hath voluntarilie and of his owne accord undertaken and begunne the same worke and to have the sole profitt thereof to him and his heires if the same work prove well and take good effecte as is wished So the said Hughe Midleton his heires and assignes are to stand unto abide and undergoe the sole and onely hazard and adventure of the said worke without looking for having or expectinge any manner of recompence from the said Maior and Coialtye and Citizens or their successors as aforesaid

AND FINALLIE it is condiconed and agreed by and betweene the said ptyes that if the said worke shall not be effected and performed within the said space of seaven yeares next after the said one and twentyeth day of Aprill next ensuing the date of theis psntes then theis psntes as also all and every the Lres of Attorney and Deputacon made to the said Hughe Midleton and all covenntes and agreements had and made betweene him and the said Maior and Coialtye and Citizens concerning the premises shalbe voyd and of none effecte

IN WITNES whereof to the one parte of theis psnte Indentures remayninge with the said Hughe Midleton the said Maior and Coialtye and Citizens have putt their comon seale and to th'other parte remayninge with the said Maior and Coialtye and citizens the said Hughe Midleton hath sett to his hand and seale Yeouen the day and yeares first above written

L S

C. Compensation Receipts 1610–1615

C.1 I Thomas Hassall Clarke vicar of much Amwell in the Countie of Hartfs doe by theis presents give and graunte unto the Maior and Communaltie of the Cittie of London and to Hugh Middelton cittizen and goldsmith of the Cittie of London their deputie free passage for the new ryver through all my grounds conteyning in length Thirty Eight pole or thereabout moved therto for the utter love I beare to the said Cittie being borne therein Sealed with my seale this 2d daie of January 1609 Annoq Regis Jacobi septimo

Tho: Hassall L S

Sealed & delivered in the psnce of

H. Cocke	Tho: Thorowgoode
Geo: Michel	G Fordham
Edw: Hughs	Rich: Roocke

C.2 Receaved by me Willm Manton of Wormley in the Countie of Hartford yeoman of the Maior and comynaltie of the Cittie of London by the handes of Hugh Middleton cittizen and goldsmith of London in full satisfaction for ye passage of the newe Ryver by Acte of plament through my grounde in [*illegible*] Wormley conteyning in length fifty one poles [*illegible*] the some of twentie shillings of currante Englishe money Sealed with my seale the 27th day of January 1609 Annoq Regis Jacobi septimo

Willm Manton L S

Sealed and delivered in ye psence of

H Cocke	
G Baylye	Tho: Thorowgoode
E Michel	G Fordham
Edw: Hughs	Rich: Roocke

C.3 Recd by mee Thomas Collyns of Edmonton in ye Counetye of Middx husbandman of the Mayor & Comynalltie of the Cittie of London by the handes of Hughe Midleton citizen & goldsmith of London fyve shillinges of lawfull moneye of England, in full satisfaction of all my damages susteyned in my grasse by reason of a trench cutt throughe the same conteyning xxtie poles nowe filled in againe being allowed for two yeares losse of my grasse In wittness whereof I have hereunto putt my hand & seale the xiijth daye of December 1612

The mk + of Thomas Collyns
L S

Sealed & delyvered in the
presence of
Edw: Pond

C.4 Recd by mee William Hollyday of London Marchaunte of the Maior & Comynalltie of ye Cittie of London by the handes of Hugh Mydleton Citizen & goldsmith of London fyve poundes fyve shillings of lawfull money of England in full satisfaction of all my damages susteyned in my Meadows & Landes in ye p/ish of Islington in ye County of Middx by reason of the cutt & Bankes or otherwise for a trench cutt through my land conteyning one & twenty poles for the passage of a streame of running water to ye North ptes of the Cittye of London In wyttnes whereof I have hereunto putt my hand & seale the xxijth of Aprill 1613

By me William Hallidaie
L S

Sealed & delyvered in the psence of
Willm [*illegible*]

C.5 Receaved by me Samuel Backhouse of Swallowfield in the county of Berk Esquire of the mayor & comminalty of the city of London by the handes of Hugh Middleton citizen & goldsmith of the same Threescore & five poundes of lawfull mony of England in full satisfaction of all my Dammages & trespasses whatsoever as well by reason of the cutt & bankes or otherwise for a trench cutt throughe my landes called the Mantles lieng & being within the parish of Clerkenwell in the county of Middx for the passage of a streame of running water to the northe partes of the sayd city conteyning xviij poles & three footor thereabouts As also in consideration of all my dammages & trespasses whtsoever susteyned by reason of a brick wall & cesternehouse built in & upon the sayd landes called the Mantles for conveyinge of the aforesaid streame of water into the city of London In witness whereof I have hereunto put my hand & seale the iijd day of May Ao 1614

Sa: Backhouse
L S

Sealed & delivered in presence of
Francis Deane
Rich: Daly
Phill: Warrick Exmer

C.6 Mr Lewyn I praie you paie Mr Nichols the 3li 6s 8d and take his acquittance upon this arbattrement 30th June 1615

Hugh Myddelton

The xxxth of June 1615

Recd by mee Edmond Niccolsonne of Bushe Hilles in the pishe of Enfeild in the Counetye of Myddx gent of Hughe Middleton Citizen & goldsmith of London three poundes sixe shillings and eight pence of lawfull moneye of England in full payemente & satisfaction of all my damages & trespasses whatsoever susteyned in my groundes by reason of a cutt made through the same for the passage of a streame of Runneinge water to the Northe ptes of the Cittye of London as allsoe for all other damages susteyned by meanes theirof In wittness whereof I have hereunto putt my hand & seale the daye & yeere above written

iij^{l} vjs viiid

Ed: Nicholson
L S

Sealed & delivd in the presence of
Will: Lewyn
Edw: Michell

D. Royal Investment

2 May 1612

THIS INDENTURE made the second daie of May in the yeare of the Raigne of our Soveraigne Lord James by the Grace of God King of England Scotland ffraunce and Ireland Defendor of the Faith that is to say of England ffraunce and Ireland the tenth and of Scotland the five and forteth BETWEENE Our said Soveraigne Lord the Kinges Maiesty of the one parte and Hugh Middleton Citizen and Goldsmith of London of the other partie WHEREAS by certeyne Articles of Agreement indented made and agreed uppon the first daie of November last past before the date hereof Betweene the Right Honorable Robert Earl of Salisbury Lord High Treasorer of England for and on the parte and behalfe of our said Soveraigne Lord the Kinges Maiestie of the one partie and the said Hugh Midleton of the other partie [*Agreement recited*]

NOW for the better performance and accomplishement of all and singular the covenants promises grantes and agreements in the before mentioned Articles aswell on the part and behalfe of our said Soveraigne Lord the Kinges Maiestie his heires and successors as on the parte and behalfe of the said Hugh Midleton his heires executors and administrators to be performed accomplished and fullfilled according to the tenor effecte and true meaning of the said Articles

THIS INDENTURE WITNESSETH thatt our said Soveraigne Lorde the Kinges Maiestie for him his heires and successors doth promise and graunt to and with the said Hugh Midleton his heires executors and administrators by these presents that his Maiestie his heires and successors shall and will at all tymes hereafter doe and performe all such lawfull and resonable acts deeds and thinges at the costs charges and travell of the said Hugh Midleton his executors administrators and assignes which may tende to the helpe and furtherance of the bringing and conveighing the said springes and waters of Chadwell and Amwell and other springes in the Countie of Hertford to the said Citty of London and for the continuance of the said ryver being once brought thither And Will also as much as in his Maiestie shall lye by his Royall powers and authoritie withstand and remove all such iniuste and unlawfull impediment which shall or may give lett disturbance and hinderance to the bringing of the said waters and springes to the said Citty or to the continuance of the said current and ryver being once brought thither And his Maiestie doth also by theise psents for himselfe his heires and successors give and graunte unto the said Hugh Midleton and his assignes full power and authoritie by the view and directions of some person for that purpose to be appointed by our said Soveraigne Lord the Kinges Maiestie or by the Lord Treasorer of England for the tyme being to carry and convey the said springes and waters through any the mannors parkes landes tenements and hereditaments of his Maiestie and for effecting thereof by like view and directions to enter into any of the said mannors landes parkes tenements and hereditaments in places fitt and convenient with his and their workemen carts carriages and other necessaries and there to digge cutt and cast uppe the soyle thereof as shall be fitt and necessary for the effecting and performance of the said worke and that without compounding or paying anything to his Maiestie his heires and successors and afterwards at all tymes and from tyme to tyme to doe all and everie acte and thing whatsoever which shall be needefull and expedient to be done within the said mannors parkes landes tenements and hereditaments of his Maiestie his heires and successors for the pserving of the said ryver or newe Cutt and the free passage and continuance thereof through the said mannors parkes landes tenements and hereditaments of his Maty his heires and successors And for the better effecting of the said worke our said Soveraigne Lord the Kinge for himselfe his heires and successors doth by theise presents straightlie charge and comaund the Lord Chauncellor of Englande or Lord Keeper of the greate seale of England for the tyme being upon the request of the said Hugh Midleton his heires or assignes to grant and cause to be made forth such and so manie Commissions under the great seale of England as shall be thought necessarie by the said Hugh Midleton his heires or assignes for the laying out of convenient limitts of ground for the making of the trench of the said ryver and doing of other things by the said Acts of Parliament made in the said third and fourth yeares of his Maiesties raigne of England appointed or by anie Acte of Parliament hereafter to be made to be appointed

AND further our said Soveraigne Lord the King for himselfe his heires and successors doth by theise psents graunte unto the said Hugh Midleton his heires executors and assignes thatt if any tumultuous or other rude or unlawfull courses by force sleight clamors or otherwise shall be at any tyme or tymes hereafter used attempted or put in use by any pson or psons to the hinderance lett or opposition of bringing of the said springs and water to the said Citie of London or to the pservacon of the continuall passage and current of the said ryver after it shall be once brought thither that then in such cases his Maiestie will uppon the information and request of the said Hugh Midleton his heires or assignes cause the same by some due course to be suppressed and reformed

AND therefore our said Soveraigne Lord the King doth by theise psents for himselfe his heires and successors straightlie charge and comaunde all and everie the subiects of his Maiestie his heires and successors whatsoever that they nor anie of them doe at any time or times hereafter molest inquiett trouble or hinder the said Hugh Midleton his heires executors and assignes or anie of them in the doing and effecting of the premises according to the true intente and meaning thereof nor attempt use or put in use any unlawfull courses by sleight clamor or otherwise to the hinderance lett or opposicon of bringing of the said springs and water to the City of London or to the preservacon of the continuall passage and current of the said ryver uppon payne of his Maiesties high displeasure and uppon such other paines and penalties as by any lawes or statutes of this Realme are or may be inflicted uppon them or anie of them for their disobedience and contempt in that behalfe

AND our said Soveraigne Lord the King is also further pleased and contented and by theis psents for him his heires and successors doth graunte unto the said Hugh Midleton his heires executors and assignes that if hereafter at any tyme any Bill or Peticon for any Acte of Parliament to redresse or supplie anie defecte in the former mentioned Acts of Parliament or for the better or more effectual bringing of the said springes and waters to the Citie of London or continuance of the same or for the setling conveying and assigning of the interest of the said ryver and newe Cutt or of the benefitt profitt and comoditie that may arise and growe by reason and menes thereof to the use of the said Hugh Midleton his heires and assignes or to the use of such Adventurers in the said worke to whome the said Hugh Midleton or his heires shall assigne and graunte or shall have assigned and graunted the same or anie parte thereof shall pass or be agreed uppon by the Lords and Comons in Parliament that then our said Soveraigne Lord the Kinge his heires and successors will give his and their free and royall assent thereunto to the end the same may be and have the full force and effect of an Acte of Parliament

AND our Soveraigne Lord the King doth likewise for him his heires and successors with the assent consent and agreement of the said Hugh Midleton give full power and authoritie unto his wellbeloved servaunt Myles Whiteacres Gent. to acquaint and inform himself of all and everie the payment and disbursement that have bene heretofore from the foure and twentieth daie of August last past before the date hereof and shall hereafter be laied out and made by the said Hugh Midleton his heires and assignes in about or concerning the following finishing and bringing of the said worke within one myle of the said Citty of London

AND IT IS fullie concluded and agreed aswell by our said Soveraigne Lorde the Kinge as by the said Hugh Midleton That the said Myles Whiteacres and the said Hugh Midleton his heires and assignes or such other person as the said Hugh Midleton his heires or assignes shall nomynate to be his Expenditor of the monies shall kepe one or more bookes of accompte as they shall thinke best wherein the said payement and disbursement shall be entred and subscribed aswell with the hande of the said Myles Whiteacres as with the hande of the said Hugh Midleton his heires and assignes or his Expenditor which subscription shall be a sufficient warrant to the Lord Treasorer of England for the tyme being to allow of the said accompt

AND our said Soveraigne Lorde the Kinge for him his heires and successors doth by theis psents give full power and authoritie and doth also straightlie charge and comaunde the Lord High Treasorer of Englande for the tyme beinge within twentie daies after tender made of everie suche accompte as aforesaid as well for the disbursementes laide out before the date of the said Articles as for those which have been made or shall bee made since the date of the same unto the said Lord Treasorer for the tyme being to paie and deliver or cause to be paid and delivered unto the said Hugh Midleton his heires executors and administrators from tyme to tyme to his and their owne uses out of the treasure of his Highnes his heires and successors remayning in the Exchequer as well the one halfe of the monie already disbursed as the one halfe of the mony to be disbursed in and about the pmsses And theise psentes or the inroulmente thereof shall bee from tyme to tyme to the said Lord Treasorer sufficient warrante and discharge in that behalfe

AND further his Maiestie is pleased and contented and by theis psentes for him his heires and successors doth give full power and authoritie unto the Lord Treasorer of Englande for the tyme being at all tymes after the said springes and water shall be broughte within one myle of the said Citie of London to nomynate and appointe some such one person as is aforesaid who shall be made acquainted and privie to all and everie the paymentes and disbursementes that shall hereafter be laied oute and made by the said Hugh Midleton his heires and assignes in aboute and concerning the bringing of the said springes and waters from thence and the dispersinge of the saide water in and through severall pipes into severall houses and places in or near the said Citty and in and aboute the pservacon maintening and continuance of the same currente of the saide ryver into the said Cittie of London for ever after and of the pondes pipes cesternes and other things necessarie for the dispersing thereof into severall houses as is aforesaid and maintenance thereof which person as shall be appointed by the said Lorde Treasorer and the said Hugh Midleton his heires and assignes or such other person as the said Hugh Midleton his heires and assignes shall nomynate to be Expenditor of the mony shall kepe one or more bookes of accompt as they shall think best wherein the paiment and disbursement last mentioned shall be entred and subscribed in manner and forme as before in these presentes is declared and expressed which subscription shall be from tyme to tyme sufficient warrant to the Lorde Treasorer of England for the tyme being to allow of the said accompt last mentioned

AND his Maiestie doth hereby also for him his heires and successors give full power and authoritie and doth straightlie charge and comaunde the said Lord Treasorer of England for the tyme being within twentie daies after tender made of such accompt or accomptes unto the said Lord Treasorer for the tyme being to paie and deliver or cause to be paied and delivered unto the said Hugh Midleton his heires executors and administrators to his and their owne uses at the receipt of his Maiesties Exchequer at Westminster out of the Treasure of his Maiestie his heires and successors there remayning the one halfe of such costs and charges from tyme to tyme to be disbursed in or aboute the bringing of the said springes and waters from the said places within one myle of the said Citie and the dispersing preservacon continuance and maintenance of the said ryver and of the pondes pipes cesternes and other necessarie thinges aforesaid and theise psentes or the the inroulmente thereof shall be unto the Lorde Treasorer of England for the tyme being a sufficient warrant and discharge in that behalfe

AND his Maiestie doth further for his Highnes his heires and successors covenaunt promise and graunte to and with the said Hugh Midleton his heires and assignes by these psentes that his Maiestie his heires and successors shall at all tymes after the said newe Cutt or streame shall be brought to London or within one myle of the said Citty susteyne and beare the one moitie or halfe parte of all and everie the somes of money costs damages losses and charges that shall or may bee susteyned undergone or borne by the said Hugh Midleton his heires executors administrators or assignes by force or virtue of the said covenaunt before mentioned in the said dede made between the said Lord Maior and Cominaltie and Citizens of the Citty of London of the one parte and the said Hugh Midleton of the other part bearing date the said eight and twentyeth day of March conteyned And his Maiestie is pleased and contented and doth give and grante unto the said Hugh Midleton full and free licence libertie and authoritie at his proper cost and charge to derive a quill out of the mayne pipe that shall convey the water to the said City of London to serve the poor people gratis about Saint Johns Streate and Aldergate Streate which are not able nor fitt to paie for their water to be enioied by the said poore perpetuallie

AND the said Hugh Midleton for and in consideration of the said powers liberties priviledges authorities payments and other thinge to him the said Hugh Midleton his heires executors and administrators by theise presentes given graunted and to be paied and performed Doth by theise presentes for him his heires executors administrators and assignes covenant promise and grante to and with our saide Soveraigne Lorde the Kinge his heires and successors by theise presentes for ever the one halfe of the benefitt profitt and comoditie of the said water and of the conveying of the same to and from all places and that the said Lorde Maior Cominaltie and Citizens of the said Citie of London and their successors and the said Hugh Midleton his heires executors administrators and assignes shall and will from tyme to tyme doe and suffer to be done all actes and thinges for the assuring and sure making of the same to some such person or persons and in such manner and forme as his Maiestie his heires and successors shall nomynate and appointe and that the same assurance shall be from tyme to tyme renewed altered or amended as shall be appointed by his Maiestie his heires or successors or any of them or by his Councell learned in the lawe so as the interest shall and may still be setled and kepte in the subiecte and not in His Maiestie his heires or successors according to the purporte effecte or true meaning of any of the covenants or agreements of the said Maior and Cominaltie and Citizens in the aforesaid dede betweene them of the one parte and the said Hugh Midleton of the other parte bearing date the foresaid eight and twentyeth daie of March conteyned

IN WITNESS whereof to the one part of theise indentures remayning with the said Hugh Midleton our saide Soveraigne Lorde the Kinges Maiestie hath caused the great seale of England to be putt and to the other part thereof remayning with our said Soveraigne Lorde the Kinge the said Hugh Midleton hath put his seale Yeouen the daie and yeare first above written

L S

E. Share Issue

8 May 1612

THIS INDENTURE made the eighth daie of Maye in the yere of the raigne of our soveraigne Lord James by the grace of God of England Scotland ffraunce and Ireland Kinge Defendor of the faithe that is to saie of England ffrance and Ireland the tenth and of Scotland the five and fortyeth Betweene Hugh Middleton Cittizen and goldsmith of London of the one parte And Sir Henry Nevill of Billingsbear in the countie of Berks Knight of the other parte WITNESSETH

That whereas heretofore Two severall actes of Parliement were made [*statutes recited*]

AND whereas the said Maior and Comonaltie and Cittizens of the Cittie of London [*transfer of powers recited*]

AND whereas by an Indenture with covennts made between the Kinges most excellent matie of the one parte and the said Hugh Middleton of the other parte [*Royal investment recited*]

AND whereas the said Sir Henrie Nevill is and hathe beene an adventurer in the said worke according to the rate and proportion in these presents expressed

NOW FURTHER witnesseth theis presents that for and in consideracon as well of the some of two hundred pounds to him the said Hugh by the said Sir Henry Nevill paied and delivered longe before the sealinge and deliverie of theis presents as of other covenants thereafter by theis presents made by the said Sir Henry Nevill for hym his heires and assignes and by hym and them to bee performed touchinge further payment to the said Hugh Middleton his heires or assignes towards the effectinge and performinge of the said waterworks by him alreadie begunne and to be expended and imployed therein

THE SAID Hugh Middleton for him and his heires doth by theis presents graunt and assigne unto the said Sir Henry Nevill his heires and assignes for ever two full and intire six and thirtieth partes of the said waterworks river and new cutt made and to be made and of the profitt benefitt gaigne comoditie and advantage which (such moietie or halfe of the profitts and comodities thereof due and to be due to the Kinges Matie aforesaid according to the true meaninge thereof excepted and allowed) at anie tyme herafter shalbe made or raised by or out of the said river water streame or new cutt and by and out of all and everie cesterne mills milldams ponds pooles staynes pipes and conduits and conveiance of water to be made thereby or thereupon or from or out of the same to be deduced drawne or derived and of all rents somes of monie and other profitte and advantages which shalbe upon anie contracts or agreements or demises of or for anie such pipes or derivacons of water had taken obteyned or paid or aniewaie by meanes or occasion thereof received bargayned contracted for or agreed to be yealded or paied and of all fynes or amerciaments by anie comissioners of Sewers or others lawfullie authorized to be laied imposed or adiudged upon anie person or persons for or in respect of anie acte obstruction hurt or impediment by them or anie of them done to the said river or new cutt or anie of the premisses And of all other liberties powers authorities and advantages in the said severall writings conteyned or expressed

AND the said Hugh for him his heires and assignes doth covennt promise graunte and agree to and with the said Sir Henry Nevill his heires and assignes in manner and forme followinge That is to saie That the said Sir Hugh his heires executors administrators or assignes shall imploy the said two hundred pounds and soe much more as shall be needfull in and about the effecting and perfectinge of the said worke And that hee his heires and assignes shall use their best and uttermost endeavor as speedilie as may be to accomplishe the same entended worke And that there shalbe noe defecte nor willfull defaulte in the said Hugh Middleton his heires or assignes in accomplishinge and perfectinge of the said entended worke

AND that neither hee the said Hugh his heires nor assignes shall at anie tyme hereafter without the assent and consent of the said Sir Henry Nevill or his heires in writinge thereunto first had and obteyned surrender relinquish or yeeld up unto the said Maior comonaltie and Cittizens of the said Cittie of London or to the said Cittie his or their said autoritie deputacon factorshipp or agencie in the premisses to him comitted as aforesaid nor shall doe or comitt anie thinge whereby the same shall or may be forfeited lost repealed annihilated or revoked And that yf by or through anie impossibilitie in the said worke or other impediment or hinderance which the said Hugh his heires or assignes cannot nor shall not be able to remove or withstand the said worke shalbe staied and not proceeded in or not be effected and perfected before the first daie of Aprill which shalbe in the yeare of our Lord God according to the computacon of the Church of England one thousand six hundred and thirteen THAT then he the said Hugh his heires or assignes shall within one moneth after request to him or them in that behalfe made or for him or them leafte in writinge at his or their most usuall place of abode repaie unto the said Sir Henry Nevill his heires executors or administrators soe muche monie as the said two hundred pounds shalbe in surplusage over and above the sixteenth parte of the monie disbursed and to be disbursed about the said worke as aforesaid

AND that neither he the said Hugh nor his heires shall grant out of the profitt of the premisses or charge the same with more then sixe and thirtie partes The totall and entire to be accounted and devided into sixe and thirtie parts and the parts in this present grant and others formerlie made being accompted AND that he the said Hugh his heires and assignes shall once every yeare upon the request of the said Sir Henrie Nevill or his heires make true and iust accompt to him and his heires aswell of all the coste and charges of the said worke as of the gayne benefit and advantage thereafter arisinge out of the same when the same shalbe brought to good effecte and shall permitt and suffer the said Sir Henry Nevill his heires and assignes to have receave and take two full sixe and thirtieth parts of the gaine profitt and advantage accordinge to the true intent and meaning of these presents

AND that he the said Hugh and his heires shall from time to tyme for ever hereafter doe his and their best endeavour to procure and gett a good and absolute estate and interest in the premisses and also shall at all tymes hereafter at the costs and charges of the said Sir Henrie Nevill his heires or assignes doe all and every such further and other lawfull and reasonable acte and thinge for the better and fulle assuring and securinge of the said part parts profitt comoditie and interest hereby meant and intended to the said Sir Henrie Nevill his heires and assignes And of two sixe and thirtith parts of the same when the said Sir Hugh Middleton or his heires shall have or procure a further or better estate or interest in the same to be by him and them had held and enioyed accordinge to the purporte true intent and meaning of theis presents as by the said Sir Henry Nevill his heires or assignes or by his or their Councell learned in the lawe shalbe reasonablie devised advised and required so that the same extend not to anie statute or recognizance bond nor obligacon

AND whereas there are assigned or extended to Edmond Colthurst of the Cittie of Bath Gent in consideracon of greate labour and endeavour by him bestowed about the said worke fower partes in sixe and thirtie parts to be devided of the said profit and benefit to be raised as aforesaid which said Edmond Colthurst may disburse anie thereof for and toward the discharge of the said worke as the same is entended and concluded by and betweene the said parties to theis presentes And the said Hugh Middleton for him his heires executors administrators and assignes doth covennt graunt and agree to and with the said Sir Henrie Nevill his heires and assignes that after the effectinge of the said worke and as sone as it is brought to yeeld profitt and benefitt the whole gayne and advantages thereof arisinge by or out of anie fynes [*illegible*] rents or other profitte [*illegible*] Mills or derivacon of water by pipes and conduits or otherwise shall goe and be devided into sixe and thirtie parts ffower parts whereof shalbe to the said Edmond Colthurst for terme of his naturall life and after his decease two of the said ffower parts shalbe and remayne to the said Hugh Middleton his heires and assignes in respecte of the great industrie travell and paynes takinge of the said Hugh Middleton in and about the performing finishing and effecting of the said worke And the other two partes of the said ffower partes soe appointed and allotted to the said Edmond Colthurst shalbe and remayne to the said Edmond Colthurst his heires and assignes yf the said Edmond Colthurst shall live untill the said entended worke shalbe finished and perfected as aforesaid But yf the said Edmond Colthurst shall happen to die before the finishing and perfectinge of the said worke then the two partes so intended and appointed for the said Edmond Colthurst his heires and assignes shalbe shared devided and secured by and amonge the said Sir Henry Nevill and Hugh Middleton and the other adventurers in the said worke and their heirs and assignes according to the severall rate and proporcon of their share advanture and disbursements that is to say the full seaventeenth parte thereof shalbe and remayne to the said Sir Henry Nevill his heires and assignes for ever and the residue thereof according to the true intent and meaninge of theis psntes

AND the said Sir Henrie Nevill for him his heires executors and administrators doth covennt promise grant and agree to and with the said Hugh his heires and assignes that yf the charge of the said worke shall amounte unto more than three thousand and two hundred pounds that then he the said Sir Henry Nevill his heires executors and administrators shall uppon a full and perfecte accompte thereof and thereupon yerely made after the said three thousand and two hundred pounds expended shall paie unto the said Hugh his heires or assignes a full sixteenth parte of all such suprlusage or charge soe by the said Hugh Middleton his heires or assignes further disbursed or expended or to be disbursed or expended according to the true intent and meaninge of theis pntes

AND the said Hugh Middleton for him his heires and assignes doth covennt and graunt to and with the said Sir Henry Nevill his heires and assigns that he the said Hugh Middleton his heires executors and assignes shall from tyme to tyme and at all tymes upon reasonable request make a true accompt to the said Sir Henrie Nevill his heires and assignes of all such somes of monie as shalbe paied to him the said Hugh Middleton his heires or assignes by the Kinges matie his heires or successors or by the Lord Treasurer for the tyme beinge by force and vertue of the covennts or agreements in the said indenture conteyned And shall from time to time paie and allowe to the said Sir Henry Nevill his heires and assignes a full sixteenth parte of all such some and somes of monie so paid as aforesaid

AND lastlie it is concluded agreed and explaned by the said parties that both the two six and thirtieth parts herein limitted unto the said Sir Henry Nevill and the ffower six and thirtieth parts limitted unto the said Edmond Colthurst of the said river and streame of water And of the gayne profitt and comoditie of the said river streame of water and premisses aforementioned are entended and meant to be onlie of the gayne profitt and comoditie thereof as shall remayne apperteyne and belonge to the said High Middleton his heires and assignes after the halfe share of or in the profitte of the same due and payable to the Kinges matie his heires and successors by force of the covennts aforesaid shalbe paied abated and deducted

IN WITNES whereof the said parties hereto to theis present indentures their hands and seales interchangeably have put the daie and year first above written

Hugh Myddelton L S

Sealed signed and delivered
in the presence of
Ni: Hyde
Will: Staverton
Wm: Neast

F. Incorporation

21 June 1619

JAMES by the Grace of God Kinge of England Scotland ffraunce and Ireland Defender of the ffaith etc. To All to whome theise presents shall come Greetinge

WHEREAS two severall Actes of Parliament were made [*statutes recited*] By virtue and authority of which Act and Acts the Mayor Cominaltie and Cittizens of our Cittie of London and their successors have libertie given them and are thereby enabled to bringe a freshe Streame of runninge Water to the north partes of our said Cittie of London from the springs of Chadwell and Amwell and other springs in the Countie of Hertf not farre distant from the said Springs either in an open cutt or in close Truncke vaulte of bricke or stone which work upon view was found verie fezible and was like to be profitable to manie As by the said Actes more at large appeareth; nevertheless the said Mayor [etc.] weighinge the great charge and expence the said Worke would require and doubtinge what damage and losse might fall upon the Chamber of the said Cittie in case the Work should not fall out to be both beneficiall and gainfull did thereupon forbeare at theire comon charge to undertake that Worke so as the same lay longe neglected and unlike by them to be performed:

AND WHEREAS Hugh Middleton Cittizen and Gouldsmith of London well affectinge the good of our said Cittie of London and being moved with a desire and zeale to perform soe publique necessary and worthie a Worke to that Cittie whereof he is a member was willing to adventure and upon his own private charge to undertake the said Worke and did out of a pyous and comendable purpose make offer to the Lord Mayor Aldermen and Comons of our Cittie of London assembled in a comon Councell houlden within the said Cittie the eight and twentieth daie of March in the seaventh yeare of our Raigne of England ffraunce and Ireland to undertake the said Worke and fully and perfectly to do execute and performe at the proper coste and charges of him his heires and Assignes whatsoever on the parte and behalfe of the said Mayor [etc.] by and accordinge to the Acts of Parliament or the true Intent and meaninge of the same Acts or either of them was or should be necessary and convenient to be done and performed and withall to save and keep harmles the said Mayor [etc.] for ever of and from all charges and damages losses hinderances and expences that should or might anie way arise or growe by occasion or meanes of the foresaid Worke or anie thinge thereto belonginge or thereupon followinge and to make such Agreements with everie partie interessed in any soile through which the said river or streame should be brought and to give such recompence satisfaccon and amends to any partie which should be dampnified putt to a losse or hindred by the said Worke as the said Mayor [etc.] might anie ways be charged withall either by reason of the said Actes of Parliament or either of them or anie thinge done in the pformance thereof or whatsoever should arise by meanes or occasion of the said Workes so alwaies as he the said Hugh Middleton his heires and Assignes might be constituted and appointed ioyntlie and severally the lawfull Deputy or Deputies Attorney or Attornies Agents or Assignes to and for the said Mayor [etc.] to doe execute and performe whatseover by vertue of the said Acts or either of them the said Mayor [etc.] had power libertie or Authoritie to do by them or their Deputies or workmen; and soe as the said Mayor [etc.] would condescend and agree to graunt convey and assure to the said Hugh Middleton his heires and Assignes for ever the whole and entire profitt benefitt and comoditie that should or might arise come or growe by the said River or Water and the disposicon or distribucon thereof and of every or anie part or parts thereof into the several parts and places of the said Cittie and Suburbes thereof and that he the said Hugh Middleton his heires and assignes should and might have libertye for layinge of pipes for conveyance of Water in by and through all partes and places where the said Mayor [etc.] had power and Authoritie to doe and license the same to be done; and that all Contracts Bargaines and Agreements to be made for the said Water or anie part thereof and whole benefitt profitt and comoditie thereby cominge growinge or arisinge from tyme to tyme should and might be to and for the sole use and behoofe of the said Hugh Middleton his heires and assignes for ever; Whereupon the said Lord Mayor Aldermen and Comons in the said comon Councell assembled well weighinge and consideringe the offer made by the said Hugh Middleton as afores[d] after longe and deliberate consultacon and advisement had and taken among themselves in the said cause declared their verie good likinge thereof and willingly accepted and embraced the said offer as a thinge of great consequence and worthie of acceptacon for the good of the said Cittie as by the said Acte of Comon Councell more fully may appeare; And thereupon the said Mayor [etc.] by their Indenture under their comon Seale [*recites transfer of powers*]

AND WHEREAS the said Hugh Middleton by vertue of the said Acts of Parliament and of the power and Authoritie graunted to him by the said Mayor [etc.] had begun to convey the said Springs in a new Channell and River towards the said Cittie of London and soe farr proceeded therein as he had brought the same Waters divers myles towardes the said Cittie yet findinge the charge of the said Worke greater and heavier than at first was expected the Successe thereof doubtfull and the Opposicons made against it very stronge besides many other difficulties thought fitt to joyne unto him for helpe therein some other ffriends such as were well affected to the said Worke and willing to adventure and joyn in contribucon towards the charge thereof whereupon divers our lovinge Subjects hereafter named well affectinge the said Worke made severall Agreements with the said Hugh Middleton to pay disburse and contribute towards the charge of the said Worke both past and to come for such ratable partes and porcons in the said Worke as was agreed between them and in regard thereof it was likewise agreed That the severall Adventurers should have and receave severallie to them and their heires ratable shares and parts out of the profitts to growe and arise out of the same accordinge to the proporcon of their severall Disbursements and Adventures; after which time the said Hugh Middleton and the said Adventurers at their great Charge proceeded soe farr in bringinge the said River towards the said Cittie of London that it not only appeared to be feazible but likewise also to be a Worke of great use benefitt and comfort to the comon wealth and especially to our said Cittie of London which Wee considering out of our Royall and gracious Inclination being willing to give our Ayde [*recites royal investment*]

AND WHEREAS the said Hugh Midleton and the said Adventurers with great Expences and Charge both of us and of themselves in particular have proceeded in the said Worke and after many Difficulties and Opposicons undergon therein have by our aid and ffurtherance and with the speciall Labor Care and Industrie of the said Hugh Midleton longe since brought the said freshe streame into our said Cittie of London and into the Suburbes thereof And also into our Cittie of Westminster and distributed the same by pipes through manie partes thereof all which notwithstanding the said worke hath not hitherto yeilded such profitt as was hoped for partly by reason of the Expences dailie arisinge farr greater and heavier than by the said Adventurers was expected and partly for want of power in them to settle the carriage and Government thereof in such order and form as is fitt and convenient;

KNOW YEE THEREFORE THAT WEE for the settlinge and establishinge of the said Worke and the profitts and comodities thereof in tyme to come to such intents uses and purposes as are herein menconed (that is to say) for and concerninge the one moietie thereof (all necessarie Charges and Expences deducted) to the use of us our heires and Successors and for the other moietie to the use of the said

Hugh Middleton and the said Adventurers their heires and Assigns ratablie and respectivelie accordinge to the proporcons of their severall Disbursements Adventures and parts therein, And to the end they maie be the better encouraged to take paines hereafter in perfectinge and preservinge the said Worke and enabled to make and execute good Orders for the maintayninge and continueinge of the same and to receive assurance of their severall partes and shares of the cleere benefitt and profitt of the said Worke to them their heires and Assignes for ever: And upon the humble Peticon of the said Hugh Middleton and the rest of the said Adventurers of our especial grace certaine knowledge and meer mocon have willed graunted ordained created and appointed and by theis presents for us our heires and Successors doe will graunt ordaine create and appointe That our wellbeloved subjects Hugh Midleton Cittizen and Gouldsmith of London Sir Henry Mountague Knight Lord Chief Justice of our Court of Kings Bench Sir Robert Killigrewe Knight Sir William Burlacie the elder Knight Sir Thomas Midleton Knight Cittizen and Alderman of London Sir Lawrence Hide Knight Sir William Burlacie the younger Knight Sir Henry Nevill Knight Nicholas Hide of the Middle Temple London Esquier John Packer Esquier Samuel Backhowse Esquier John Backhowse his Sonne and heire Esquier Robert Bateman of London Skynner Henry Midleton sonne and heire of David Midleton late of London Gent deceased Humfrey Hall of London Girdler Peter Vanlore Merchant stranger Rowland Backhowse of London Mercer Timothie Midleton of London Esquier Hugh Midleton sonne and heir of Hugh Midleton Gouldsmith William Midleton of London Draper Richard Midleton of London Grocer William Midleton of London Gouldsmith Marmaduke Rawden of London Clothworker Henry Vincent of London Letherseller William Bateman of London Grocer John ffaror of London Skinner Edward Prichard of London Skinner James Bearblocke of London Gent and Gabriell Newman of London Gouldsmith and all and every person and persons which hereafter accordinge to the true Intent of theise presents shall be elected and chosen into the roome or place of them or anie of them which shall die or be removed for ever hereafter be and shalbee by force of these presents one body corporate and politique in Deed fact and name and by the name of **The Governor and Company of the New River brought from Chadwell and Amwell to London:** And them by [*that name*] one body corporate and politique really and fully for us our heires and Successors Wee doe erect make ordaine create constitute and declare by these presents and that by the same name they shall have perpetuall Succession and that they and their Successors for ever by [*that name*] be and shalbee for ever able and capable in lawe to have receive take purchase and possesse to them and their

Successors Mannors Landes Tenements Rents Revenues possessions liberties priviledges Rights Jurisdiccons franchises and hereditaments and also goodes and Chattles whatsoever of what kind nature of Qualitye soever they be in fee and perpetuitie or otherwise howsoever And alsoe to demise lease assigne lett give graunt sell or dispose of the said Mannors [etc.] or anie of them and that they and their Successors for ever by [*that name*] may pleade and be impleaded answeare and be answeared unto defend and be defended in all manner of Courts and places that now are or hereafter shalbe within our Realme or elsewhere as well spirituall as Temporall in all manner of Accons suits pleas matter or causes whatsoever of what kinde sorte or qualitie soever they be or shalbe called or knowne in the same and in as large and ample manner and forme to all Intents construccons and purposes as anie other person or persons bodies politique or corporate of this our Realme of England beinge able and capable persons in lawe may doe;

And further [*to have a common seal and*] That there shalbe for ever hereafter one of the most sufficient and discreete persons of the said Companie in manner and form hereafter in these presents expressed from tyme to tyme elected and chosen which shalbe and shalbe called the Governor of the said Companie for the callinge of Courts Assemblies Councells and Consultacons and for the better direccon and necessary dispatch of the affaires and busineses concerninge the same Companie

And that there shalbe also one other sufficient person of the said company in manner hereafter in these presents expressed elected and chosen which shalbe and shalbe called the Deputy Governor of the said Company who shalbe usually resident within our said Cittie of London or the Suburbs thereof and shall in the absence of the Governor supplie his place and room and have the like and same Authoritie as the Governor hath and that there shalbe also one other person of the said Company in manner and forme also in the presents expressed to be elected and chosen which shalbe and shalbe called the Treasurer of the said Company who shall from tyme to tyme have the receipts of all the rents and profitts arisinge and cominge of and by the aforesaid Worke and the thinges thereunto belonging as also the disbursinge and layinge forthe of the same or so much thereof as shalbe necessary for the charges and Occasions touchinge and concerninge the said Worke by direccon of the said Companie accordinge to the Intent of these presents and the Distribucon and payment of the residue of the cleare gaine and profitt thereby arisinge (all necessary charges and Expences and the Officers ffees and Allowances first deducted) That is to the one moietie thereof to us our heires and Successors and the other moietie thereof to the severall parties interessed in the said Worke accordinge to their severall partes shares proporcons and Interests and accordinge to the true meaning of these Presents

And further Wee doe by these presents for us our heires and Successors graunt unto the said Governor and Company and their Successors That it shall and may be lawfull to and for the persons before in these presents named and appointed to be of the said Company together with the Deputy Governor for the time being and all others hereafter accordinge to the true meaninge of these presents which shalbe of the said Companie and their Successors or anie five or more of them (whereof the Governor of the said Companie or his Deputie for the tyme being to be one) from tyme to tyme to meete and assemble themselves together in some such meete and convenient place within our said Cittie of London or the Suburbes thereof as to them shall seem best and as often as they shall thinke convenient and there being so well mett together to hould Courts Councells and Consultacons and in them from tyme to tyme conclude and agree upon and make demises and leases of anie parte or partes of the Water coming from the foresaid new River or streame or anie profitt or advantage of or by reason of the said river or streame to anie person or persons either to be derived or conveyed out of the pipes of the said Worke or otherwise for anie Terme or Estate not exceedinge the terme of one and twentie yeares or three lives or anie number of yeares determinable upon one two or three lives and for such fines and rents uppon such covenaunts and condicons as they shall from tyme to tyme thinke fitt and also to hear and handle and determine all and all manner of businesses matters and things concerninge the well preserving ordering and maintayning of the foresaid Workes streame and Water and the collecting and receiving of the whole profitt gaine and benefitt arisinge or cominge thereof and thereby;

And as touchinge the charges expences [etc.] for the needfull Occasions and businesses touchinge the foresaid Worke streame and Water or anie thinge thereto belonginge as for the Officers to be used and employed in or about the said Worke [etc.] or for the Affaires concerninge the same and ffees and wages to be to them paid and allowed for the same And also in the same Courts Assemblies Councells and Consultacons in forme aforesaid to be houlden from tyme to tyme to name make and constitute Stewards Clarkes and such and soe manie other Officers and Ministers for the said Company as well for the writing and registring of their Graunts Acts and Constitucons and for the Oversight repayringe maintaininge and preservinge of the said Worke [etc.] as for the dispatch of other the businesses concerninge the said Company and Worke [etc.] as they shall think fitt and to give and minister unto every of the said Officers so to be nominated and appointed his oath for the true due honest and faithfull execucon and discharge of his or their place or Office appointed to him or them so long as hee or they shall continue in the same for the most profitt benefitt and advantage of the said Worke [etc.] and of the Owners thereof and the affaires and businesses of the same and for makinge true Accompts of all matters and things within their severall Offices and ymployments And further [*power to five or more including Governor or Deputy*] to make ordaine and sett downe orders Ordinances Acts of comon Councell lawes and Constitucons whatsoever reasonable and convenient in writinge which according to their discrecons shall seeme to be good [*the same to*] stand in full force and strength in lawe to all Construccons Intents and purposes untill such tyme as by other ordinances orders and Constitucons to be made by the said Company the same shalbe altered revoaked or repealed so as the same Orders [etc.] be not repugnant to the lawes and statuts of the Realme nor to our Prerogative Royall;

And for the better execucon of our will and pleasure herein Wee have nominated [etc.] and by theis presents for us our heires and Successors do nominate [etc.] the said Hugh Middleton to be the first and present Governor of the said Companie and our welbeloved Subject Robert Bateman to be the first and present Deputy Governor of the said Company and our welbeloved Subject Rowland Backhowse to be the first and present Treasorer of the said Companie to remaine and continue in the the said Offices severally and respectively until the Tuesday next after the ffeast of All Saints which shalbe in the yeare of our Lord God one thousand sixe hundred and twentie and from thence untill some other sufficient and discreet person shalbe chosen in their roomes and places accordinge to the true meaninge of these presents; The said present Governor takinge first his corporall Oath for the due Execucon of his Office and place in all things concerninge the same before the cheife Baron of our Court of Exchequer for the time being or any other of the Barons of the same Courte for the tyme being unto which said cheife Baron or other of the Barons Wee doe hereby give and graunt full power and Authoritie to minister an Oath to the said first Governor for the true and due execucon of his Office without anie further or other Warrant from us our heires and Successors in that behalfe to be had procured or obtained [*other officers to take oath before Governor; latter empowered to administer*]

And further our will and pleasure is and Wee doe hereby for us our heires and Successors graunt unto the said Governor and Company and their successors that it shall and maie be lawfull to and for all and every person and persons now being or hereafter to be of the said Companie accordinge to the true meaninge of these presents or anie seaven or more of them (whereof the Governor or his Deputy for the tyme being to be one) to assemble and meete together within our said Cittie of London or the suburbs of the same as is aforesaid yearely and every yeare on the Tuesday next after the ffeast of All Saints as aforesaid or within tenn daies after and there to elect [etc.] one fitt sufficient and discreete person of the said Company to be Governor [*the like for the other officers*] And the same severall persons havinge so taken their and every of their Corporall Oathes shall and may lawfully have use and execute the same their severall Offices roomes and places for one whole yeare from thence next ensuinge and untill some other fitt psons shalbe unto the said Offices respectivelie nominated [etc.; *power to administer oaths to clerks etc.*] And if it should happen at anie tyme or tyme hereafter the Governor Deputy Governor or Treasorer or anie other Officer or minister of the said Company to dye departe or be removed from the execucon of anie their places respectively (whom for cause reasonable Wee wil shalbe from tyme to tyme removeable at the will and pleasure of the said Company or anie twelve or more of them) That then and so often it shall and may be lawfull to and for anie twelve or more of the said Company then remayninge with as convenient speede as they may after such death departure or removinge to nominate elect and choose one or more other person or persons unto the roome or roomes place or places of the [*Officers*] for the residue of the yeare then to come and [*power to administer oaths*]

And further of our especiall grace [etc.] Wee have given [etc.] and by these presents for us our heires and Successors (for the consideracons aforesaid) as much as in us is Wee doe give [etc.] unto the said Governor and Company of the new River [etc.] and their Successors the said new River cutt and streame soe as aforesaid brought from Chadwell and Amwell to London with the appurtenances and all manner of profitts Advantages and Comodities thereof or by reason thereof in any sorte to be made raised or gotten To have hould and enjoye the said new River Cutt or Streame and premisses with the appurtenances to the said Governor and Company of the new River [etc.] and their Successors for ever accordinge to the true meaninge of these presents; To be holden of us our heires and Successors as of our Mannor of Eastgreenwich in our Countie of Kent in free and comon Socage by fealty only and not in chiefe nor by knights service

And further Wee will and by these presents for us our heires and Successors doe ordaine that the said [*Company*] and their Successors at all and every tyme and tymes hereafter shall well and sufficiently maintaine repayre preserve and scoure the said new River and

Streame and all the Bancks and Bridges of and belonging to the same as now it is And that the said Governor and Company and their Successors shall and may lawfully alter and change the said new River or cutt in by and through anie of the Groundes or soyle of us our heires or Successors without any ympeachment or Impediment or further or other warrant in that behalfe; And further that it shall and may be lawfull for the said [*Company*] and their Successors and to their Officers and Workemen and Servants to take and use the earth digged and cast up out of the said new River or Trench already made or hereafter to be made and to carry the same to anie place or places for the good of the said worke streame or water or for the benefitt of the said Companie of and from the Grounde or Soile of us our heires and Successors;

And further of our more especiall grace [etc.] Wee doe for us our heires and Successors hereby give and graunt unto the said [Company] and their Successors full power license and Authoritie to purchase have receave take and enjoy to the use of the said [Company] and their Successors for ever aswell of the Mayor [etc.] of the said Cittie of London as from the said Hugh Middleton his heires and assignes and of and from all and every other pson and psons having or clayminge anie thinge into or concerning the said New River Streame Water and premisses such Estate Right Title and Interest liberties and priviledges whatsoever as they or anie of them have or ought to have and which may be lawfully passed conveyed graunted or anie waie transferred to the said Governor and Company and their Successors; And likewise Wee doe hereby for us our heires and Successors give and graunt unto the said [*Company*] and their Successors full and free license libertie power and Authoritie to purchase have receive take enjoy and possesse from or of us our heires or Successors or of and from anie other pson or psons whatsoever one convenient Messuage Tenement or howse with the Appurtenances within our Cittie of London or Suburbes of the same for a hall or meetinge place To hold their Councells [etc.] so as the same be not holden of us our heires or Successors by knights service in Capite; The Statute of Mortmaine or anie other Act or Statute to the contrary notwithstanding;

And to the end that the Company may have perpetuall Continuance and the psons unto whome anie partes or porcons in the moiety of the benefitt arising by the said Water Worke shall come or fall by purchase discent or otherwise maie in equall and respective measure for every parte and share accordinge to their severall parts and shares in the said Worke have a severall voice and dealing in the said Company and worke; Wee doe hereby for us our heires and Successors will ordaine and appoint That whensoever and so often as it shall happen anie of the said psons before menconed to have anie share or shares out of the moiety of the said new River and of the cleare yearely profitt from thence arisinge accordinge to the true meaninge of these presents to depart withall or so much of the said share or part as that hee shall not still retayne a full thirtie sixth part or share of the moiety of the benefitt or proffitt of the said worke Then and soe often it shall and may be lawfull to and for the same Governor and Company to remove such pson from being of the said Companie and to elect such pson or psons to whom such share or part shalbe transferred or some other pson or psons to whom a thirtie sixth parte or share of the benefitt or profitt of the said worke shall apptaine into the room or place of him that is or shalbe so removed and also that upon death or avoydance of the place of any of the said Company then such heire or person unto whom the Inheritance of such part porcon or share shall come or some other pson or psons beinge lawfully Intituled to a full thirtie sixth parte of the benefitt of the said Worke shalbe by the Governor and Company for the tyme being elected and taken into the said Company and be a Member thereof in the roome of him soe deceasinge or whose place shalbe voyde

And further Wee doe by these presents for us our heires and Successors straightly charge and comaund all pson and psons whatsoever that they or anie of them doe not hereafter cast or putt into the said new River anie Earth rubbish soyle gravell stones dogges Catts or anie Cattle Carrion or anie unwholesome or uncleane thinge nor shall washe nor clense anie Clothes wooll or other thinge in the said River nor hurt abate breake pull downe take or carrie away anie the howses pipes pondes banckes or bridges of or belonging to the said new River made or to be made or anie parte of them nor shall doe anie Act or thinge that shall or may hinder lett stopp or annoye the said water or the current or passage thereof nor shall make or convey anie sincke sewer ditch Tanhowse dying howse or seege into the said River or to have anie fall into the same; And further that they or anie of them doe not hereafter presume to lay or place anie pipe or pipes or make anie devise to drawe or convey or otherwise to fetch or carry away turne or divert anie the water out of the said River nor out of anie pipe or quill graunted or to be graunted to anie pson or psons by the said Companie without the lycence and consent of the said Governor and Companie for the tyme being or of their lawfull officers and Ministers thereunto to be authorized first had and obtayned in writinge nor do hereafter make or digge any new ditch pond pitt or trench neere the said new River whereby the water of the same may fall or drayne away nor doe hereafter plant or sett anie Sallowes Willowes or Elme within five yardes of the said River at the least nor doe anie other Nusance or Annoyance whatsoever to the said river nor attempt or go about to bringe to the said Citties of London and Westminster and to the borough of Southwark or to either of them anie other river or pipe for conveyinge or bringinge of water from anie place whatsoever without the lycense and Assent of the said [*Company*] or their successors upon payne that every pson and psons offendinge in all or anie of the premisses shall incurr our high displeasure and such paines penalties and punishments as by the lawes or statuts of this our Realme of England or by our Prerogative Royall can or maie be Inflicted and Imposed upon such Offenders as breakers and Contemners of our royall Comaundement given for the preservacon and Continuance of this soe great and necessary a worke tendinge so much to the publique good of our said Cittie of London:

And further Wee will and ordaine by these presents for us our heires and Successors That such pson or psons as Wee our heires or Successors shall hereafter name and appoint to take and receive to our use of and from the said Governor and Company and their Successors such somes of money and profitts as shall accrue and belong to us our heires and Successors for or by meanes of the said Water Worke shall have full power and Authoritie and him and them Wee doe hereby authorize upon receipt of the same monies and profitts to make and deliver to the said Governor and Company and their Successors from tyme to tyme such Acquittances and Releases in writinge under his and their hand and seale of and for the same moneys and profitts soe received as aforesaid which said Acquittances and releases Wee will shalbe from tyme to tyme good and sufficient exoneracons and Discharges to and for the said Governor and Company and their Successors against us our heires and Successors of and for the same moneys and profitts so paid as aforesaid without other or further warrant to be had or obtained from us our heires or Successors in that behalfe;

And likewise Wee will and by these presents for us our heires and Successors doe graunt unto the said Governor and Company and their Successors That theis our lres patents or the Inrollment of them and all and every thinge and things in the same contayned shalbe in and by all things firme strong effectuall and avayleable in the law against us our heires and Successors aswell in all our Courts as elsewhere soever; Notwithstanding the not reciting or misreciting of the foresaid Actes of Parliament or of the foresaid Acts of Comon Councell or of the said Indenture made between the said Mayor [etc.] and the said Hugh Middleton or of the said Indenture made between us and the said Hugh Middleton or misreciting of the dates or tymes of them or any of them And notwithstanding the statute concerninge landes and tenementes not to be putt to Mortmaine and notwithstanding anie other defect Impfeccon matter cause or thing whatsoever;

And further Wee doe for us our heires and Successors (in consideracon of the long travell and attendance of our welbeloved subject William Lewyn Gentleman in and about the said Water Worke) appoint name constitute and make him the said William Lewyn to be the first Clarke of the said Companie; to have hould execute and enjoye the said Office by himself or his sufficient Deputy for and during the naturall life of the said William Lewyn (hee behaving himself well and honestly in the execucon of the same) And after the decease of the said William Lewyn Wee will and appoint That it shall and may be lawfull to and for the said Governor and Company and their Successors or anie seaven or more of them (whereof the Governor or his Deputy for the tyme being to be one) to name elect and choose some other meete pson to the said Office of Clarke of the said Company who shalbe and continue in the same place for and during the pleasure of the Governor and Company and their Successors or the greater part of them The said William Lewyn and all other person hereafter to be chosen to the said place of Clarke of the said Company first taking his and their Oath before the Governor or Deputy Governor of the said Company as aforesaid for the execucon of his and their place of Clarke of the said Company; although expresse mencon of the true yerely value or certenty of the premisses or anie of them or of anie other Gifts or Graunts by us or anie of our Progenitors or Predecessors to the foresaid Governor and Company of the new River [etc.] before theis tymes made in theis presents is not made or any Statute Acte Ordinance provision proclamacon or restraint heretofore had made sett forth ordained or provided or anie other matter cause or thing whatsoever to the contrary in anie wise notwithstandinge;

In witnes whereof Wee have caused theis our lres to be made patents Witnes ourselfe at Westminster the one and twentieth daie of June in the seaventeenth yeare of our Raigne of England ffraunce and Ireland and of the Scotland the two and fiftieth

per breve de privato sigillo

[*Endorsement*]

To the Right Honourable the Master of the Rolls

The humble Petition of the Governor and Company of the New River

Sheweth

That by letters Patent under the Great Seal of England bearing date the one and twentieth day of June in the seventeenth year of the reign of King James the first Sir Hugh Middleton Knight and severall other persons in the said letters Patent named were incorporated and made a Body Corporate and politick by the name of the Governor and Company of the New River brought from Chadwell and Amwell to London. That the said King by the said letters Patent made and constituted the said Sir Hugh Middleton to be the first and then present Governor and also constituted the Deputy Governor and other Officers of the said Company therein particularly named.

That the said then Governor and the other persons so by the said letters incorporated did accordingly forthwith proceed in the Execution of the severall powers and Authorities therein and thereby granted to them; And that they and all their successors ever since have acted under the said letters Patent or Charter. And your Petitioners the present Governor and Company by right of succession do act under the same And by no other Charter or letters Patent of incorporation whatsoever.

That your Petitioners have lately discovered that by some omission or neglect the said letters Patent and Charter so granted as aforesaid were never to this time Recorded or Inrolled.

Your Petitioners therefore to prevent any damage that by any accident may attend the loss of the said letters Patent upon which the Properties of many persons depend And the Inconveniences that by any such loss may ensue to the Inhabitants of London Westminster and other places who are supplied with water in their houses from the said New River humbly pray Your Honour will be pleased to order that an Inrollment may be forthwith made of the said letters Patent under the Great seal and affixed to the Patent Rolls of the same year wherein they bear date.

And your Petitioners shall ever pray &c.
28 March 1737

Be it so

J. Jekyll

Inrolled on the Patent Roll amongst the Patents of the seventeenth year of the reign of King James pursuant to an Order made by that purpose by the Right Honourable the Master of the Rolls dated 28th March 1737. Rooke.

Examined in the Chapel of the Rolls with Mr William Rooke and compared with the record consisting of eleven membranes this twenty first day of April 1737.

Jasper Bull
Clerk of the Company within mentioned

G. Crown Clog

18 November 1631

THIS INDENTURE TRIPARTITE made the eighteenth day of November in the seaventh yeare of the raigne of our Most Gracious Soveraigne Lord Charles by the grace of God Kinge of England Scotland ffraunce and Ireland Defender of the Faith etc. BETWEENE our said Soveraigne Lord the Kinges most excellent Maiestie of the first part Henry Viscount Falkland Sir Robert Naunton Knight Master of the Court of Wardes and Liveries and Sir Julius Cesar Knight Master of the Rolles of the seacond parte And the Governor and Companie of the Newe River brought from Chadwell and Amwell to London and Sir Hugh Middleton Baronett of the third parte

WHEREAS by an Indenture dated the eight and twentyeth day of October in the seaventeenth yeare of the raigne of our late soveraigne lord Kinge James over England made betweene the said Governor and Companie of the one parte and the said Henry Viscount Falkland by the name of Sir Henry Carie Knight Comptroller of his said late Maiesties most honorable household Sir Robert Naunton Knight nowe Master of the Courte of Wardes and Liveries by the name of Sir Robert Naunton Knight one of his said late Maiesties principall secretaries ffulke Lord Brooke since deceased by the name of Sir ffulke Grevill Knight then Chauncellor and Undertreasurer of his said late Maiesties Exchequer Sir Julius Cesar Knight Master of the Rolles and Giles Mompesson by the name of Sir Giles Mompesson Knight on the other parte reciting [*Letters Patent of incorporation*] Nevertheless it was the true intente of His said Maiestie and of the said persons so incorporated forasmuch as his said Maiestie had formerly susteyned and borne and was still from time to time to susteyne and beare one full and equall Moety of all manner of charges disbursements and somes of mony whatsoever expended or to be expended in or about the making or mayntayning of the said river and waterworke That his Maiestie his heires and successors should have receive and take from tyme to tyme one full moiety or halfe parte of all cleare benefitt profitt and comoditie that should and may arise or be had made or gotten of and by the said waterwork The said Governor and Companie of the said New River in performance and accomplishment of the premises did by the said Indenture fullie clearlie and absolutelie give grant bargain and sell at the nomynacon of his said late Maiesty and for the use and benefitt of his said Maiestie his heires and successors to the said Henry Viscount Falkland by the name of Sir Henry Carie Knight the said Robert Naunton the said Lord Brooke by the name of Sir ffulke Grevill and the said Sir Julius Cesar and Giles Mompesson being persons especially named in trust for his said Maiesty and to their heires and assignes one full and entire moytie or halfe parte of all such ffynes somes of mony Rent Reservacons benefitt profitt and comodities whatsoever as over and above all necessarie charges and expences that then were or thereafter from tyme to tyme should in any way be raised had made leavied or gotten of or by meanes of the said Newe River or waterworke or of or by reason of the conveyance of the water thereof in or by anie part or parts place or places or unto or for any person or persons whatsoever

TO HAVE hould receive perceive take and enjoy the said moytie or half part of all and every the said ffynes somes of mony [etc.] in the said Newe River or waterworke and premisses to the said Henry Carie nowe Viscount Falkland Sir Robert Naunton Sir ffulke Grevill Sir Julius Cesar and Giles Mompesson their heires and assignes to the onely use and behoof of the said Sir Henry Carie now Viscount Falkland Sir Robert Naunton Sir ffulke Grevill since Lord Brooke Sir Julius Cesar and Giles Mompesson their heires and assignes for ever upon trust for the profitt and comoditie of our said late Soveraigne Lord the Kinge his heires and successors for ever As in and by the said recited Indenture amongst divers covenants and clauses therein conteyned more at large it doth and may appeare

AND WHEREAS the said Giles Mompesson by his indenture or deede indented bearing date the seaventh day of October in the seaventh yeare of His nowe Maiesties Raigne made betweene the said Giles Mompesson of the one parte and the said Viscount Falkland Sir Robert Naunton and Sir Julius Cesar of the other parte for the consideracons therein expressed hath for him the said Giles Mompesson his heires and assignes and every of them graunted remised released assigned and sett over unto the said Viscount Falkland Sir Robert Naunton and Sir Julius Cesar all the interest right use trust propertie claymes and demaunde whatsoever of him the said Giles Mompesson of in and to the said recited indenture and of in and to the said Moytie or halfe parte of all and everie the said ffynes somes of mony [etc.] of the said Newe River waterworke and premises to them the said Viscount Falkland Sir Robert Naunton ffoulke Grevill Lord Brooke deceased Sir Julius Cesar and Giles Mompesson their heires and assignes by the said recited indenture given and granted as aforesaid and of in and to everie parte and parcell thereof As in and by the said recited indenture more at large it doth and may appeare

AND WHEREAS our late Soveraigne Lord Kinge James of blessed and happie memorie by His Highnes Letters Patent under the great seale of England bearing date the nyneteenth day of Januarie in the ffifteenth yeare of his raigne of England ffraunce and Ireland and of Scotland the one and fiftieth reciting as therein is recited and for the reasons and consideracons therein particularlie specified and declared did by the said Letters Patent make ordeyne name constitute and appoint his trulie and wellbeloved servaunt Edward Ball Esqr one of the groomes of his said late Maiesties privy Chamber to be Expenditor or Surveyor on the behalfe of his said late Maiestie his heires and successors of the said river expressed by the name as therein appeareth TO HAVE and to hould the said office or place of Expenditor or Surveyor on the behalfe of his said late Maiestie his heires and successors of the said waterworke current or river and of the receipt profitt payment and disbursement to be from time to time thereby had or made Unto the said Edward Ball for and during his naturall life To be held by himselfe or his sufficient deputie or deputies during the natural life of the said Edward Ball And for the continual travell charge and attendaunce of the said Edward Ball to be from time to time bestowed expended and imployed in or about the executon of the said office or place His said late Maiesty was graciously pleased and did by the said Letters Patent for His Highnes his heires and successors give and grant unto the said Edward Ball one yearely ffee or Penson of one hundred poundes of lawfull mony of England To be yearely and everie yeare had taken and payde out of the issue rent and profitt of and by the said waterworke to his said late Maiestie his heires and successors from tyme to tyme arrising growing accrewing and belonging as aforesaid at the four usual ffeasts or termes in the yeare that is to say the ffeast of the Birth of Our Lord God the Annunciacon of the Blessed Virgin Mary the Nativitie of St John Baptist and St Michaell the Archangell by even and equall porcons everie yeare during the naturall life of the said Edward Ball as by the said recited Letters Patent among other things therein conteyned more at large appeareth

NOW THIS INDENTURE WITNESSETH that our said Soveraigne Lord the Kinge for and in consideracon of the rent covenants and agreements hereafter by these presents specified to be made by the said Sir Hugh Middleton and for divers and sundry other good causes and consideracons His Maiestie thereunto especially moving of His Maiesties speciall grace certen knowledge and meere mocon hath given and granted and by these presents doth give and grant unto the said Sir Hugh Middleton his heires and assignes all the trust use benefitt profitt interest and comoditie that doth or may appertayne to our said Soveraigne Lord the Kinges Maiestie his heires or successors of or in the moytie or halfe parte of the said waterworke and all His Maiesties parte in the same and of all and everie the said ffynes somes of mony [etc.] of the said Newe River [etc.] and all arrearages thereof whereof noe accompt hath beene made to His Maiestie or for his use and all right concerning the same and our said Soveraigne Lord the Kinges Maiestie of his more especiall grace [etc.] for himselfe his heires and successors by these presents requires wills and comaunds the said Viscount Falkland Sir Robert Naunton and Sir Julius Cesar and everie of them to grant convey and assure the Moyty or halfe of the said cutt and everie the said ffynes somes of mony [etc.] of the said Newe River [etc.] and all that to them appertayning and all writings conveying the same to the said Sir Hugh Middleton his heires and assignes to the onelie use and behoofe of the said Sir Hugh Middleton his heires and assignes for ever and our said soveraigne Lord the kinges Most Excellent Maiestie of England of his especiall grace [etc.] for himselfe his heires and successors doth by these presents acquitte release and discharge the said Henry Viscount Falkland Sir Robert Naunton and Sir Julius Cesar and their heires of and from the said trust in the premises and herein willeth that the said Viscount Falkland Sir Robert Naunton and the said Sir Julius Cesar and their heires be for ever hereafter thereof discharged and acquitted against his Maiestie his heires and successors and the said Henry Viscount Falkland Sir Robert Naunton and Sir Julius Cesar in whom the whole interest of the premises granted to his Maiesties use as aforesaid is for the accomplishment of the good pleasure of our said Soveraigne Lord the King and by the direccon and appointment of his said Maiestie have granted assigned and set over and by these presents for themselves their heires and assignes doe hereby grant assign and set over unto the said Sir Hugh Middleton his heires and assignes the said recited Indentures bearing the said date the eight and twentyeth day of October in the seaventeenth yeare of our late Soveraigne Lord King James and the said moiety or halfe parte of all and every the said ffynes somes of mony [etc.] in the said Newe River [etc.] to them the said Viscount Falkland Sir Robert Naunton Lord Brooke Sir Julius Cesar and Giles Mompesson their heires and assignes by the said recited indenture given and granted as aforesaid and of and in every parte and parcell thereof and all writings concerning the same and all their right tytle use trust and demaunde in the same

AND THE SAID Henry Viscount Falkland for himselfe his heires and assignes and everie of them doth covenant promise and graunt to and with the said Sir Hugh Middleton his heires and assignes by these presents that he the said Viscount Falkland hath not made anie other grante or grants assignement or assignements of the premises to any other person or persons whatsoever nor hath nor will doe nor suffer to be done any acte or thing whatsoever touching or concerning the premises but onlie unto him the said Sir Hugh Middleton his heires or assignes according to His Maiesties direccon as aforesaid and that he the said Viscount Falkland his heires or assignes and all other person or persons clayming by from or under him shall and will from tyme to tyme upon request to him to be made and by the direccon of His Maiestie his heires or successors in that behalfe doe execute and suffer all or anie other act and acts thing or things for the further and better assuring and sure making of the premises and every parte and parcell thereof unto him the said Sir Hugh Middleton his heires and assignes as by him the said Sir Hugh Middleton his heires and assignes or by his or their or any of his or their Councell learned in the lawe shall be reasonably devised or advised and required [*the like covenants by Sir Robert Naunton and Sir Julius Cesar*]

PROVIDED ALWAYS and the said Sir Hugh Middleton in consideracon of the premises doth for himselfe his heires and assignes covenant promise and graunt to and with his Maiestie his heires and successors by these presents that he the said Sir Hugh Middleton his heires and assignes shall and will yearely and every yeare for ever yeilde and paie or cause to be yeilded and paied unto the Kinges Maiesties Receivor Generall of the Citty of London for the tyme being or into the receipt of His Maiesties Exchequer at Westminster to and for the use of His Maiestie his heires and successors the yearely rent or some of five hundred poundes of good and lawfull mony of England at the ffeasts of St Michaell the Archangell and the Annunciacon of the Blessed Virgin Mary by equall and even porcons or within fortie daies next after either of the said ffeasts for ever to be paid the first payment thereof to be made at the ffeast of the Annunciacon of the Blessed Virgin Mary next ensewing the date hereof

AND the said Sir Hugh Middleton for him and his heires covenanteth with our said Soveraigne Lord the Kinge his heires and successors that he the said Sir Hugh Middleton his heires and assigns shall and will paie or cause to be paied unto the said Edward Ball or his assignes yearely and every yeare during the naturall life of him the said Edward Ball at such daies and tymes as by the before recited Letters Patent is lymitted and appointed the said yearely ffee or Penson of one hundred poundes by the yeare and alsoe shall and will paie or cause to be paied all and singular other the rents and paiements which by his Maiestie his heires or successors or by the said Viscount Falkland Sir Robert Naunton Sir Julius Cesar Giles Mompesson or anie of them and their heires out of or by reason of the premises or anie of them shall be due or payable except onelie such some and somes of mony and other payment as are or shalbe due and payable to the said Giles Mompesson of which his Maiestie is graciously pleased to discharge the said Sir Hugh Middleton his heires and assignes for ever And alsoe shall and will from tyme to tyme and at all tymes for ever hereafter discharge or save harmeles his Maiestie his heires and successors as well of and from the said yearely ffee of one hundred poundes payable unto the said Edward Ball as aforesaid and all and singular other the rent and payment due and payable of or for the said waterworke or anie parte of the premises by His Maiestie his heires and successors or by the said Viscount Falkland Sir Robert Naunton and Sir Julius Cesar other than to the said Giles Mompesson as aforesaid as alsoe of and from all and singuler expences burthens and charges whatsoever in or concerning the premises or anie of them

And the said Sir Hugh Middleton for the consideracons aforesaid doth likewise hereby for himselfe his heires and assignes covenant promise and grant to and with His Maiestie his heires and successors by these presents that he the said Sir Hugh Middleton his heires and assignes shall and will paie or cause to be paied into the receipt of the Exchequer at Westminster to and for His Highnes use the some of five hundred poundes of lawfull mony of England for one yeares rente due at the ffeast of St Michaell the Archangell nowe last past before the date hereof within two daies after the date of these presents and alsoe shall and will paie or cause to be paied untoe the said Edward Ball or his assignes all such some and somes of mony which were arrears due and payable out of or by reason of the said penson of one hundred poundes unto him the said Edward Ball at the said ffeast of St Michaell the Archangell last past before the date of these presents

AND his Maiestie for and in consideracon of the said yearely rent payment and other the premisses doth for himselfe his heires and successors covenant promise and grant to and with the said Governor and Companie and their successors and to and with the said Sir Hugh Middleton his heires and assignes by these presents that His Maiestie his heires and successors shall and will from tyme to tyme and at all tymes hereafter be ayding and assisting unto the said Governor and Companie and their successors and to the said Sir Hugh Middleton his heires and assignes aswell for the preservacon of the worke of the Newe River and the waters drawne thereout both in the said citty and without the same as alsoe for the preservacon of the bankes bridges pipes and other necessaries in and about the said Newe River and waterworke

AND because manie misdemenors and offences have beene and are daylie comitted by sondry ill affected persons which cannot be proceeded against really by the ordinary proceedings at lawe therefore for the more speedy redresse and reformacon of such abuses and the better to enable the said Sir Hugh Middleton his heires and assigns to paie and satisfie unto His Maiestie his heires and successors the said yearely rente or some of five hundred poundes per annum His Maiestie is graciously pleased and doth by these presents for himselfe his heires and successors authorise require and comaunde the Lordes and others of his privie counsell and of the privie counsell of his heires and successors for the tyme being or any five or more of them at the humble request of the said Sir Hugh Middleton his heires or assignes or at the request of such others as shall be authorised by him in that behalfe to grant all warrants from tyme to tyme for the apprehending and bringing before them of all such person or persons as shall offend in unlawful cutting or spoyling the bankes or pipes or bridges belonging to the river or letting out the said river in waste or to any other unlawfull purpose whatsoever in the passage as it cometh to London or that shall unlawfully convey any pipes or extremities thereof into their houses or other places as reasonably shall be required by the said Sir Hugh Middleton his heires or assignes or by the said Governor and Companie or any of them and alsoe upon just cause of complaint or suspicion to graunt warrants from tyme to tyme to search in anie house or houses to some of His Maiesties officers and ministers whereof one at least shall be a constable for the discoverie of such as shall be suspected to have stolen or secretlie derived any braunches from the pipes carrying water from them unto their howses to the intent their Lordshipps maie thereupon inflict such deserved punishment upon the offenders therein as in their wisedomes and judgement shalbe though fitt upon just cause of complaint

AND these presents or the inroulmente thereof shalbe unto the said Lordes and others of the privy counsell for the tyme being for the doing and performing of this His Maiesties pleasure and comaunde therein signified a sufficient warrant and discharge in that behalfe

AND His Maiestie doth alsoe hereby for His Highnes his heires and successors covenant promise and grant to and with the said Sir Hugh Middleton his heires and assignes by these presents that His Maiestie his heires and successors shall and will from tyme to tyme release acquit discharge or save harmeles the said Sir Hugh Middleton his heires and assignes and everie of them of and from all and all manner of paiement some and somes of mony due and payable and hereafter to be due and payable to the said Giles Mompesson his heires and assignes out of or for the premisses before by these presents granted or any of them or out of any profitt coming thereof

AND His Maiestie doth hereby further for himselfe his heires and successors covenant promise and graunt to and with the said Sir Hugh Middleton his heires and assignes That His Maiestie his heires or successors shall not nor will not give grant assign or set over unto any person or person whatsoever the aforesaid yearely rente or some of five hundred poundes nor anie parte thereof in and by these presents reserved or agreed to be paid to our said Soveraigne Lord the Kinge his heires and successors as aforesaid but shall and will for ever hereafter kepe and continue the same and everie parte and parcell thereof to our said Soveraigne Lord the Kinge his heires and successors as to their Crowne united and annexed for ever

AND OUR SAID Soveraigne Lord the Kinges Maiestie for the consideracons aforesaid doth by these presents for his Highnes his heires and successors pardon release exonerate discharge and quiteclayme the said Governor and Companie and their successors and the said Sir Hugh Middleton his heires executors administrators and assignes of and from all and singular the rente duties somes of mony arrearages and other profitt by them or anie of them heretofore had received or taken for or by reason of the said waterworke and other the premises aforesaid (other than are of and for the somes of mony and other paiements in these presents reserved and due and payable or agreed to be paid as aforesaid) and of and from all and singular reckoninge accompte paiement and satisfactions whatsoever to his Highnes his heires or successors by them the said Governor and Companie and their successors and the said Sir Hugh Middleton his heires executors administrators or assigns or anie of them to be rendered paid made or given for the same or anie parte thereof and all actions suites extents execucons and demaundes whatsoever which his Maiestie his heires or successors nowe have or hereafter at any tyme or tymes will or may have against the said Governor and Companie and their successors or against the said Sir Hugh Middleton his heires executors administrators or assignes or their or any of their lordshipps mannors landes tenements hereditaments goods or chattels for touching and concerning the said rent duties some and somes of mony and other the premises aforesaid or anie of them or the said reckoninge accompt satisfaction and demaundes and other the premises hereby mentioned to be acquitted pardoned remised released exonerated discharged and quiteclaymed as aforesaid or anie of them

AND His Maiestie doth alsoe for his Highnes his heires and successors further grant by these presents unto the said Governor and Companie and their successors and the said Sir Hugh Middleton his heires executors administrators and assignes that neither they nor anie of them their nor anie of their heires [etc.] shalbe in anie sorte called to accompt sued molested in quieted or troubled nor his or their or anie his or their lordshipps mannors [etc.] in anie wise to be taken seised or extended by his Maiestie his heires or successors or by any commissions officers or mynisters of his Highnes his heires or successors for or by reason of the said rent dueties some and somes of mony aforesaid and other the premises or anie of them before by these presents mentioned to be pardoned released and discharged But that aswell the said Governor and Companie and their successors as the said Sir Hugh Middleton his heires [etc.] and everie of them and their and everie of their lordshipps [etc.] be and shalbe forever hereafter altogether and whollie thereof freed cleared pardoned [etc.] against his Highnes his heires and successors by vertue of these presents

AND TO THE END that thus his Maiesties pleasure maie take the better effect his Highnes doth hereby for himselfe his heires and successors will require and comaunde the Treasurer Chauncellor Undertrsr and Barons of the Exchequer the Auditors of the Imprest and all other the officers and mynisters of his Highnes his heires and successors whatsoever for the tyme being whome it shall or maie concern to take notice of these presents or the inroulmente constat or exemplification of them and to give allowance to the same according to his Highnes pleasure herein specified and declared AND these presents or the inroulmente constat or exemplification of them shalbe unto all men whom it shall concern a sufficient warraunt and discharge in that behalfe without any further or other warraunt from his Highnes his heires and successors to be had presented or obteyned

AND his Maiestie doth further for the consideracons aforesaid for himselfe his heires and successors covenant promise and grant to and with the said Governor and Companie and their successors and the said Sir Hugh Middleton his heires and assignes by these presents that all and singular the pipes and channels alreadie laied or made within his Maiesties waste soyle within the Citty of London and Counties of Middlesex and Hartford or anie of them or elsewhere for or concerning the said waterworke shall and maie stand be and continue as nowe they are without the lett or interruption of his Maiestie his heires or successors or anie other person or persons whatsoever

AND his Maiestie doth hereby for himselfe his heires and successors give and grant full power libertie and authoritie unto the said Governor and Companie and their successors and the said Sir Hugh Middleton his heires and assignes from tyme to tyme and at all tymes hereafter to laie or cause to be laied or to make or cause to be made any new pipe or pipes or channells in anie place or places convenient within his Maiesties waste soyle either within the said Citty or Counties and also to amend as well the pipes that are nowe laied or shalbe laied hereafter for carrying on anie of the water of the said waterworke as their channell when and as often as neede shall require

IN WITNESS WHEREOF three partes are made of these presents and to one of those partes remayning with the said Viscount Falkland Sir Robert Naunton and Sir Julius Cesar the said Governor and Companie and the said Sir Hugh Middleton our said Soveraigne Lord the Kinge hath putt the great seale of England to one other parte remayning with our said Soveraigne Lord the King the said Viscount Falkland Sir Robert Naunton Sir Julius Cesar the said Governor and Companie and Sir Hugh Middleton have putt their seales And to one other parte thereof remayning with the said Governor and Companie and Sir Hugh Middleton the said Viscount Falkland Sir Robert Naunton and Sir Julius Cesar have putt their seales the daie and yeare first above written

L S

H. Waterlease

30 December 1669

THIS INDENTURE MADE the Thirtieth day of December in the one and twentieth yeare of the Reign of our Soveraign Lord Charles the Second by the grace of God, of England, Scotland, France and Ireland King Defender of the Faith &c.

BETWEEN the Governour and Company of the New River brought from Chadwel and Amwel to London on the one part; and Robert Chevill, Sadler on the other part;

WITNESSETH, That the said Governour and Company for, and in consideration of the Sum of six and twenty shillings and eight pence in hand paid, in the name of a Fine or income (the Receipt whereof the said Governour and Company do by these presents acknowledge) and for and in consideration of the Covenants and Conditions hereafter in these presents expressed, Have Demised and Granted, and by these Presents do Demise and Grant unto the said Robert Chevill One Water-course, conveniently furnished with Water running in and through one small Branch of Pipe of Lead containing half an Inch of Water or thereabouts, and in and through one small Cock of Brass souldred and set unto the same, and placed in the cellar of the now dwelling-house of the said Robert Chevill and in manner hereafter expressed, for the only proper use and service of the said Lessees Family inhabiting and dwelling in the house aforesaid; the said Branch to be laid from the main Pipe that lyeth in Fleete Street at his the said Lessees own proper Costs and Charges, by one of the known Plumbers appointed, or to be appointed by the said Governour and Company, in and about the Water-works of the said New River.

TO HAVE AND TO HOLD the said Branch or Water-course in form aforesaid unto the said Robert Chevill for the term of eleven Years now next ensuing the Date hereof, and fully to be compleat and ended, if the said Robert Chevill shall so long dwell and continue in the said House, and use it no otherwise than as it is hereby Granted, and not using any other way for greater expence of Water, without the consent of the said Governour and Company:

YIELDING and paying therefore yearly during the said Term, unto the said Governour and Company, their Successors and Assigns, at the House scituate in the Parish of St James Clerkenwel, in the County of Middlesex, commonly called the New-River-Water-House, the sum of six and twenty shillings and eight pence of lawful money of England at the Feasts of the Nativity of St John the Baptist, St Michael the

Archangel, the Birth of our Lord God, and the Annunciation of St Mary the Virgin, by even and equal portions, without abatement for any Tax or Rate whatever, imposed, or to be imposed; the first payment to begin at the Feast of the Annunciation of the Blessed Virgin Mary next coming after the date hereof; The which yearly Rent the said Lessee doth for him, his Executors and Administrators, Covenant, Promise and Grant, by these Presents to and with the said Governour and Company, for them, their Successors and Assigns, well and truly to pay by even and equal portions unto the said Governour and Company, their Successors and Assigns at the feasts aforesaid yearly, during the continuance of this Demise, or within seven days after every of the said Feasts at the New-River-Water-House in Clerkenwel aforesaid.

AND the said Governour and Company for them, their Successors and Assigns, do Covenant and Grant by these presents to and with the said Lessee, That the said Lessee shall or may peaceably and quietly during the said Terme enjoy the said Branch or Water-course, conveniently furnished with Water, to be turned on by the Turncock three days in every week at least, according to the usage and manner of the said Governour and Company (time of needful Reparation, and of mischance, and casualty of Fire excepted).

PROVIDED always and the said Lessee doth Covenant, Promise and Grant to and with the said Governour and Company, their successors and assigns, by these Presents, That the said Governour and Company, their Successors and Assigns, or their Officer or Servants for that purpose appointed, or to be appointed, shall or may peaceably and quietly come into the said House of the said Lessee in the day time as often as shall be convenient to view the said Cock and Pipe for the said Water-course, or any other Pipe or Branch that shall be derived into any other House from the said Lessees Branch, and to see that the said Water shall not be given, sold, taken away, or run at waste: And further, that the said Lessee shall and will from time to time during the said Term repair and maintain the said Cock, and so much of the Pipe of Lead serving for the said Water belonging to the said Lessees House, at his own proper Costs and Charges.

PROVIDED always, That if the said yearly Rent shall be behind, or unpaid, in part, or in all, by the space of fourteen days next after any of the said Feasts, contrary to the tenor and true meaning of these Presents, the same being demanded at the House of the said Lessee by the said Governour and Company, their Successors and Assigns, or their Servants, Attorney or Officer for that purpose appointed, on any day after such respective Feast whereon the same was due; Or if the said Water shall run at waste at any time (except in time of Frost a quarter Cock) the said Lessee shall for every such default of payment of the said Rent, and for every such Waste at the finding thereof by the said Governour and Company, their Successors, Officers, or Servants, upon request or demand pay, or cause to be paid, to the said Governour and Company, their Successors or Assigns, or to their Officer demanding the same, the sum of Two shillings six pence Nomine poenae; Or if the said Pipe or Cock shall be enlarged, altered, or taken away, or be neglected to be repaired within Ten days next after notice given at the House of the said Lessee, or any part of quantity of the said Water issuing by and through the said Branch or Pipe shall happen to be conveyed, given, sold, or converted to any place or places, person or persons, use or uses whatsoever, other than for the necessary use and service of the said Lessee his Servants and Family inhabiting within the Tenement aforesaid, or any other Water-course shall be drawn or derived out of the said Pipe or Cock by the said Lessee, or other his Tenants, or by any other person or persons, by his consent or procurement, contrary to the true tenor and meaning of these Presents; Or that the said Lessee shall not pay and satisfie to the said Governour and Company the said sum of Two shillings six pence upon demand, so often as the same shall become due and payable as aforesaid, That then it shall and may be lawful to and for the said Governour and Company, their Successours or Assigns, or their Officer or Servants for that purpose by them appointed, to cut off and stop the said Quill or Branch, and sever it from the main pipe at their will and pleasure, without any manner of lett, trouble or denial, claim or demand of the said Lessee, or any other person or persons whatsoever; And that then and from the time of such cutting off or stopping of the said Quill or Branch, this present Demise and Grant, and every Covenant, Article and Agreement tending to the advantage or benefit of the said Lessee shall be utterly void and frustrate to all intents and purposes, any thing in these Presents contained to the contrary thereof in any wise notwithstanding.

AND LASTLY the said Governour and Company for them, their Successors and Assigns, do further Covenant, Promise and Grant to and with the said Lessee by these Presents, That if the said Lessee shall happen to be unserved with Water into his said Pipe, in manner aforesaid, through the default of the said Governour and Company by reason of any lett or impediment in the main Pipe, and the same shall not be amended within fourteen days (except in time of Frost) after notice given to the Governour, or to the Members that meet weekly at the Clerks Office near Puddle-Dock: That then it shall and may be lawful for the said Lessee to detain and keep to his owne use the Quarters rent that shall next grow due, and always after till the fault be amended, without any forfeiture of the said Demise or Grant made to the said Lessee as aforesaid.

IN WITNESS whereof to the one part of these Present Indentures remaining with the said Lessee, the said Governour and Company have set to their common Seal; and to the other part thereof remaining with the said Governour and Company, the said Lessee hath set to his Hand and Seal the day and year first above written Annoq; Dom. 1669

L S

I. Dividends and Prices 1633–1903

[Dividends estimated to the nearest penny (halfpence counted up) gross of poll and land tax, net of income tax. Unless otherwise stated, share prices are of the Neville holdings: see Chapter 4.3. The two types are distinguished by the letters A and K.]

Date	*Dividend*			Price (£)	Date	*Dividend*		
		s.	*d.*				*s.*	*d.*
1633	11	19	1		1662	77	12	7
1634	3	4	2		1663	61	9	11
1635	14	14	3		1664	70	9	2
1636	19	10	11		1665	64	16	7
1637	22	19	9		1666	74	16	11
1638	26	5	10		1667	51	16	11
1639	28	14	5		1668	53	12	6
1640	33	2	9		1669	56	18	9
1641	30	14	8		1670	70	14	2
1642	31	19	5		1671	97	9	4
1643	27	13	6		1672	103	10	2
1644	27	10	6		1673	108	3	3
1645	32	3	1		1674	129	4	7
1646	36	10	0		1675	127	4	1
1647	38	12	11		1676	134	13	6
1648	38	3	5		1677	143	2	5
1649	35	14	9		1678	149	18	2
1650	39	18	9		1679	151	9	0
1651	39	9	5		1680	145	1	8
1652	44	2	3		1681	169	1	1
1653	52	4	1		1682	172	9	3
1654	52	3	7		1683	168	13	8
1655	54	16	10		1684	172	4	5
1656	43	14	6		1685	195	17	5
1657	61	8	6	500K[a]	1686	206	6	0
1658	60	3	8		1687	226	3	7
1659	65	18	11		1688	231	10	7
1660	68	15	0		1689	237	1	1
1661	81	9	11		1690	222	9	4

[a] Chapter 5.2

Date	Dividend	s.	d.	Price (£)	Date	Dividend	s.	d.	Price (£)
1691	212	15	3		1729	189	13	7	
1692	255	2	9		1730	199	12	7	
1693	217	0	2[b]		1731	178	7	0	
1694	199	6	7		1732	160	9	2	5,000A[c]
1695	207	17	4		1733	216	17	4	
1696	113	7	6		1734	226	1	5	
1697	183	13	9		1735	241	16	1	
1698	180	19	5		1736	220	0	7	
1699	206	10	4		1737	234	3	2	
1700	211	16	7		1738	189	17	10	
1701	208	12	10		1739	195	1	10	
1702	186	7	11		1740	166	8	3	
1703	162	0	10		1741	170	17	2	
1704	178	7	0		1742	206	15	5	
1705	183	6	4		1743	198	18	6	
1706	186	3	5		1744	213	4	1	
1707	183	10	9	3,900A	1745	216	6	10	
1708	153	13	8		1746	213	11	2	
1709	156	5	5		1747	251	1	9	
1710	150	0	0		1748	245	15	1	
1711	157	17	1		1749	247	11	7	
1712	164	8	5		1750	244	8	3	
1713	209	0	8	7,000A	1751	263	12	7	
1714	241	11	6		1752	278	4	10	
1715	229	4	7		1753	262	13	4	
1716	217	17	9		1754	255	9	6	
1717	224	0	8		1755	280	11	4	
1718	230	2	6		1756	279	3	3	
1719	217	16	3		1757	268	11	4	
1720	214	15	8		1758	256	7	7	
1721	228	15	6		1759	265	9	10	
1722	228	13	11		1760	268	12	4	
1723	249	10	8		1761	285	6	1	
1724	246	10	8		1762	288	4	5	
1725	257	17	8		1763	260	10	1	
1726	236	18	9		1764	263	7	10	
1727	214	7	4		1765	260	16	6	
1728	190	3	1		1766	240	7	10	

[b] Competition by York Building Co. and Hampstead Waterworks.
[c] Abstract of title of R. S. Smith: TW, NR file 2/55.

Date	Dividend			Price (£)	Date	Dividend			Price (£)
		s.	d.				s.	d.	
1767	248	18	2		1804	396	19	10	
1768	236	18	11		1805	486	0	1	
1769	257	0	7		1806	450	2	11	
1770	255	13	11		1807	440	13	2	
1771	256	3	9		1808	472	1	0	
1772	232	6	5		1809	472	5	9	
1773	297	17	0		1810[e]	465	0	7	
1774	308	5	7		1811	282	12	10	
1775	316	6	9	6,923A[d]	1812	220	13	3	
1776	284	17	3		1813	113	18	8	
1777	311	3	4		1814	23	2	7	
1778	325	2	9		1815	60	3	0	
1779	322	17	2		1816	85	0	0	
1780	316	15	2		1817	120	2	9	
1781	343	5	11		1818	159	4	10	
1782	339	0	0		1819	199	10	11	
1783	350	19	11		1820	266	3	8	
1784	363	6	6		1821	341	19	2	8,740K[f]
1785	390	4	6		1822	402	5	3	
1786	390	13	9		1823	447	17	1	
1787	384	17	11		1824	489	0	3	
1788	405	18	3		1825	501	13	8	
1789	409	17	5		1826	490	12	11	
1790	400	9	9		1827	516	11	11	15,200A[g]
1791	411	17	0		1828	536	6	5	
1792	426	5	10		1829	546	17	5	
1793	441	12	10		1830	568	11	8	
1794	431	5	8		1831	583	17	10	
1795	425	14	4		1832	598	14	11	
1796	445	0	4		1833	617	15	5	
1797	470	12	8		1834	639	1	11	
1798	456	11	2		1835	647	9	6	
1799	457	12	6		1836	646	8	3	
1800	462	12	1		1837	650	9	10	
1801	471	9	1		1838	660	9	1	
1802	451	4	4		1839	682	16	0	
1803	445	6	3		1840	706	12	0	

[d] Calculated from GL MS 4161 (sale of thirteen-twelfths).
[e] For the competition see Chapter 7.2.
[f] Auction contract: TW, Strongroom B6, box 86/169.
[g] Abstract of title R. S. Smith: TW, NR file 2/55.

Date	*Dividend*			Price (£)	Date	*Dividend*		
		s.	d.				s.	d.
1841	726	9	2		1857	846	0	0
1842	755	19	1		1858	846	0	0
1843	791	5	11		1859	846	0	0
1844	820	6	0		1860	851	0	0
1845	834	8	0		1861	856	0	0
1846	849	17	8		1862	876	0	0
1847	864	10	4		1863	896	0	0
1848	873	4	1		1864	969	0	0
1849	878	14	10		1865	1,150	0	0
1850	847	18	8		1866	1,290	0	0[h]
1851	847	3	0		1867	1,300	0	0
1852	846	0	0		1868	1,320	0	0
1853	846	0	0		1869	1,530	0	0
1854	846	0	0		1870	1,625	0	0
1855	846	0	0		1871	1,625	0	0
1856	846	0	0					

Date	Water (£)	Estates (£)	*Total*			Price (£)
			£	s.	d.	
1872	1,685	107	1,792	0	0	
1873	1,900	76	1,976	0	0	
1874	2,015	64	2,079	0	0[i]	
1875	2,093	45	2,138	0	0	
1876	2,100	44	2,144	0	0	
1877	2,110	39	2,149	0	0	
1878	2,110	39	2,149	0	0	
1879	2,201	39	2,240	0	0	
1880	2,330	39	2,369	0	0	
1881	2,430	38	2,468	0	0	
1882	2,465	40	2,505	0	0	
1883[j]	2,520	40	2,560	0	0	95,000A
1884	2,520	40	2,560	0	0	
1885	2,520	40	2,560	0	0	
1886	2,520	40	2,560	0	0	
1887	2,520	40	2,560	0	0	86,000A

[h] Bonus £1,400 per share from sale of Dorset lease.
[i] Estate bonus £1,008 per share.
[j] Sale prices 1883–1901 taken fron Arbitration Transcript Table JS1.

Date	Water (£)	Estates (£)	Total £	s.	d.	Price (£)
1888	2,520	40	2,560	0	0	85,000A
						92,500A
						90,000A
						95,000A
						95,000A
						81,000K
1889	2,520	41	2,561	0	0	122,800A
						112,000A
1890	2,520	42	2,562	0	0	
1891	2,520	43	2,563	0	0	100,000A
1892	2,520	44	2,564	0	0	
1893	2,540	44	2,584	0	0	83,200K
1894	2,610	44	2,654	0	0	96,000A
						94,900A
1895	2,610	44	2,654	0	0	103,000A
1896	2,680	44	2,724	0	0	105,000A
						122,500A
						125,250A
1897	2,740	44	2,784	0	0	122,000A
						120,000A
						121,500A
						125,500A
						115,000K
1898	2,810	44	2,854	0	0	125,352A
						115,500K
1899	2,880	44	2,924	0	0	124,000A
						122,500A
						114,000K
1900	2,880	44	2,924	0	0	
1901	2,660	43	2,703	0	0	120,000K
1902	2,660	42	2,702	0	0	
1903	2,660	44	2,704	0	0	

Table of Statutes

1850	Kent Waterworks Act, 13 & 14 Vict., c. lix	136
	River Lee Trustees Act, 13 & 14 Vict., c. cix	35
1851	City of London Sewers Act, 14 & 15 Vict., c. xci	133
1852	Metropolis Water Act, 15 & 16 Vict., c. 84	118, 133, 159
	Chelsea Waterworks Act, 15 & 16 Vict., c. clvi	147
	Grand Junction Waterworks Act, 15 & 16 Vict., c. clvii	147
	Southwark and Vauxhall Waterworks Act, 15 & 16 Vict., c. clviii	147
	West Middlesex Waterworks Act, 15 & 16 Vict., c. clix	147
	New River Company's Act, 15 & 16 Vict., c. clx	10, 118, 161–3, 170–2, 185
	East London Waterworks Act, 15 & 16 Vict., c. clxiv	147
1853	East London Waterworks Act, 16 & 17 Vict., c. clxvi	136
1854	New River Company (Hertford Sewerage Diversion) Act, 17 & 18 Vict., c. xxxix	118, 164
	East London Waterworks Act, 17 & 18 Vict., c. lxv	136
	New River Company's Act, 17 & 18 Vict., c. lxxii	118, 163–4
1855	Metropolis Management Act, 18 & 19 Vict., c. 120	133
	Nuisances Removal Act, 18 & 19 Vict., c. 121	133
	Grand Junction Waterworks Act, 18 & 19 Vict., c. xxi	136
	Southwark & Vauxhall Waterworks Act, 18 & 19 Vict., c. xxiv	136
	River Lee Act, 18 & 19 Vict., c. cxcvi	35, 133, 164
1856	Joint Stock Companies Act, 19 & 20 Vict., c. 47	225, 234, 237
	Lambeth Waterworks Act, 19 & 20 Vict., c. x	136
	Grand Junction Waterworks Act, 19 & 20 Vict., c. cxvi	136
1857	New River Company's Act, 20 & 21 Vict., c. cxlii	118–19, 165, 176–7
1860	West Middlesex Waterworks Act, 23 & 24 Vict., c. i	136
1861	Grand Junction Waterworks Act, 24 & 25 Vict., c. cli	136
1862	Joint Stock Companies Act, 25 & 26 Vict., c. 89	225, 234
	Metropolis Management Act, 25 & 26 Vict., c. 102	133
	East London Waterworks Act, 25 & 26 Vict., c. xxii	136
	Kent Waterworks Act, 25 & 26 Vict., c. xliv	136
1863	Waterworks Clauses (Amendment) Act, 26 & 27 Vict., c. 93	133
1864	Judgments etc. Law (Amendment) Act, 27 & 28 Vict., c. 112	219
	Southwark & Vauxhall Waterworks Act, 27 & 28 Vict., c. viii	136

Table of Cases

Works Cited

1 Manuscript Sources

Bodleian Library

Tanner MS 98 fos. 47–9, 113 (papers on the 1610 bill).

British Library

Additional MS 29974 fos. 61–6 (Pitt correspondence).
36051 fos. 153–60 (Hardwicke papers).
36056 fos. 100–10 (Hardwicke papers).
36063 fo. 130 (Hardwicke papers).
Additional Chancery 40379, 40380 (Waterleases).
Hargrave 70 fos. 95–118 (copy Dodd's Reports).
71 fos. 37–224 (copy Dodd's Reports).
Harleian 3604 (New River Treasurer's accounts 1670–84).
Stowe 796 fo. 43b (Plumbers' Company dispute 1644).

English Legal Manuscripts

(Microfiches ed. Dr J. H. Baker; references in footnotes).

Greater London Record Office

Middlesex Deeds Register (references in footnotes).

Guildhall Library

MS 173/1–4 (papers on London Water).
4161 (title deeds etc. of fractions of New River shares).
4883 (1686 inventory of New River deeds).
11314 (Land Tax papers 1824–5).

Kent County Archives

Sackville MS 621 (1622 Commission first report).
1177 (draft letter, Cranfield to Derby).
2422 (1622 Commission second report).

New River Company

Charter under Great Seal 1619.

Accounts 1609–30.
Register of Proprietors (8 vols.).
Copy Deeds (7 vols.).
Minute Books, deeds, abstracts, accounts, cases to counsel, etc. (references in footnotes).

Public Record Office

LR 2/27–44 (New River ledgers etc. 1609–30).
27–33 (expenditure; 9 vols.).
35–43 (income; 9 vols.).
34 (draft deeds, estimates, Hugh Myddelton's abstract of accounts 1609–19, etc.)
44 (list of arrears with William Lewyn's oath).
Req 1/76 (Court of Requests draft Order Book).
Fines and Recoveries (references in footnotes).

Thames Water Authority

Terriers 2035, 2036, 2232, 2516.
New River Minute Books 1769–1884.
New River General Court Minute Books 1817–1904.
New River letter book 1770–1814.
New River disbursement books 1770–1829.
Revelstoke Arbitration 1904 transcript.
Fry Arbitration 1903–5 transcript.
Numerous deeds and other documents (references in footnotes).

2 Parliamentary Papers

1821	v	HC SC Metropolitan Water Supply.
1828	viii	HC SC Met. Water Supply.
1828	ix	RC Met. Water Supply.
1829	x	Real Property Commrs. (lst Rept.).
1830	xi	Real Property Commrs. (2nd Rept.).
1831–2	xxiii	Real Property Commrs. (3rd Rept.).
1833	xxii	Real Property Commrs. (4th Rept.).
1834	li	Telford Rept. Met. Water Supply.
1834	xv	HC SC Met. Water.
1840	xii	HL SC Met. Water Supply.
1842	xxvi	Poor Law Commrs. Sanitary Rept.
1845	xviii	RC State of Large Towns (2nd Rep.).

1846	xii	HC SC Private Bills.
1850	xxii	General Bd. of Health Rept. Met. Water Supply.
1851	xv	HC SC Met. Water Bill.
1851	xxiii	Met. Water Supply Commission Rept.
1852	xii	HC SC Met. Water Bills.
1852	xxi	HL SC Met. Water Bill.
1854	lxi	Met. Water Co's Repts.
1854–5	liii	Met. Water Co's Repts.
1856	lii	Met. Water Supply Repts.
1857	xiii	Met. Water Supply Rept. of A. H. Hassall.
1868–9	xxxiii	RC Sources of Water Supply.
1871	xi	HC SC Met. Water Bill.
1873	xxxviii	Bd of Trade: Regulations.
1880	x	HC SC Met. Water Supply.
1884–5	lxxi	Met. Water Supply Repts. to Local Govt. Bd.
1890–1	xii	HC SC London Water Bills.
1893–4	xl, pts. 1 and 2	RC Met. Water Supply.
1896	xi	HC SC London Water Co's Bills.
1899	x	HC SC Met. Water Bill.
1899	xli	RC Met. Water Supply lst Rept.
1900	xxxviii, pts. 1 and 2	RC Met. Water Supply Final Rept.
1900	xxxix	—— Plans etc.
1901	iii	Water Bill.
1902	iii	Water Bill.
1902	vi	Joint SC on Water Bill.

3 Books etc.

[Unless otherwise indicated, London is the place of publication.]

ANDERSON, A., *An Historical and Chronological Deduction of the Origin of Commerce* (2nd edn., 4 vols., 1787).

ANGELL, J. K., *A Treatise on the Law of Watercourses* (3rd edn., Boston, Mass., 1840).

ASHLEY, M., (1) *England in the Seventeenth Century* (rev. edn., 1967).

—— (2) *Life in Stuart England* (rev. edn., 1967).

ASHLEY, W. J., *An Introduction to English Economic History and Theory* (2 vols., 1894).
ASHMOLE. E., *Notes and Correspondence* (ed. C. H. Josten, 5 vols., Oxford, 1966).
ASHTON, A., *Water for London* (1956).
ASHTON, R., (1) *The Crown and the Money Market 1603–1640* (1960).
—— (2) *The City and the Court 1603–1643* (1979).
ASHTON, T. S., *The Industrial Revolution 1760–1830* (Oxford, 1970).
Attorney's Practice Epitomized (anon. 1822).
AUBREY, J., *Brief Lives* (1898, 2 vols., ed. A. Clark; 1949 ed. O. L. Dick).
BACON, M., *A New Abridgment of the Law* (8 vols., 1832).
BAKER, J. H.: *see* Spelman, Sir J.
BARTON, N., *The Lost Rivers of London* (1962, repr. 1982).
BAXTER, W. T. and DAVIDSON, S., *Studies in Accounting* (3rd edn., 1977).
BERLE, A. A. and MEANS, G. C., *The Modern Corporation and Private Property* (rev. edn., New York, 1968).
BERRY, G. C., 'Sir Hugh Myddelton and the New River', *Transactions of the Honourable Society of Cymmrodorion for 1956*, 17–46.
BINNIE, G. F., *Early Victorian Water Engineers* (1981).
BLACKSTONE, Sir W., *Commentaries on the Laws of England* (1st edn., facsimile, 4 vols., Chicago, 1979).
BOSWELL, J., *Boswell's Life of Johnson* (eds. G. B. Hill and L. F. Powell, 6 vols., Oxford, 1934–50).
BOURDIN, M. A., *The Land Tax* (3rd edn., ed. S. Bunbury, 1885).
BRACTON, H. DE, *On the Laws and Customs of England* (ed. S. E. Thorne, 4 vols., Cambridge, Mass., 1968–77).
BRAUN, P., *Sir Hugh Myddelton, Practical Idealist* (1980).
CARR, C. T., (1) *General principles of the law of Corporations* (1905).
—— (2) *Select Charters of Trading Companies* (28 Selden Society, 1913).
CARTER, J. C., *Rogers on Elections* (13th edn., 1880).
CAYLEY, A., *Principles of Bookkeeping by Double-entry* (1894).
CHALLIS, H. W., *Real Property* (1st edn., 1885; 2nd edn., 1892; 3rd edn., ed. C. Sweet, 1911).
CLAPHAM, J. H., *Economic History of Modern Britain* (3 vols., Cambridge, 1930–8).
Clarendon Letters: *see* Singer, S. W.
CLIFFORD, F., *History of Private Bill Legislation* (2 vols., 1887).
COKE, Sir E., *Commentary upon Littleton* (19th edn., ed. C. Butler, 2 vols., 1832).
COLLYER, J., *A Practical Treatise on the Law of Partnership* (1832).
COMYNS, Sir J., *Digest of the Laws of England* (5th edn., ed. A. Hammond, 8 vols., 1822).
COOKE, C. A., *Corporation, Trust and Company* (1950).

CORY, I. P., *Practical Treatise on Accounts* (1839).
CRABB, G., *The Law of Real Property* (2 vols., 1846).
CRONHELM, F. W., *Double Entry by Single* (1818).
CRUISE, W., (1) *A Digest of the Laws of England respecting Real Property* (2nd edn., 7 vols., 1818; 4th edn., 7 vols. ed. H. H. White, 1835).
—— (2) *An Essay on the Nature and Operation of Fines and Recoveries* (2nd edn., 1786).
—— (3) *A Treatise on the Origin and Nature of Dignities and Titles of Honour* (2nd edn., 1823).
DANIEL, W. B., *Recollections comprising the Chronicles of two New River Shares* (1811).
DAVIES, K. G., *The Royal Africa Company* (1957).
DEVON, F., *Issues of the Exchequer* (1836).
DICKINSON, A. L., *Accounting Practice and Procedure* (1914).
DICKINSON, H. W., *The Water Supply of Greater London* (1954).
DICKSON, P. G. M., *The Financial Revolution in England* (1967).
DIETZ, F. C., *English Public Finance 1558–1641* (1932).
DOWELL, S., *History of Taxation and Taxes* (2nd edn., 4 vols., 1888).
DUBOIS, A. B., *The English Business Company after the Bubble Act* (1938).
ELLIOTT, G. P.A., *A Practical Treatise on the Qualifications and Registration of Parliamentary Electors in England and Wales* (2nd edn., 1843).
ENTICK, J., *History and Survey of London* (1761).
EVELYN, J., *Diary* (ed. E. S. de Beer, 6 vols., Oxford, 1955).
Exposition of the Act for a Contribution on Property, Professions, Trades, and Offices (anon. 1803).
FEARNE, C., *An Essay on the Learning of Contingent Remainders and Executory Devises* (1st edn., 1772; 10th edn., ed. J. Smith, 2 vols., 1844).
FINER, S. E., *The Life and Times of Sir Edwin Chadwick* (1952).
'FITZGIBBON, E.' (pseud. of GIBNEY, S.), *The New River: a Romance of the Time of Hugh Myddelton* (1885).
FLINTOFF, O., *The Law of Real Property* (2 vols., 1839).
FOORD, A. S., *The Springs, Streams and Spas of London* (1910).
FORDE, Sir E., *A Design for bringing a Navigable River from Rickmansworth in Hertfordshire to St Giles's in the Fields* (1641).
FORMOY, R. R., *The Historical Foundations of Modern Company Law* (1923).
GARNETT, W., *A little book on Water Supply* (Cambridge, 1921).
GEORGE, J., *A View of the Existing Law affecting Unincorporated Joint-stock Companies* (1825).
GIBNEY, S.: *see* 'Fitzgibbon, E.'.
GOODE, R. M., *Commercial Law* (1982).
GOWER, L. C., *Principles of Modern Company Law* (1979).
GOUGH, J. W., *Sir Hugh Myddelton: Entrepreneur and Engineer* (Oxford, 1964).

GRANT, J., *A Practical Treatise on the Law of Corporations* (1850).
GRAY, J. C., *The Rule against Perpetuities* (4th edn., ed. R. Gray, Boston, Mass., 1942).
HASSALL, A. H., *A Microscopic Examination of the Water supplied to the Inhabitants of London* (1850).
HECKSCHER, E. F., *Mercantilism* (tr. M. Shapiro, 2 vols., 1934).
HERBERT, W., *History of the Twelve Great Livery Companies of London* (2 vols., 1837).
Hertford Records, *Extracts from the Books of the Mayor and Aldermen of Hertford relating to the River Lea* (1734).
HOLDSWORTH, Sir W. S., *History of English Law to 1700* (17 vols., 1922–72).
HOWES, E., *Continuation of John Stow: Annales or a General Chronicle of England* (1631).
How Long is London to be Victimized by its Sewage? (anon. 1854).
HUNT, B. C., *The Development of the Business Corporation in England 1800–1867* (Cambridge, Mass., 1936).
HURRELL, H. and HYDE, C. G., *A Treatise on the Law of Joint-Stock Companies* (1883).
HURST, J. W., *The Legitimacy of the Business Corporation* (Charlottesville, Va., 1970).
IMPEY, W. J., *A Treatise on the Law and Practice of Mandamus* (1826).
Inspector-General of Stamps and Taxes, *A Guide to the Property and Income Tax Act* (1842).
JENKINS, R., *Collected Papers* (Oxford 1936).
JEPHSON, H. L., *The Sanitary Evolution of London* (1907).
JONES, E., *Accountancy and the British Economy 1840–1980* (1981).
JOSTEN, C. H., 'William Backhouse of Swallowfield', *Journal of the Society for the Study of Alchemy and Early Chemistry* (*Ambix*) 4 (1949–51) 1–33.
KENYON, J. P., *Stuart England* (1978).
KYD, S., *A Treatise on the Law of Corporations* (2 vols., 1793–4).
LAMBERT, S., *Bills and Acts: Legislative Procedure in Eighteenth-Century England* (1971).
LARKIN, J. F. and HUGHES, P. L., *Stuart Royal Proclamations*, vol. i, (Oxford, 1973).
LEVY, A. B., *Private Corporations and their Control* (2 vols., 1950).
LEWIS, R. A., *Edwin Chadwick and the Public Health Movement 1832–1854* (1952).
LEWIS, S., *The History and Topography of the Parish of St Mary Islington* (1842).
LINDLEY, Sir N., (1) *The Law of Partnership* (1st edn., 2 vols., 1860).
—— (2) *The Law of Companies* (6th edn., ed. Honb. W. B. Lindley, 2 vols., 1902).

LITTLETON, A. C. and YAMEY, B. S., *Studies in the History of Accounting* (1956).
LITTLETON, T., *Tenures* (ed. T. E. Tomlin, 1841).
LYSONS, D., *The Environs of London* (4 vols., 1792–96).
MAITLAND, F. W., (1) *Constitutional History of England* (1909).
—— (2) 'The Law of Real Property', *Collected Papers* (1879) ii 162.
MAITLAND, W., *History of London* (1739).
MALCOLM, J. P., *Anecdotes of the Manners and Customs of London from the Roman Invasion to the year 1700* (2nd edn., 2 vols., 1811).
MALYNES, G., *Consuetudo vel Lex Mercatoria* (1622).
MANBY, R., *The Law and Practice of Fines and Recoveries* (1738).
MATTHEWS, W., *Hydraulia* (1835).
Metropolitan Water Board, *The Water Supply of London* (1949 and 1961).
Middlesex County Records, ed. J. C. Jeaffreson (2 vols., 1886–7).
MILL, J. S., *Principles of Political Economy* (ed. W. J. Ashley, 1921).
MILLER, J., *An Inquiry into the Present State of the Civil Law of England* (1825).
MILNER-GIBSON-CULLUM, G., 'Myddelton Family', *Miscellanea Genealogica et Heraldica* 3rd Ser. vol. 2 (1897), 49–54, 66–72, 270–9.
MORRIS, J. H. C. and LEACH, W. B., *The Rule against Perpetuities* (2nd edn., 1962).
MYDDELTON, W. M., (1) *Chirk Castle Accounts* (1910).
—— (2) *Pedigree of the Family of Myddelton* (1910).
NELSON, J., *History and Antiquities of the Parish of Islington* (1823).
NELSON, W., *An Abridgment of the Common Law* (3 vols., 1736).
NICHOLS, J., *The Progresses, Processions, and Magnificent Festivities of James I* (4 vols., 1828).
NOTTINGHAM, Lord, *Manual of Chancery Practice* and *Prolegomena of Chancery and Equity* (1 vol., ed. D. E. C. Yale, Cambridge, 1965).
NOYES, C. R., *The Institution of Property* (New York, 1936).
ORME, R., *A Practical Digest of the Election Laws* (1796).
OVERALL, W. H. and H. C., *Analytical Index to Remembrancia of the City of London* (1878).
PECKWELL, R. H., *Cases of Controverted Elections* (2 vols., 1805).
Pell Records: *see* Devon, F.
PEPYS, S., *Diary* (eds. R. Latham and W. Matthews, 11 vols., 1970–83).
PETTUS, Sir J., *Fodinae Regales* (1670).
PENNANT, T., *History of London* (1790).
PINK, W. D., *Notes on the Myddelton Family* (Chester, 1891).
Practitioner, A, *The Attorney's Clerk's Assistant* (1819).
PRESTWICH, M., *Cranfield: Politics and Profits under the Early Stuarts* (Oxford, 1966).

PRIDEAUX, W. S., *Memorials of the Goldsmiths' Company* (2 vols., 1896–7).
RALEIGH, T., *Outline of the Law of Property* (1890).
Remembrancia: *see* Overall, W. H. and H. C.
RICHARDS, H. C. and PAYNE, W. H. C., *The London Water Supply* (2nd edn., ed. J. P. H. Soper, 1899).
ROBERTS, Sir W., (1) *An Answer to Mr Forde's Book* (1641).
—— (2) *A Proposition for the serving and supplying of London with water from Hoddesdon* (1641).
ROPER, R. S. D., *A Treatise of the Law of Property arising from relations between Husband and Wife* (2nd edn., ed. E. Jacob, 2 vols., 1826).
RUSSELL, Lady [CONSTANCE], *Swallowfield and its Owners* (1901).
RYDE, W. C., *The Law and Practice of Rating* (2nd edn., 1904).
SABINE, B. E. V., (1) *A History of Income Tax* (1966).
—— (2) *A Short History of Taxation* (1980).
SALZMAN, L. F., *Building in England down to 1540* (repr. 1967).
SCOTT, J., *Amwell: a Descriptive Poem* (1776).
SCOTT, W. R., *The Constitution and Finance of English, Scottish, and Irish Joint-stock Companies to 1720* (3 vols., 1910–12).
SEALY, L. S., *Cases and Materials on Company Law* (2nd edn., 1978).
SHADWELL, A., *The London Water Supply* (1899).
SHARPE, R. R., *London and the Kingdom* (3 vols., 1894).
SHEPPARD, W., (1) *Corporations, Fraternities, and Guilds* (1659).
—— (2) *A Touchstone of Common Assurances of the Kingdom* (7th edn., 2 vols., 1820).
SHORTT, J., *Informations (Criminal and Quo Warranto), Mandamus, and Prohibition* (1887).
SINGER, S. W., ed. *Correspondence of the Earls of Clarendon and Rochester* (2 vols., 1844).
SISLEY, R., *The London Water Supply: a Retrospect and a Survey* (1899).
SMILES, S., *Lives of the Great Engineers* (illustr. edn., 1904).
SMITH, A., *The Wealth of Nations* (2 vols., Oxford, 1908).
SOMBART, W., *Der moderne Kapitalismus* (2 vols., Munich, 1916).
SPELMAN, Sir J., *Reports* (ed. J. H. Baker, 2 vols., 93 and 94 Selden Society, 1977 and 1978).
SPRING, E., 'The Settlement of Land in Nineteenth-Century England', (1964) *American Journal of Legal History* 209.
STACEY, N. A. H., *English Accountancy 1800–1954* (1954).
STOW, J., *Survey of the Cities of London and Westminster* (1603; ed. C. L. Kingsford, 2 vols., 1908; ed. J. Strype, 2 vols., 1720).
STRAHAN, J. H. S., *A General View of the Law of Property* (1895).
STRINGER, G. F., *Some Descriptive Notes on the New River Head* (1927).
TAPPING, T., *The Law and Practice of the High Prerogative Writ of Mandamus* (1848).

TAWNEY, R. H., *Business and Politics under James I* (1958).
THOMPSON, F. M. L., *English Landed Society in the Nineteenth Century* (1963).
TINDALL, G., *The Fields Beneath* (1980).
TUDOR, O., *A Selection of the Leading Cases on Real Property, Conveyancing etc.* (1856).
UNWIN, G., *Industrial Organisation in Sixteenth- and Seventeenth-century England* (1957).
VINER, C., *A General Abridgment of Law and Equity* (23 vols., 1741–57).
Water vol. 1, 1883–4 (weekly until 2 August 1884).
WILLIAMS, J., (1) *Law of Real Property* (1st edn., 1845; 24th edn., ed. R. A. Eastwood, 1926).
—— (2) *Law of Personal Property* (1st edn., 1848).
WILLISTON, S., 'A History of the Law of Business Corporations before 1800', (1888–9) 2 *Harvard Law Review* 105 and 149.
Wills from Doctors' Commons (eds. J. G. Nichols and J. Bruce, Camden Soc., OS, vol. 83, 1863).
WOOD, A. À, *Athenae Oxonienses* (3rd edn., ed. P. Bliss, 4 vols., 1813–20).
WORDSWORTH, C. F. F., *Law of Joint Stock Companies* (1st edn., 1836).
WREN, Sir C., 'Thoughts concerning the Distribution of the New River Water', *Gentleman's Magazine*, 23 (1753), 114.
YAMEY, B. S., EDEY, H. C. and THOMSON, H. T., *Accounting in England and Scotland 1543–1800* (1963).
YOGEV, G., *Diamonds and Coral: Anglo-Dutch Jews and Eighteenth-century Trade* (Leicester, 1978).

Index